UNDIANS

UNS

VANDALS

OSTROGOTHS

VISIGOTHS

•Sirmium

BLACK SEA

•Trapezus

DACIA

Naissus•

THRACIA

Philippopolis •

PONTUS

Constantinople

Ilium
(Troy)

AEGEAN
SEA

ASIA

PERSIA

TIGRIS

EUPHRATES

MACEDONIA

•Antioch

•Athenae

ORIENT

CYRUS

•Damascus

CRETE

ANEAN   SEA

•Hierosolyma
(Jerusalem)

Alexandria• •

ARABIA

EGYPT

•Memphis

NILE

N EASTERN
N ROMAN
E EMPIRE

RED

SEA

The Genius
of Venice

Piazza San Marco and
the Making of the Republic

The Genius
of Venice

Piazza San Marco and
the Making of the Republic

Dial Parrott

Rizzoli
ex libris

First published in the United States of America in 2013
by Dial Parrott
in association with Rizzoli Ex Libris
an imprint of
Rizzoli International Publications, Inc.
300 Park Avenue South
New York, N.Y. 10010
www.rizzoliusa.com

Cover: WESTERN FACADE OF THE BASILICA SAN MARCO,
watercolor triptych by Alberto Prosdocimi.
Used with the kind permission of the Procuratoria di San Marco, Venice.

2013 2012 2011 2010 / 10 9 8 7 6 5 4 3 2 1

Distributed in the U.S. trade by Random House, New York

Printed in China

ISBN-13: 978-0-8478-4053-3

Library of Congress Control Number: 2012947644

Illustration Credits

Art Resource: *Figs. 2, 3, 4, 6, 8, 9, 10, 11, 12, 13, 15, 17, 18, 19, 24, 26, 29, 35, 39, 40, 41, 42, 44, 45, 47, 50, 51, 56, 57, 61, 62, 63, 64, 65, 75, 80, 86, 94, 95, 98, 100, 101, 108, 109;* Author's photos: *Figs. 7, 21, 34, 36, 37, 38, 48, 49, 52, 54, 55, 60, 66, 69, 70, 71, 72, 73, 74, 77, 78, 81, 83, 89, 90, 91, 92, 96, 102, 104, 105, 107;* Bridgeman Art Library: *Figs. 43, 46, 58, 59, 67, 68, 76, 82, 84, 87, 88, 93, 97, 103, 106, 111, 112;* Hand Made Maps Ltd: *Front and rear end paper maps, Figs. 1, 5;* Piloti Press: *Figs. 20, 22, 23, 25, 27, 28, 53, 79, 85, 99, 110;* Procuratoria di San Marco: *Figs. 14, 16, 30, 31, 32, 33.*

To Sally, Sam, and Max,
who made the journey with me

CONTENTS

Introduction

Nineteen eighty-two was a year of important firsts for me. During those twelve months, I got married, was fired from my first job as a lawyer, and saw Venice for the first time—interrelated events, as it turned out. Barely out of law school, I was working feverishly to prove to my Boston firm that I was a young attorney worth keeping. At the same time, I was determined that even if it cost me my job, my new wife and I were going to have a full two-week honeymoon, the first week in Paris and the second in Venice. I had never visited either place.

On the night train from Paris, I was unable to fall sleep and arrived in the Venetian lagoon in a semi-delirious state. My experience during those first few hours was nothing less than a waking dream. To the extent the rational part of my brain was working at all, it kept repeating the same involuntary questions. What could possibly explain the fantastical scenes passing before my eyes? How could anything so beautiful and improbable ever have come to be? Since almost nothing I saw seemed to conform to what I had been taught to revere in college art courses, I contented myself with gathering gorgeous, inchoate sensations. Sally and I danced across the moonlit Piazza San Marco to the music of three small orchestras. We took a *vaporetto* to the deserted island of Torcello, where we explored the chaste, unguarded beauty of the cathedral of Santa Maria Assunta and its enchanting companion, the little octagonal church of Santa Fosca. We stayed in a small, ground-floor room of a magnificent medieval palazzo. In the morning, we walked up a massive stairway to breakfast in an enormous second-story chamber overlooking an elegant neighborhood *campo*. As we ate, small birds flew through the Gothic windows and circled the ornate ceiling.

Upon returning to Boston, I made two quick discoveries. The first was that in my absence, one of the bond deals assigned to me had hit a major snag and ended up on the desk of a very unforgiving senior partner. I was given a few months to find another job. The second was that my experience in Venice had been transformative. I really did need to find answers to the dilemmas my mind instinctively threw up in those original, dazed hours. I began reading the literature of Venice and discovered this passage, which seemed to offer a burst of genuine insight:

Where else have a handful of fugitives driven at sword point into a muddy lagoon, without vegetation, without drinkable water, without materials with which to rebuild their lives—or even the necessary space in which to build—come in time to establish the highest example of stable, consistent government, extracting from their swamp an endless naval arsenal with which they conquer a great empire and reap the riches of the East. When one watches such refugees seize the political levers of Italy, dominate the seas, reduce whole nations to the status of dependents, and, in the end, render impotent the combined might of all Europe leagued against them, one can be certain that he is observing an enlargement of human intelligence that merits study.

This is my translation of Count Pierre Daru's remarkable *Histoire de la république de Venise*, published in eight volumes from 1815 to 1819. Daru's vision of a unique city formed out of the void by the sheer determination of her people, the offspring of bold, calculating men who seized the main chance wherever they found it, fired my imagination. Part of the reason for this, I realized, was that its heroic view of Venice made me think of the origins of the United States. Like early Americans, Venetians were "new men," refugees who abandoned their ancestral homes and staked out fresh lives in an unknown wilderness. Both nations initially served as pioneer outposts for large, powerful empires and ultimately rebelled against and defeated their colonial fathers. Neither had a feudal past; both were originally seagoing, trading societies whose national characters were strongly stamped with the versatility and adaptability demanded by maritime enterprise. Each displayed a native genius for moneymaking, self-government and rapid, efficient organization. Each devoted enormous intellectual and political capital to forming a constitution that would promote collective decision making and impede rule by a single individual or dominant faction. And while both were often seen by other nations as ruthless, arrogant, greedy, ignoble, and vulgar, each typically saw itself as a divinely blessed people with a God-given right to success and prosperity.

Such analogies were certainly intriguing, I thought, but was it entirely fair to compare a millennium and a half of Venetian experience with the brief history of a country little more than two centuries old? This was an important distinction. The much longer trajectory of Venetian history had exposed the lagoon city to later, more despairing strains of historical interpretation. Indeed, not long after the publication of Daru's magisterial work, a host of writers began to envision Venice not as the heroine of an epic tale but as an archetypal symbol of decadence and decay. She was portrayed as an exhausted relic from a vanished past, a lovely but passive victim before the brutal onslaught of modern civilization. Authors described the pathos they felt watching her aging monuments crumble and disappear beneath the encroaching sea.

It was no accident that this wave of literary pessimism emerged in the wake of Napoleon's 1797 invasion and despoliation of the city while she was still suffering the ongoing shame of Austrian military occupation. French forces destroyed the Venetian navy and looted more than eighty churches, monasteries, convents, and guilds, crippling the city's economy for over a century. During the four decades of Austrian rule that followed Napoleon's fall in 1815, Venice was often viewed by the rest of Europe as little more than a stagnant backwater, a city of inundation and ruin whose vast artistic heritage was now ripe for acquisition at bargain prices. In many ways, Venice has never recovered from this prolonged treatment as an icon of exhaustion and decline. This is still the essential portrait found in today's mass media, where Venice is typically pictured as a city in constant peril from rising seas, mass tourism, residential depopulation, global warming, and every other affliction, real or imagined, that haunts the contemporary imagination. The ultimate logic of this all-too-common perspective is that however mysterious and lovely she may seem, in the end we must treat her as nothing more than a transient curiosity unworthy of our sustained intellectual attention.

Of course, the story that a writer disinters from sixteen centuries of historical evidence is inevitably a reflection of his own core values. For myself, having confirmed that the fugitives who built Venice actually did accomplish everything that Daru attributed to them, I realized that her modern image as a passive victim, a convenient symbol of decay and looming catastrophe, is one to which I could not subscribe. Indeed, based on many years of research, I believe it is a revisionist fallacy completely at odds with the overall arc of Venetian history. Throughout most of her long existence, Venice has been an example of astonishing success. During her first millennium, she was almost always rightly regarded by jealous rivals as a vanguard state. Viewed through the lens of her fifth-century beginnings as a handful of frightened, bickering refugees from the terrorized Italian mainland, it is much more accurate to see Venice as an archetypal symbol of rebirth and renewal, forging from within her lagoon a truly new people, the product of an accelerated national consciousness that a few centuries later was to transform the rest of Europe. Looked at objectively, this rekindling of faith and purpose after catastrophic loss, followed by the construction of a great city on a desolate mass of swampy islets, is one of the truly memorable examples of human courage and applied intelligence in Western history.

This was the story I wanted to tell. The question was how to create a special focus that would offer something not already available in the thousands of existing books on Venice. Fortunately, at this point in my research, I made two surprising discoveries. First, I found that there was no single work in English that told the overall creation story of the Piazza San Marco in anything like the degree of fascinating detail available in specialized volumes focused on a particular building or period. This was a critical realization because it suggested that there might be room for a new book on the city's oldest and most resonant architectural site, the one that would necessarily have the most revealing connections with sixteen centuries of Venetian history. Second, I discovered that although there were already wonderful single-volume histories, such as Deborah Howard's *The Architectural History of Venice* and John Julius Norwich's *A History of Venice*, there was nothing that specifically paired an account of the eight-century creation of the Piazza San Marco with a detailed chronological narrative of the entire social, political, military, and economic history of Venice. This was crucial because, by this point in my investigation, I had become convinced that the best way to understand the course of Venetian history in general and to appreciate the architectural and artistic value of the Piazza ensemble in particular was by interweaving parallel treatments of both subjects. I had also come to see that there is a necessary connection between the modern pessimistic view of Venice and the fact that many contemporary writers concentrate their attention on the sixteenth-century Venetian Renaissance and give relatively little notice to the preceding millennium of accelerating Venetian wealth and power. Beginning or centering the story there, near what is commonly regarded as the high-water mark of Venetian cultural achievement, inevitably makes what follows seem like a tale of deterioration and decline.

Gradually, my idea for a work on the development of the Piazza San Marco and the major monuments of which it is composed—the Basilica of San Marco, the Doge's Palace, the Campanile, the Marciana Library, and the apartments of the procurators of Saint Mark—began to take shape. The book would offer simultaneous accounts of these brilliant architectural achievements and the growth of the city's political and commercial arrangements, presented as twin facets of that remarkable "enlargement of human intelligence" with which Daru had credited Venice. Properly done, it would allow readers to grasp the evolution of Venetian self-identity from the early Middle Ages to the Age of the Renaissance in an immediately apprehensible form—as manifested in the creation and development of the city's oldest and most culturally significant architectural site. It would contain extensive background material describing the ancient imperial city of Constantinople and its monuments, particularly the Augusteum, the Late Classical forum that was the model for the Piazza San Marco, as well as frequent comparisons between Venice, which experienced a proto-Renaissance in the twelfth and thirteenth centuries, and contemporary architectural developments in Florence and Rome. The goal would be to enable readers to see Venice's greatest architectural masterpieces as the living books of history they were always intended to be, to adopt John Ruskin's memorable phrase. After two decades of careful research and seven years of writing, I believe this volume fulfills these goals.

A Word About Architectural Terminology

To avoid confusing either American or British and European readers, I have refrained from using the term "first floor," which to the former audience means the ground floor of a building, and to the latter, the floor directly above the ground floor. Instead, when directing attention to building levels, I have specifically referred to the ground floor or to upper floors or stories.

Acknowledgments

I have received generous support and good counsel from loved ones, friends and colleagues at every stage of this venture. There is nothing like staying up night after night struggling to push forward with a project whose end point can only dimly be discerned to clarify just how dependent on those around us our quicksilver emotions truly are. Above all, I have come to realize what a fateful day it was thirty years ago when I sat down in the wrong seat next to an alluring young woman (my future wife) at Fenway Park in Boston. From that time to this, Sally has been the guiding presence around whom I have gladly organized my life. Her instinctive sympathy toward everyone she meets as well as her keen intelligence, sense of humor and passionate enjoyment of art and foreign travel have made me a very lucky man. Not surprisingly, these qualities have also provided her with a large circle of talented friends. One of them, Peggy Burhoe (who was sitting next to Sally at that Red Sox game) gave me the best writing advice I ever received: "Keep telling stories, Dial. That's what you do best." And it was another friend, Terry Hackford, who introduced me to my brilliant, infinitely resourceful editor and literary agent, Janet Adams Strong. Working under the corporate name of Piloti Press, Janet and her amazingly talented book designer colleague, Linda Zingg, bring great intelligence, fierce dedication and exacting standards to the task of shaping their clients' books. My association with them has been a revelation and a delight. Not the least of all her many contributions, it was Janet who introduced me to David Morton and Alessandra Lusardi at Rizzoli, both of whom have been invaluable in preparing this book for publication. And, among many other things, Linda is responsible for the book's splendid non-color maps. David Atkinson of Hand Made Maps in London produced the volume's beautiful color maps.

I want to acknowledge a feeling of special gratitude to my friend Michael Broderick whose fascinating lectures and tours (available at www.venicescapes.org) are one of the finest in-depth introductions to Venetian art and architecture and the city's rich political and social history available to English-speaking visitors. One December day ten years ago, Michael and I waded through *acqua alta* to meet each other at the Adam and Eve corner of the Ducal Palace, then spent six hours discussing Venetian constitutional arrangements in various Palace chambers where the temperature could not have exceeded 40 degrees F. As Michael enthusiastically fielded question after question, a friendship was born, and from that time to this, I have been the fortunate recipient of his rare knowledge and unflagging support.

I also wish to offer special thanks to John Freely (author of numerous books on Istanbul, Byzantine architecture, the Greek islands, and Venice) for his generous encouragement. When introduced to John by Sukru Yarcan, a former student of his who is now the leading tour guide in Istanbul, John was kind enough to invite me to his home and attempt to throw open the mysteries of the publishing world. As we chatted high above the Bosporus, John said that he thought the basic idea of my proposed work was a very good one which might sell thousands of copies annually for years to come—a statement which I eagerly hoarded and repeatedly played back to myself during periods of doubt and indecision. My thanks as well to the medieval scholar John Aberth whose gripping translation of mid-fourteenth-century Venetian plague accounts (de Monacis, *Chronicon de Rebus Venetis*) was extremely helpful in composing Chapter Nine; to my friend Stoney Conley who helped me correct the discussion of Venetian Renaissance painting in Chapters Ten and Twelve; and to my copy editor Ann Kirschner whose remarkable attention to detail has been extremely valuable. I also wish to thank the following friends for their interest and suggestions over the years: Mary Armstrong, Stacey and David Brodsky, Hilary and Miller Brown, Dick Burhoe, Mally Cox-Chapman, Rick Dighello, Kane Ditto, D Gorton, Tom Gugliotti, Betsy Mankin Kornhauser, Harlan Levy, Jim and Blakes Lloyd, Paul Mc-Cormick, Noel Polk, Robert Sacks, and Pattie Weiss.

Much of the research for this book was done at the Biblioteca Marciana and the Biblioteca della Fondazione Querini Stampalia in Venice and the Yale University Library and the Brown University Library in the United States. I also received kind assistance from the Reference Department of the Welles-Turner Memorial Library in Glastonbury, Connecticut, and have benefited greatly from the resources of the Connecticut Inter-Library Loan system.

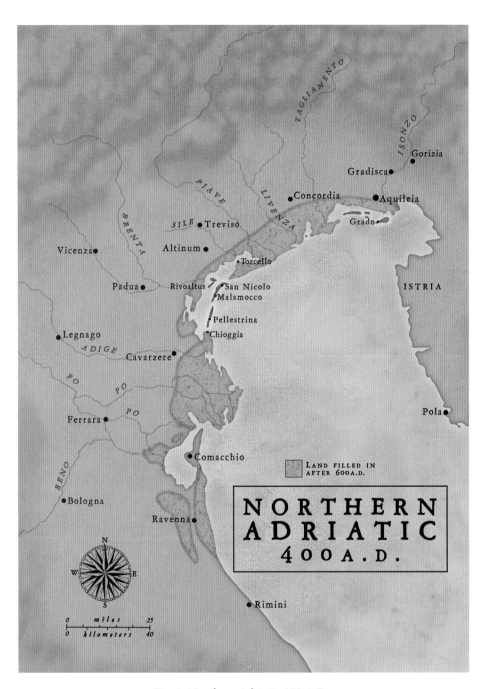

Fig. 1: Northern Adriatic 400 A.D.

CHAPTER ONE

Origins (400–810)

An Arc of Splendid Roman Cities

By the fifth century A.D., the architectural marvels of imperial Rome had spread far beyond the great capital itself. Centuries of continual military expansion had led emperors and proconsuls to replicate large portions of Roman material splendor in a host of conquered and colonized cities ranging over three continents from the Black Sea to the coasts of Britain, Spain, and North Africa (*see front endpaper map*). Indeed, so much imperial wealth had been lavished on new colonial settlements that it had become necessary to establish several regional capitals to effectively manage the empire's far-flung dominions.

One of the most brilliant examples of this elegant urban civilization was an arc of splendid cities in the northeastern corner of Italy, set slightly inland from the Adriatic Sea. Fourth-century Padua, Altinum, Concordia, and Aquileia, beneficiaries of a vibrant provincial culture centered on commerce and sea trade, were among the richest municipal centers in the Roman Empire (*Fig. 1*). Behind massive, fortified walls, they gleamed with magnificent marble temples, churches, palaces, law courts, stadiums, circuses, and amphitheaters that, for refinement of style and material, were almost the equal of anything to be found in Rome itself. Without, the fields were lush with olive groves, vineyards, and great country houses. As inhabitants of the Roman province of Venetia, their citizens were connected to Rome and every other part of the empire by a network of superbly engineered highways on which a fast-moving chariot could travel a hundred miles in a single day. Many of the cities had impressive artificial harbors linked to rivers and canals that flowed directly into the Adriatic and from there to the lucrative trade markets of the eastern Mediterranean.[1]

Immediately south and east of these cultivated centers lay a large, desolate lagoon, a nether region of marsh and tidal pool, six to twelve miles wide and originally 140 miles long (four times its present length since, at that time, it stretched as a continuous geographical feature from the Po River delta in the south to the northeast corner of the Adriatic). The lagoon formed a strange, forbidding interstice between the thriving, populated mainland and the open sea. Except for brief hunting and fishing expeditions, northern Italian urbanites would never have dreamed of leaving their magnificent creature comforts to penetrate its mud-drenched solitude.[2]

Then, beginning in the early fifth century, this complex, refined civilization was repeatedly invaded by wave after wave of lethal barbarian hordes. Legions of Goths and Huns were followed by throngs of Vandals and Longobards, all drawn by the same tempting prospects for plunder and slaughter. In many cases, their initial targets were the northern cities of Venetia. Thus, in 452, after advancing along a splendid Roman road to the very gates of the regional capital of Aquileia at the head of the Adriatic, Attila the Hun (*Fig. 2*) and his warriors stopped and laid siege to that city. Constructing stone and earthen embankments next to the city walls, they swarmed over its ramparts, reduced its splendid buildings to ash and rubble (*Fig. 3*) and murdered and enslaved its exhausted defenders. Then, their wagon trains groaning with booty and captives, the Huns turned south, eager to impose an equally destructive butchery on the citizens of Concordia, Altinum, and Padua. That these cities escaped the worst of Aquileia's fate was entirely due to their immediate capitulation before the advancing barbarian horde. Believing that resistance was useless, in exchange for preserving their lives, the Huns' latest victims simply opened their gates and submitted to unlimited plunder.[3]

In theory, none of this should have been possible, since Aquileia had been built to serve as an impregnable Roman fortress. With a population of over 200,000, it was not only a major regional capital but the ninth-largest city in the empire. More than two dozen Roman emperors, beginning with Augustus himself, had, at one time or another, temporarily resided within its sumptuous imperial palace. Encircled by a double set of towered walls, the city had been specifically sited to prevent an invading army from entering northeast Italy. In 238, during a civil war between rival imperial candidates, it had successfully withstood the fierce assault of a major army of veteran Roman legionnaires from the Rhine and the Danube.[4]

Fig. 2: Attila the Hun

Fig. 3: Ancient Roman Aquileia, ruins of river port

Part of the explanation for their startling success lay with the Huns themselves. These nomadic intruders from the steppes of central Asia were trained from birth as relentless, cold-blooded killers with a legendary capacity to ignore physical hardship. The men had ritually scarred faces and large deformed heads misshapen at birth to fit the war helmets they wore as adults. They dined on raw meat tenderized with horse sweat and wore tunics woven from the skins of mice. To the Roman imagination, they personified pure horror. Stories circulated that they ate the flesh of children and drank the blood of women. In addition to their unsurpassed skill as mounted warriors and their deadly accuracy as bow-men, tales of their pitiless savagery, both true and exaggerated, helped to overwhelm the psychological defenses of their refined victims. Of equal importance was the fact that by the time of the Hun invasion, the spectacular architectural monuments of northern Italy only served to mask a military and political vacuum. If we are to believe the best-known authority on the subject, much of the blame for this state of affairs can be traced to one preeminent individual. According to Edward Gibbon's magisterial eighteenth-century classic, *The Decline and Fall of the Roman Empire*, the collapse of Roman power in the West was directly attributable to two fateful decisions by the fourth-century emperor Constantine the Great (*Fig. 4*).[5]

Fig. 4: Monumental head of Constantine the Great,
Capitoline Museum, Rome

Constantine the Great

This ruthless, domineering man, arguably the most influential secular leader in European history, became emperor in 312 and died in office a quarter century later, in 337. His accession to the Roman throne was bitterly contested. From an original field of six contenders, he alone managed to survive the deadly struggle for control of the empire. When faced with military opponents and conspiracies, real or imagined, he never flinched from doing whatever he believed was required to acquire and maintain supreme power. Over the course of his reign, this involved the execution of his wife, his son, his father-in-law, his brother-in-law, his nephew, and many of his closest associates within the imperial entourage. Having chosen this bloody path to the imperial purple, Constantine then dumbfounded his subjects by declaring that he owed his throne to none other than the Christian God who had revealed His true nature to erring man in the life of Jesus of Nazareth. Coming from a supreme political opportunist such as Constantine, this was a profoundly shocking statement, since nothing could have been better calculated to undermine his standing in the Roman world it was now his task to govern.[6]

In 312, Christianity was still a small, suspect religious cult whose adherents, constituting no more than five percent of the imperial population, had been subjected to intense persecution during the previous decade. Scorned by both the patrician elite and the vast majority of Roman subjects, faith in Jesus as a divine savior was regarded as one of the abject superstitions of the poor, the ignorant, the gullible, and the criminal. Constantine set out to change this completely. He began by eliminating the penalties the Senate and earlier emperors had imposed on the despised sect. In 313, he granted Christianity full legal recognition throughout the empire and announced a policy of official neutrality toward the numerous religions practiced across the Roman world. But his ultimate goal was far more ambitious: the exclusive public triumph of the Christian faith within his dominions. In this astonishingly bold endeavor, the first of the two fateful actions highlighted by Gibbon, Constantine initially enjoyed only partial success.[7]

Despite the growing popularity of Christianity following the emperor's conversion (which did not formally occur until just before his death in 337), paganism remained firmly entrenched in the wealthy patrician class whose members made up the Roman Senate. Although shorn of any true political authority, this traditional elite retained sufficient cultural veto power within the city of Rome to block one of Constantine's most cherished ambitions. Even as the emperor successfully constructed a half dozen major new Christian churches, he felt compelled to restrict them to existing Christian burial sites outside the city walls or to imperial private property near the municipal periphery. Pagan resistance was so strong that even a will as fierce as Constantine's was forced to give way, and his building initiatives had only minimal effect on the architectural transformation of Rome from a pagan to a Christian city. This led to the second of the major historical actions cited by Gibbon: the emperor's decision to transfer his throne to the East, where military and political strategy also dictated that the imperial headquarters should be located. There, it would be possible to erect a New Rome, a distinctively Christian capital of a new Christian empire.[8]

Accordingly, Constantine built a spectacular imperial metropolis on the breathtaking site of the ancient city of Byzantium at the mouth of the Black Sea. Constantine's city, to which he gave his own name, occupied a large, easily defended promontory that was also the natural juncture for the major land and water trade routes between Europe and Asia. Having established himself at this strategic crossroads, the emperor then ransacked both continents to adorn Constantinople with the finest artistic works the Roman world could offer. In a few centuries, the Eastern capital grew to become Christendom's greatest city, fabled for its wealth and architectural splendor and larger by far than any Western competitor.[9]

In the West, although Christianity and paganism continued to struggle for supremacy during the reigns of Constantine's immediate successors, by the beginning of the fifth century Christianity had clearly triumphed. At this point, even in Rome itself, paganism had been suppressed, and the old aristocratic families had been forced to convert. In Gibbon's mind, this was a fatal turn of events. As he saw it, Christianity's ultimate victory led to crippling social discord and an otherworldly indifference to impending danger at the very moment when repeated barbarian invasions were beginning to subject the empire's internal cohesion and external defenses to their greatest test. Thus, when Rome was sacked by the Goths in 410, many Christians saw this as no more than God's just punishment for pagan sinfulness. Rather than calling for decisive military action to protect Roman lives and security, Church leaders preached that worldly government, being inherently evil, should be abandoned altogether. To them, God's message was clear: the end of the world prophesied in Christian revelation was finally at hand. The terrifying aliens who swarmed across frontier borders to destroy the ordered world of Roman civilization were merely the agents of

His Divine Wrath. Against such a force, earthly defenses were futile. And some Christians went even further. They openly celebrated the prospect of watching Rome devoured in flames and witnessing the mass slaughter of her arrogant, narcissistic inhabitants.[10]

In such a fractured Roman world, Constantine's decision to transplant his capital to the city of Byzantium, thereby transforming the East into the locus of imperial power, amounted to a slow death sentence for the West. After 330, the year Constantine formally dedicated Constantinople to the Virgin Mary, no emperor ever returned to take up permanent residence in Rome. The old capital was left to a penniless rabble under the direction of a well-educated but feckless nobility that frequently declined government office, preferring to devote its wealth to the pleasures of private life. Over time, the necessary energy and discipline to maintain a Western Empire simply vanished. As spiraling inflation impoverished millions, the rich used their political connections to avoid taxation, causing the public burden to fall with crushing weight on small landowners and leading to a progressive depopulation of the countryside. Lacking sufficient taxes, nothing resembling the professional Roman army that had once maintained imperial order could be sustained, with the result that in the contested border provinces of the West, effective military power was left to local peasant militia. Poorly trained and equipped, they were easily routed by the barbarian legions pouring into northern Italy.[11]

Thus, Italians of the fifth and sixth centuries grew to adulthood accustomed to terror, hunger, plague, and the sight and smell of violent death as barbarian and scarcely Christianized warlords fought for temporary gain in an endless succession of meaningless conflicts. Men and women who had founded their lives on the assumptions of Roman law and culture watched these verities dissolve before their eyes. In 476, the last Roman emperor of the West, a mere boy, was deposed and exiled. For the next three centuries, there would be no successor.[12]

Flight to the Lagoon

In the midst of this carnage, Italians in the northern Adriatic sought temporary refuge in the unlikeliest of havens. Because the alien hordes that terrorized them seemed to have no naval skills, some of those who survived the initial onslaughts commandeered boats or built crude rafts and pushed off into the neighboring lagoon. Initially, the terrified fugitives who entered this strange region of mud and solitude merely camped out in rude huts built by coastal fishermen and trappers. When they perceived that the latest threat had passed, they returned to the mainland, dug up their buried treasure, and rebuilt their destroyed homes. But over time, a different pattern emerged. As the fifth century gave way to the sixth, short-lived flights of temporary refugees were succeeded by larger migrations of permanent settlers. These were men and women who, after bitter and repeated losses, had finally relinquished all hope of ever reclaiming their former lives in a cultivated urban environment, concluding that their sole remaining option was voluntary exile to a region so forlorn and inaccessible that the barbarity of the mainland could no longer reach them.[13]

The best description of "the wild and solitary scene" that greeted these Roman pilgrims as they penetrated the lagoon is by the English writer John Ruskin. Ruskin asks his readers to envision small bands of frightened city dwellers picking their way across "a great plain of calcareous mud" crisscrossed by "torturous channels...choked with slime." He then asks us to imagine an hour when "the bright investiture and sweet warmth of sunset are withdrawn from the waters, and the black desert of their shore lies in the darkness beneath the night, pathless, comfortless, infirm, lost in dark languor and fearful silence.... [For only then will we] be enabled to enter in some sort into the horror of heart with which this solitude was anciently chosen by man for his habitation."[14] There must have been an initial period of profound depression when it was impossible for such exiles to think of anything but the sheer absurdity of their predicament, since who could imagine the renewal of civilized life under such appalling conditions? At some point, however, fresh energies did begin to seep back into broken lives, and the lagoon people found the courage to begin reclaiming their personal histories from the vast surrounding nothingness. In time, when they had regained their strength and creative imagination, they slowly rebuilt their shattered lives with an earnest resolution that paid tribute to the collective memory of that brutally painful beginning.

At the heart of this recovery was a process of deep psychological transformation, greatly assisted by the shaping power of myth. Just as the lagoon dwellers imported the stones of their toppled cities to erect new buildings in the swamp, so they also began to recast their new lives in images salvaged from the world of Roman and Christian legend. They came to see themselves as divinely inspired exiles chosen to relive the rebirth and revival of a great urban civilization. In part, they saw themselves reenacting the creation story of Rome told by Virgil in the *Aeneid* as well as the historical mirroring of that original foundation by

Trojan refugees which occurred when Constantine transferred the seat of Roman power back to the East in the fourth century. But at a deeper personal level, Venetians came to feel that only the ancient biblical myth of Noah adequately conveyed the unique travail of their national rebirth after the total devastation of the fifth and sixth centuries. They came to see this story of God's deliverance of his chosen people—by directing them to build an ark of refuge amidst the surrounding waters—as their special heritage.

It was a rebirth that could never have taken place under mainland conditions. Only by escaping to the lagoon did Venice avoid the feudal ideology, founded on the martial values of the German war band, which everywhere else in the West had replaced the lost universalist culture of the Romans. Without that fundamental new beginning, the lives of her people would have been constricted within the same narrow tribal loyalties that shackled the rest of Europe, where men were subject to the dictates of a local chieftain and bound to particular plots of arable land. Venetians would have been forced to find their rank in a fixed hierarchy based on military prowess in the service of rival warlords. They would have become entangled in the same incessant quarrels between petty belligerent fiefdoms that plunged the rest of Italy into despair, poverty, and chaos for many dark centuries. But the men of the lagoon refused to permit any leader to exercise sovereignty over the ownership and transfer of property within the Venetian state and, consequently, were never enslaved to the military servitude and backbreaking toil of subsistence agriculture on which the mainland feudal system depended. Instead, they transformed themselves into skilled mariners and enterprising traders forever in search of profit along the Adriatic coast and up the inland rivers of northern Italy. Venetians also became prosperous by skimming salt, a precious natural resource, from the frothy surface of the waves. This bent toward trade, distant markets, foreign climes, and new technologies—the avid search for wealth wherever it could be found—came early, and it was fundamental to the nature of the lagoon enterprise.

Rival Settlements

Initially, of course, there was not a single Venetian lagoon community; there were many. There was a lagoon settlement on the island of Grado, populated by survivors of the destruction of Aquileia; on the island of Torcello, peopled by refugees from Altinum; at Caorle, the refuge of exiles from Concordia; and at Malamocco, a city on one of the long, sandy barrier islands or *lidi* forming the Adriatic shore of the lagoon, which became a haven for survivors from the ancient city of Padua (*Figs. 1, 5*). During the sixth through the eighth centuries, the leading families of these widely scattered island communities (governing as elected magistrates called tribunes) competed with each other for political and cultural dominance, basing their claims to preeminence on the former size and importance of the original mainland cities from which they had fled. Whatever solidarity these rival elites may have shared was imposed upon them by their common protector, the Byzantine Empire.[15]

Thanks to the efforts of Constantine and his successors, the Roman Empire (and the imperial military on which it depended) still existed in the East, albeit recast in the form of a Greek-speaking court, people, and Church. In fact, after the disappearance of the Western Roman Empire in 476, the Eastern Roman Empire's growing absorption of the surrounding Hellenistic culture of ancient Greece became so marked that it led to the adoption of a new name. This Eastern or Greek Empire began to be referred to as Byzantium, a term that had originally meant no more than the site of the original Greek city on which Constantine built his great fourth-century imperial capital. Wealth was more widely dispersed in the Byzantine East. A relatively prosperous peasantry supplied ample recruits to the Byzantine army, which was supported by an efficient bureaucracy and taxing system. As a result, the Eastern Empire not only defended itself, but during the reign of the Emperor Justinian (493–565), its generals Belisarius and Narses were able to retake Italy from the Goths. Following several appallingly bloody campaigns that inflicted as much butchery and suffering as any of the barbarian invasions themselves, the Greek commanders established a Byzantine government in Ravenna.[16]

In 697, the Venetian lagoon itself was made a separate Byzantine military command under a *dux* or doge appointed by the Eastern Emperor. The doge initially ruled from the provincial capital of Heraclea, an imperial outpost on the Adriatic which was named for the Emperor Heraclius (r. 610–640). However, within a half century, the doge became an elected officeholder chosen in a general assembly of citizens from all of the lagoon settlements. The early doges possessed both civil and military authority and were intended to embody whatever collective resolve the separate lagoon communities were capable of forming. Although elected, like most Western sovereigns of this early period, the doge's public authority was virtually unlimited in scope. He treated with foreign powers, decided questions of war and peace, was master of the state's military forces, controlled

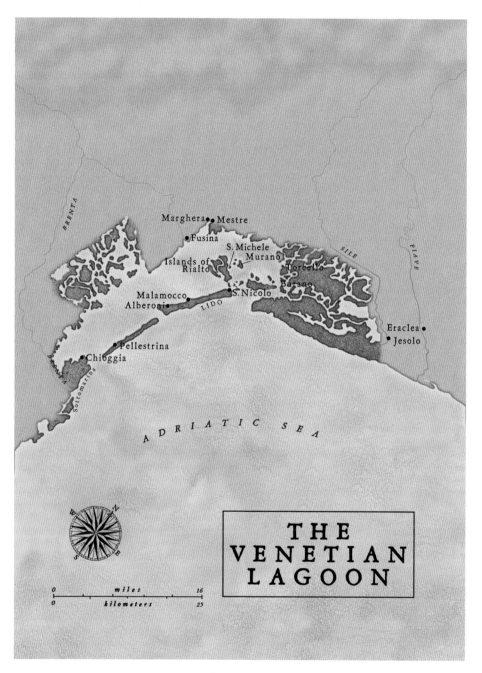

Fig. 5: The Venetian Lagoon

its finances as well as its judiciary, appointed and directed the clergy, and presided over the general assembly of the people, which he alone was authorized to convene. Amounts necessary to carry out his public policies and support his private needs were met by mandatory contributions of land, money, and service imposed on the inhabitants of the lagoon.[17]

Unfortunately, the process of choosing a common leader did little to unify the separate lagoon cities. On the contrary, electoral competition among contending candidates only quickened what were already sharp and often violent power struggles among the principal families of the rival settlements. The early chronicles report that of the first six doges, five were violently deposed: two by blinding, two by death, and one by blinding followed by death. And the situation only worsened when, at end of the eighth century, the Franks, under Charlemagne (742–814), vanquished the scattered Germanic kingdoms that had battled the Byzantine Empire for Italian supremacy during the past two hundred years and used their new-won dominance to begin meddling in the lagoon's internal governance. What had formerly been a local feud among rival clans from separate island settlements now escalated into a contest between two opposing imperial camps—a traditional pro-Byzantine party concentrated at Heraclea and a clerical, pro-Frankish faction centered on Malamocco.[18]

Charlemagne heartily disliked the lagoon dwellers. He saw no reason why they should not be forced to abandon their historical Eastern allegiance and join the rest of feudal Italy as part of his Carolingian kingdom, which he trumpeted as the revived Roman Empire of the West. Nor, by the end of the year 809, did he foresee much effective opposition to such a design. Byzantium had lost its Italian beachhead at Ravenna, and the Venetian throne was shared by a trio of co-doges, the Antenori brothers, who were willing pawns of the Frankish court. Indeed, one of the Antenori had even taken a Frankish bride. Altogether, it seemed like a very opportune moment for Charlemagne's headstrong son Pepin, the king of Frankish Italy, to use an armada he had gathered in nearby Ravenna to subdue Venice. As if anything more were needed, Pepin learned that the three Antenori were now actively imploring him to transform the lagoon communities into a Frankish province. Wasting no time, he hastily prepared his invasion force and hurried north.[19]

The Shift to Rivoaltus

The Antenori's shocking act of ducal treachery and Pepin's armed threat to Venetian independence finally galvanized the lagoon cities into concerted action. After falling back from all the outlying settlements, Venetians stoutly defended their capital at Malamocco, in the center of the line of sandy barrier islands that separated the lagoon from the Adriatic. And when that, too, proved indefensible, they carried out a deliberate retreat into the very heart of the lagoon. Here, on the barely populated islands of the Rialtine archipelago, ringed with oozy shoals and inscrutable underwater passages, they continued to defy the Frankish aggressors. Across the way, sensing that victory was near, Pepin ordered his infantry to seize boats and cross the short distance separating them from this seemingly defenseless mass of spongy islets. But as the invading host closed on this last Venetian refuge, they discovered that just below the placid surface lay a labyrinth of hidden channels and clay banks. As tidal waters dipped ever so slightly, the Frankish vessels began to run aground on half-seen muddy reefs. Frustrated and confused, the Franks climbed over the gunwales and attempted to free themselves from the treacherous muck. Sagging under heavy armor, their feet slipping and sinking in the mire, Pepin's soldiers were immediately attacked by Venetian marines and naval archers fighting in their native element. Many Franks were drowned or cut to pieces as they floundered and cursed near a channel known forever after as the Canal of the Orphans. The following summer, when disease broke out among the invaders (who had not anticipated a long struggle against resolute defenders), Pepin terminated the campaign and departed.

Venetian reaction to the victory was more reflective than ecstatic. Even as the lagoon dwellers offered prayers of thanksgiving, they brooded on the narrow margin of their deliverance and their continuing vulnerability. The nature of the problem was clear. The barbarian invasions had caused individual refugee bands to flee to separate islands, leaving the lagoon federation in a state of perpetual disunion that made it susceptible to even an improvised attack by a second-rate commander like Pepin. What was needed was a radical new start, a wholesale concentration of forces in an impregnable site free from the tribal animosities of the past. And if unity and national security were the criteria, there was really only one choice. The islets making up the Rialtine cluster were centrally located and sparsely inhabited. Their approach channels were narrow and sufficiently treacherous to make them impenetrable to anyone not intimately familiar with their peculiar tidal shifts. Equally important, the archipelago was unassociated with any of the rival factions.

Of course, there were major drawbacks as well, defects serious enough to explain why development of *rivus altus* ("deep stream" in the Latin of the old chronicles, referring to the serpentine river, the Grand Canal to be, whose deep channel formed a backward S as it coursed north to south through the 117 islets making up the Rialtine group) had lagged behind the other settlements. Unlike Torcello, Heraclea, and Malamocco, which were built on solid, dry ground, the Rialtine islands were low and waterlogged. Large portions were really no more than seaweed-covered mud reefs subject to frequent tidal submersion. It would require extensive land reclamation before the archipelago could accommodate an influx of new settlers, and the primitive methods available for draining, enlarging, and reinforcing low, saturated land masses ensured that this would be an arduous, time-consuming process.[20]

However, in 811, having made the decision to relocate to Rivoaltus, the Venetians' most immediate task was not material; it was political. Although the Antenori doges made a last-minute attempt to undo their treason by pretending to oppose the very invasion their betrayal had invited, no one was fooled. The three brothers were deposed and exiled, one being sent in chains to Constantinople and the others to Dalmatia across the Adriatic. Thus, at the threshold of what would hopefully be a new era of national unity, the lagoon had to choose a fresh leader. The ideal candidate needed to meet two essential criteria. He should be an outstanding patriot; that is, he should have taken a leading role in the heroic repulse of the Franks. And he should be free from even the slightest taint of foreign alliance, a requirement that, practically speaking, meant that he should be a native of the Rialtine islands. Fortunately, there was just such a man to whom the lagoon dwellers could turn, and it was upon his head that the citizens of Venice decided to bestow the ducal powers.

The patrician roots of Agnello Participazio went back to the lagoon settlements' earliest beginnings. The Participazi had originally settled in Byzantine-oriented Heraclea, where a succession of family members had served as that city's elected municipal tribune. Then, at the beginning of the eighth century, the clan had migrated to the frontier islands of Rivoaltus, where they settled on the north bank of the archipelago's great, curving river. A hundred years later, when the Franks encircled the lagoon, Agnello had immediately volunteered for military service. His courageous leadership of Venetian marines helped ensure that the enemy never gained the final redoubt that was also his family home. As a native, he understood both the merits of Rivoaltus as a defensive stronghold and the amount of painful struggle it would require to transform that cluster of swampy islets into a unified urban center. After weighing the pros and cons, he had strongly advocated relocating the seat of government to the Rialtine archipelago. His selection was a near unanimous choice, and, as future events would prove, a wise one.

Chapter Two

New Beginnings (811–976)

Reflections of the New Doge

As the eighth doge of Venice, Agnello Participazio was initially forced to govern from his small, fortified house near the present-day Campo Santi Apostoli in the northern part of the archipelago. Given its total inadequacy as even a temporary ducal palace, the doge must have wasted little time before scouting sites for the construction of a new governmental center. Ideally, such a complex needed to be positioned at the southern end of the broad serpentine river that ran through the central mass of the Rialtine islands before emptying into a large basin which served as the city's main harbor. Such a location, midway along the southern rim of the archipelago, provided an excellent view of the lidi and the open sea beyond, the direction from which any naval invasion force would approach the lagoon. There was an existing site that met this criterion, and it was to this spot that the doge ordered his boatman to steer one bright, sunlit morning.

As he stepped into the waiting vessel, Doge Agnello must have been all too aware of the heavy responsibilities that his fellow citizens, most of whom resided in older, richer settlements, had laid upon him. He was charged with the daunting task of transforming his home, a largely uninhabited group of boggy islets and sandbars roughly two and a half miles long and half as wide, into a united political and commercial capital. During the past two centuries, while the principal cities of the lagoon—Torcello, Malamocco and Heraclea—were growing and prospering, Rivoaltus had slumbered virtually undisturbed. As a result, there was little to distract the doge's thoughts from the cares of office as his boat swerved along the great curving river between banks of soft mud and an occasional plot of reclaimed soil.

Rather than a continuous arc of marble or brick palaces rising above a grand canal, the doge passed solitary timber-framed houses with reed-thatched roofs and wooden outbuildings, scattered along mazy, swampy shores. Occasionally, there might also be a small stone church. Fishermen standing on wooden docks or in small boats cast their nets into the wide stream and its many tributaries. Here and there amid the surrounding clumps of land, the doge could recognize the faces of men he knew tending vines or tilling small fields while pigs and cattle lazed along the muddy banks. Gazing into the morning sun, there was nothing to block his view all the way out to the lidi with their as-yet-uncut stands of pine forest visible against the eastern horizon. North toward the mainland, the sharp blue pyramids of the Dolomite Mountains appeared magnified in the crystalline air.

Abruptly, this view of the mountains triggered an entirely new train of reflections in the doge. Ceasing to obsess about his public burdens, his thoughts suddenly converged on the geophysical wonder surrounding him on every side, and he began to perceive the lagoon as the natural marvel it truly was: a unique aquatic environment whose very existence constituted a kind of miracle. A whole series of improbable steps had led to its formation. In the beginning, minute bits of Alpine debris had washed down and become dissolved in streams like the Piave, the Sile, and the Brenta, which watered the thirty miles of open plain between the Dolomites and the Adriatic. If the sediment were too heavy or the current dried up for lack of rain, the particles ended up on the river bottoms; if the rivers flooded, the suspended deposits ran off and became alluvial soil. In either case, they never reached the coast. To keep the process going, sediment that completed the long river journey and reached open water had to receive precisely the right surge of both freshwater and marine currents. Under ideal conditions, water-suspended sand would be thrown back repeatedly just before it entered the open Adriatic, and in time a long series of sandbars would be formed, partially sealing off a body of water between such lidi and the mainland. As sand and mud were increasingly trapped within this encapsulated area, a shallow lake dotted with small muddy islands and crisscrossed with intricate fresh- and saltwater rivulets would gradually be formed. Finally, if conditions were truly perfect, as they had been at Venice, waves from the Adriatic would scour openings or ports through the sandbars, flushing the lagoon with daily tidal action and transforming it into a harbor with access to the open sea.

To Doge Agnello, the meaning of this astonishing process was inescapable. Over the course of countless millennia, God had directed the powers of nature to prepare this miraculous environment for the deliverance of the Venetian people.

The Original San Marco Site

At the end of his reverie, the doge looked up to see that his boat had reached the point where the great river flowed into the open waters of the archipelago's principal harbor. After coursing east for several hundred yards, the boatman turned left toward a small island. The approaching concave shoreline was low and muddy, with harbor waters frequently encroaching on what passed for dry ground. On a protruding spit of land to his right, Doge Agnello could see the decrepit remains of an early Byzantine castle, an abandoned outpost of the Eastern Empire. The boatman pulled past the ancient fortress before gliding to a halt against the far end of the incurving waterfront. Stepping ashore and walking straight ahead, the doge entered a "cloister-like"[1] green field or *campo* in the middle of an L-shaped island. To the left, the island ended abruptly at the bank of a small tree-lined stream.[2]

On the right, there was a small stone church built on a central Greek-cross plan imported from Constantinople. This was the church of San Teodoro, which, according to the early chronicles, was erected in the mid-sixth century by the Byzantine general Narses during his campaign to retake Italy from the Goths. The church was named for Saint Theodore of Amasea, also known as Saint Theodore Tyro. Theodore had been a recruit (a *tyro* in Latin) in the Roman army. He was also a Christian martyr. In 306, while serving in the province of Pontus near the Black Sea, he protested the persecution of Christianity under Diocletian by setting fire to a pagan temple dedicated to Cybele, the Great Mother, for which he was himself condemned to death by burning.[3]

In Byzantium, Theodore was highly venerated as one of the Eastern Church's three warrior saints; within Constantinople alone, there were thirteen churches bearing his name. As an Eastern soldier martyr, Theodore would have been a natural choice for the patron saint of a church originally serving the needs of a Byzantine military encampment. According to early sources, after recognizing the Venetian harbor's strategic naval advantages and anchoring his large war fleet there before returning to Constantinople, Narses had built San Teodoro and resided within its walls for a short time. The church was probably crowned with a central dome and preceded by a Byzantine vestibule or narthex; its interior was celebrated for its stately columns and sumptuous marbles.[4]

Walking across the San Teodoro campo and peering through the tree line that formed its western boundary, the doge would have found a crude wooden bridge over the narrow stream that separated the first island from its neighbor. Looking across, the doge could see that the second island was essentially a large orchard surrounded by open fields. Within this orchard was another small Greek-plan church built in brick. This was San Geminiano e Mena, which the early chronicles report was also built by Narses in the mid-sixth century. The church's first namesake, Saint Geminian, was a mid-fourth-century deacon of Modena, who gave shelter to Saint Athanasius, one of the Eastern Church's greatest theologians. The second namesake, Saint Menas, was an Egyptian martyr and Byzantine military saint.[5]

That was all. There was no Molo, no Campanile, no Piazzetta, no Ducal Palace, no Basilica San Marco, and no Piazza. In fact, there was no urban landscape of any kind. In 811, this future scene of Venetian power and glory was nothing more than a rustic island landscape of fields, vines, and fruit trees containing a ruined castle and a few scattered monuments to Greek soldier-saints and church fathers. What little architecture existed gave evidence of an exclusively Byzantine military and religious culture. Clearly, before a new Venice, with its own distinctive form and identity, could emerge, some fresh, far more original ingredient would have to be supplied.

Having completed his inspection tour, Doge Agnello decided to construct a new ducal "palace" on the site of the disintegrating Byzantine castle. However, the building he erected, constructed of thick stone blocks, enclosed by water on every side, and bristling with battle ramparts, fortified gates, and corner towers to control the harbor and safeguard ducal authority, was much closer to being a moated fortress than a palatial residence. The chambers within its dark, dank interior were used as ducal sleeping quarters, meeting halls, stables, an armory, a military barracks, and a prison, all connected by low, narrow passageways. It was very similar to its counterparts on the feudal mainland, built to keep hostile forces at bay rather than to serve as the busy center of an open communal government.[6]

Meanwhile, on an adjacent site just to the northeast, the Greek emperor was constructing a splendid new Byzantine sanctuary on a parcel of ducal land donated to the project by the Participazio family.[7] The project was under the control of a Greek master builder and employed a host of highly skilled artisans, all imported from Constantinople, almost fourteen hundred sea miles to the east. When completed, the church would contain another imperial gift: the remains of Saint Zaccarias, the father of John the Baptist. Although by this time Byzantium was no longer able to project its military power into the Adriatic without Venetian naval assistance, it still possessed enormous cultural capital, including an extraordinary number of priceless Christian relics, which it could choose to bestow on those it perceived as faithful allies. The emperor must have hoped that his resplendent new church would be received by grateful Venetians as a major addition to their architectural patrimony but, unfortunately, his timing could not have been worse. Since the defeat of the Franks and the decision to move the governmental center to Rivoaltus, Venetians seem to have experienced a rapid and intense surge of national imagination. They were beginning to feel secure in their new island stronghold, and the sense of relief this brought allowed them to compare the city's future prospects with their original plight as terrified mainlanders huddled in desolate, forbidding swamps. Looking back at that brutal lopping-off of all that had come before, that beginning from absolute zero in a maze of mud and water, they could only marvel at the distance they had already traveled. In addition to a profound sense of gratitude, they must have experienced a kind of collective euphoria, a feeling that literally nothing was impossible. In any event, they were in no mood to rest content with colonial hand-me-downs and tokens of imperial largesse.

The Theft of Saint Mark

What occurred next, in the year 828, was a marriage of cold, calculated conception and breathtakingly audacious execution. The body of Saint Mark the Evangelist lay in a lightly guarded tomb in Alexandria, Egypt, a city well-known to Venetian merchants. This magnificent ancient capital had been founded by Alexander the Great but was now under Muslim control. Mark is credited with being in the Garden of Gethsemane when Jesus was arrested by Roman soldiers shortly before his crucifixion. He accompanied Paul and Barnabas on their first missionary journey to Asia Minor and later served as Peter's assistant in Rome. He authored a gospel believed to have been written specifically for Italians, and he founded the Church of Alexandria, the city where he was martyred in the seventh decade of the new Christian era. Tradition also credited Mark with extending his missionary efforts to the northern Adriatic, where he was said to have founded the See of Aquileia. Thus, to Venetians of the early ninth century, Mark was not only an epic figure in the general history of early Christianity, he was the creator of the lagoon Church in particular. This mattered because only a year earlier, Venice had suffered an alarming setback in her continuing struggle for ecclesiastical dominance in the northern Adriatic.[8]

In 827, the same year that Doge Agnello Participazio died, the Pope had restored the supremacy of the church of Aquileia, which was under the influence of the Frankish Empire, over the See of Grado, which was controlled by Venice. The Patriarch of Aquileia, who was rebuilding a magnificent municipal basilica with heavy financial support from the Franks, was determined to crush Grado, and establishing Mark as the uncontested patron saint of Aquileia would have advanced his purpose admirably. In this situation where demand for the credible remains of major Christian saints clearly exceeded supply, the theft of relics from sites with important Christian associations such as Alexandria had become a common practice, often involving the employment of professional thieves.[9]

Given the international prestige that the Evangelist's remains would instantly convey to an upstart city like Venice and the risk of allowing the Patriarch of Aquileia or his Frankish allies, who were actively promoting the development of a cult of saints throughout their dominions, to act first, there was no hesitation. In 828, two Venetian merchants sailed into the great Alexandrian harbor (*Fig. 6*) prepared to execute a daring plan. In the shadow of the city's great lighthouse towering four hundred feet above their masts, the conspirators waited for nightfall before entering the huge metropolis and proceeding to the saint's burial site located not far inland. After co-opting the Christian sentinels guarding the tomb, the Venetians lifted the heavy lid of the sarcophagus, carefully removed Mark's mummified body from his funeral shroud, and lowered the sacred remains into a basket. Then, slipping another corpse into the Evangelist's grave clothes and placing that in the empty stone casket, they spirited the precious relics away to their waiting ship.

Of course, the tomb robbers still had to worry about possible detection by Egyptian customs inspectors controlling the Alexandrian harbor. To meet this threat, they filled the basket containing Saint Mark with a thick layer of pig's flesh and cabbage. Attempting to leave the port, the Venetian ship was boarded and searched; however, as soon as the lid of the basket was lifted, the orthodox Muslim officials recoiled in horror and fled overboard uttering cries of "Swine! Swine!" (*Fig. 7*).[10] In the confusion, the Venetian merchants made a rapid departure for the lagoon, where, after crossing almost fifteen hundred miles of open sea, they were hailed by the new doge, Giustiniano Participazio (Agnello's son) and his court. Following a thorough cleansing, the precious relics were deposited in an improvised chapel in a corner tower of the recently completed ducal fortress. Like much Venetian behavior to follow, the action was swift, shameless, and supremely effective.

Fig. 6: Great lighthouse and harbor of ancient Alexandria

In burgling the lagoon's future patron saint before he could be seized by a rival city, the pious thieves were almost certainly acting at the direction of the new doge, perhaps according to plans passed down from his recently deceased father. In any event, this brazen act of body snatching proved to be a powerful spur to city's mythic imagination. For, once interred in the center of the lagoon, Saint Mark became much more than a venerated relic held under close guard in a ducal chapel. He was transformed into a new and uniquely Venetian symbol. In future centuries, whether emblazoned on a crimson banner, enthroned on a towering pillar, or staring majestically from an intricately carved Gothic doorway, it was the Winged Lion of Saint Mark with its bold gleaming eyes, poised for soaring flight and dominion over other mere terrestrial creatures, that fully expressed the expansive scope of Venetian aspirations. In its fully realized form, this is the arrogant creature who stares back at us in Vittore Carpaccio's famous painting of the Winged Lion (*Fig. 8*), daring us even to think about questioning the predestination legend that later generations invented to explain the transfer of Mark's relics to Venice. That myth is encapsulated in a brief Latin phrase (*Pax tibi, Marce, evangelista meus*) written on the pages of a book that the Lion holds up for our inspection. The words refer to the prophecy that an angel is supposed to have delivered to Mark after the saint's boat was blown off course during a missionary voyage across the lagoon, leaving him stranded on the Rialtine islands. "Peace to you, Mark, my evangelist. Here [on the islands of Rivoaltus], your body shall rest," the divine messenger is said to have assured him.[11]

The Original Church of San Marco

In 829, only a year after Saint Mark's removal to Venice and a scant two years after taking office, Doge Giustiniano Participazio discovered that he was terminally ill. Knowing that he had only a short time left, the doge devoted his remaining days to ensuring that the sacred relics would be enshrined in a magnificent new church. He ordered that the collection of ancient Roman columns, reliefs, and other precious building spoils which he had lovingly scavenged from the mainland to enrich his private residence should instead be used to ornament the new sanctuary. But the decisions of the dying doge in those last few months of life did much more than determine the appearance of the first church of San Marco. By establishing the purpose as well as the site of the original building, they permanently shaped the form and function of the entire Piazza complex to come. As Doge Giustiniano conceived of it, the new shrine would be constructed as an annex to his father's imposing ducal fortress. Since it would be built on ducal land on the easternmost of the two San Marco islands, the reigning doge would control Saint Mark's sanctuary as his personal chapel and administer it through ducal appointees without interference by Roman Church officials.

Thus, from the beginning, Venice chose to integrate its principal church and its chief governmental building in one central location, a pattern distinctly at odds with the practice of mainland Italian cities such as Padua, Vicenza, Verona, Florence, and Siena, where separate civic and church squares were located some distance apart. In concentrating the two functions in a single unified setting, Venice was modeling herself on Constantinople,

Fig. 7: "Swine! Swine!" Seventeenth-century lunette mosaic,
western façade, Basilica San Marco

Fig. 8: The Winged Lion of Saint Mark *by Vittore Carpaccio*

where the state cathedral, Haghia Sophia, as well as the Senate building and the imperial palace all opened onto the same splendid classical square, an imperial forum known as the Augusteum. This Late Antique Byzantine model was, in turn, derived from an even earlier classical prototype: the Roman Forum. In the Forum, altars and temples to a host of gods and deified Romans were indiscriminately packed into the same constricted space shared by shops and major public buildings of the state, including the Senate house, the state archives, the law courts, and a prison. Indeed, in the Forum, religious and government functions were sometimes housed in a single building; for example, the basement of a religious edifice like the Temple of Saturn contained the Roman public treasury. Moving back another step in time, this classical mix of political, religious, and commercial uses in a single setting was a pattern derived from the ancient Greek agora.[12]

The decision to make San Marco an annex to the ducal fortress also meant that the new church would be constructed on a severely constricted site owned by the Participazio family, a parcel hemmed in by San Teodoro to the north, San Zaccaria to the east, and the ducal castle to the south. In fact, part of the land previously donated for the construction of San Zaccaria had to be reacquired in order to meet even minimal site requirements for the new church, since San Marco was designed to be a very grand building by the standards of ninth-century Venice. Although not as tall as the church we see today, its total floor area, including its attached atrium, was almost as great. Such impressive dimensions are less surprising, however, when we understand the grand Late Antique model on which it was based. The Participazi envisioned something fundamentally different from the standard basilica-plan church, with its prominent longitudinal axis or nave, which had previously been adopted throughout most of Italy, including the lagoon.[13] They patterned their building on the church of the Holy Apostles in Constantinople (known as the Apostoleion), one of the Greek capital's most magnificent structures.[14]

Originally erected by Constantine the Great as his own imperial mausoleum, the Apostoleion[15] had been completely rebuilt in the sixth century by the emperor Justinian as an apostolic shrine chiefly devoted to Mark's fellow evangelist Luke. In its reconstructed form, it was an eminent example of the fundamental change in Christian church design wrought at this time by Eastern architects. While earlier churches were typically based on the horizontal, longitudinal, timber-roofed designs of Roman meeting halls known as basilicas, the new Justinian churches had a centralized, often cruciform, plan and were frequently capped with magnificent central domes. Their emphasis on a unified central vertical space allowed Byzantine churches to mirror the Greek conception of the cosmos by transforming the cupolas, suspended over the congregation of earthly worshipers standing below, into symbolic representations of the heavenly spheres.

Justinian's Apostoleion served several functions. It was an apostles' church, housing the remains of no less than three apostles, and it served as an important state church as well as a dynastic chapel for the imperial families that ruled Byzantium. Since the Participazi intended San Marco to serve these same religious, political, and dynastic purposes, they logically decided to imitate, to the degree their means allowed, this great Byzantine original. Such emulation was facilitated by the close alliance ninth-century Venice enjoyed with the Eastern Empire. Members of the Participazi, like many prominent Venetians, were frequent visitors to Constantinople, where they had ample opportunity to view its architectural monuments in person. In return, Byzantium sent some of its finest artists and architects to work on major projects in the lagoon, as the emperor had done during the construction of San Zaccaria.[16]

The Apostoleion had a Greek-cross floor plan and was topped with five large brick domes, one erected over the square-shaped central bay and another over each of the building's four equal arms. To make this innovative architecture possible, Greek builders had perfected a Syrian method for making a smooth transition from a square or rectangular floor space to an overhead cupola. These beautiful and efficient structures—elegant concave spandrels that connected perpendicular supporting walls to the bottom of the circular drum on which the dome rested—were called pendentives (*Fig. 10*). They had been virtually unknown to Roman imperial builders, who almost always erected domes over circles, as in the Pantheon (*Fig. 9*). The four arms of the Apostoleion interior were surrounded by generous side aisles and imposing upper-story galleries, and their walls were covered with intricately patterned marble panels. Immediately below the mosaic-covered central dome was the shrine containing apostolic relics. Visitors passed into the church through a colonnaded portico or atrium. Dominating the crest of the fourth of Constantinople's seven hills, with a magnificent view of the capital's long, bow-shaped harbor, the Apostoleion was a spectacular sight even in a city bursting with architectural wonders.[17]

Of course, given the complexities of a cramped island site and the limited resources of a pioneer state such as ninth-century Venice, San Marco could never be a literal copy of its

Byzantine prototype. In addition, there were differences in the rites of worship practiced in the Eastern Church and those adopted in the lagoon (where Western forms prevailed) that dictated changes in architectural practice. For instance, in a Byzantine church, the altar was usually located under the central dome. This followed from the fact that in the Greek liturgy, the sanctuary's entire central bay was reserved for the performance of the Mass by a professional priesthood, with the laity restricted to observing from the surrounding aisles. In the Italian practice, which Venice followed, rather than being centrally located, the altar and the principal relics were typically placed in a presbytery at the eastern end of the church, where the Mass was also celebrated.[18]

And, as always, there was the human factor, perhaps the most formidable obstacle of all to the realization of Doge Giustiniano's dying ambition. As the doge knew all too well (being the son of a doge himself), an incipient dynastic tradition had now begun to guide the people's choice of a new ducal leader upon the death of his predecessor. Unfortunately, if this model were followed when he died, Giustiniano's successor would be none other than his younger brother Giovanni, a man for whom he had always displayed nothing but open contempt. In fact, at one point, relations had become so bitter that the doge had exiled his brother from Venice. Nevertheless, as death neared, Giustiniano understood that it was into the hands of this unworthy sibling that he would now have to commit the faithful execution of his life's goal; he could only hope that God would be merciful. As anticipated, Giovanni was elected to fill his brother's empty chair, but fortunately, whatever resentment he may have felt over half a lifetime of sibling persecution did not prevent his carrying out the San Marco project in full accord with Giustiniano's expansive vision. Giovanni adopted his brother's plan as though it were his own and finished the new church in 836 after a building process of only seven years. Until then, Saint Mark's relics remained in a corner tower of the ducal fortress.

The Construction Process

The doge's architect began the construction process by drawing San Marco's cruciform ground plan in the muddy ground between San Teodoro and the ducal castle. Foundation trenches were then dug, passing though the thin, wet soil just below the surface to the dense clay layer lying nine to ten feet down, with wooden buttressing used to keep the dirt walls from collapsing. Thousands of oak and larch pilings were then driven vertically into the hard clay at the bottom of the trenches, and rafts of thick wooden planks were laid horizontally on top of that. The foundations themselves were formed of massive stones lowered onto the planking. Since the harbor waters ran inland along the entire western flank of the ducal fortress, this created a small marina and dock at the northern end where small boats could transport enormous foundation stones to the very edge of the construction site. These included ancient Roman stones salvaged from Aquileia and Altino. On top of this heavy stone base, masons laid alternating rows of brick and smaller stones up to ground level.

Since scholarly opinion differs about the form of San Marco above its foundations, what follows is a consensus account of the scene Doge Giovanni Participazio would have witnessed as he kept watch on the project from the towers of the ducal fortress. The church's ascending brick walls would have formed four equal arms of a Greek cross, with each arm topped by a gabled timber roof. The eastern arm would have been attached to a triad of projecting apses, creating the effect of an extended eastern wing, with the altar located within the curve of the middle apse. Rising above the central crossing was a large but shallow brick dome resting on four massive barrel vaults with pendentives. The vaults were supported by huge stone-and-brick piers, each of which rested on four legs. Missing entirely were the four lateral domes, continuous side aisles, and upper-story galleries that would have allowed the interior of San Marco to rival the grandeur of the Apostoleion in Constantinople. However, if San Marco's single dome was hardly a match for the five-domed magnificence of its Byzantine original, in Venice the erection of even a single cupola, with its immensely heavy vaults, pendentives, and pier supports, was a very problematic undertaking. Since their structural integrity depended on an inflexible support system, such constructions were particularly prone to stress and collapse from the lagoon's continuous ground settlement. To counteract this rigidity, masons used slow-drying soft-lime mortar to cement the bricks in the dome and vaults, with the result that Venetian cupolas were likely to lose their original spherical shape in the process of curing, which could take several seasons.[19]

The church was preceded by an arcaded courtyard. Normally, such atriums were open to the public, but in this case San Marco was a private chapel built on ducal grounds with a number of interior passages running directly between the church and the inner sanctums of the ducal castle. Thus, to allow unrestricted public access from the public square into

Fig. 9: Interior of the Pantheon, Rome

the courtyard and the church beyond would have created serious security problems within the ducal residence, risks that Doge Giovanni, who had become a distinctly unpopular leader, was not prepared to run. To allay such fears, he built a large two-story guardhouse, complete with interior stairs, into the outer wall of the courtyard, and there he stationed an armed garrison to control entry into the atrium and the church.[20]

Viewed from the outside, the completed church was deceptively plain. But, in the typical Byzantine manner, San Marco's unornamented brick façade belied the decorative wealth within. If admitted beyond the guard station and atrium courtyard, visitors passed into a glowing interior suffused with light from windows encircling the base of the central dome and adorned with stately ancient columns, brightly colored mosaics, and elegant Roman

Fig. 10: Interior of Haghia Sophia, Constantinople, showing
pendentives supporting the great dome

and Byzantine reliefs collected from ruins as far away as Sicily. Rising at the far end of the church, in the precise middle of the central apse, was Saint Mark's burial shrine, a massive slab of red Verona marble balanced on four thick columns topped with heavy green marble capitals. Here, in 836, Doge Giovanni presided over a service in which the Evangelist was formally laid to rest in his new Venetian home.[21]

Threats to the Lagoon

Having completed this historic Participazio family achievement, Doge Giovanni apparently concluded that his ducal labors were over. Thus, he took no countermeasures even as Venetian ships passing up and down the Adriatic were repeatedly attacked and plundered by Dalmatian pirates, thereby reinforcing the misgivings Venetians had always harbored about his suitability for high office. Finally, when the people had endured enough, they forcibly retired Doge Giovanni and elected a new leader who they believed would at least try to meet the new dangers the city was facing. This established a precedent that held true for most of the next century. The principal criterion for electing a new doge would almost always be his projected fitness to protect Venetian lives and property from a continual series of threats—Slavic pirates, Saracen naval raiders, and nomadic Magyar armies—operating just outside the lagoon. In this long effort to protect the upper Adriatic (the so-called Gulf of Venice) from piracy and foreign invasion, the city experienced several major scares. In 899, a barbarian army of Magyars from central Asia overran northern Italy and successfully repeated Pepin's encirclement of the lagoon nearly a century earlier. Advancing from the south, the Magyars captured several key settlements on the lidi before being repulsed by a combined Venetian land and naval force commanded by Doge Pietro Tribuno. Victorious, but alarmed by another dangerously close incursion, Venice decided to construct whatever was required to deal with the ultimate nightmare scenario—an enemy naval penetration of the lagoon, particularly one able to reach the ducal center on Rivoaltus.

Thus, Doge Tribuno devoted his reign (888–912) to building a formidable defensive system. He constructed the foundations for a massive tower or campanile next to the small canal, the Rio Batario, which separated the two islands making up the San Marco precinct. When raised to a serviceable height, this huge structure would function as both a watch tower for detecting foreign fleets and a beacon to returning Venetian ships. Across the entrances to the principal canals, the doge installed a network of heavy iron chains that, when winched up from the bottom and pulled taut, would close such vital access points. Above all, the doge constructed a long battlemented wall along the harbor front from the eastern end of Venice to a point well west of the ducal fortress. At San Marco, the main wall ran across the harbor front, while a branch turned inland to enclose the two islands of the ducal center and to merge with key defensive strongholds such as the ducal castle and the campanile. The building of Tribuno's wall was another major milestone in the development of Venetian identity, marking the point when the settlement at Rivoaltus became a *civitas*, a separate enclosed space that provided its citizens with a fresh sense of security and collective purpose.[22]

The Revolt Against the Candiano Dynasty

A century after the move to Rivoaltus, Venice could look back with satisfaction at what she had accomplished. Her ducal center was fortified, her trade was expanding from the Italian mainland to the Mediterranean and Black seas, and her growing naval power made her an increasingly valuable ally to both the Eastern and Western empires. The trick, she would soon discover, was preserving the conditions that had nurtured this astonishing resurgence. Experience had shown that successful Venetian governments followed two basic rules. They did everything in their power to ensure internal harmony within the lagoon community, and they steered clear of entangling foreign alliances, particularly any close association with the alien feudal culture of mainland Europe. Yet somehow, in 959, Venice elected a leader whose personal ambitions were a blatant contradiction of this successful formula.

Pietro Candiano IV was the fourth member of his family to be elected doge during the previous seventy years.[23] While he displayed the same energy, aggression, and dynastic ambition that had characterized earlier Candiani, in his case these qualities had combined with a blind and willful insolence that caused them to metastasize into something distinctly more sinister. His haughty, despotic personality had more in common with the arrogant feudal barons who ruled the Italian *terraferma* than with the earlier ducal leaders of the Venetian lagoon. From his youth, this latest Candiano had been a source of factional strife within the city, having repeatedly led his personal gang of thugs in violent public attacks against the rule of his father. After this earned him a sentence of exile from Venice, he grew to manhood as an embittered refugee, a frequent guest in mainland courts, where he came to relish the unbridled power wielded by his autocratic hosts. Then, astonishingly, upon the death of his father, the Venetians chose this banished son to become their new leader. The dynastic tradition, which had gained increasing currency in Venice during the tenth century, was undoubtedly a major factor. However, in the face of such a staggering failure of collective judgment, one can only surmise that some other cause must also have been at work. The values of Western feudal culture exemplified by Candiano IV—its pomp and splendor, its emphasis on personal aggrandizement, its freedom from the boring restrictions of prudent government—must have begun to have their corrosive appeal within Venice herself.

But whatever may have propelled Venetians to make such a choice, the new doge wasted little time in demonstrating just how rashly they had acted. He divorced his Venetian wife and remarried the Western emperor's German niece, who was also sister to one of the greatest of all mainland barons. Since her dowry included immense landholdings in northern Italy, the doge of Venice instantly became a feudal vassal of the Holy Roman emperor. Not content with this outrage, the doge also appointed his son to a series of lucrative ecclesiastical posts with major Italian landholdings. Based on such behavior, it became increasingly clear to a large number of Venetians that in the eyes of their doge, Venice herself had become nothing but a convenient launching pad for Candiano family glory. Unless something changed, the city would probably end up as only a minor appendage to the interlocking power structure of feudal Europe. And Doge Pietro seems to have been keenly aware of just how unpopular his actions had now become. Whether holding court in his fortified castle or riding through the city on horseback, he was always surrounded by a large bodyguard of foreign troops recruited from his feudal estates. To most Venetians, it felt like an occupation.

By the summer of 976, the situation was grave. Doge Pietro was forcing Venice to decide just how far she would tolerate the dismantling of her immensely successful political and economic institutions. Many of the community's merchant leaders could see that unless prompt corrective action were taken, their profitable way of life based on commercial enterprise, Eastern trade, and mobile, nonlanded capital might well be destroyed. It was at this point that Doge Pietro had the stunningly bad idea to try to draft lagoon residents into his personal army and force them to defend his family property on the Italian mainland. It was the final insult. Having been pushed too far, the people, including the merchant nobility, rose up in violent revolt. Determined to put an end to Candiani misrule, they charged past Tribuno's crenellated wall and began to assault the ducal fortress. From the top of the castle towers, the doge's foreign troops looked down on a campo swarming with armed, enraged Venetians. Of course, given the inherent defensive strength of a medieval castle, this initial frontal attack was a failure, but its bloody repulse only increased the populace's anger and frustration. Changing tactics, they decided to burn the hated leader out of his lair. Realizing that some of them would be destroying their own homes, they set fire to the wooden houses around the fortress, and, as hoped, the flames soon spread to the castle and the annexed ducal chapel.

To escape the choking smoke that soon engulfed the fortress, Candiano and his wife and infant son plunged into one of the stone passageways leading from the castle into the church. After struggling through the burning chapel, they emerged into the atrium courtyard, only to encounter a grim welcoming committee—Venetian nobles with drawn swords and bloody axes who had just hacked their way past the guardhouse portal. Pleas for mercy resulted in a decision to spare the wife only. Without another word, the assassins closed in and butchered the cornered doge where he stood. Determined to ensure that no Candiano would ever again rule in Venice, they ripped the child away from his mother and thrust a spear through his tiny body.

The killers then retraced their steps through the guardhouse portal into the smoke-filled campo. From there, they watched as the conflagration continued to spread freely, leaping from building to building until it engulfed the entire San Marco neighborhood. When the blaze was finally extinguished, the area of destruction was immense. Flames had gutted the ducal fortress, the churches of San Marco, San Teodoro and San Zaccaria, and hundreds of shops and residences in and around the government center. Venice had saved herself from a would-be tyrant, but the price had been enormous. In a single summer's day, she had lost 150 years of accumulated architectural development. Nor, in the immediate aftermath of the inferno was it even clear that the priceless relics of the Evangelist himself had survived.

Chapter Three

Saint Mark's Basilica (976–1094)

The Aftermath of the Revolt

Venetians entering the San Marco district the morning after the Candiano uprising would have found only a single intact structure: the squat brick stump of Pietro Tribuno's partially completed watch tower. If they climbed to the top of the unfinished Campanile, they could have peered down through the gutted walls of the ducal fortress and the attached chapel of Saint Mark. Resting in heaps on the stone floors were the smoldering embers of what had once been the roofs and upper stories. A few dozen yards away stood the equally devastated hulks of San Teodoro and San Zaccaria. From the tower, there was also a clear view of the long, straight line of the Tribuno defensive wall, largely undamaged as it ran down the harbor front toward the eastern end of the archipelago. But within the area where this barrier forked inland to enclose the two islands of the ducal center, all was ashy desolation. The rubble of incinerated houses and shops ringed both sides of its scorched brick walls.

Meanwhile, the bloody corpses of the doge and his infant son lay unburied in a butcher's stall in the city's central market, where their murderers had dragged them as flames were engulfing San Marco. Determined not to repeat the same disaster twice, the Venetians' choice of a successor fell upon a very different type of man. Thus, the new doge, Pietro Orseolo I, was a wealthy and successful merchant known for his sincere religious devotion and ascetic habits. But in the agitated political air that now prevailed in Venice, nothing could prevent the circulation of slanderous rumors. There was talk that it had been Doge Orseolo himself who had first suggested setting fire to the houses surrounding the ducal fortress. It was even whispered that he had made the ringleaders of the revolt promise that if he began the blaze by torching his own house, they would elect him doge after Candiano IV was eliminated. Whatever the truth of the first rumor, the second seems quite false, since we are told by the leading modern historian of Venice that Orseolo's dwelling was located well down the harbor front and away from the ducal center and, accordingly, that it survived the conflagration. More important, even if Orseolo and the other leaders of the uprising had wanted to strike a bargain, it is doubtful that they would have felt confident of their ability to impose its terms on the rest of the city. In 976, the general assembly of the people, called the *arengo*, was still the mainspring of Venetian politics. The congress of the people not only elected new ducal leaders by direct popular vote; upon occasion, it also established fundamental state policy. Once in office, a doge whose actions were in sync with the popular will possessed almost unlimited executive power. On the other hand, as the career of Candiano IV so clearly demonstrated, a doge who continually challenged strongly held majority views was playing a dangerous game. The Venetian political system did not yet recognize a distinct class of leading families whose judgment and experience were expected to channel, and frequently temper, the collective views of the people at large.[1]

Architectural Recovery

Since the ducal castle was still a smoldering shell, Doge Orseolo was forced to govern from his private home located along the walled harbor front stretching east from San Marco. His first act was to order the burial of Pietro Candiano IV and his son. Only then did his thoughts turn to rebuilding the charred ruins of the ducal precinct, which would be expensive no matter how economical a renovation plan might be adopted. Accordingly, he began by announcing that he would donate a large portion of his great personal wealth to the effort.[2]

Because the historical record is almost nonexistent, we can only deduce the form and scope of Doge Orseolo's rebuilding of the ducal fortress from the few general facts that we do have. We know that Venice needed a new government center as soon as possible and that reconstruction funds were limited. We know that the only reason the ducal castle had to be rebuilt at all was its destruction in an act of mob violence. From this, we can reasonably conclude that, for reasons of security, economy, and speed, the new ducal residence was a straightforward restoration project, closely modeled on the purely defensive citadel it replaced. As it had been for the past hundred and fifty years, the new structure remained the doge's almost exclusive preserve. The need for a more open and accessible form of public architecture containing new types of interior space would not arise for another two centuries, after the city had begun to experiment with genuinely communal forms of government.[3]

The replacement church of San Marco also seems to have been a work of repair or restoration rather than a complete rebuilding. After clearing away the debris from the collapsed upper regions of the original Participazio church, masons no doubt tried to save and reuse as much of the building's wall and pier structure as possible. In any event, they certainly would have avoided altering the ground plan, a change that would have necessitated digging costly and time-consuming new foundations. Thus, from the outside, the completed Orseolo church no doubt strongly resembled the Participazio edifice—a Greek-cross, central-domed building with three apses at the end of its eastern arm. We do not know if the church of San Teodoro was also rebuilt at this time or if its ruins were simply left in place or perhaps even incorporated into the northern wall of the reconstructed San Marco. As to San Zaccaria, Otto Demus has made a persuasive case that not long after the Candiano fire, portions of that ruined church were used to build a replacement structure on the present site of San Zaccaria, several hundred yards to the east. Part of its original fabric may also have been used to restore San Marco. In addition, Doge Orseolo raised the San Marco Campanile to a serviceable height and initiated the construction of a pilgrim hospice that, in the view of most scholars, was a two-story edifice fronted by a portico of round arches on square piers which extended from the western edge of the Campanile to the Rio Batario. If this view is correct, the Campanile and the adjoining hospice created the nucleus of an architecturally organized southern boundary to the small campo fronting the rebuilt church and began the transformation of the square into an arcaded forecourt to San Marco, an intention which would be given much clearer, bolder form in the centuries to come.[4]

Survival of the Relics

But what did the fire do to the body of Saint Mark, the whole reason for creating and restoring the ducal church of San Marco in the first place? We know that the conflagration destroyed the building's vaults and ceilings and undoubtedly portions of the upper walls and pier supports as well. As these structures buckled and crashed to the ground, what damage did they do to the exposed tomb memorial containing the saint's relics in the center of the eastern apse? We know that Venetian chroniclers consistently denied that the saint's body was destroyed in the blaze, but the view of most contemporary non-Venetians must have been the same as that articulated many centuries later by John Ruskin, who could not have been more blunt. "The body of St. Mark ..., without doubt, perished in the conflagration of 976," and everything that Venetians later said and did in response to this undeniable fact "appears to have been one of the best arranged and most successful impostures ever attempted."[5] This included inventing a story that sometime prior to the revolt of 976, Doge Candiano had sensed impending trouble and transferred the saint's relics from the tomb monument in the eastern apse to a new, safe location whose exact whereabouts had, of course, been lost when the doge and his ducal chaplains, the only three people to know of the body's removal, were killed in the rebellion. Such a tale, so completely at odds with the well-known character of Doge Pietro, must have done little to convince a skeptical world. Thus, at precisely the moment when Venice was devoting scarce resources to rebuild Mark's architectural shrine, she was also under pressure to prove that she still possessed his intact earthly remains.[6]

Intriguingly, it was at precisely this point that the restorers of San Marco made the only significant change that we know of to the interior arrangements of the original Participazio church. Until the fire of 976, Saint Mark's tomb had been an unenclosed memorial located on the ground floor of the central apse. But in reconstructing the church, the Orseolo builders did something different; they erected brick vaults over the tomb monument, encasing it below a ceiling of protective masonry. This created a semi-crypt, a covered relic chamber below the now raised floor of the chancel, to which worshippers could descend and view what were said to be the intact remains of Saint Mark. It was an extremely costly undertaking, involving as it did raising the floor level of the church's eastern arm,[7] so expensive, in fact, that it seemed to act as a sufficient rebuttal to anyone impertinent enough to assert that the Evangelist's body had been destroyed or permanently lost. Would anyone, even the Venetians, incur such expense if there were nothing left to protect from future danger?

Factional Warfare

Doge Orseolo's personal generosity made him the ideal leader to initiate the architectural recovery of Venice, but he was temperamentally unsuited to solving the city's more fundamental problem: its unresolved, increasingly lethal political strife. By murdering Doge Candiano, the majority of the nobility had served notice that it would do whatever was required to protect the city's status as a rising commercial power, oriented toward the East and firmly outside the orbit of European feudalism. And although in the immediate aftermath of the revolt the Candiano party was now out of power in Venice itself, it remained a force to be reckoned with. Fresh from the butchery of her husband and infant son, Candiano's wife, the redoubtable Waldrada, had fled to the court of her uncle, the Western emperor, and from there, she was able to cow Doge Orseolo into repaying every ducat of the huge dowry she had brought to her assassinated spouse. As a result of giving in to such demands, Orseolo's popularity plummeted, and in 978, only two years after his election, he abandoned the ducal throne and fled to a monastery. At this point, the pro-Western party in Venice lost no time in trying to regain its position. The next two holders of the ducal throne were Candiani by blood or marriage, but they were too weak to tip the balance of power one way or another. As a result, the years 978–991 were a period of open warfare between the city's two major factions: a mercantile, pro-Byzantine party, headed by the Morosini clan, and a feudal, pro-Western camp led by the Coloprini family.[8]

The political cohesion that, a century and a half earlier, had been strong enough to repel a Frankish invasion seemed to have vanished entirely. The head of the Coloprini family plotted with the Western emperor to make Venice an imperial vassal in exchange for establishing a Coloprini dogate, an act of treason that came to nothing only because the chief conspirator suddenly died of natural causes. Other members of the Coloprini family were not as fortunate. In 991, a group of Morosini swordsmen attacked three Coloprini as they were entering boats near the rebuilt ducal fortress. After swiftly dispatching their victims, they tossed the bleeding corpses into the harbor in plain view of anyone who might care to watch. This open assassination of political opponents, perpetrated in the very heart of the restored governmental center, marked a low point in the city's political affairs. Victimized by such entrenched dynastic quarrels, most Venetians must have felt themselves sickeningly adrift, a potentially great people unable to break free from the greed and myopia of their would-be rulers. Then, just when blind clannishness seemed about to sink the lagoon enterprise altogether, this same dynastic principle suddenly produced a remedy.[9]

A Leader of Genius

When he fled the cares of office, Pietro Orseolo I left behind an adolescent son. And in 991, thirteen chaotic years later, it was to this Orseolo offspring, Pietro II, that Venice turned when her latest doge resigned in the teeth of the city's seemingly intractable political problems. What must Venetians have seen in Pietro II—a mere thirty years of age, completely untested, and son of the first of a long line of recent ducal leaders to buckle under pressure? Whatever it was, their judgment was superb. "Statesman, warrior and diplomatist of genius,"[10] from the moment of his election, the new doge brought the healing grace of true leadership to his demoralized people. The vicious internecine warfare that had infected the Venetian body politic like a seemingly ineradicable curse suddenly vanished as though it had never existed. Pietro Orseolo II instinctively understood that for a commercial power like Venice, being asked to choose between East and West was both self-defeating and completely unnecessary. In order to prosper, the city needed the friendship of both sovereigns: the Western emperor, who controlled river access and trade rights within the adjacent Italian mainland, and the emperor of the East in Constantinople, ruler of the world's most lucrative international trading preserve. Thus, his first actions were to reestablish profitable commercial relations with each of these two great empires and to enter into other beneficial trading arrangements with the Islamic kingdoms of Spain, Sicily, and the Middle East.

Nor did the new doge neglect critical problems closer to home. He understood that his brilliant diplomatic achievements, procuring open markets and lower tariffs in distant Byzantine and Levantine ports, would be of little value if Venetian merchants were afraid to venture forth and take advantage of such opportunities. Yet, for most of the past century, Venetian ships traversing the Adriatic had been the constant prey of Croatian pirates operating from their lairs along the Dalmatian coast. The Croats were a formidable military power; in repelling punitive missions led against their chief base near the mouth of the Narenta River, they had already slain one doge and kidnapped the son of another. And in 946, according to tradition, the Slavic raiders had even been bold enough to venture into the lagoon itself, where, after steering their boats to the eastern end of the Rialtine archipelago, they had landed near the cathedral church of San Pietro di Castello, a remote area unprotected by the Tribuno defensive system. By chance, the church at that moment contained a large number of Venetian maidens gathered for a collective marriage ceremony. Before the grooms could arrive, the pirates abducted the brides-to-be and sailed for open water; however, according to the story, the kidnappers were swiftly overtaken and the brides returned. Whether legendary or true, the episode clearly illustrates just how seriously Venetians felt forced to treat the Croatian menace. During the latter half of the tenth century, Venice regularly made large annual protection payments to allow her ships to pass Croat bases unmolested.[11]

With Pietro Orseolo II, this extortion came to an abrupt end; it simply did not comport with either his character or his conception of Venetian destiny. When agents of the Croatian chieftains arrived in Venice to receive their yearly tribute money, the doge answered that he did not want to deal with intermediaries—he would bring the Venetian response himself. Then, with the blessing of the Byzantine emperor, he summoned a general assembly of the Venetian people and proposed a military expedition to suppress Slavic piracy once and for all. Following the plan's enthusiastic reception and the celebration of a mass in San Pietro di Castello (the very church where, according to tradition, Croatian buccaneers had seized the brides of Venice), the doge led a formidable armada out of the lagoon. The day was May 9, 1000—Ascension Day in the Christian calendar and a date that in future years would be marked by a uniquely Venetian national ritual. Believing in the value of decisive early action, Orseolo steered his ships to the main pirate citadel of Lagosta, where his army stormed the heavily fortified city, slew all of the inhabitants, and toppled its walls and buildings. Then, relying as much on the threat of force as its actual application, the doge quickly liberated the Dalmatian coast from a scourge that for centuries had become an accepted fact of life. Suddenly freed after years of affliction, the non-Croatian peoples of the region were naturally quite eager to enter into the closest possible relationship with this new naval powerhouse from the northern Adriatic. Of course, in all his diplomatic gestures, Orseolo was careful to respect the area's nominal subjection to the Byzantine Empire, but it was to Venice that Dalmatian cities now looked for protection and economic alliance.[12]

These new relationships brought immediate tangible benefits. Henceforth, when Venetian merchants made voyages down the Adriatic to distant Mediterranean ports, their ships would find welcome in friendly Dalmatian harbors where they were encouraged to build profitable trading posts and warehouses. Equally important, many of these new allies produced in abundance the very types of natural resources that matched the city's critical needs. For instance, while the Venetian islands contained little arable land, the ample fields and vineyards of the eastern Adriatic produced plentiful crops of grain, olive oil, and wine. Once Venice had finished harvesting the pine forests on the lidi, the lagoon was almost treeless. But now the lush groves of oak, ash, beech, larch, pine, and fir that covered the plains and mountains of Dalmatia and its coastal islands could supply timber for the city's naval fleets and building projects for centuries to come. In addition, the upper Dalmatian coast contained large amounts of a dense, intensely white limestone (commonly referred to as Istrian stone), whose combination of hardness and workability made it the equal of marble as a building and sculptural material.

Thanks to Orseolo's brilliant Dalmatian campaign, the idea of what constituted Venetian home waters expanded exponentially, far beyond the lagoon itself. At a minimum, the entire upper Adriatic, as far south as Ravenna, was transformed into the Gulf of Venice, a fact that the city began to celebrate each Ascension Day with its own uniquely maritime ritual. Originally a fairly modest service, the doge and his retinue would gather on the open sea where a simple prayer and hymn of thanksgiving were offered. But over time, this became transformed into a much more elaborate and imperial ceremony known as the *Sposalizio del Mar* or Marriage of the Sea. In its fully evolved form, the doge, in his golden galley, would be rowed into the Adriatic, followed by thousands of ships carrying virtually the entire population of Venice. There the doge would toss a golden ring into the waves and announce, "We wed thee, O Sea, as a sign of our true and perpetual dominion."

In 1002, it was a Venetian fleet that rescued Bari, the largest Byzantine city in Italy, from a Muslim siege and helped to halt Islamic expansion up the peninsula. Building on her Adriatic naval superiority, Venice enjoyed lucrative commercial ties with both the Western and Eastern empires throughout the eleventh century, a period when her population was growing rapidly. By the end of the century, it had reached sixty thousand, two to three times that of Florence, her closest rival among the burgeoning Italian city-states. The city had also begun to expand her habitable land mass, a slow and arduous process that required staking out submerged areas with wooden palisades, then draining off the water and liquefied mud until something approaching solid soil was left. Over time, these soft, spongy sites would be further built up and consolidated with stones, debris, and mud from excavated canals, so that by 1100, Venice had created enough additional ground surface to support thirteen new parishes.[13]

Robert Guiscard and the Normans of Southern Italy

Throughout this long period of accelerating Venetian growth and success, another new power, the hyperaggressive Norman kingdom of southern Italy, was also rising with meteoric speed. The Norman warriors who first reached the far end of the peninsula around 1015 were landless adventurers, but men who, however penniless they might be, possessed keen swords, hardy mounts, and fierce native cunning. Their great-great-grandfathers had been pagan sea pirates, Vikings who guided their splendid war galleys up the rivers of northern France in search of easy prey and finding the opportunities to their liking, put down roots. A hundred years later, the Norsemen (shortened to Normans) were now calling themselves Christians, but their goals were still the same. The only real change was that they now preferred to do their fighting and killing on land rather than sea, although this in no way lessened the thrill they felt from watching terrified inhabitants scatter in helpless panic before their murderous plunder raids.[14]

In 1046, one of the nomadic wanderers who departed France and trekked over the Alps into southern Italy was Robert de Hauteville. Blue-eyed and fair with a large powerful body, the sixth son of a minor provincial baron, de Hauteville began his Italian career in standard Norman fashion, as a thief and a killer. Operating from a series of caves in the hills of Apulia, he and his band of fifteen cutthroats visited a reign of terror and extortion on defenseless peasants and monks. His victims looked in vain for protection from their nominal sovereign, the declining Byzantine Empire. Next came a stint as a small landowner and occasional brigand on a dirt-poor estate given to de Hauteville by his half-brother Drogo in sultry, stifling Calabria at the tail end of Italy. It was here that Robert began to display the quick-wittedness that led to his recognition as one of the most gifted soldiers of his age and earned him the nickname of Guiscard ("the Crafty"). By 1053, he had risen to command an entire wing of the Norman military force that crushed and humiliated a papal army in southern Italy. Six years later, when a reluctant pope recognized him as Robert, Duke of Apulia, Calabria, and Sicily, he, in turn, pledged to serve as the pope's military shield against a hostile Western emperor. In 1071, Guiscard led a victorious land and naval force against Bari, transforming that final Byzantine stronghold in southern Italy into a Norman citadel. The following year, he mounted an equally successful amphibious assault against Palermo, a city of 250,000 inhabitants that until then had been the Saracen capital of Sicily. Upon its fall to the Normans, this magnificent Byzantine-Arabic metropolis became the second-largest city in Christendom.[15]

During thirty years of continuous fighting, Guiscard had defeated papal armies, driven the Byzantine Empire off the Italian peninsula, and broken the Muslim occupation of Sicily. Then, finding that none of this could satisfy his restless spirit, he began to conceive of an even grander design. In 1078, at the age of sixty-three, he began to make deadly serious preparations to conquer the Byzantine Empire, whose culture and sophistication his barbarian soul both envied and despised. As usual, his timing could not have been better, for by the end of the eleventh century, the Eastern Empire was battered and tottering, its territories under continual assault by another band of nomadic warriors whose military brilliance resembled nothing so much as that of the Normans themselves. The Seljuk Turks were recent converts to the Muslim faith who, after taking Persia, had erupted into the critical Byzantine province of Anatolia (eastern Asia Minor). In addition to being the Greeks' principal granary, Anatolia was the chief recruiting ground for the imperial navy's most capable seamen, the army's toughest military conscripts, the cream of the officer corps, and the elite civil servant cadre that administered the Byzantine state. In 1071, in the midst of a life-and-death struggle for Asia Minor, Turkish forces had annihilated a major Byzantine army at the battle of Manzikert in Armenia. This appalling disaster, the greatest military defeat in Byzantine history, crippled imperial military strength at its very source. It was a blow from which the Eastern Empire never recovered, and it occurred the same year in which Guiscard put an end to five centuries of Greek rule in southern Italy.[16]

Seeing no reason why he should not one day realize his cherished dream, de Hauteville began to adorn himself in gold-brocaded robes carefully copied from those worn by the Eastern emperor within his sumptuous palace in Constantinople. Not only had Guiscard never been defeated in regular land combat, he had been victorious in a series of innovative amphibious assaults against major coastal strongholds in southern Italy and Sicily. Now he planned to use these same inventive tactics to seize the eastern Adriatic port of Durazzo opposite the Italian boot, from which he and his unbeaten Norman army would then march directly east to Byzantium along an eight-hundred-year-old Roman road. In May 1081, Duke Robert crossed the Adriatic at the head of a formidable armada and quickly established a base at Corfu, south of Durazzo. Meanwhile, in Constantinople, Emperor Alexius Comnenus, all too aware that his army and navy were severely overmatched, wasted no time in urgently requesting Venetian support. This was aid which it was very much in the city's self-interest to supply, since Venice could hardly remain passive while an adventurer of de Hauteville's mettle seized the straits controlling passage from the Adriatic into the Mediterranean Sea. Worse still, what if Guiscard achieved his grand obsession? An Eastern Empire run by a bickering Greek bureaucracy more interested in esoteric theological disputes than reviving imperial military and naval capacity was one thing. Such a state posed no threat to Venetian interests; in fact, the city had prospered mightily by filling the power vacuum left by waning Byzantine naval strength, all the while playing the role of a faithful ally. But what if Venice were forced to confront a nation of emboldened Norman warriors after they had absorbed the vast resources of the Eastern Empire? This would present a different risk entirely.[17]

Thus, one evening as they rode becalmed after dropping anchor just off Durazzo, Guiscard's ships were suddenly set upon by a Venetian war fleet commanded by the doge himself. Almost immediately, de Hauteville learned the difference between the improvised naval skills his Norman soldiers had lately begun to display and the consummate ship-handling mastery of a genuinely maritime nation. After transforming their vessels into concentrated fighting platforms by hoisting teams of archers to the tops of the masts, the Venetians broke the enemy line and sank a large number of Norman ships before withdrawing into the Durazzo harbor. However, this decisive naval defeat did not discourage Guiscard in the slightest. He ordered the unimpaired Norman army to lay siege to Durazzo, and eight months later, after a battle in which his infantry and cavalry shattered the Byzantine land force led by Emperor Alexius Comnenus, he forced the city to surrender. Within weeks, all the neighboring provinces had capitulated, and Norman soldiers were soon pushing their way into the Balkan interior, only three hundred and fifty miles from the walls of Constantinople. Then, in 1082, Guiscard was forced to leave the campaign and take part of his army to Rome to protect his ally the pope from the menaces of the

Western Emperor. Although he was back in the Balkans by 1084, in his absence, the seemingly invincible Norman army had been outwitted and defeated. A Venetian naval force had retaken Durazzo and Corfu, erasing all of the campaign's previous gains.[18]

Completely undeterred, Guiscard immediately launched a second offensive. Again, his initial objective was Corfu, where, this time, he was soundly defeated by a combined Venetian and Byzantine armada. However, at this point, because Norman naval losses had been so large, Robert knew that the last thing the Venetians would expect was a surprise attack by his small remnant of surviving vessels. When this was precisely what he ordered, the timing was perfect. Being totally unprepared to defend themselves, all the largest Venetian war galleys were sunk or captured, and Venetian dead were said to total thirteen thousand. Corfu was recaptured, and the unfortunate Doge Domenico Selvo, who presided over this debacle, was deposed and sent to end his days in a monastery. Then fate miraculously intervened. Typhoid broke out in the Norman army the following winter, and by spring, five hundred Norman knights were dead, and much of Duke Robert's army was unfit for fighting. Unphased as always, Guiscard pushed ahead with the campaign until the summer of 1085 when he too was stricken with the disease, dying on July 17 at age seventy. Without his leadership, the Norman military threat to the Eastern Empire abruptly collapsed.[19]

But while the Norman danger loomed, the Greeks gave ample demonstration of their gratitude for Venetian naval assistance. In the midst of the crisis, Emperor Alexius Comnenus issued an imperial charter (called a *Chrysobull* or Golden Bull because it was literally written in golden ink) in favor of the city's merchants. It granted them permission to establish their own trading quarter, with Venetian-owned docks, warehouses, markets, shops, and churches, on the southern shore of Constantinople's great harbor, known as the Golden Horn. Most importantly, the Golden Bull of 1082 declared that Venetian trade would henceforth be completely exempt from the heavy customs duty and sales tax imposed on other commerce within the Byzantine Empire. The customs duty alone was normally ten percent, and it was zealously imposed on all nonexempt transactions. Thus, while other Italians merchants had to add these costs of doing business to their selling price just to break even, Venetian traders operating anywhere within the Eastern Empire from the Adriatic to Constantinople could either undercut their competitors' prices or pocket the difference as pure profit. All that Venice had to do in exchange was to continue using her formidable naval power to defend the Byzantine imperial system that was the source of her enormous new advantage. As the city's merchants began exploiting this lucrative trade monopoly, attempts to compete with them were doomed to failure, and many Venetian families quickly grew very wealthy. As the historian John Julius Norwich has emphasized, it is hard to exaggerate the importance of the emperor's generous concessions, which literally "flung open to [Venice] the gates of the Orient."[20]

A Lingering Political Dilemma

Observing how Norman plans to seize the Greek Empire suddenly evaporated after the death of Robert Guiscard only reinforced a growing tendency in Venetian political thinking. The city was becoming increasingly reluctant to have her public policies and civic tranquility depend on the purely personal qualities of a single individual leader, regardless of his talent, energy, or genius. As Venetians reflected on recent events, they realized that even the brilliant achievements of Pietro Orseolo II eight decades earlier underscored this lesson. Certainly, as much as any single individual ever could, Doge Orseolo had demonstrated the unique, transforming powers of genuine political leadership. But he also showed how rare and ephemeral such individual genius truly was. After marrying or associating his sons into the royal families of both the Eastern and Western empires, Doge Orseolo had aspired to settle the city's political future by founding a dynastic monarchy. However, when the plague struck Venice in 1006, two of its victims were the doge's eldest son (and intended successor) and the doge's grandson, his hope for the next generation. Crushed by the total collapse of his plans, at the age of forty-eight, Doge Orseolo's astounding vitality vanished overnight, and he spent his last two years locked in the dark recesses of the ducal fortress paying little attention to public affairs. None of his surviving family members proved capable of realizing the dying patriarch's hereditary dream, even with the assistance of well-placed imperial relatives.

Yet, if the dynastic model had been tried and found wanting, as it certainly had in view of the city's long, disillusioning experience with the Participazi, the Candiani, and now the Orseoli, what was the alternative? By 1084, there had been thirty Venetian doges, each supposedly elected for life. Yet no more than twelve had died a natural death in office. Of the rest, one was slain in battle, three were murdered, four were deposed and blinded, five were deposed and merely exiled, and five resigned from office rather than face a more gruesome fate. The explanation for this raft of sudden departures was simple. Pure popular election of the doge meant that the ducal leader, once chosen, possessed powers that it was almost impossible to challenge except by the threat of violent removal. The question for the future was plain. Could Venetians devise new, more stable political arrangements which did not depend on either the failed dynastic principle or the personal vagaries of a single popularly elected leader?

The Third Church of San Marco

As it did throughout her history, accelerating commercial success fed the desire of Venetian leaders to make the city more beautiful and resplendent. Thus, in 1063, Doge Domenico Contarini resolved to reconstruct the church of San Marco (as rebuilt by the Orseoli after the fire of 976) in a form whose magnificence would eliminate any question of a future replacement. The Orseolo restoration project had been a hasty affair, a frugal patch job rather than a proper repair of the damage done by the Candiano conflagration. Although the building's condition was not so bad that it called for immediate intervention, Doge Contarini inherited a ducal church with serious structural problems that would have to be addressed sooner or later. Competitive pressures also played a part in his decision. In the second half of the eleventh century, a large number of Italian cities were reconstructing their cathedrals on a much grander scale. For instance, Pisa, Venice's most important commercial rival at the time, began construction of a splendid new cathedral in 1063. In addition, Venice had recently been engaged in a series of hard-fought battles with the patriarch of Aquileia in the ongoing struggle for ecclesiastical supremacy in the northern Adriatic, and one of the patriarch's major achievements had been rebuilding Aquilea's cathedral as a magnificent basilica-plan church.[21]

But the primary aim in rebuilding San Marco was to give architectural expression to a new, enlarged vision of Venetian destiny. When the original ninth-century church was constructed, Venice was an ambitious frontier community with strictly limited resources. Not surprisingly, then, her first version of the grand building model chosen by the Participazi, the Emperor Justinian's splendid sixth-century church of the Holy Apostles in Constantinople, lacked many essential features of its imperial Byzantine archetype. Two centuries later, the city was considerably larger, wealthier, and more united, and she naturally wished to rebuild the church of her patron saint on a scale more in keeping with her expanded powers.[22] To ensure that the builder would be thoroughly familiar with the great Greek original which had inspired the San Marco project from its inception, Doge Contarini chose a Greek architect from Constantinople.[23] But, as we shall see, this Byzantine master was also an architect of consummate adaptive skills, capable of balancing the merits of faithfully duplicating the imported imperial model with attention to the intricacies and practical necessities of the Venetian site.

In carrying out this extraordinary commission, the first step would have been to separate the usable from the unusable portions of the hastily reconstructed Orseolo church and the extensive remains of the ninth-century Participazio church incorporated within it. Of course, the city's already well-established preservationist aesthetic would have dictated that, wherever feasible, the sound and beautiful parts of the old building should be saved and recycled into the new project. Thus, workers would have demolished and removed only those parts that were too weak and unstable to be safely integrated into the fabric of the replacement church or that were completely at odds with the pattern of the Apostoleion model. For instance, builders would certainly have been instructed to avoid, whenever possible, the enormous expense (up to one-third of total construction cost) of replacing the ninth-century foundations. In addition, one scholar has estimated that as much as sixty to seventy-five percent of the original Participazio building fabric escaped demolition and became incorporated into the new Contarini church. This would have included a substantial part of the Participazio central dome with its supporting vaults and piers, an adaptation made easier by the fact that the central bay of the Participazio church was approximately equal in size to the central bay of the imported Apostoleion model.[24]

Architectural Dilemmas and Necessary Adjustments

After reducing the building site to its reusable elements, the Greek architect would have imaginatively projected the plan and elevation of the Apostoleion over the church's surviving fabric. The principal features of Justinian's church were a Greek-cross floor plan from which massive four-legged piers and barrel vaults rose to support five large domes, one over the central crossing and one over each of the building's four equal arms. Between the giant supporting piers, two-story arcades screened off continuous side aisles and upper-story galleries. Visitors entered the church through a lateral vestibule or narthex attached to the western arm. In pursuing this grand form, Justinian and his architect had been unconstrained by any existing site restrictions, since the Apostoleion had been built in an undeveloped part of the imperial capital near the old Constantinian walls.[25] But in adapting this magnificent scheme to Venice, the Contarini architect faced a number of additional challenges. To satisfy even the minimal requirements of his great classical prototype, he had to find sufficient lateral space within the confines of a very cramped ninth-century footprint to build four additional domes, one over each of the new building's four reconstructed cross-arms. At the same time, he had to preserve and assimilate a number of highly valued remnants from adjoining structures, some of which were not very adaptable to the Apostoleion model.

It was the four-fold increase in the number of stately domes resting on imposing brick vaults that made the interior of the new San Marco appear so much loftier and spacious to contemporary Venetians. But these additions also greatly multiplied the project's inherent structural problems. Rigidly supported architectural forms such as vaults and domes were always a risky business in Venice, since they were particularly vulnerable to stress and failure from the lagoon's continuous ground subsidence. In addition, the fabric of San Marco was subject to a special form of destabilization from the city's enveloping waters. After the great fire of 976, the area surrounding Saint Mark's tomb had been transformed into a subterranean enclosure through the construction of overhead brick vaulting. Because part of the resulting crypt was below sea level, it behaved like a kind of giant floating caisson, acted upon by every tidal rise and fall from the surrounding lagoon. Ultimately, all of these constantly shifting forces were transmitted to the vulnerable vaults and domes.[26]

The Contarini architect also faced particular architectural dilemmas in reconstructing each of the building's four cross-arms. For instance, in order to install a dome and its supporting vaults above the eastern arm, it was necessary to demolish the existing central apse and rebuild a new one to the east. This, in turn, required extending the subterranean crypt chamber located below the apse an equal distance eastward, which could be done only after constructing expensive new foundations to support the entire enterprise. To carry the weight of the new eastern dome, enormous barrel vaults had to be erected high above the side apses (now used as lateral chapels), and these massive new structures somehow had to be integrated with a series of fragile, preexisting arches which supported the lateral chapels' delicate cross-vaulted ceilings. All of this complex, heavy reconstruction had to be carried out without damaging Saint Mark's tomb monument, which was located immediately below the work site.[27]

Adding a dome above San Marco's northern arm was complicated by the wish to preserve certain building remnants from the church of San Teodoro located on that side of the site. Likewise, the difficulty of installing a cupola over the southern arm was increased by the large, intrusive presence of the ducal fortress, including an abutting corner tower revered as the original repository of Saint Mark's body. The decision not to demolish these venerable historical structures created severe space constraints and physical integration problems, particularly in the design of satisfactory support systems for the northern and southern domes. There simply was not sufficient room to build a full set of the massive piers used to bear the lateral domes in the Apostoleion model. The Venetian solution was to integrate the preexisting historical structures into the outer walls of the new church and to use these reinforced walls as an alternative means of support. Moreover, finding sufficient space to install lateral domes equal in width to the existing central cupola was a physical impossibility, and the span of the northern and southern domes had to be reduced by approximately fifteen percent.[28]

Extending the western arm of San Marco to accommodate a dome system required demolishing the ninth-century atrium originally attached to that side of the church. However, the Contarini architect did decide to save one valuable artifact from the outer wall of the courtyard: the guardhouse portal that Doge Giovanni Participazio had built to control access into the ducal chapel and the connecting ducal fortress. This remnant, an "apse-like niche" constituting a "foreign body...encased within a wholly different system of architecture,"[29] was retained to serve as the central portal leading into the church from the narthex or vestibule that would soon be added to the western end of San Marco *(Fig. 11)*. However, part of this incongruous relic (an apse superimposed above the portal) was much higher than the shallow barrel vaults that made up the rest of the narthex ceiling. This meant that in order to accommodate the portal remnant, it was necessary to insert the salvaged two-story guardhouse shaft into the upper regions of the narthex central bay. This anomalous structure became the famous *pozzo* or inverted well that rises through the narthex ceiling directly into the church interior. The portal relic also contained twin interior stairways that formerly conveyed the doge's soldiers to the upper story of the guardhouse. These were also retained and adapted to provide access to the women's galleries which encircled the upper story of the Contarini church interior.[30]

As these examples demonstrate, the Greek master chosen by Doge Contarini was a brilliantly adaptive builder who generally held true to the Apostoleion architectural pattern despite a host of formidable obstacles. Otto Demus, the world's foremost authority on the subject, has called the Contarini church "a very sensitive adaptation of a great model"[31] and concluded that of all the churches which used the Apostoleion as their archetype, San Marco is the most faithful to the parental form. However, not even the genius of the Contarini architect could perform the impossible, and certain deviations from the Byzantine original became unavoidable. For instance, the requirement to align the walls of the new church with the surviving walls of preexisting structures such as San Teodoro and the ducal castle made it impossible to maintain strict right angles, and the result of these necessary adjustments was to throw the building's east-west axis out of kilter. Incorporating preexisting historic structures also left no room for side aisles along the end walls of the northern and southern arms. In a similar fashion, preservation of the lateral chapels and the erection of massive overhead barrel vaults prevented the construction of arcaded side aisles in the eastern bay of the church. Finally, San Marco's constricted floor plan was too cramped to allow its domes to rest exclusively on the type of four-legged pier system that supported all of the Apostoleion cupolas. As a result, the Venetian builder was forced to devise a number of alternative support methods, including special load-bearing arches erected on twin columns, particularly for the four lateral domes.[32]

The versatile Contarini architect also knew how to make creative use of certain necessary deviations. For instance, to incorporate the two-story guardhouse portal and other remnants of the original ninth-century courtyard into the narthex, the western arm of the church was lengthened by approximately thirty feet, thereby imparting a semibasilical east-west axis to the building *(Fig. 12)*. Taking this departure from a perfect Greek-cross floor plan as a starting point, the Contarini architect then installed a pair of vaults on twin columns above the eastern end of the church. In addition to providing much-needed support for the eastern dome, these prominent archlike structures helped frame a vista that sweeps the full length of the sanctuary from the main entrance to the altar of Saint Mark. San Marco's nave is almost two hundred feet long and ninety feet wide, while the shorter, narrower northern and southern arms, which act as transepts, measure a collective 160 feet from end to end. Unlike an Eastern church with its perfect Greek-cross contours, where the central square would have been reserved for the performance of the Mass by a professional clergy, San Marco's central bay was given over to the Venetian laity. As in Western basilical churches, the Mass was celebrated in San Marco's eastern presbytery.[33]

On the upper story above the side aisles, the nave and transepts were encircled by galleries reserved for women and members of the doge's family; the latter made their entrance from corridors in the eastern end of the church that led directly from the adjoining ducal castle. A visitor could use the women's galleries to circumnavigate the entire interior of the church with the exception of the central apse. Except for the aisles beneath the galleries, which remained in deep shadow, the main body of the church was magnificently illuminated by a system of large, regular windows. There were sixteen openings lining the base of each dome, with three windows in the eastern apse and eight windows piercing each of the other eleven walls making up the four cross-arms—a total of 171.[34]

San Marco's basic structural fabric, including its walls and piers, was completed in only eight years, that is, by 1071, the same year that Doge Contarini died. Contemporary reports tell us that as part of his coronation ceremony, the new doge, Domenico Selvo, left his shoes in the western campo and walked barefoot into the church, where he accepted his office amid the dust and scaffolding of ongoing construction. Once installed, Doge Selvo directed Venetian merchants traveling in the East to bring back precious marbles and building reliefs to ornament the new Basilica. He also imported skilled mosaicists from Ravenna, including the artists who created San Marco's earliest mosaics: portraits of the Madonna, eight Apostles, and the four Evangelists, set in individual niches above and beside the central portal leading from the narthex into the interior *(Fig. 11)*. But for all his personal commitment to the enrichment of the new church, Selvo did not remain in office to see it completed. He was the hapless doge who lost an entire fleet and the lives of a reported thirteen thousand Venetian seamen in Robert Guiscard's surprise attack off Corfu in 1084, for which he was promptly deposed. It fell to his successor, Vitale Falier, to carry the Basilica project to final construction and consecration in 1094.[35]

Fig. 11: *Central entrance portal, narthex of
the Basilica San Marco*

Fig. 12 (opposite): *The Basilica San Marco's
semibasilical east-west axis*

The Miraculous Reappearance of the Relics

Although the record is not clear, it seems very likely that whatever relics were reburied in Saint Mark's tomb after the Candiano fire and the Orseolo reconstruction of San Marco were transferred to a safe place during the extensive alterations to the eastern bay that were part of the Contarini rebuilding project. In any case, we do know that on October 8, 1094, as part of the consecration ceremony for Mark's third and final church, what were universally regarded as the saint's remains were re-entombed in the now fully enclosed crypt under the main altar. Then, sometime during the thirteenth century ("that most prolific period of state-controlled mythogenesis"),[36] these simple facts became the basis for a major Venetian invention, the story of the *apparitio* or miraculous reappearance of the relics. According to this highly imaginative legend, just when the completed Contarini church was on the verge of final consecration, it was suddenly discovered that Saint Mark's body had been inexplicably lost during the process of reconstruction. Fortunately, after three days of fasting and prayer for its recovery, the location of the misplaced relics was miraculously revealed during High Mass in the newly completed Basilica. As the congregation gazed in amazement, the wall of a giant pier suddenly broke open to expose an extended human arm, which was soon discovered to belong to Mark himself, who seemed to be beckoning to the assembled worshippers.[37]

What is one to conclude about a story which tries to make us believe that Venice misplaced the body of her patron saint at the very time when she was raising a magnificent new shrine to celebrate its possession? Just as late tenth-century Venice refused to acknowledge the seemingly undeniable fact that Mark's relics were destroyed in the Candiano fire of 976, so, in the thirteenth century, the city appears to have gone out of her way to claim a loss that almost certainly never occurred. What can explain such a reversal? Why would Venice want to invent a legend that, if accepted as true, seemed to stress her own negligence in caring for the precious remains? To answer these questions, we need to understand certain core medieval beliefs about a saint's power over his earthly body. Christians of the Middle Ages believed that it was impossible to appropriate or retain the relics of a departed saint without the saint's active collaboration. Even after their deaths, saints remained powerful, vital beings who continued to control the fate of their earthly remains. If a saint did not wish his relics to be possessed by a particular church or city, no force on earth could make that happen.[38]

Thus, inventing a story that recounted the loss and miraculous reappearance of Mark's body in 1094 was a way of underscoring the unique, unbreakable connection between Venice and her patron saint. The predestination legend or *praedestinatio*, that other major thirteenth-century product of the Venetian mythic imagination (briefly described in the section titled "The Theft of Saint Mark" in Chapter Two), had made it clear that Saint Mark's original removal to Venice was divinely ordained. In addition to confirming this point, the apparitio demonstrated that Mark himself was a participant in the process, that he actively desired to remain in Venice and assist her people to claim their destiny. Even if Venetians were negligent, even if they proved careless and misplaced his earthly body, Mark forgave their failings and miraculously reappeared in their midst. Whatever might happen, the Evangelist was indissolubly wedded to the lagoon city.

The Spirit of Justinian Art

A visitor approaching the completed Basilica soon after its consecration would have encountered a large, imposing building set in an unpaved, disproportionately small public square. Approximately two hundred feet to the west, the campo ended abruptly at the shore of the Batario canal; immediately to the south, it was compressed by a narrow, free-flowing inlet from the Venetian harbor. Visitors arriving by boat, as most did, would have docked at a small marina on the northern bank of the inlet, located only a few yards from the Basilica's southern flank. They would have entered San Marco not by walking around the building into to the western square but by passing directly from the water into a large, apse-shaped portal cut into the southern or harborside face of the church. This grand ceremonial entranceway was called the *Porta da Mar* or Sea Gate, and as befitted the chief sanctuary of a great maritime nation, its arch of brightly colored bricks was mirrored in the waters of the lagoon.[39]

Viewed from the outside, San Marco's four cross-arms conveyed an impression of chaste and uncluttered symmetry. Seen from the western campo, the vestibule's austere rectangular brick exterior was pierced by five large, round-arched portals, and raised above that, one saw the shallow curve of five large brick domes perched on the imposing bulk of their brick support vaults. As was normal for Byzantine-inspired sanctuaries, the Basilica's external surface consisted almost entirely of unadorned brick, relieved by only a few subtle niches and scattered patches of colored stone. As they passed through the narthex, visitors would have noticed that four doges were already buried in the vestibule, evidence of another practice borrowed from the church's Byzantine model. In the interior, the volumes of the five vaulted and domed bays were of truly Justinian dimensions, and the overall impression was one of Late Antique spaciousness, clarity, and order. As with the exterior façades, the plain brick interior surfaces were almost entirely devoid of marble, mosaic, or other ornament, making the sumptuous color of the veined marble columns lining the nave and transepts particularly striking.[40]

Thus, by the end of the eleventh century, Venice, a small land-restricted city, had succeeded in erecting a shrine to her patron saint whose grandeur and proportions "breathe[d] much of the spirit of Justinian art."[41] Moreover, she had built this adaptation of an authentic classical prototype not in subservience to the Eastern Roman Empire but to proclaim, in unmistakable terms, an accelerating independence from her former imperial mentor. It was a separation that had begun with the acquisition of Mark's body in 828, a bold act which fueled a progressive revolt against the city's initial status as a Byzantine cultural and economic dependent. Two and a half centuries later, her decolonialization was complete. Whatever small trace might be left of the church of San Teodoro, that original token of Greek supremacy, had now been wholly absorbed into the fabric of the Basilica. Economically, Venice had long since ceased to be an imperial satellite; she was now Byzantium's most important commercial ally. Her merchants, who resided in their own thriving quarter in the heart of Constantinople, were amassing phenomenal wealth from their privileged position within the Greek Empire. And in military and naval affairs, there had been a complete reversal of roles; it was the Byzantines who now sought the promise of Venetian protection. In Chapter Five, we will explore in some detail what this new independence meant for the historic Veneto-Byzantine relationship in the century following the consecration of the Contarini Basilica. But first, we need to examine twelfth-century Venice in a nearer context, to compare her dynamism and her cultural and political cohesion with other medieval city-states on the Italian peninsula.

CHAPTER FOUR

Venice the Vanguard State

Medieval Florence

Well before entering its gates, a Venetian merchant visiting twelfth-century Florence would have understood that he was on the threshold of a very different urban environment. Gazing down from the crest of the surrounding hills, he would have seen a forest of shockingly tall stone towers clustered behind the city's brick ramparts. Descending from the heights, he could have counted more than a hundred of these enormous vertical citadels, some of whose rectangular shafts soared over two hundred feet. Inside the city gates, the atmosphere turned dense and claustrophobic. Narrow, dirty streets made abrupt, ill-lit turns between ravinelike walls. Massive tower bases protruded into roadways, making it impossible to see more than a short distance ahead. At the point where the base of a shaft, composed of huge irregular stone blocks, gave way to higher levels of cobble and brick, the trunk was often engrafted with horizontal walkways extending to the top floors of neighboring houses. These sprawling, multitentacled complexes were so large that they made it difficult for sunlight to reach the unpaved streets. Looking up from the city's dark, constricted alleyways into this dense network of overlooming fortresses must have been a disturbing experience to a visitor from the open, brilliantly sunlit waterways of the Venetian lagoon.[1]

These were the tower societies of the feudal nobility, recent émigrés to Florence and other growing cities of the Italian mainland *(Fig. 13)* who brought within urban walls the same armed habits that governed their violent lives in the rural hinterland, including the blood feud and the vendetta. As protection against the resulting mayhem, these provincial warriors organized themselves into defensive clans and constructed family compounds

59

Fig. 13: Medieval towers of San Gimignano in Tuscany

centered around one or more fortified towers. Neighboring clans frequently leagued themselves into larger mutual defense pacts, linking their separate tower complexes by connecting bridges. Given such extended alliances, all the towers in several adjacent neighborhoods could suddenly erupt in violent civil war at any moment. At the sound of an alarm, archers and crossbowmen would appear on crenellated roofs, firing at anything that moved in the enemy complexes across the way. Streets would be barricaded, making large areas of the city impenetrable as long as the fighting continued, which could be for weeks or months. One tactic was to barricade enemy clans within their towers and starve them into submission; if that proved unsuccessful, catapults could be brought out to fire huge stones against the base of a tower at point-blank range. Given sufficient time, it might be possible to batter down the stoutest foundations, perhaps causing the entire shaft to collapse, killing everyone inside. Meanwhile, the defenders above would hurl or fire down stones, spears, arrows—whatever was at hand—at the besiegers below.[2]

In their native countryside, Italian nobles had long operated as little more than glorified brigands, preying on the rich merchants whose caravans passed through their separate fiefdoms. However, once they understood just how decisively the towns in their midst had become centers of swelling economic growth and potential political power, they also began to carve out places for themselves within these urban outposts. The result was a scramble for supremacy among a class of men long accustomed to dictate the terms of law and property within their private domains and to seize whatever they desired by force of arms. Thus, while life in twelfth-century Florence was vital and energetic, it was also a place where every action was performed in the teeth of rampant violence and lawlessness, under a social compact that was crude and volatile at best. The merchant class, on which the city's economic vibrancy depended, had no political power. Instead, the Florentine streets were ruled by the menace and swagger of armed gangs, and the feudal chieftains who could unleash this violence at any moment also controlled the government. In such circumstances, it is hardly surprising that Florentine architectural expression in the twelfth century was quite basic. The city contained no imposing public space, and the public architecture of the period was limited to remodeling the municipal Baptistery, building a single wooden bridge over the Arno, and constructing the city's massive new defensive walls (expanded at enormous cost in 1173). In the furious disorder of the time, a large public space or monumental civic building would have been a waste of resources. Except for necessary trips to church, cathedral or market, what could have enticed Florentines to leave the safety of their tower compounds and voluntarily expose themselves to danger in such unprotected environments?[3]

Florentine architecture would not begin to exhibit the spaciousness and regularity of a true urban aesthetic until the end of the thirteenth century. In 1255, when the city built its first town hall, the Palazzo del Popolo (now known as the Bargello), it was a small, fortresslike building architecturally indistinguishable from the mass of surrounding towers. When Florence's principal square, the Piazza della Signoria, began to assume its earliest form in 1268, its shape was a pure accident: an irregular hole in the city's tangled building fabric left by destroying the sprawling tower complex of an exiled family. The Florentine Cathedral or Duomo, begun in 1294, would be the medieval commune's first monumental public building project, and except for certain purely decorative features of the municipal Baptistery and the church of San Miniato al Monte, no Florentine building would take its inspiration from classical architecture before the 1420s. Not until the urban middle classes—the merchants, manufacturers, shop-owners and artisans—became strong enough to subdue the feudal nobility and win control of the government could the city begin to give architectural expression to a new communal political vision. In Florence, this did not begin to happen until after 1250, with the rise of the earliest Florentine democracy, the *primo popolo*, and the establishment in 1282 of a new mercantile magistracy, the Priorate of the Guilds. But even after these events, the city's extraordinary penchant for domestic quarrels continued to erupt in wars of extermination between the two principal political factions: the Guelphs (the pro-papal party) and the Ghibellines (who were allied with the Western emperor in Germany). Even when the Guelph faction had finally triumphed, there were still two warring camps within that victorious party, the Blacks and the Whites, who remained locked in brutally destructive combat.[4]

A similar pattern of delayed architectural expression characterized Italy north of Florence. In the late twelfth century, when the northern Italian communes emancipated themselves from the yoke of the German emperor, the construction of spacious new public squares and council buildings was not a prominent feature of life within these independent urban centers and would not become one until after 1240. In many cases, it took several centuries to complete such projects, and efforts to impose a uniform design during such lengthy construction periods were only marginally successful.[5]

Medieval Rome

Twelfth-century Rome was also characterized by continual violence and disorder. The battlemented compounds and enormous towers of the great Roman clans, clustered on the crests of the city's seven hills, loomed over dark, crowded tenements holding most of the thirty-five thousand people who lived in this former imperial capital of a million inhabitants. These medieval elites, many of whom claimed an ancestry reaching back to the great senatorial families of the ancient city, were continually engaged in bloody street battles as they vied with each for a chance to seat a family member on the papal throne. And the German emperor often took sides in these domestic quarrels. In 1167, Emperor Frederick Barbarossa, who invaded Italy for the express purpose of ending the papacy of Alexander III, stormed his way into Saint Peter's basilica and left the nave strewn with the bodies of the pope's murdered defenders. Moreover, when semidemocratic forces first began to make their presence felt at mid-century, all that this achieved was to increase the number of contestants in the city's violent power struggles. When the urban middle class rose in revolt in 1143 and reconstituted the Roman Senate after demanding that the pope abdicate all temporal power, the result was forty years of bloody skirmishing between the new communal government and a papacy dominated by the leading noble families. Each party frequently implored the German emperor to intervene militarily on its behalf, providing that prince with a convenient excuse for pursuing his own ends south of the Alps.[6]

As in Florence, twelfth-century Roman architecture largely reflected the chaos and bloodshed of the era. Almost all secular and many important ecclesiastical buildings, including the Vatican palace, were heavily fortified. When the Roman Republic of 1143, violently opposed by the papacy, the old medieval families, and the German emperor, decided to erect a senatorial palace on the Capitoline Hill, the building it constructed was a fortresslike structure framed by irregular stone towers. Not until the High Renaissance of the 1530s would political conditions allow Michelangelo Buonarroti (1475–1564) to rebuild the Capitoline Hill in conformity with ideas of classical grandeur, elegance, and symmetry. In the meantime, a great deal of the antique splendor of the ancient Roman capital lay crumbling into dust, and some of the largest classical monuments, such as the Colosseum, the Theater of Marcellus, the Arch of Titus, and the Arch of Constantine, were seized by the great clans and turned into family citadels. More often, important antique structures were plundered for their building materials, a process that often involved stripping away the building's marble revetment and shipping it off to distant building sites or melting it down in lime kilns. At the same time, a huge portion of the area within the old imperial walls, once pulsing with the constant ebb and flow of a million people, stood virtually uninhabited. This was the *disabitato*, a great unbroken expanse of open fields and architectural ruins stretching north, south, and east of the Colosseum, which had been abandoned when most of the city's shrunken medieval population moved west into the bend of the Tiber after the aqueducts ceased to function.[7]

Venetian Exceptionalism

The Venetian historical pattern was quite different. Although the city had endured the brief reign of Pietro Candiano IV in the tenth century, she had been spared the long, bloody conflict with a powerfully entrenched feudal order that delayed the arrival of independent communal government in Florence and other mainland cities. From the ninth century onward, the Rialtine islands' impregnable physical separation from continental Italy ensured that Venice would continue to enjoy a rare isolation from the fury and disorder that plagued the rest of medieval Europe. As a result of this precious autonomy, mercantile Venice began to experiment with communal government much earlier than other major Italian cities. By the second half of the twelfth century, her fledgling communal institutions were maturing rapidly, at a time when Florence and most of the peninsula remained trapped in the savage turmoil of the tower societies. Able to maintain her distance from the mainland's feudal anarchy, Venice cast her gaze eastward toward the open sea, where she discovered a profusion of lucrative trading markets. Exploiting these rich opportunities, she projected her naval power into the Adriatic and the distant Mediterranean.

By the twelfth century, her seaborne strength and mercantile wealth had made Venice an international power with an international foreign policy. She had become the principal intermediary for commerce between the feudal West and the Byzantine East. As the favored ally of the Eastern Roman Empire, she possessed her own special harbor, wharves, warehouses, market, and residential quarter in Constantinople, the world's largest and most splendid metropolis. As the greatest maritime power in Europe, Venice negotiated directly not only with Byzantium but with the Western Roman Empire, the papacy, and the great Muslim kingdoms of North Africa and the Middle East. Her lagoon population of one hundred thousand (not counting at least twenty thousand Venetians living abroad) made her the largest city in Western Europe, at least twice the size of Paris and over three times that of Florence. Part of the explanation for this success was that medieval Venice was the direct inheritor of an ancient Mediterranean worldview that had all but vanished on the feudal mainland. Like ancient Greece and Rome, Venice empowered her citizens with unique private property rights, and the accelerated economic activity which grew out of this birthright enabled Venetians to develop a network of commercial relations throughout the Mediterranean world. In contrast, under mainland feudalism, with its glorification of warrior values, trade was a disfavored occupation. It was viewed as a contemptible activity practiced by low and dishonest men, and the complicated legal relations required to support it were resisted at every turn.[8]

While open violence and political fragmentation were the norm in mainland cities such as Florence, twelfth-century Venice experienced a sustained period of physical, political, and architectural unification. When the capital was transferred to the Rialtine islands in the early ninth century, most of the archipelago's 117 islets were uninhabited. Untouched by human labor, they were small and boggy, full of swampy ponds and separated from each other by broad expanses of open water. In time, small groups of settler families ferried themselves over to these scattered cays and began to build houses, fishing docks, and eventually churches. Over time, these separate pioneer outposts became distinct communities, each with its own patron saint and particular parish identity. In 900, Venetians had settled thirty such island-parishes; by 1100, the number had more than doubled, to sixty-eight. As newcomers continued to arrive, parish settlers persevered with the arduous work of enlarging their habitable land mass. Ponds and swamps were drained, and intervening waterways were filled in so that the shores of neighboring islands began to approach each other. When distances had shrunk sufficiently, rude planks and wooden bridges were laid over the narrowed water channels, permitting residents to walk or ride horses and mules from enclave to enclave. Along her muddy new streets, the commune installed small wooden tabernacles where Venetians lit candles and left devotional offerings to their parish saints, making Venice the first city in Western Europe to be regularly lit at night. By 1150, the city's physical integration had progressed to a point that its overall outline assumed something close to its present shape, a dolphinlike form two and a half miles long and half as wide.[9]

On the individual parish-islands, buildings were erected around open fields, and each campo typically contained its own small market. But as Venice became a world power and began to import exotic goods from the distant corners of the Mediterranean and Black seas, she needed to create a citywide market devoted to this thriving international commerce. In response, two trading centers arose on opposite banks of the first bend in the deep serpentine stream (the Grand Canal) that coursed through the center of the archipelago, just where the river currents narrowed as they passed between two of the city's earliest island settlements. Not surprisingly, the area was also a major convergence point for the city's expanding network of bridges, footpaths, and horse trails. In 1097, the family that owned the private market located on the far or northwestern bank of the Grand Canal (an area which by then had become known as the Rialto)[10] donated a large portion of this property to the Venetian state, which then built a primitive boat bridge linking this Rialto market to the southeastern or San Marco side of the canal.[11]

Like her individual parish markets, the first Venetian shipyards were small, privately owned enterprises scattered throughout the archipelago; however, the city's rapid growth as a maritime power prompted the government to intervene in this area as well. To ensure a sufficient supply of naval vessels to support the city's far-flung mercantile ventures, the government in 1104 began to construct a national shipyard known as the *Arsenale* (from the Arabic phrase for factory) in an area of marsh and stagnant pools near Venice's eastern extremity. Although the original twelfth-century nucleus of the Arsenale was modest in size, it provided the government with a fundamentally new ability to organize and control overall Venetian ship production. In future contests for naval supremacy, on which the continued expansion of Venetian commerce would depend, this represented an enormous advantage. As the owner of the Arsenale, the Venetian state could commit to the rapid construction of a large trading caravan or a great war fleet of a hundred vessels or more and be confident of having them available when they were needed. Until well into the thirteenth century, she was the only Italian state possessing this capacity. And by locating her national shipyard on the desolate, uninhabited tip of the archipelago, Venice made certain that she could always double or even quadruple the size of this critical facility as future conditions warranted.[12]

The Growth of Communal Government in Venice

Although specialized physical infrastructure such as the Arsenale would be crucial to the city's future success, twelfth-century Venice's most important advantage resulted from the strides she took to broaden and unify her political institutions. Before 1100, a doge, once elected, normally functioned as a sovereign of virtually unlimited discretionary power. For while a vote of the general assembly of the people or arengo was decisive on any issue actually placed before it, this council of the entire populace could only deliver its verdict if and when it was summoned. For the election of a new doge or a declaration of war, the convening of the arengo was mandatory, and for the making of new laws, it was at least customary. But beyond such occasions, the general assembly was typically called only in the case of true emergencies, and the decision about when to convene it was left to the doge's discretion. Popular involvement in state affairs on such a fleeting and impromptu basis was virtually guaranteed to provide hasty and inconsistent counsel, all the more so as the population soared toward one hundred thousand during the twelfth century. And since the general assembly was unlikely to be of much practical help in forging public policy, there was a strong incentive for the doge not to summon the arengo except when the law strictly required it.[13]

But there was an even more troubling flaw in the existing system, one that only grew worse after Venice received the huge Byzantine trade concessions contained in Alexius Comnenus' Golden Bull of 1082 and the number of families who grew rich from Eastern trade swelled substantially. Under existing political arrangements, this wealthy new class had no regular opportunity to participate in the decisions of state that vitally affected their economic future; once the people had elevated a single man to be the sovereign leader of Venice, the rest of the merchant aristocracy had no constituted role in public affairs apart from their membership in the general assembly. Thus, even where the doge's authority was exercised with great wisdom and tact, the enormous gap between the power of the man chosen to sit on the ducal throne and all of his former peers inevitably placed a severe strain on the city's political cohesion. And for a small city-state such as Venice—aspiring, as she did, to commercial domination of the East, rising influence in the West, and an architectural distinction undreamed of in the rest of Europe—political solidarity was an absolute necessity. Unless some solution could be found, this problem threatened to undermine the city's development as a medieval vanguard state.

Earlier efforts to remedy these basic constitutional defects had failed. Men of wealth and social standing who wished to express their views on public matters made it a point to appear in the ducal court, but since they had no official position, either individually or collectively, their influence was necessarily limited. This changed slightly in the tenth and eleventh centuries, when the doge began to select a few members of his court to serve as ducal judges. However, since he had every incentive to choose only men who already supported his policies, this hardly resulted in a fundamental power shift. A second change occurred in 1032, when the general assembly began to elect two ducal councilors who, by attending the doge at all times, were supposed to somehow prevent the worst abuses of autocratic rule. However, since these new councilors lacked a well-defined means of exercising their assigned role, very few of them even made a serious attempt to restrict the doge's unilateral authority.[14]

The first effective change did not come until well into the twelfth century, during the dogate of Pietro Polani (1129–1148), when influential members of the merchant nobility formed a permanent body, the *consilium sapientium* or council of the wise, and forced the doge to begin consulting with them before making important decisions. Members of this new council of nobles now had a formal right to participate in making state policy, which permitted them to begin carving out a separate sphere of power between the doge and the underlying assembly of the people. Doges had to compete with the rest of the merchant aristocracy for political authority and were increasingly forced to treat their office as a public trust whose powers had to be exercised in a manner that satisfied the new communal councilors. However, this power-sharing arrangement did nothing to alter the underlying prerogative retained by the general populace on a fundamental question like war or peace. If public opinion was nearly unanimous, the general assembly of the people could all too easily overwhelm the judgments of both the doge and the new council.[15]

As we shall see in more detail in Chapter Five, relations between Venice and Byzantium deteriorated precipitously during the twelfth century, reaching a final rupture point in 1171 when Emperor Manuel Comnenus jailed and confiscated the wealth of over ten thousand Venetians living within Byzantine territory. Although the initial reaction of Doge Vitale Michiel II and his councilors was to dispatch a diplomatic mission to Constantinople to sound out imperial terms for releasing the hostages and their property, the Venetian people would have none of it. Without waiting to be summoned, they poured into the streets demanding revenge, and feeling powerless to resist this direct expression of the popular will, the doge summoned and led a war fleet of 120 ships into Greek waters. But once there, he again changed his mind and decided to see if negotiations might lead to an acceptable outcome. Unfortunately, in the midst of what the Byzantine emperor made certain were long, inconclusive deliberations, plague struck the Venetian armada. His offensive totally crippled and the death toll mounting, the doge ordered the fleet to return to the lagoon, where the Venetian people once again seized control of events. Convinced that the entire debacle was caused by Doge Michiel's cowardice and vacillation, an angry mob assembled before the ducal palace and threatened his life. When he attempted to flee for sanctuary to the nearby convent of San Zaccaria, he was overtaken and stabbed to death.[16]

Following this public assassination of their elected leader, repentant Venetians took a hard look at themselves and came to two definite conclusions. First, a set of political arrangements incapable of ensuring which group—the people at large or the doge and his councilors—should have final say over an issue as basic as whether to wage war or pursue diplomacy was a recipe for recurring disaster. Second, in the complicated, rapidly changing world in which Venice now found herself, the assembly of the people was simply too large and capricious to be trusted with the city's most important decisions. In 1172, this collective self-assessment resulted in the most fundamental constitutional changes in Venetian history. The first was a decision to withdraw the power to elect a successor to the murdered Vitale Michiel II from popular control. Instead, the people merely ratified the makeup of a special eleven-man electoral commission established by the council of the merchant nobility, and the commission then selected the new ducal leader. Within a few years, the council devised a more elaborate process for choosing ducal electors, but its principles remained the same: the election of the doge was to be initiated and controlled by members of the council, leaving the general assembly with no more than a nominal confirmation role. As a result, the Venetian aristocracy could now be confident that whoever became doge would owe his election to fellow members of the merchant elite and not to the popular assembly. Feeling obligated to his peers, such a man was much more likely function as a team player when making important decisions. The Venetian state was being transformed from an elected monarchy into a constitutional Republic.[17]

An equally critical change was to transform the existing council of nobles into an expanded body of 480 leading citizens, eighty from each of the six *sestieri* or districts into which the city was now divided. To this congress of Venetian notables or Great Council was entrusted the all-important power to elect every other public official and to prepare legislation for submission to the general assembly of the people. Members of the Great Council were initially appointed by democratically elected representatives of the six sestieri and limited to a one-year term. However, at the end of their first year in office, members of the initial Great Council proceeded to choose the twelve new electors who would, in turn, name the members of the next year's council. Repeated time after time, this created a self-perpetuating system of aristocratic control that excluded popular participation. Finally, the authority of the ducal councilors, who were required to attend the doge at all times, was greatly strengthened. Their number was increased from two to six, and they were given explicit power to veto ducal actions in certain circumstances.[18]

Over the next two decades, these radically new constitutional arrangements developed into a robust system of checks and balances between the doge and the communal bodies by which his power was now restricted. Chief among these new institutions were the Great Council and the six-man council of attending ducal advisers, first known as the Minor Council and later, with a few additional members, as the *Signoria*. Fortunately, we have a detailed picture of just how this new power-sharing functioned at the end of the twelfth century in the form of the *promissione* or written oath of office sworn by Enrico Dandolo, the man elected to the ducal chair in 1192. Although similarly binding oaths were no doubt imposed on earlier doges, their documentation has not survived. What the 1192 promissione reveals are the drastic changes in the doge–council relationship wrought by the constitutional revisions of 1172. For instance, Doge Dandolo's 1192 oath of office contained specific promises that he would not conduct foreign policy, dispose of state property, or even administer communal business without the approval of a majority of the Great Council. The Doge agreed that his judicial decisions could be stayed by a majority of the Great Council, and that if any matter coming before him even appeared to tempt his self-interest, in order to be enforceable, his decision would have to be supported by all six councilors of the Minor Council and a majority of the Great Council.[19]

By the end of the twelfth century, the doge and his two advisory councils, one large and one small, had become an interlocking series of decision makers. Policy was made and judgments reached through the constant interaction of these three organs of government. With the ability of the general populace to intervene severely curtailed and the doge transformed into only one of several power centers, politics in the Venetian Republic had begun to assume its full-fledged oligarchic form. Yet, it is important to understand that however much the doge's unilateral authority may have been reduced, a ducal leader of intellect and vision who won the trust and assent of his councils could still be an extremely powerful figure. Two of the doges elected immediately after the political transformation of 1172, Sebastiano Ziani (1172–1178) and the aforementioned Enrico Dandolo (1192–1205) whose oath of office contained so many specific new restrictions, would be among the most important and forceful leaders ever to guide the Republic.

Embellishing the Basilica Interior

The same overflowing vitality that rapidly reshaped the Republic's political institutions at the end of the twelfth century was also evident in the transformation of the Basilica San Marco's bare brick interior. When the Contarini church was consecrated in 1094, the impression conveyed to a visitor standing in the nave was one of stark clarity and un-adorned rational order. The only dash of color interrupting the plainness of the exposed brick surfaces came from the tall, stately columns of veined Greek marble lining the sides of the nave and transepts. By 1200, this had totally changed. The floor had been paved in bright, intricately patterned stone, large parts of the interior walls had been covered in continuous sheets of rich, luminous marble, and an ambitious program of golden mosaic had been spread across the vaults and domes *(Fig. 14)*. As befitted a shrine modeled on Justinian's sixth-century church of the Holy Apostles, San Marco's century-long embellishment was carried out in accordance with essential principles of Byzantine interior decoration, including the use of contrasting materials to create a strict dichotomy between two distinct architectural zones: a lower, earthly zone consisting of the walls and floor and the upper, celestial zone of the vaults and domes *(Fig. 15)*.[20]

Once the church fabric was sufficiently complete, skilled craftsmen (probably imported from Constantinople) began laying the Basilica's marble floors. When they were done, twenty thousand square feet of floor space were covered with brightly colored patterns of sharply cut marble, ranging from the tiny chips employed in *opus tessellatum* work (floral and animal figures) to the larger pieces employed in the much more common *opus sectile* (geometric) designs. In addition, enormous slabs of Proconnesian marble were laid directly beneath the central and western domes. Although the overall effect was that of a complex network of geometric shapes, the margins were varied by elegant representational figures such as peacocks sipping from classical vases. Along the building's east-west axis from nave to apse, large, linear designs predominated, enhancing the semibasilical impression created by the surrounding architectural framework.[21]

To complete the Basilica's earthly zone, large portions of the lower brick walls and piers were covered in rare and beautiful marble revetment. Seen from a distance or poorly lit, this marble sheathing appears gray or dark brown. But when viewed up close or in better light, the eye becomes fascinated by smoky shades of cream, blue-gray, green, ruby, red-

Fig. 14: INTERIOR OF THE BASILICA SAN MARCO *(looking east toward the altar) by Alberto Prosdocimi (with the kind permission of the Procuratoria di San Marco, Venice)*

Fig. 15 (opposite): Interior of the Basilica San Marco (looking west toward the main entrance)

brown, orange, and porphyry. This revetment surface is mottled in every direction, its patterns of gorgeous veining acting to dissolve the rectangular shapes of the individual marble slabs *(Fig. 16)*. To achieve this effect, the artisans of San Marco would cut a particularly beautiful piece of marble into half or quarter slices and then arrange the sheets on the wall so that their almost identical veining patterns radiated from a common center, sometimes giving the impression of butterfly wings. Slightly different techniques were used to create strange melting effects, imparting a mysterious, almost metaphysical air to the Basilica

interior. Over time, this process transformed San Marco into one of the world's finest examples of the antique art of marble incrustation. Ultimately derived from the Romans, this classical technique was also a prominent interior feature of San Marco's model, the Apostoleion, and of other Late Antique Byzantine masterpieces such as Haghia Sophia in Constantinople *(Figs. 10, 17)* and San Vitale in Ravenna. Its highly skilled use within the Basilica is one of the major reasons San Marco seems to "breathe much of the spirit of Justinian art."[22] However, in San Marco, this lower zone of precious marble sheathing does not extend as far up the walls and piers as it often does in pure Byzantine church interiors. As a result, in the Basilica, a great deal of the emphasis is on "beauty of surface, of tone, of detail, of things near enough to touch and kneel upon and lean against—it is from this that the effect proceeds,"[23] in the words of Henry James *(Fig. 18)*.

At the same time that this transformation of the church's lower levels was under way, additional teams of skilled artists were gradually filling San Marco's celestial zone with a set of imposing mosaic programs. Work proceeded rapidly, so that by 1200, stunning mosaics covered all of the Basilica's domes and vaults. At times only a single team might be at work, suspended on a light scaffold in the arc of a dome, toiling at its exacting art in the church's cavernous upper spheres. At other times, there might be as many as five separate teams (each composed of a master mosaicist and his assistants) working on the same vault or dome, with each group free to express its individual artistic style. Mosaicists created the raw materials for their art by applying gold and other colors to clear glass plates, then breaking the glass into small shards called *tesserae*. Buckets of tesserae were then hoisted up to the domes and vaults whose brick surfaces had previously been covered with cement, where an image small enough to be finished in a single day was then traced. After a thin layer of fresh mortar was applied, the traced image was painted in full color and detail. Then came the highly demanding task of creating a high-quality mosaic image. As the tesserae were pressed into the mortar, care had to be taken to continually vary the angles at which the individual pieces were set so that the glass fragments would refract light in different directions. At the same time, in order to create a realistic effect when viewed from the nave floor, the mosaic artist had to leave different widths between the tesserae. And, being limited to a small, only slightly graduated color palette, he had to be able to model very large, realistic figures solely through subtle variations in hue and tone.[24]

Like the surrounding architectural framework, the general designs for San Marco's original mosaic programs were very likely derived from the Apostoleion, and it is almost certain that the earliest versions of this Byzantine iconography were installed by Greek mosaicists, who began their work in the church's apse and eastern dome. These Byzantine mosaic artists and the Venetians who succeeded them had to overcome challenges of creative adaptation similar to those faced by the Greek architect who designed and built the Contarini church in the previous century. All Byzantine mosaic programs were based on the placement of particular images in specific architectural locations. Yet the Greek masters who initiated San Marco's mosaics at the beginning of the twelfth century were working in a building whose structure was fundamentally different from the Byzantine churches in which these artists had been trained. Compared to the Basilica and the sixth-century Apostoleion on which it was based, the contemporary Greek churches with which these mosaic artists were familiar were smaller and simpler, with far fewer domes—in fact, quite commonly with only a single central cupola. Thus, the Greek mosaic artists assigned to San Marco knew only three types of dome composition, and they used this limited repertoire on the three cupolas making up the Basilica's main east-west axis, leaving the design of the two transept domes to be invented by their local Venetian successors.[25]

Fig. 16: Detail of the marble revetment on the north nave wall of the Basilica San Marco (with the kind permission of the Procuratoria di San Marco, Venice)

Fig. 17: Interior of Hagia Sophia

*Fig. 18 (opposite): Western narthex of the Basilica
San Marco ("things near enough to touch")*

In general, the purity of San Marco's imported mosaic programs began to weaken in the years after 1118, when the influx of Greek artists, styles, and techniques into Venice began to wane during the progressive deterioration of the Veneto-Byzantine economic and military alliance. Byzantine mosaic practice was based on a clear, unvarying hierarchy of standard elements in which specific mosaic images were theologically assigned to particular architectural spaces. In buildings of a specific type, neither the architectural location of each image nor the precise sequence of images within a given area varied from church to church. The earliest San Marco mosaics possessed a number of these essential Byzantine characteristics, and those which have survived intact are, like standard Greek mosaics, generally framed by the building elements of their immediate architectural context—the niches, partitions, angles, and wall borders where they were installed. However, Venetians never shared the same passionate interest in abstract theological speculation that obsessed the Greek mind and from which the Byzantine commitment to strictly ordered decorative systems drew its inspiration. Thus, as Greek artistic influence began to recede toward the middle of the twelfth century, this original Byzantine style of mosaic construction was displaced by a so-called transparent style. In this new, more expressive mode, framing devices disappeared, leaving the mosaic images to float on an all-encompassing golden background rather than being contained within a defined architectural space *(Fig. 19)*.[26]

The local Venetian workshops that created this new transparent style were passionately committed to exploring its full artistic potential. In their excitement, they began to extend a seamless golden skin over the Basilica's entire celestial region. The result of spreading this gilded mantle over every dome and vault was a series of mosaic paintings that Otto Demus has called one of the richest monuments of medieval art ever produced. But it was also a program whose completion required the bricking over of more and more windows. Originally, each wall of the Contarini church was pierced by eight large windows, but as Venetian mosaicists added wave after wave of golden surface, the number of openings in a typical wall shrank to no more than three or four—or, in some cases, to none—and the interior became substantially darker. Of course, this expansion of ornamental surface at the expense of original illumination could only proceed so far before compensating steps had to be taken. In time, it would lead to the most important structural change ever made to the medieval San Marco interior: the removal of the women's galleries located above the aisles of the nave and the northern and southern transepts. The elimination of these upper floors and their replacement by narrow catwalks, occurring in two phases between 1170 and 1230, transformed the interior perimeter. Decorative ornament could now be extended to well-lit aisles, areas of the church that had formerly been obscured in deep shadow.[27]

Another Audacious Leap into the Future

Venetian exceptionalism took many forms in the twelfth century—physical integration, accelerating commercial success, the creation and refinement of communal political institutions, the development of critical facilities like the Rialto market and the Arsenale shipyard, and the extraordinary exuberance of the Basilica's interior decoration. But important as these achievements were, none fully expressed the unique changes occurring in the city's collective psyche. Venice remained a society of "new men" descended from

Fig. 19: The Basilica San Marco's dome and vault mosaics

refugee bands who had been forced to re-create their lives in a barren, unpopulated wasteland. Her people, always readier to make bold new beginnings than other nations, were now preparing themselves for another audacious leap into the future, one equally as brash as her seizure of Mark the Evangelist three centuries earlier when the city was only a fledgling frontier state living in the narrow margin between two giant empires. In giving form to this expanded sense of her high destiny, the spare brick façade of the Basilica San Marco, the small bucolic field in which it sat, the grim, adjoining ducal fortress, and the area's surrounding waterways would be the tabula rasa on which Venetian genius would act. Over the course of the following century, the Republic would transform these original rude elements into a related pair of classically inspired piazzas. Spared the huge expense of building ever-expanding defensive walls, Venice would merge her architectural efforts into one all-encompassing achievement: the creation of the largest and most splendid public square in medieval Europe. In so doing, she would prove herself to be a true vanguard state, achieving an authentic antique grandeur on a scale that other Italian cities would not attempt for another two centuries.

CHAPTER FIVE

A World Stage (1095-1200)

Western Crusaders Arrive in Constantinople

Beginning in the late eleventh century, Western Christendom launched a series of holy wars, known as the Crusades, that were intended to wrest control of Biblical Palestine from the Muslim rulers who had conquered and held it for the previous four and a half centuries. Only the first of these adventures was even a partial military success, but to the Greek Christians of the Byzantine Empire whose homes and fields lay in the line of march by which these Western armies reached the Holy Land, efforts to distinguish the various Crusades with words like success or failure were pointless if not absurd. To them, every Crusade was a hostile incursion into imperial territory by foreign troops who returned Eastern hospitality with regular sprees of pillage and murder. To his abiding regret, it was the Byzantine emperor Alexius Comnenus himself (r. 1081–1118) who had initially invited this swarm of Latin soldiers to the gates of his capital. In 1094, the emperor had faced a dire threat: the Seljuk Turks had seized three-quarters of Asia Minor, Byzantium's principal source of foodstuffs and military recruits, from his overmatched Greek armies. Responding to this immediate danger, Alexius had suggested to Pope Urban II that some of the surplus men-at-arms then plaguing Western Europe might be useful in rolling back the infidel tide.[1]

What the emperor hoped to attract was a steady supply of professional soldiers who, in exchange for excellent pay, would enlist under his command in a campaign to return Asia Minor to Greek control. What arrived on his doorstep in the period 1096–1097 were a hundred thousand freebooting adventurers, at least a third of whom were part of a fanatical rabble with virtually no military skills. As for the experienced fighters within this crusading horde, some of the best belonged to an army of aggressive Normans led by Robert Guiscard's son Bohemond, whose declared goal in joining the First Crusade was to carve out his own kingdom in historic Greek territory. These initial Crusader bands had paid dearly to reach Constantinople, and they were not prepared to be led into battle by a Byzantine commander to achieve Greek military goals. To take part in the First Crusade, a typical knight needed to raise almost four times his annual income, forcing many to sell or mortgage a large part of their feudal estates to the Church, usually at a steep discount. If these Crusaders made the twenty-five-hundred-mile trip by land, the journey took eight grueling months. Those who could afford the expense of a sea voyage reduced their travel period to six weeks, but they spent most of this time in utter squalor and occasional mortal terror, rolling from side to side in the dark, damp underbelly of a small, cramped ship. And for most of these Western pilgrims, the odds were very high that their Eastern odyssey would end in death, enslavement, or financial ruin. Between thirty-five and fifty percent of all Crusader knights died from shipwreck, hunger, or disease, or were killed on the battlefield, and the mortality rate was of course higher for the common soldiers who followed in their train. Not surprisingly then, when these Latin wayfarers reached Constantinople, they hoped to cram in as much luxury and carnal pleasure as possible before moving on to confront the Muslim armies waiting for them on the other side of the straits separating the imperial capital from Asia. Having heard of Byzantium's fabled wealth, they expected to have all of their physical needs eagerly attended to by their rich co-religionists.[2]

In planning the First Crusade, there seems to have been a general hope by leaders on both sides that, in spite of the formal schism that had existed between the Roman and Eastern Churches since 1054, the armies of Western Europe and Byzantium would be able to unite against a common Moslem foe. Alexius Comnenus, himself a splendid general and the aristocratic offspring of a great Eastern feudal family, may well have believed that this background would give him a special kinship with Western chivalry. If so, he was sadly mistaken. From the moment the Latin warriors of the First Crusade arrived before the Greek capital, deeply engrained differences overwhelmed any nominal similarities and caused the two cultures to view each other with extreme suspicion and hostility. In the feudal West, political and military power was decentralized, and local lords of every degree jealously guarded the autonomy they had won by force of arms. In the East, on the other hand, the feudal organization of landed estates was counterbalanced by a universal belief in the infallibility and absolute authority of the Byzantine emperor, who, whatever his personal merits or defects might be, was recognized as both national sovereign and commander in chief of all Greek military forces. In the tradition of Constantine the Great, the emperor was even viewed as God's vicar on earth, king and priest in one, infallible in both the temporal and spiritual realms. Consequently, in vivid contrast to Western Europe, the Eastern Empire was governed from a splendid metropolitan capital whose imperial court was staffed by a highly educated state bureaucracy. The great wealth and population of Constantinople had generated a complex social hierarchy, including a large class of urban intellectuals who were passionately interested in art, architecture, and abstruse theological debate.[3]

Nothing like these fruits of a sophisticated metropolitan culture existed in the medieval West, at least not on a remotely comparable scale. Major European cities such as Paris, London, and Milan were little more than country towns in comparison to the great capitals of Byzantium and Islam. And rather than responding sympathetically to the magnificent cultural and intellectual life of the Byzantine capital, the Crusaders viewed the Greeks as effete guardians of a decadent, exhausted civilization. For many of these untraveled French and German warriors, it was genuinely difficult to detect a difference between the foreign-looking, strange-sounding inhabitants of the Eastern Empire and the Muslim and Jewish unbelievers they had come to exterminate. When the Crusaders first encountered indigenous Eastern Christians during their land march to Constantinople, they had mistakenly butchered them in large numbers.[4]

Thus, at the very moment when he hoped to mount a counteroffensive against the Turks who had seized his countryside, Alexius Comnenus had to divert precious manpower to protect his capital from the greed and rapacity of Western Christians. The earliest arrivals belonged to the so-called People's Crusade, an unruly mob of thirty thousand thieves and rapists led by an unwashed fanatic named Peter the Hermit. The emperor promptly ferried this predatory band over to Asia Minor and was not sorry to learn, a few months later, that ninety percent of them had been slaughtered in a Turkish ambush. However, Alexius employed a very different approach with later contingents of the First Crusade, totaling about seventy thousand men, who reached Constantinople in the years 1096–1097. Since these contained a large proportion of first-class fighting men led by some of Europe's greatest feudal lords, the emperor made a straightforward offer to buy their military allegiance. Unfortunately, this only revealed the profound ethical gulf dividing the two cultures, since nothing could have been better designed to earn the Latin knights' bitter contempt. Although they felt no qualms about accepting Alexius' expensive gifts, the Crusaders haughtily refused to acknowledge any return obligation to place themselves under imperial command, since this would have violated the warrior ethos on which their whole existence was based. In their eyes, military combat could never be the matter of a mere business contract. It was a mystical act, a joyous bloodbath whose carnage and mutilation were to be revered for their own sake. By his liberal offer, the emperor had only revealed himself to be a coward and a wily tempter. To enlist as mere mercenaries, as he had proposed, would have been to pollute the sacred ideals on which these feudal warriors had grounded their lives.[5]

Naturally, Alexius Comnenus saw matters very differently. He had performed the duties of a gracious host and munificent ally under the most trying of circumstances. He had showered his uncouth guests with lavish gifts and subtle diplomacy. In response, these Latin intruders had not only rejected his generous enlistment terms, they had openly discussed establishing independent Crusader kingdoms on historic Byzantine soil. In imperial eyes, the Westerners were coarse, greedy men whose fickle, untrustworthy natures made them an ever-present danger to Greek lives and property. And he certainly was not prepared to look on passively while Venice, a nation on which he had bestowed huge trade concessions, assisted the Crusader cause rather than Byzantine interests. Therefore, he made it clear to the Republic that if she used her naval might to help the Crusaders, as she was now being urged to do, the enormous tax and customs exemptions Venetian merchants had received in the Golden Bull of 1082 would instantly be terminated. Venice had to choose. She could continue to reap the benefits of a valuable existing alliance or she could abandon her current position as the major intermediary between the Greek East and Western feudalism to pursue tempting new opportunities, but she could not do both. Initially, Venice tried to put off a decision, but when Genoa and Pisa stepped forward to exchange their naval support for lucrative trade benefits within future Crusader kingdoms, she knew she had to act. The risk of allowing her rivals unrestricted freedom to establish new commercial bases in the East, formerly an exclusive Venetian preserve, was simply too great. She decided to throw in her lot with the crusading adventurers, and having done so, became a major contributor. Her fleet of two hundred ships and nine thousand men made her the largest Italian participant in the First Crusade. Two decades later, a Venetian armada of 120 ships and fifteen thousand men (one quarter of her male population) smashed the Egyptian navy in a decisive battle from which there were few if any surviving enemy vessels, thereby ending the Muslim naval threat. The following year, the doge himself led an army that conquered the important Muslim coastal stronghold of Tyre.[6]

As her reward, Venice received one-third of Tyre as well as trade and political concessions in Acre and Sidon, the right to establish her own Venetian quarter in Jerusalem, and an exemption of Venetian commerce from all tolls and customs within the new Crusader kingdoms. And Venetians enjoyed these generous benefits free of traditional feudal obligations. Compare this to the typical fate of other Western Crusaders who fought exclusively on land. Of those fortunate enough to survive the hazardous journey, the brutal Middle Eastern killing fields, and the enslavement that routinely followed military defeat, most struggled home penniless. Nor were such results unanticipated or deemed entirely undesirable. In preaching the First Crusade, one of the pope's principal goals had been to purge Western Europe of its surfeit of belligerent warriors and landless peasants. In this respect, the Crusades were a great success. They devastated much of the feudal nobility and killed between 300,000 and 1,000,000 of the nonlanded poor who joined the armies' rank and file.[7]

The Collapsing Byzantine Alliance

In spite of his threats, Emperor Alexius Comnenus did not punish Venice for her assistance to the Crusades because he remained dependent on Venetian naval power to ward off the threat of a new Norman invasion. Although he granted Pisan merchants their own quarter in Constantinople and cut Pisan customs duty to four percent, Venetian traders continued to receive the full ten percent exemption they had enjoyed for the past three decades. This arrangement remained in place until Alexius' death in 1118, when his son John Comnenus (r. 1118–1143) took the throne and refused to renew the Venetian concessions. Since exploitation of her special trading privileges in the Eastern Empire was the cornerstone of Venetian economic policy, the Republic felt she had no choice but to respond aggressively, and she initiated a war of deliberate piracy against imperial interests. After seven years of watching Byzantine ships and ports plundered by Venetian raiders throughout the Mediterranean and Aegean, John Comnenus grudgingly reinstated the exemptions of 1082, and Venetian merchants once more began to enrich themselves in the Greek capital.[8]

But the years of open hostility had wrought a fundamental change in the relationship. The Byzantines now saw the Venetians not as loyal allies but as a coarse, commercial people, oblivious to anything beyond the world of monetary values. Greek aristocrats, with their keen interest in philosophy and theology, looked on trade as a servile activity fit only for uneducated vulgarians. In their eyes, Venetians would always be the lowly offspring of greasy fishermen, and no amount of wealth heaped up as international merchants could ever disguise their origins. On the other hand, Venetians felt nothing but scorn for such Greek snobbery. Of course, they were traders and mariners; they would never think of denying such facts. Commerce and naval prowess were the foundations of their entire society and its unparalleled economic, political, and architectural achievements during the last three centuries. Citizens of the Republic were shocked that there could be a culture foolish enough to denigrate such critical skills. Far from being intimidated by Greek disdain, it only deepened the contempt Venetians felt for the Byzantines themselves, a people they believed had become too lazy and self-indulgent to protect their vital interests. In order to retain the wealth and power they had inherited from distant ancestors, the Greeks now depended on youthful, emerging nations such as Venice, whose people had repeatedly sacrificed their blood defending imperial territory and commerce.[9]

In the political realm, while medieval Venetians still admired many of the ancient Roman ideals on which the Byzantine state had been founded, they were far too practical to cling to a governance model that was proving to be increasingly dysfunctional. To this point, an astonishing sixty percent of all Byzantine emperors had been either been forced to abdicate or were poisoned, smothered, strangled, or stabbed to death while in office. As one scholar has observed, Greek imperial authority was absolute power tempered only by assassination. This type of extreme political instability had led directly to Byzantium's loss of eastern Asia Minor to the Seljuk Turks, an outcome that fed a growing Venetian distrust of concentrated power. As we have seen, by the middle of the twelfth century, the Republic's political constitution was moving in the opposite direction, away from the Byzantine concept of an all-powerful, divine emperor toward an oligarchic model—a deliberate dispersal of authority among an inner circle of the city's most powerful merchant families.[10]

When Emperor John Comnenus died in 1143, he was succeeded by his son Manuel, who would reign for the next thirty-seven years. Manuel waited four years before confirming the Republic's vital trade exemptions, and when he did so in 1147, it was only because he needed Venetian naval assistance to roll back another Norman invasion of Greek territory. But in the course of joint Venetian and Byzantine naval operations in the Adriatic, an incident occurred that revealed just how deep the schism between the two nominal allies had become. During their attack on Norman-held Corfu, spontaneous fighting broke out between the Venetian and Greek assault forces. After losing an initial skirmish in the town's central square, the Venetians retreated to the harbor, where they burned several Greek cargo vessels and seized the emperor's flagship. While searching the royal galley, the Venetian boarding party discovered that Manuel had left one of his imperial robes on board. In short order, Venetian sailors draped the robe over the shoulders of a black slave and staged an on-deck parody of Manuel's imperial coronation ceremony. This racist taunt, a deliberate mockery of sacred Byzantine rites, was performed in full view of the imperial fleet and Manuel himself, who was famously vain about his dark, handsome features. The Venetians must have intended it as both a personal insult and a calculated affront to Greek political ideals, an action that would be all but impossible to forget or forgive.[11]

In spite of the deep humiliation he must have felt and the size of the five-hundred-ship Greek armada he commanded, Manuel wisely decided to avoid an immediate all-out clash with the Mediterranean's most formidable naval power. Not surprisingly, however, after this ugly Corfu episode, the historic Veneto-Byzantine alliance began to unravel completely. Venice signed a nonaggression treaty with the Greeks' traditional enemies, the German emperor and the Norman kingdom of Sicily, and Manuel reestablished Byzantine sovereignty over Dalmatia and Croatia, which the Republic had come to regard as part of her Adriatic sphere of influence. When Venice refused to supply naval assistance after the Greeks were threatened with renewed Norman aggression, Manuel responded by granting liberal trading concessions and commercial quarters in Constantinople to both Genoa and Pisa. In reaction, Venetian merchants attacked and destroyed the new Genoese district in the imperial capital and threatened to renew the piracy campaign that had forced the emperor's father to capitulate forty years earlier. Strangely, however, the final rupture that seemed so imminent failed to occur. In fact, the emperor seems to have deliberately interrupted hostilities by offering assurances that citizens of the Republic could continue to lead their privileged lives in the Greek East without fear of reprisal, and for the next several months, Venetians appear to have believed this fantasy.[12]

Then, on April 12, 1171, the emperor's trap sprang shut. Without warning, imperial troops marched into the Venetian quarter of Greek cities throughout the empire, killing some residents and arresting everyone else they found. After rounding up an estimated ten to twenty thousand prisoners, Manuel seized the captives' homes, shops, warehouses, ships, and cargos, all of which instantly became Byzantine property. Venetian capital losses were immense. Men and women accustomed to a life of wealth and elegance in one of the world's supremely beautiful cities now sat incarcerated in darkness and filth, knowing that if they were ever released from their squalid cells, they would walk out penniless. By not responding immediately after the insult at Corfu, by refusing to react until every component of his intricate plot was firmly in place, Manuel believed that he had made himself immune from Venetian retaliation. Should the Republic elect a direct military assault on the Greek capital, the emperor knew that in more than eight centuries, the walls of Constantinople had never been breached, having withstood repeated assaults by Goth, Persian, Slav, and Muslim armies much larger than anything Venice could muster. And if the Republic decided to attack some other more vulnerable part of the empire, Manuel now held at least ten thousand Venetian hostages, many of whom were members of the city's wealthiest aristocratic families.[13]

Doge Vitale Michiel II and his councilors also understood the reality of such constraints, and their first reaction was to try diplomacy, not military action, to secure the hostages' release. However, six months later, after surrendering to popular pressure, the doge led a war fleet of 120 ships into the Aegean Sea, at which point he paused and once again began to pursue negotiations. While imperial diplomats deliberately stalled talks in the Greek capital, the Republic's fleet, sitting idle in the harbor of Chios, was struck by a lethal attack of plague, which rapidly crippled the powerful armada. It was at this point that Emperor Manuel, well informed of the ongoing Venetian catastrophe, sent a message to Vitale Michiel. After taunting the doge with accusations of gross stupidity, Manuel declared how much he enjoyed watching the parvenus of Venice make themselves the laughingstock of the whole world. Jeered at by the enemy he had been sent to punish and threatened with mutiny by his dying crews if he remained in Eastern waters, Doge Michiel chose to lead his shattered fleet, still infected with plague, back to the Venetian lagoon. There, accosted by an angry mob, he fled from the ducal castle only to be assassinated before he could reach sanctuary.

However, from this abject low point, Venice displayed astonishing powers of recovery. The following year, she adopted the most far-reaching constitutional reforms in her history, and five years later, her exceptional new doge, Sebastiano Ziani, masterminded the 1177 Peace of Venice which ended the long, bitter power struggle between Pope Alexander III and the German emperor Frederick Barbarossa. This historic reconciliation had the collateral effect of crushing any hope the Greek emperor may have had to strip Italy from the Western emperor's grasp by posing as the pope's protector. Venice had the double satisfaction of knowing that her brilliant diplomatic coup was also the final, shattering blow to one of Manuel Comnenus' most deeply cherished ambitions.[14]

For several years after Manuel's death in 1180, the Republic's relationship with Byzantium remained one of open enmity as thousands of Venetians continued to languish in Greek prisons. However, in 1182, this turned out to be a blessing in disguise when a Greek mob, seething with anti-Latin hatred, burst into the foreign colonies nestled along the Golden Horn, raping, torturing, and eventually killing everyone who fell into their hands. It is estimated that of the seventy thousand Latins then living in Constantinople, over fifty thousand men, women, and children (mostly Pisans and Genoese) were murdered, and four thousand were sold into Turkish slavery. Not long after, the new emperor, the same Andronicus Comnenus who had incited the mob to commit this act of mass butchery, realizing that he was now exposed to the hostility of Pisa and Genoa as well as the resurgent Normans, decided that he needed to reestablish relations with the Republic if he intended to survive. He therefore ordered a general release of Venetian hostages, and the Republic's merchants began to return to their profitable trading districts in Constantinople and other Byzantine cities. Several years later, when the mob turned on Andronicus (he was subjected to a series of slow, ghastly tortures before dying), imperial rule passed into the hands of the Angelus family whose first representative, Isaac II, allowed the Byzantine navy to shrivel to a few decrepit ships before being deposed and blinded by his brother Alexius III Angelus, an unbalanced megalomaniac who rose to power on a wave of venomous anti-Venetian sentiment. After ordering his tax and customs officials to ignore Venetian trade exemptions, Alexius began to shower favors on the Republic's commercial rivals, Genoa and Pisa; he also encouraged Pisans living in the capital to attack Venetian ships docked along the shore of the Republic's trading quarter.[15]

Thus, Venetians residing in Constantinople at the end of the twelfth century lived in the midst of a Greek rabble whose bitter hatred of foreigners could erupt into homicidal fury at any moment. At the head of this volatile mob sat an unstable, duplicitous ruler who had openly repudiated the Republic's hard-won commercial rights and cheered on the murder and plunder of her citizens. Yet, in spite of this, the capital teemed with Venetians, many of whom saw themselves as the true masters of the Eastern Empire. In their eyes, it was Venetian entrepreneurial energy which ensured Constantinople's commercial vitality and continued to make it the center of world trade. For centuries, Venetian naval power had served as the critical prop in preserving the entire Byzantine imperial system. Indeed, after 1187, Venice held Byzantine naval defense almost entirely within her control.[16]

Origins of the Medieval Piazza San Marco

In the twelfth century, Venice took the first serious steps toward transforming herself from a state ruled by monarchical doges and popular assemblies into a communal oligarchy where decision making was shared among the members of a large and powerful merchant aristocracy. With the ascendancy of the mercantile nobility, the Republic began to assert a much more independent foreign policy, uncoupling her goals from those of Byzantium, her historical mentor and ally, in favor of new, more experimental alliances with states and kingdoms she had formerly opposed. With her wealth and power continually expanding, by the final decades of the twelfth century, Venice was pursuing her own expansive dreams on a worldwide stage. She was beginning to see herself as nothing less than the legitimate heir to the riches of the Byzantine East.[17]

However, during the first half of the twelfth century, the extraordinary energy that propelled the Republic to these remarkable political and economic achievements failed to leave its mark on the public face of the San Marco precinct (*Fig. 20*). For instance, nothing like the Basilica's exuberant interior decoration had spilled out onto its spare, brick exterior. The church remained what it had always been, a ducal chapel, connected by private corridors to the adjoining ducal castle, the doge's heavily fortified residence and government headquarters. The church, the fortress, and the partially completed San Marco Campanile sat within or protruded from a small, L-shaped island. A canal, the Rio Batario, located just west of the tower, a lagoon inlet that washed ashore just south of the church, and the

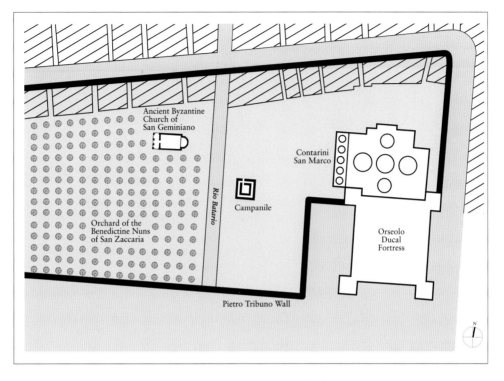

Fig. 20: Plan of San Marco precinct in 1150 (after drawing by A. Pelanda)

other watery barriers that enveloped these central district monuments severely reduced the surrounding open space. In fact, this constricted island campo still gave off a semirural air; its irregular grassy surface was crisscrossed with intersecting dirt paths running between clumps of bushes and small trees (*Fig. 21*). The overall San Marco precinct was composed of this L-shaped island and a second island to the immediate west containing an ancient church and a pilgrim hospice. The two islands were separated by the intersecting Batario canal but united by the old Pietro Tribuno fortified wall that formed the district perimeter. The sides of this weathered, tenth-century brick rampart blocked any clear view into or out of this central governmental area. Just inside its defensive walls, the San Marco district

*Fig. 21: In 1150, the San Marco precinct had the same
semirural air as the present-day island of Torcello.*

was bordered by the houses and shops of wealthy merchants, all built after 1106, the year that a devastating fire had spread to the area from the city's northern neighborhoods. The inferno's destructive power could still be seen in the scorched brick and stone exteriors of the Basilica and the ducal fortress.[18]

In the 1160s or 1170s, Venice began a radical reconstruction of these two walled-off islands, a century-long project whose final form, the medieval Piazza San Marco, would reflect some of the most profound economic and political changes in Venetian history. Yet what is striking, given the extreme dynamism of this period, is that from the beginning this was a project of remarkable conceptual unity and architectural coherence. There are two basic reasons for this. First, Venice knew what she wished to accomplish and remained committed to her objectives throughout the lengthy construction period. She wanted to build a large public square where her state church, her government palace, and her most important communal rituals would all be merged in a single magnificent setting. She wanted to do this on a grand classical scale, in an authentic antique style derived from ancient Roman models, and she wanted to use the project's classical grandeur and elegance to lend prestige to the Republic's new communal political institutions. In particular, she wanted to convert the old, forbidding ducal fortress into an open, inviting, public meeting place for the city's expanding communal councils and judicial system and to transform the Basilica from a private chapel into a national sanctuary.[19]

The other reason for the medieval Piazza's extraordinary coherence is that virtually its entire hundred-year development appears to have been under the general direction of a single, quasi-public office. Just as political power in twelfth-century Venice gravitated from the doge to communal magistrates and councils, so control of public architecture in the San Marco area passed into the hands of a new communal entity known as the Procuracy of Saint Mark. This position, initially held by a single nobleman, probably originated about the time of the consecration of the Basilica in 1094, although the earliest verifiable record of its existence dates from 1152. In the beginning, the procurator's responsibilities were restricted to the maintenance, renovation, and decoration of the Basilica only. But sometime during the dogate of Vitale Michiel II (1156–1172), when workers began clearing and enlarging the area directly opposite the church to create San Marco's monumental new piazza, it was the Procuracy of Saint Mark that began to assume overall management of the huge new project.[20]

As with any other major architectural undertaking, Venice needed to begin with a useful model. The ideal archetype would be a ceremonial square directly bordered by a national church and governmental palace, all constructed on a grand classical scale as part of a unified complex owned and managed by the state. The Roman Forum itself was proof that the Romans had built many such ancient piazzas throughout Italy, but due to the routine architectural cannibalism practiced by medieval builders, none of these classical sites had survived in a sufficiently intact state to be of much direct use. Fortunately, Venice was not limited to Western models.

Constantinople's Great Classical Square

Medieval Venetians were intimately familiar with Constantinople. As early as the eighth and ninth centuries, some of Venice's leading settlers began making long journeys to the Greek metropolis, and the length and frequency of these sojourns increased dramatically after 1082, the year the emperor granted Venetian traders a series of lucrative financial incentives to live and work in Byzantine dominions. By 1150, an estimated ten thousand Venetians, many of whom belonged to the Republic's wealthiest, most influential merchant families, had taken up residence in the Byzantine capital. Most lived within the Republic's private trading colony, a short, narrow strip of land along the southern shore of the Golden Horn.[21] What was the daily experience of these overseas Venetians? What did they witness as they walked through the streets and public squares of the great Eastern metropolis? Above all, they would have been conscious that they were living in an authentic, function-ing classical city. Constantinople was the majestic fourth-century architectural creation of the Roman emperor Constantine, rebuilt on an even larger scale in full Late Antique grandeur by the sixth-century Roman emperor Justinian. Unlike medieval Rome, whose population had shrunk to thirty-five thousand and whose classical buildings were, in many cases, vandalized heaps of brick and rubble, the Greek capital had sustained its original commercial vigor, and most of its Justinian-era monuments remained intact throughout the twelfth century. As late as 1203, with a population between 600,000 and 1,000,000, the huge city was a vital, living expression of classical Roman civilization, "the still beating heart of antiquity."[22]

Constantine had founded his city on a wedge-shaped promontory jutting eastward from the European landmass at the very point where the Bosporus, the long, narrow strait run-ning north to the Black Sea, and the city's bow-shaped harbor, the Golden Horn, poured into the Sea of Marmara (*Fig. 22*). Directly east of the city, over a mile of open water, lay the opposing continent of Asia. On the European side, the waves of the Marmara broke against encircling city walls which rose to an average height of forty feet and were braced with two hundred stout towers. Behind the sea ramparts, rising steadily to the crest of the first hill, then sweeping west for several miles over a succession of valleys and ridges, was a breath-taking panorama of palaces, temples, gardens, baths, classical porticos, public squares, ceremonial columns, and domed churches. Constantine had ransacked his empire to adorn the city's monumental forums and avenues with the finest art of the Greco-Roman world.

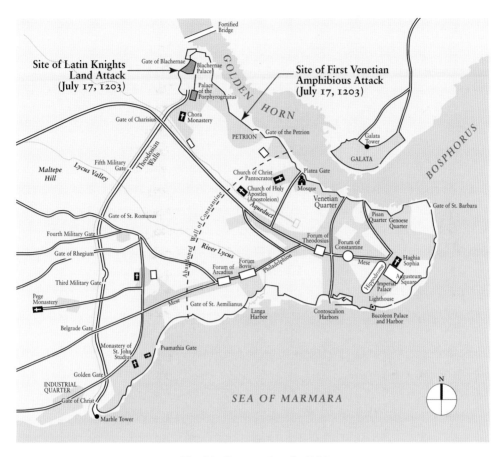

Fig. 22: Constantinople 1203

On a plain at the top of the first hill, overlooking the surrounding sea, Constantine built the capital's principal public square, a spacious enclosure lined with stately columns, paved with dark marble, and filled with masterworks of classical sculpture. He named it the Augusteum in honor of his mother Helena, whose ceremonial title was the Augusta, and placed her statue at the top of a large porphyry column in the middle of the square. Constantine's site was the heart of the old Roman town constructed on ancient Greek foundations by the Roman emperor Septimus Severus at the end of the second century.

Constantine rebuilt this modest Severan center (which contained a small forum as well as a racing arena or hippodrome, a bath, and an assortment of other public buildings) on a much grander scale. He added a sprawling imperial palace complex, a huge new Hippodrome, a Senate House, and a magnificent new basilica, the Haghia Sophia or Church of the Holy Wisdom, all of which adjoined the Augusteum courtyard. He then filled the district with freestanding classical statues and relief sculpture as well as a second column surmounted with his own imperial likeness.[23]

Virtually all of these Constantinian buildings and monuments, with the significant exception of the enormous Hippodrome (three-fourths as large as the Circus Maximus in Rome and capable of seating up to eighty thousand spectators), burned to the ground in 532 during the Nika Revolt against Emperor Justinian I, whose reign (527–565) marked the zenith of the Byzantine Empire. Confronted with this extraordinary threat to his life and sovereignty, Justinian responded decisively. He crushed the rebellion in a single blow by ordering imperial troops into the Hippodrome, where they methodically slaughtered thirty thousand conspirators. Having restored imperial authority, he then reconstructed the entire Augusteum area in unrivaled Late Antique splendor. Re-erected on the charred site of Constantine's original building complex, it would have been Justinian's magnificently restored square (a huge public space at least several times the size of an American football field) and his incomparable replacement church of Haghia Sophia that dazzled the eyes of twelfth-century Venetians. And because the empire as he conceived of it was still the Roman Empire of ancient times, Justinian's architectural monuments were imbued with the authentic antique grandeur of classical Rome. Like Constantine before him, Justinian "strove to revive the glory of old Rome" by making her architectural daughter, Constantinople, even "more ravishing than the mother."[24]

From the age of Constantine to the twelfth century, the Augusteum and the three great monuments which surrounded it constituted the symbolic heart of the Eastern Roman Empire (*Fig. 23*). Above all, the great square served as a forecourt to the domed vastness of Justinian's Haghia Sophia, the national cathedral of a passionately religious people and one of the world's supreme building achievements, containing what is arguably the most sublime interior space ever constructed. On its opposite flank, the Augusteum led directly into the hushed beauty of the ancient Imperial Palace. Although by 1081 this sprawling complex of halls and pavilions had ceased to be the emperor's main residence, it was here

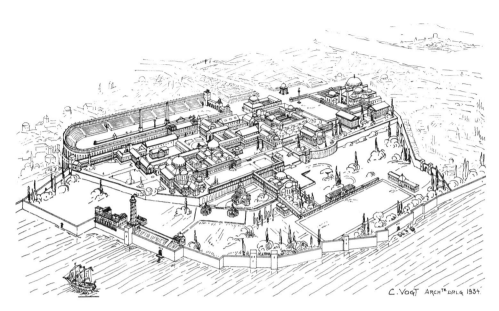

C. VOGT ARCH^TᵉDᴿ·ᴸ·ɢ 1934.

Fig. 23: Reconstruction drawing of the Augusteum square, Hippodrome and Imperial Palace in post-Justinian Constantinople, by Charles Vogt

that foreign visitors had been awed by carefully staged court rituals for over seven centuries. Adjoining the palace to the west stood the Hippodrome, the great arena (over fifteen hundred feet long and four hundred feet wide) where the emperor employed a mixture of political, athletic and religious spectacle to divert the fickle emotions of the urban mob. The Byzantine state operated these three monuments as an integrated complex. An emperor's coronation ceremony began in the Augusteum, where the new sovereign was seated on a battle shield and hoisted aloft to the acclaim of the people before being carried into Haghia Sophia to receive his robes of office. In subsequent public appearances, the emperor often entered the Great Church via private corridors and stairs leading from the Imperial Palace. The emperor also used another connecting stairway from the Imperial Palace to ascend to the *kathisma*, his private viewing stand in the Hippodrome, from which the enormous central dome of Haghia Sophia, its outer shell poised almost two hundred feet above the ground, was visible to spectators in the top rows.[25]

The Augusteum square contained a magnificent bronze equestrian statue of the Emperor Justinian, three times life size, dressed in the armor of Achilles and carrying the globe of the world in his left hand. The courtyard also held a large bronze statue of Athena by the Greek sculptor Phidias, and the bordering colonnades were filled with additional statues of emperors, classical gods, and heroes. But the Augusteum was more than a vast outdoor art museum and the center of Byzantine ritual; it was also infused with the capital's thriving business energies. The classical arcades enclosing the piazza housed busy shops run by proprietors who lived above their storefronts. In this respect, the Augusteum was modeled on the ancient Roman Forum and the classical Athenian *agora* or central marketplace, where the city's vigorous commercial life was on full display beside the state's most important political and religious functions.[26]

Adapting the Byzantine Model

Medieval Venice was deeply attracted to the Augusteum's magnificent classical architecture, the most faithful reflection of ancient Roman splendor then in existence. For a parvenu state like herself, eager to discover just how far an ambitious republic of expert mariners and bustling merchants could rise in the world of nations, the lure of Constantinople's unparalleled imperial grandeur must have been all but irresistible. The immense size of the Augusteum also helped Venetians decide that the Piazza San Marco would be a very large public space. For instance, the Piazza is almost twice the length of the Forum of Trajan, the largest of the imperial forums built in ancient Rome. Indeed, the Piazza's extraordinary size only makes sense when it is compared with the truly monumental dimensions of its great classical prototype in the Byzantine capital. The Augusteum encompassed an estimated 387,000 square feet, approximately three times the area covered by the Piazza and its smaller companion square (the Piazzetta) when they were completed in the thirteenth century. The Augusteum was also a very useful archetype because it mirrored an existing Venetian peculiarity. Its classical mingling of political and religious life in a single central district was the same model that Venice had chosen to follow in the early ninth century when Doge Giustiniano Participazio created the first church of San Marco as a ducal chapel annexed to his father's fortified castle rather than as a physically separate national shrine. From the beginning, this merger of functions in one integrated complex distinguished Venice from other Italian cities in which separate architectural centers for church and state, built some distance apart, were the norm.[27]

But there was one important feature of the Augusteum complex that the Venetians deliberately chose not to incorporate into the Piazza San Marco. Virtually all of Constantinople's architectural monuments, particularly those in the Augusteum, were expressions of the Eastern Empire's traditional belief in absolute imperial infallibility. It was an ideology that began with the founder Constantine, who believed that in addition to being an imperial sovereign, he was also God's vicar on earth and, to some degree, a divinity himself. Not surprisingly, then, many of the freestanding statues that filled the Augusteum and the city's other great public squares were effigies of past emperors or imperial family members. Whether installed at the summit of huge columns or placed at ground level next to statues of gods and heroes, collectively they offered vivid artistic testimony of the Byzantine commitment to a governing order in which infallible emperors were revered as semideities who ruled by divine right.[28]

As we have seen, such a belief system was totally at odds with political developments in twelfth-century Venice, where communal institutions based on carefully crafted checks and balances had replaced the city's original monarchical system. Indeed, one of the fundamental changes made by the medieval Republic was the deliberate creation of a powerful new senatorial class, the antithesis of Constantine's action effectively terminating the power of the old Roman Senate by transferring the imperial capital to the East. The builders of the medieval Piazza San Marco were acutely conscious of these critical differences between the two societies, and, as one would expect from a nation of discriminating businessmen, they were highly selective borrowers. While they consciously designed the Venetian complex to evoke the Augusteum's classical elegance and grandeur, they were careful to ensure that this magnificent new public space would only strengthen the city's prevailing political creed. Thus, they deliberately rejected any notion of duplicating the Eastern capital's wealth of freestanding sculpture raised to glorify powerful individual rulers. It was the medieval Piazza project that first established a strict prohibition against the glorification of individual Venetians in the public space of San Marco, a rule which thereafter guided Venetian architectural practice for many centuries. As a result, it was Saint Mark, not the doge, who became the symbol of Venetian sovereignty. It was in Mark's name that Venetian fleets won victories and returned to the lagoon laden with trophies. Because he borrowed the cut of his ceremonial robes and the style of his public rituals from the Byzantine emperor, a doge might look like a monarch. But increasingly, his office symbolized not individual or personal authority but the collective power and majesty of the communal Republic and her divine guardian, Mark the Evangelist.[29]

The Piazza Project in the Twelfth Century

The Piazza project began shortly after mid-century during the dogate of Vitale Michiel II, who occupied the ducal chair for sixteen years before his assassination in 1172. Work then accelerated under the expanded communal government led by his brilliant and fabulously rich successor, Sebastiano Ziani (1172–1178). By the time the Republic hosted the internationally celebrated Peace of Venice reconciling the pope and the Western emperor in the summer of 1177, a radical alteration of the two walled islands making up the San Marco precinct was well under way. The cramped field in front of the ducal chapel was being transformed into an impressively large public space in which the citizens of Venice could assemble and view themselves as a collective enterprise. A start had been made in converting the ducal fortress into a communal palace, and, after more than two centuries of fitful progress, the shaft of San Marco's Campanile had finally been raised to its full height and roofed. These achievements had necessitated a number of fundamental site changes. First came the demolition of Pietro Tribuno's antiquated defensive wall, which for centuries had blocked sightlines into and out of the two islands making up the San Marco district. This was undoubtedly accompanied by the demolition of a large number of houses and shops adjoining the battlemented relic. Occurring at roughly the same time that Florence was building a new circuit of fortified ramparts three times the length of its original Roman walls, the two initiatives underscored fundamental differences between Venice and other powerful city-states on the Italian mainland. By the twelfth century, Venice had no need to incur this particular type of costly defensive expenditure. She could devote her resources to a more discretionary, openly aesthetic type of architecture, recreating the grandeur of a classical Roman forum within her own small archipelago in the northern Adriatic.[30]

Having released the site from its fortified brick encasement, the San Marco builders created a deep rectangular opening in the city's urban core by more than doubling the length of the campo in front of the Basilica.[31] This required purchasing the land parcels making up the western island lying on the other side of the Rio Batario, including a large orchard belonging to the Benedictine nuns of San Zaccaria, who sold it for a handsome profit; as one of the richest men in Venice, Doge Ziani reportedly used his own money to buy many of these properties. The next steps were to fill in the Rio Batario, which ran directly between the two islands making up the project site[32] and to clear the newly acquired western island of buildings and natural obstructions. This meant demolishing the ancient church of San Geminiano e Mena, which, according to early chronicles, was already two hundred years old when the lagoon dwellers had first moved their capital to Rivoaltus three and a half centuries earlier. Although a replacement church of San Geminiano was quickly constructed at the far western end of the huge new square, this destruction of sacred property did not go unnoticed. The pope immediately condemned the Venetians for their action and quickly followed up by declaring the first of many papal interdicts against the Republic. In contrast, the pilgrim hospice built by Doge Pietro Orseolo I at the end of the tenth century (which, according to the majority of scholars, extended west from the rear of the recently completed Campanile, forming a partial southern border to the square) remained in place.[33]

The traditional view has been that most of the new Piazza complex (including the adjoining public space of the Piazzetta and most of the new or reconstructed buildings erected in and around the two squares) was built or at least substantially begun during the brief six-year dogate of Sebastiano Ziani, which began in 1172. In this view, Doge Ziani was the moving force behind both the project's overall design and its rapid completion. Just as he became a symbol of the Republic's remarkable political recovery after the assassination of his predecessor, so Ziani has received the lion's share of the credit for the Piazza enterprise. However, recent scholarship has substantially modified this conventional assessment. It reveals that work on the medieval Piazza complex began roughly a decade before Ziani became doge and lasted far beyond his brief term of office, and that basic direction of the century-long project reposed not with any particular individual but with the communal office of the Procuracy of Saint Mark. Certainly, it is hard to believe that a single leader could have completed the major part of such an enormous undertaking in a mere six years. And there is documentary evidence to support this revised interpretation, in the form of construction authorizations for three of the buildings forming the southern Piazza perimeter, which were issued in 1231, 1239, and 1261, all many years after Ziani's death. Finally, the extraordinary unity of the finished Piazza argues for a strong degree of control by a permanent public entity such as the Procuracy, beginning early in the process and continuing through its estimated completion by 1280, rather than an effort directed by a succession of individual doges. We know that by 1268, there were four procurators, two of whom seem to have functioned much like a typical mainland *opera* or municipal office of the works with specific responsibility for long-term supervision of major architectural efforts in the San Marco precinct like the Piazza project.[34]

However, even after correcting for the latest scholarship, there is still a solid basis for regarding Ziani as a figure of particular importance in the development of the Piazza project, particularly in its early stages. For one thing, his enormous fortune, rapidly accumulated in the Eastern silk trade,[35] allowed him to purchase many of the land parcels on which the enlarged square was constructed, and as we know, critical financial support often translates into major design influence. For this reason, it seems highly likely that Ziani was an influential member of the inner circle that imposed the Piazza's striking architectural coherence on early project development. But the case for Ziani's singular influence on the Piazza's fundamental design also has another basis. There is a general consensus that between 1172 and 1176, Ziani personally initiated the transformation of the ducal castle into a communal palace, employing an architectural form and vocabulary derived from antique Roman buildings. After its initial application to the facade of the ducal palace, this new classically derived model became the prototype for the other buildings constructed around the Piazza perimeter, including the thirteenth-century apartments that would be built as office and residential quarters for the procurators of Saint Mark. Given the importance of Ziani's early ducal palace design to the subsequent development of the entire Piazza enclosure, one can make a strong argument that he was, in fact, the essential architect of the medieval square.[36]

We have a good idea of what the façade of the new Ziani ducal palace looked like following its construction in the last quarter of the twelfth century. Round, high-stilted arches springing from delicate marble columns extended from corner to corner across two floors, with every ground-floor arch matched by two half-size arches on the top story. These long, running porticoes were flanked at both ends by crenellated corner towers, and the roofline of the upper-story arcade was crowned with an ornamental parapet. In other words, Ziani's new palace façade looked very much like another early Veneto-Byzantine edifice, the Fondaco dei Turchi (*Fig. 24*), whose heavily restored form can still be seen today along the northern curve of the Grand Canal.[37]

Fig. 24: Fondaco dei Turchi

After the demolition of a great part of the existing ducal castle walls, Ziani's new architectural form was erected on two sides of what remained of the old fortress. This created a
new southern wing known as the *palatium consilium* or palace of the commune and a new
western wing known as the *palatium justicia* or palace of justice. The communal palace,
which faced the lagoon, housed most of the expanded communal councils, and the palace
of justice, looking west toward the Campanile, held several important magistracies and a
law court. The most important new meeting space, the Great Council assembly hall, was a
two-story chamber that took up most of the ground floor and upper story of the communal
palace. Behind and east of this new harbor-front construction were the old ducal living
quarters and the prisons, both of which ran along a canal known as the Rio del Palazzo.
What had long been an entrenched ducal citadel now became a merger of three architectural complexes, two new civic palaces and the ducal residence, arranged around a central
courtyard. By substantially increasing the amount of architectural space controlled by the
Republic's new communal magistrates, it became much easier to supervise and control ducal actions, which had earlier taken place largely out of public view.[38]

Scholars agree that the architecture of the new ducal palace was based on antique
Roman models. Pointing to the direct harbor frontage, the long elegant arcades, and the
corner towers of Ziani's reconstructed palace, some have linked it to the Roman emperor
Diocletian's early fourth-century palace at Spalato in Dalmatia. Others, observing that Diocletian's palace also embodied many prominent features of a fortified Roman camp, have
instead argued that medieval Venetian palace architecture as exemplified in the new Ziani
building project is more accurately seen as a direct descendant of Late Antique Roman villa
architecture. In this view, because she did not have to rely on enclosed, fortified buildings to
ensure her physical security, twelfth-century Venice was uniquely situated to transmit the
open, unguarded Roman villa tradition to the rest of Europe. Given the unique protection
afforded by the lagoon, Venetian architects were able to create an elegant palace building
style featuring classical porticoes and loggias rather than bulky defensive ramparts. Therefore, three centuries later, when early Renaissance architects wished to design palaces and
villas in an authentic antique style, they turned first to medieval Venetian palace models
with their direct link to Roman villa prototypes. According to the architectural historian
James Ackerman, all that prevents this interpretation from being commonly accepted is the
general bias of Renaissance scholars toward believing that all fifteenth-century architectural innovations must necessarily have originated in Florence.[39]

There is also another potential source for the architectural form of the Ziani ducal palace. Fronting the Sea of Marmara on the southern shore of twelfth-century Constantinople was the stately façade of the Bucoleon Palace, also known as the House of Justinian. Serving as the seaside terminus of the vast Imperial Palace complex that covered the southeastern slope of the city's first hill, the Bucoleon adjoined the imperial boat harbor. The palace and its water landing were embellished with sculpted lions, and its name, Bucoleon, was derived from a waterfront sculpture showing a lion in a death struggle with a bull. Like the Ziani palace, the building's sea façade consisted of an arcaded loggia flanked by crenellated corner towers. In reconstruction drawings (*Fig. 25*), it very closely resembles the Fondaco dei Turchi, a building deliberately restored to exemplify the characteristic features of Veneto-Byzantine architectural form realized in the Ziani palace. Of course, reconstruction drawings are only a form of indirect evidence and even a case of striking physical similarity is not absolute proof of direct influence. But where so many other critical elements of the medieval Piazza complex were undoubtedly derived from the Augusteum, it is hard to believe that the ducal palace builders would have overlooked such a conspicuously useful prototype in such proximity to the great Byzantine square.[40]

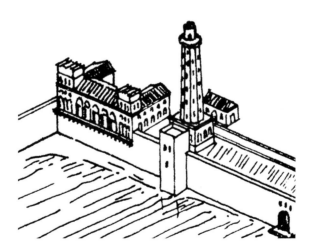

Fig. 25: Bucoleon Palace, Constantinople
(detail of Fig. 23)

Chapter Seven will provide a detailed description of the design and construction of the rest of the medieval Piazza complex; however, to fully appreciate that account, the reader first needs to have a basic understanding of the momentous events of the Fourth Crusade (1202–1204). This enterprise, which is the subject of Chapter Six, profoundly affected the ongoing development of the Piazza San Marco. In addition, as one of the most fascinating and improbable episodes in the history of the Middle Ages, it is a story well worth telling for its own sake.

Sailing for Byzantium (1201-1204)

A Contract with Venice

In the dead of winter, January 1201, six illustrious Frankish[1] knights rode through the frozen passes of the French Alps and across the plains of northern Italy until they reached the marshy shore of the Venetian lagoon. There, they left their weary horses and hired a boat to traverse the last few miles of frigid water that separated them from their hard-won destination. In the distance, they could just discern a low-lying island city punctuated by what appeared to be a host of bristling defensive towers. To these warrior chieftains, men who, in spite of their wealth and eminence, were forced for safety's sake to reside in great dirty, smoky, stone castles, the tall columns rising over the lagoon looked like telltale signs of the same ever-present violence that characterized life in their feudal homelands. But as their boats glided closer, they saw that these brick shafts were only the bell towers of peaceful parish churches. Drawing nearer in eager astonishment, these visitors from a land of crude stone citadels and wattle houses discovered an architectural marvel, an exotic metropolis larger than any town or city they had ever seen, rising up from the mud and water. But for now, there was no time for sightseeing. Stepping ashore, they hurried to make arrangements for a meeting with the doge.[2]

Dispatched by three of northern Europe's most powerful lords, these knights were men on a mission; in their eyes, the fate of Christianity in the land of the Savior's birth rested on their shoulders. A dozen years earlier, after decimating an entire Western army at the Battle of Hattin, the great Muslim leader Saladin had recaptured Jerusalem and eliminated most of the Crusader kingdoms in the Middle East. Although the Third Crusade (1190–1192), led by Richard I of England and Philip Augustus of France, did manage to reclaim a thin strip of coastal cities, the bulk of Palestine and Syria, and—above all—the city of Jerusalem, were still in Saracen hands. Now, at the urging of a new pontiff, Pope Innocent III, the West had once again resolved to drive the infidel out of the Holy Land, and the six envoys had come to Venice—the largest, richest city in Europe, with the greatest navy in the Mediterranean—to make critical transportation arrangements for a Fourth Crusade. Because a land march from Western Europe to Palestine would take eight punishing months, Crusader leaders had decided to explore the higher cost of naval transport, which, if there were no unexpected delays, would reduce travel time to about six weeks. Not that the Crusade organizers were offering to bear this enormous expense. Unlike the Second and Third Crusades, which had been largely paid for by the same European monarchs who organized them, the financing arrangements for the Fourth Crusade would resemble those of the First Crusade described at the beginning of Chapter Five: each enlisting knight would be expected to pay his own way. Although heartfelt sermons delivered by the pope and other clerics were important in igniting popular enthusiasm for the venture, the Church did not consider itself responsible for actually raising the huge sums required to launch and support this latest crusading army.[3]

The initial audience with Doge Enrico Dandolo took place in the new Ziani ducal palace, which one of the knights described as an extremely beautiful and sumptuous building. The doge was then at least ninety-three years of age and totally blind; yet in spite of his infirmities, he was a leader of great energy, high intellect, and deep political judgment. Four days after this introductory session, Dandolo convened his advisory council to hear the envoys' request. There are no surviving Venetian accounts of the meeting, and the report of Geoffrey de Villehardouin, a French emissary from the Champagne region, only states that the Franks asked the Venetians to do their best to supply the Crusaders' needs, without necessarily specifying in detail what those requirements might be. The best evidence of precisely what the Frankish envoys asked Venice to provide are the contract terms that Doge Dandolo announced a week later. The Republic offered to supply specialized transport for forty-five hundred knights and their mounts as well as for nine thousand squires and twenty thousand foot soldiers (a total Frankish force of thirty-three thousand five hundred men), plus a year's rations, for a total price of eight-five thousand silver marks to be paid in four installments. In addition, Venice would contribute her own war fleet of fifty manned galleys on condition of receiving half of all combat spoils excluding captured land;

the method for allocating conquered territory would be determined later. If accepted by the Franks and made the basis of a signed agreement, this Venetian contractual obligation would be the largest, most expensive undertaking in the history of the Republic. Indeed, it would be the greatest single commitment of national resources made by any Western state since the age of imperial Rome.[4]

At the time the six envoys left for Venice, the number of men who had already volunteered to join the Crusade was probably between eight and ten thousand, including both knights and common soldiers. It is extremely unlikely that the Frankish emissaries had a clear grasp of such figures before arriving in the lagoon, but even if they had, estimating the final enlistment total for a volatile enterprise like the Fourth Crusade would have been sheer guesswork at best. Crusading armies were fractious, disorderly masses composed of small individual bands whose commitment to a given action at any particular moment could easily be swayed by sudden fears and enthusiasms. The Second and Third Crusades had been led by kings with the presumed power to assemble and direct the military resources of their entire nations, but Richard I of England was now dead, and Philip Augustus of France had abandoned crusading. By default, the principal lay sponsors of the Fourth Crusade were three young counts not yet out of their twenties, prominent but untested leaders whose ability to recruit and command volunteers was necessarily much more limited than that of their royal predecessors.[5]

We know that the envoys immediately accepted the doge's proposal, lending support to the view that the Venetian terms must have been in response to at least some type of general Frankish estimate of their transport requirements. After winning the full consent of both the Great Council and the Venetian populace, the doge and the Franks executed a formal written contract. The campaign would open with an attack against Egypt, and the promised Venetian war galleys would be specifically designed to engage and defeat the ships of the Egyptian navy. The Franks would be required to assemble in the lagoon by April 1202, and the armada would sail the following June 29. Both sides realized that more recruits would be drawn to the Crusade if volunteers believed they would be sailing directly to the Holy Land; therefore, it was agreed that the decision to begin the campaign in Egypt should be kept a closely guarded secret. In March 1201, just before leaving Venice, the Frankish emissaries borrowed sufficient funds to make a down payment of two thousand silver marks, less than three percent of the total contract price.[6]

The doge promptly began fulfilling the city's contract obligations to the letter. But he must have realized that while these new arrangements held great financial promise, including an opportunity for Venice to become the leading commercial power in the great Egyptian port of Alexandria, they were also fraught with enormous risk. In addition to fronting the cost of a huge new fleet of specialized transport ships, Venice would be obligated to devote more than half her total manpower and virtually her entire navy to the Crusade for the next two years, a commitment that would require an almost total suspension of overseas commerce during this period. If the enterprise failed or the Franks failed to pay the contract price, the result could be financial disaster, both for the Venetian state and for her merchant aristocracy. In addition, the leaders of the Republic knew that before they could dispatch the city's fleet to the eastern Mediterranean, they would have to deal with a critical threat to Venetian prosperity in their own home waters. For the past two decades, the crucial port of Zara on the eastern Adriatic coast had been in open revolt against Venetian control, and the loss of this vital supply point had drastically curtailed the flow of Dalmatian oak to the city's busy shipyards. To maintain the large merchant fleets on which her command of international trade lanes depended, Venice needed Dalmatian timber, and this required a compliant Zara. Unfortunately, in 1201, at the time the Frankish transport contract was signed, the Zaran insurrection was more robust than ever. The breakaway city had allied itself with the powerful maritime state of Pisa, which was intent on supplanting Venice as the dominant military and commercial power in the Adriatic; to make matters worse, Zara had also received promises of military protection from the ambitious king of Hungary.[7]

Although he never raised the issue with the Frankish envoys, it is inconceivable that a leader as experienced as Erico Dandolo ever intended to allow the Venetian fleet to leave the Adriatic without first dealing with the Zaran rebellion. In deciding when and how he should announce this precondition to his Frankish partners, his thinking was no doubt colored by the fact that his father, uncle, and grandfather had all participated in earlier Crusades. Doge Dandolo knew all too well how fraught with chance and sudden shifts in direction such enterprises typically were and, therefore, how unlikely it was that the Franks would be able to fulfill every condition of their contractual bargain to the letter. And if the Franks were to fail in any particular, the doge must have thought, what was to prevent Venice from imposing a new requirement of her own—the siege and capture of

Zara—before sailing for the Holy Land? Nor would the Republic be unusual in imposing such a prerequisite. In Europe during the Middle Ages, it was a well-accepted rule that sovereign states had the right to crush revolts and stabilize their territories before being required to honor crusading obligations. For instance, before departing on the Third Crusade, Richard the Lionhearted had first pacified his dominions by launching attacks on rebellious Christian vassals in France and Sicily.[8]

Stranded on the Lido

By April 1202, the deadline for the Crusader host to assemble in Venice, it was obvious that something was seriously wrong. The Franks had not paid a single contract installment, and the influx of feudal warriors into the city still amounted to no more than a trickle. Many of the Crusaders had been late in leaving their home countries, and those who finally did arrive in Venice were quickly rowed out to bivouac on the Lido's treeless strand, two miles from San Marco. The Venetians waited until summer to conduct a final headcount, but when that turned up only eleven thousand volunteers, it became clear that any original enlistment estimates supplied by the the Franks had been wildly unrealistic. Instead of an anticipated Frankish force of thirty-three thousand five hundred, no more than fourteen thousand non-Venetians actually joined the Fourth Crusade, and three thousand of these recruits decided to use closer, cheaper embarkation points. To make matters worse, many of the poorer knights and common soldiers who did make it to Venice could not pay for their sea passage, having left home believing that some great lord would surely make up their deficiency. When all those who were gathered on the Lido had handed over everything they could spare, the Franks still owed thirty-four thousand marks, a collective shortage equal to the annual income of the king of France. Venetians angrily demanded compensation in full; at the same time, their confidence in the judgment of their aged doge, who had personally negotiated and publicly endorsed the contract with the Franks, must have also been shaken.[9]

The root of this colossal blunder went much deeper than the personal failings of six knightly emissaries; in fact, the envoys who arranged the contract with Venice had been chosen for this task precisely because they had as much experience with the recruitment and assembling of Crusader armies as any six leaders in northern Europe. The fault lay with the psyche of Western chivalry in general. In the Middle Ages, feudal aristocrats inhabited an insular, uncomplicated world that left them completely unprepared to deal with the complex commercial values of an international trading republic such as Venice. Medieval knights suffered from a particular inability to quantify their experience, stemming, in large part, from a simple failure to understand why it would be advantageous to develop such a skill. Within their small, accustomed neighborhoods, relationships were clear and easily grasped. All of the people whose rank entitled them to special consideration could be counted on the fingers of one's two hands. Anyone foolish enough to remain in school past the age of twelve was looked down upon as fit only for the priesthood. The keeping of exact time, the compiling of precise figures, or any other effort toward refined numerical thought was regarded as absurd and perhaps even suspicious or dangerous.[10]

Rather than mental exertion of any sort, a feudal knight gloried in his physical vitality and courage, the qualities which allowed him to enthusiastically embrace the hardships and cruelties of war. Battle freed him from the boredom of daily life and fed his unapologetic love of waste and destruction. He took delight in gruesome tales of heroic death exemplified by the popular songs known as *chansons de geste*. The joyful warrior ethos the chansons expressed has never been more perfectly captured than in this memorable passage:

My heart is filled with gladness when I see

Strong castles besieged, stockades broken and overwhelmed,

Many vassals struck down,

Horses of the dead and wounded roving at random.

And when the battle is joined, let all men of good lineage

Think of naught but the breaking of heads and arms.

I tell you I have no such joy as when I hear the

Groans of "Help me! Help me!"

And when I see both great and small

Fall in the ditches and the grass

And when I see the dead transfixed by spear shafts!

Lords, mortgage your domains, castles, cities,

But never give up war![11]

The ability to comprehend a number as large as thirty-three thousand five hundred would have been totally beyond the ken of those raised in such a social order. They could blithely sign a transportation contract containing such a figure with no regard for the fact that in the Third Crusade ten years earlier, the king of France himself had raised a force of no more than six hundred fifty knights and thirteen hundred squires, or that the largest French army ever assembled totaled twelve thousand men at most. Simple, naïve, highly emotional, and capable of extreme violence, an unhappy throng of eleven thousand such warriors was now impatiently milling about on the sands of the Lido, only a few miles from the palaces of Venice.[12]

Having paid over almost every scrap of cash and treasure they could spare, the Franks were anxious to abandon their foul encampments and embark on the military adventure of their lives. Therefore, rather than try to keep such a dangerously explosive force bottled up in close proximity to Venice, Doge Dandolo immediately proposed unleashing its armed might against the walls of Zara. And because they had little choice unless they wished to depart for home in disgrace with their Crusader vows unfulfilled, the Frankish chieftains rapidly accepted the doge's offer to defer payment of the final thirty-four thousand marks in exchange for returning the rebel town to Venetian control. Dandolo and the barons also agreed that, as with the plan to initiate the Middle Eastern phase of operations with an attack on Egypt, the Zaran diversion should initially be kept a secret from the Frankish rank and file. Following an emotional ceremony in the Basilica San Marco, where Venetians watched their now ninety-four-year-old doge fall to his knees and agree to personally command the Venetian fleet, the Fourth Crusade left the lagoon in early October 1202. An armada of at least fifty war galleys, fifty troop transports, and a hundred horse transport vessels, manned by an estimated twenty-one thousand Venetian sailors and marines (two-thirds of the total Crusader force of thirty-two thousand), sailed through the Lido port into the Adriatic.[13]

A Third Diversion

Doge Dandolo had personally planned the diversions to Zara and Egypt. But what he did not know was that talk of yet a third, infinitely more ambitious, diversion was already circulating among Frankish leaders before the Crusader fleet even departed the lagoon. Desperate to find some fresh source of funds to pay off their debt to Venice and to sustain the Crusade during what could well be a long, costly campaign, the barons had begun to listen to a stunning new proposal from an exiled Byzantine prince. This daring scheme called for toppling the reigning Byzantine emperor, quite possibly through the military conquest of Constantinople, whose massive fortifications had never been breached even by armies six times larger than those of the Fourth Crusade. In 1195, the Byzantine emperor Isaac II Angelus had been blinded, deposed, and imprisoned by his brother Alexius III. In the early fall of 1201, Isaac's sixteen-year-old son, whose name was also Alexius and whom historians generally refer to as Prince Alexius, escaped to the German imperial court and began to plot his uncle's overthrow. By the summer of 1202, this scheming had ripened into a tangible proposal, and the prince sent ambassadors to explain it to the Frankish chieftains languishing on the Lido. In its final form, it called for the Crusaders to use their armed might to place Prince Alexius on the Greek throne in exchange for the payment of 200,000 silver marks. The prince also promised that once he was invested with imperial power, he would contribute ten thousand Greek soldiers to the Crusader army and establish papal supremacy over the Greek Church, thereby ending the religious schism that had divided Eastern and Western Christendom since the sixth century.[14]

The Venetians did not learn of Prince Alexius' proposal until a month after the conquest of Zara, an action which had turned out to be relatively easy for a Crusader assault force equipped with wooden towers and specialized siege engines. At this point, in January 1203, German envoys arrived before the walls of the fallen rebel city to present the prince's formal offer to the entire crusading host. To Doge Dandolo and the other Venetian leaders—to everyone but a handful of Frankish chieftains—the German overture envisioned a breathtaking change in direction. Venice, which had spent the last century pondering the nature of her evolving status within the Byzantine Empire, was now confronted with a major decision. It was certainly possible, as the prince's ambassadors confidently claimed, that the mere sight of a serious military threat gathered before the walls of Constantinople would spark a coup against a feckless, incompetent sovereign like Alexius III. But it was at least equally likely that no such insurrection would materialize, or that if one did, it would be too weak to prevail against the entrenched power of an imperial incumbent, leaving military conquest as the only remaining alternative. In any case, this type of risky venture could have potentially catastrophic consequences for Venice. Two-thirds of the Republic's international trading revenue flowed from her position as a commercial intermediary within the Byzantine Empire, and there were ten thousand Venetians currently residing in Constantinople alone. In the case of a direct frontal assault, their lives and property would be at serious risk.[15]

On the other hand, Venetians also faced very real dangers if they simply tried to maintain the status quo. The current emperor, Alexius III, had ascended the throne on a popular tide of vicious anti-Venetian feeling. Like almost every other Greek ruler of the past eight decades, he regularly violated the trade exemptions guaranteed to the Republic in imperial charters, and his commercial policies consistently favored her Italian competitors, Genoa and Pisa. And looming over everything was the threat of the Constantinopolitan mob, always ready to burst into homicidal fury at the instigation of an unbalanced emperor. None of these perils could be eliminated without a fundamental change in the Byzantine government, and filling the imperial office with a pliant young emperor who owed everything to his Western allies just might enable Venetian merchants to regain the physical security and commercial dominance they had enjoyed a century earlier under Alexius Comnenus. In any event, however long the odds of success might seem, they were probably better now than they would be in any foreseeable future. Since the death of the last Comnenus emperor in 1185, Byzantine naval defense had declined to the vanishing point, and the Fourth Crusade was almost certainly as large and powerful an assault force as would ever be available for such a purpose. After careful deliberation, Doge Dandolo decided that, on balance, it was a gamble worth taking, and the Venetians made a collective decision to give the Byzantine diversion their wholehearted support.[16]

Venetian commitment to the proposed venture was decisive. It ensured that the enterprise would be supported by the full weight of the Venetian armada and Doge Dandolo's extensive diplomatic and military experience with the Byzantine Empire. The Doge's considered judgment that the Byzantine diversion was a risk worth taking confirmed the initial reaction of the Frankish barons, to whom the issue was quite simple. Without the substantial new aid Prince Alexius was offering, the Crusade would almost certainly never reach—much less retake—Jerusalem. The Franks were completely out of funds, and the term of the Venetian assistance contract on which they still owed thirty-four thousand marks would end at about the same time the Crusade was scheduled to arrive in the eastern Mediterranean to begin the initial assault against Egypt. But the Frankish rank and file saw matters quite differently for one overwhelming reason. Pope Innocent III had sent several angry letters to the Crusader host warning that anyone who joined in an attack on a Christian city would face instant excommunication, a threat that went to the very heart of the Frankish warriors' motivation. One of the principal inducements to enlist in a Crusade was the Church's promise that anyone who helped return the Holy Land to Christian hands would be guaranteed eternal salvation. When these papal missives were belatedly revealed to the common soldiers, they discovered that they had already been damned by the pope himself for their just-completed conquest of Zara. After receiving temporary absolution for this first transgression from bishops traveling with the Crusade, many refused to endanger their souls a second time by disobeying the pope's clear injunction, and almost one-fifth of the eleven thousand Franks in the expedition abandoned the Venetian armada.[17]

But for the pope's dire threats, most Franks would not have opposed diverting the Crusade to Constantinople, even if they had to fight their way into the city. They understood that Byzantium still contained two-thirds of the accumulated wealth of the entire Mediterranean world, and they shared the popular Western animosity toward Eastern Greeks, whom they regarded as indifferent Christians at best. In addition, lurking not far below the surface was the memory of the Byzantine mob's pitiless slaughter of almost every Latin in Constantinople only two decades earlier, an act of butchery that had left the narrow streets of the foreign quarters teaming with up to fifty thousand mutilated corpses. Matters finally came to a head on the island of Corfu, where the armada stopped to decide its fate. Dissent remained high, with the Crusader host split into two separate bivouacs, a minority campsite occupied by those who favored Prince Alexius' proposal and a larger encampment for the majority, which still refused to accept its terms. At this point, determined to break the deadlock, the leading Frankish barons and bishops went to the dissident majority, dropped to their knees, and tearfully begged the lesser knights and commoners to save the Crusade from imminent collapse. Against all odds, it worked; discord was overwhelmed by pity, and the pope's injunction somehow lost its previously unassailable force. On May 24, 1203, a unified Crusader force set sail for the Byzantine capital.[18]

The Still Beating Heart of Antiquity

One month later, as the two-hundred-ship expedition disembarked on the shores of Asia, the Crusader host gazed across a mile of open water to the great triangular wedge of Constantinople projecting eastward from the European landmass into the confluence of the Bosporus, the Golden Horn, and the Sea of Marmara (*Fig. 22*). Everyone enjoyed an unobstructed view of the immense metropolis whose site and monumental grandeur were unrivaled in the Mediterranean world. Each of the city's seven hills carried its own cluster of architectural wonders, with the greatest of them all, Justinian's church of Haghia Sophia, rising like a great ship on the crest of the first promontory. The largest sanctuary in Christendom, its magnificent dome, soaring 180 feet above the nave floor, was pierced by forty windows so that it appeared to be floating in a circle of heavenly light (*Fig. 10*). In addition to the Great Church, the Franks were awestruck by the city's profusion of lavish palaces and seemingly impregnable ramparts. Its streets and docks, teeming with Greeks, Italians, Arabs, Gypsies, Russians, Persians, Bulgars, Armenians, Nubians, Hungarians, Jews, and Scandinavians, held a total population between 600,000 and 1,000,000, making it eight to twelve times the size of Venice, by far the largest Western city the Franks had ever seen up to this point. One of the barons confessed that the capital's immense size made every man in the armada experience an involuntary shiver. When dusk fell and evening torches were lit, the starry night sky was matched by the glow of the city's innumerable windows.[19]

Militarily, this enormous bastion, with its massive sea and land walls, abundant grain reserves, and cavernous water cisterns, had never been conquered by foreign powers. Repeated attacks by huge Gothic, Hunic, Persian, Bulgarian, Slavic, Russian, and Islamic armies had been miserable failures. In the seventh and eight centuries, it was the walls of Constantinople that, for the first time, checked the seemingly invincible tide of Muslim conquest, at one point repelling a Saracen host six times larger than the Fourth Crusade. While the garrison of Greek regulars Alexius III had at his disposal in 1203 was of generally low quality, it boasted a troop strength of approximately fifty thousand. In addition, there were an estimated two thousand Pisan allies who were ready to fight for the Greeks, as well as at least five thousand superb ax-wielding English and Scandinavian mercenaries who belonged to the elite Varangian Guard, each member of which had personally sworn to defend the emperor with his life. In sum, Alexius III had a total force of about fifty-seven thousand to fend off approximately thirty thousand Venetians and Franks, a two-to-one ratio that heavily favored the Greek defenders. Indeed, one of the leading experts on medieval fortifications has estimated that an army defending a well-stocked fortress that was safe against famine and thirst should have been able to hold off an attacking force up to one hundred times its size. Despite the fact that Alexius III was a cowardly, unfit commander who had done nothing to prepare for the contest at hand, if it came to a conventional military struggle, the odds were still very much in his favor, and both sides knew it.[20]

Accordingly, the Crusaders spent the first nine days searching for signs of the incipient coup d'état that Prince Alexius had promised would be readily apparent once the armada appeared before the imperial capital. However, not a single supporter, not even one of the ten thousand Venetians in the city, stepped forward to welcome the invaders. On the tenth day, Doge Dandolo and the Frankish chieftains decided to make a direct appeal to the Greek populace. The doge ran a line of ships, including his own galley with Prince Alexius on board, in close to the municipal seawalls and called on the Byzantine people to rally to their rightful ruler. Far from being persuaded, Greeks standing on the ramparts began to hurl gross insults down on the imploring Crusaders, and it rapidly became clear that the mission was a humiliating failure. As they sailed back to camp, everyone in the armada understood that their only remaining hope was to conquer the huge capital by force of arms.[21]

The First Assault

While Constantinople had never fallen, even to much larger invasion armies, it had also never been assaulted by a force of specialized, supremely inventive marines like the twenty-one thousand Venetian Crusaders. Knowing that the promised coup might well prove illusory, the Venetians had devised a backup plan that capitalized on both Greek naval weakness and their own unmatched amphibious assault skills. The first phase called for using the Republic's overwhelming naval superiority to capture the northern shore of the Golden Horn. Phase two envisioned turning that captured space into a staging area for a direct attack on the southern harbor walls, a relatively unfortified stretch of thirty-foot ramparts lying less than a thousand feet away. The plan also had psychological and economic dimensions. Being forced to watch helplessly as a huge enemy armada landed so close to the city walls was certain to undermine Byzantine confidence in Alexius III, and seizure of the city's harbor would automatically shut down a substantial amount of Greek and Pisan commerce. The Venetians also devised creative tactics designed to maximize the chances for success in the final, all-important assault phase. After removing the yardarms from the masts of the transport ships,[22] Venetian sailors strung these cross-spars together lengthwise and outfitted them with wooden flooring and leather sides and tops to form covered bridges over a hundred feet in length. They then lashed these flying gangplanks to the tops of the masts so that they extended over the ship bows. During an attack, they could be pushed onto the summits of the city's walls and flanking towers, forming sheltered tubes from which to insert armored warriors into the most critical parts of the battle.[23]

Phase one of the Crusader plan went flawlessly, as the Franks and Venetians used their combined strength to seize the northern shore of the harbor; however, the Franks then balked at the idea of joining the Venetian amphibious attack across the Golden Horn. For such men, the joy of skewering their enemies while seated on a charging mount was life's supreme thrill, and they refused to give up fighting from the saddles of their splendid warhorses in order to launch themselves from the tops of tall ships. The fact that the only terrain suitable for equestrian combat was far to the west of the Venetian assault point in an area directly opposite the city's tallest and stoutest land walls (an impregnable system of three parallel ramparts preceded by a deep moat) did not seem to register. Feudal warriors honed their military skills in tournaments and other ritualized forms of combat; practical adjustments to specific tactical circumstances were not part of their training or mental makeup. For their part, the Venetians understood that any military assault faced very long odds no matter how innovative its tactics might be, and they remained firmly committed to the original plan—an amphibious thrust against the weakest point in the city's defenses. Consequently, it became necessary to split the Crusader force. On July 17, the day of the attack, the Franks marched off to begin their charge against the landward side of the Blachernae fortress at the northwest corner of the city, approximately a mile from the center of the Venetian sortie. The Blachernae complex contained Alexius III's imperial residence as well as the prison tower in which his deposed brother Isaac II was incarcerated. This citadel, with its massive stone walls fifty feet high, fifteen feet thick, and densely packed with tall, strong towers, was even more formidable than the monumental Theodosian walls that guarded the remainder of the city's western perimeter.[24]

Directed and inspired by their blind, ninety-five-year-old doge, the Venetian amphibious attack was a spectacular success *(Fig. 26)*. After rushing his galley forward and grounding it on the narrow strand beneath the walls, Doge Dandolo planted the banner of Saint Mark at the forefront of the raging battle. Supported by crossbowmen, archers, and rock-hurling catapults, Venetian marines used the flying bridges suspended from the masts of their ships to seize twenty-five towers and a large section of the harbor wall. To ward off a Byzantine counterattack, the Venetians set fire to a row of houses just inside the captured ramparts, counting on the prevailing north wind to carry the blaze a short way toward the Greek lines. But when the winds rose unexpectedly, the blaze erupted into a raging inferno that spread into the heart of the city's northwestern residential quarter; before it stopped burning, it left twenty thousand homeless Byzantines scattered across 125 acres of charred rubble.[25]

Meanwhile, the Frankish attack against the Blachernae citadel was a complete failure. Having arrayed themselves directly opposite Constantinople's most heavily fortified sector, the Franks found themselves continually on the defensive, pressed so hard by repeated Greek counterattacks that they had to sleep and eat in full battle armor, their only fresh meat coming from the Crusader horses killed in the Greek onslaughts. The would-be besiegers had become the besieged. Finally, just as the Venetians succeeded in capturing the harbor walls, the ten thousand battered and wounded Franks were set upon by a Byzantine army of thirty thousand. In response, the barons issued a frantic plea for the Venetians to abandon their hold on the city and rush west to rescue their fellow Crusaders. When the doge and his men did as they were bid, relinquishing their hard-won victory to join the Franks in front of the land walls, the emperor, his cunning stratagem having worked to perfection, quit the field and withdrew his forces within the gates.[26]

Unfortunately for Alexius III, this crafty maneuver also fooled his own people, who took the emperor's hasty retreat as a final confirmation of his inveterate cowardice and unfitness for imperial command. When the Greeks had seen him lead a huge Byzantine assault force out of the land walls, they anticipated witnessing a crushing defeat imposed on the hated Crusaders who had started the huge fire that was even then consuming the city's northern neighborhoods. Consequently, the emperor's abrupt abandonment of the battlefield triggered a dramatic shift in Greek public opinion, and that night, smelling a coup in the works, Alexius III fled the city with as much of the imperial treasury as he could carry.

Fig. 26: Venetian amphibious assault across the Golden Horn by Jacopo Palma

At this point, the Byzantines attempted to preempt further Crusader attacks by releasing Prince Alexius' father (Isaac II) from prison and reseating him on the Greek throne. Father and son were to rule as co-emperors, and Isaac promised to honor the prior commitments that Prince Alexius (now Alexius IV) had made to the Crusaders. These included payment of 200,000 silver marks to the Frankish invaders and subjugation of the Greek Church to papal authority in Rome, terms which Isaac knew at that time would never be honored. The ensuing weeks became a period of uneasy truce in which the Greeks waited to see if the Crusaders were so delusional as to insist on such impossible conditions, and the Crusaders waited for the Greeks to make good on each and every promise.[27]

The Final Conquest

The only way Alexius IV and his father were able to pay even a fraction of what had been guaranteed to the Crusader army was by appropriating the assets of wealthy Greek aristocrats and seizing precious reliquaries and icons from Greek churches and monasteries. In response, the Byzantine people not only despised the Westerners for their avarice; they came to regard the co-emperors with open contempt for their alliance with the greedy, uncouth invaders. In the middle of August, this hostility burst forth in an indiscriminate attack on the Latin colonies along the Golden Horn. The Byzantine mob torched everything in its path, sending throngs of homeless Westerners to join the Crusader camp across the harbor. Among the refugees were the city's resident Pisans, including many who, just a month earlier, had stood shoulder-to-shoulder with their Greek allies at the top of the seawalls, fighting to hold back the Venetian assault. The next day, a small squad of Pisans, Venetians, and Franks recrossed the harbor and set fire to a Greek neighborhood near the burned-out Latin quarter. Although the Europeans apparently intended nothing more than a modest retaliatory strike, they once again failed to anticipate the effect of unusually strong winds; these transformed the blaze into one of the most destructive infernos in recorded history, a huge conflagration that burned for eight days. Beginning at the Golden Horn, it moved south across some of the city's wealthiest and most populous neighborhoods. After obliterating almost the entire Forum of Constantine, it then changed direction and raged eastward along the porticoes of the great Mese avenue before stopping just short of Haghia Sophia and the Augusteum complex. After scorching the Great Church's western atrium and just missing the Hippodrome, it veered southwest and burned its way down to the seawalls lining the Marmara.[28]

The huge, lurid flames, billowing many times higher than the buildings they engulfed, made frequent, abrupt changes in direction. Whatever they surrounded—great churches, sumptuous palaces, antique porticoes, monumental columns, priceless statues, or the crowded slums of the urban poor—dissolved like wax in the all-consuming heat. When it was finally extinguished, the fire left a gigantic black scar across the heart of the city, 450 acres of smoldering ash where more than a hundred thousand Byzantines had formerly lived and worked. In its destructive fury, the blaze resembled the Great London Fire of 1666, although, given the accumulated wealth of Constantinople, the value of the property destroyed in the ancient capital was probably greater. While some dispossessed Greeks deserted the city, most set up tents and makeshift huts among the charred ruins of their former homes. Together with the area consumed in the first Crusader fire, a vast landscape of almost six hundred acres (about one-sixth of the city) had been transformed into smoking rubble. A host of architectural masterpieces and ancient art treasures as well as rare classical manuscripts had vanished in the flames.[29]

Given these grievous wounds to the imperial city, Latins who chose to remain there did so at the risk of their lives. In one particularly gruesome incident, three Venetians who failed to depart in time were caught, impaled on steel hooks hung over the seawalls, and set on fire in plain view of the Crusader camp across the harbor. The Byzantines also tried to burn the Venetian fleet, and in response, the Crusaders began to carry out plunder raids along the shores of the Marmara and the Bosporus. Amid this escalating violence, Alexius IV ceased making additional payments to the Crusaders, which elicited a warning from the doge that just as Venice had once pulled the penniless prince up from a dung heap, so she could always toss him back onto it. But the doge never had a chance to make good on his threat. Because they had never viewed their young sovereign as anything other than a Western puppet, the Byzantines readily accepted the results of a palace coup that replaced Alexius IV with an energetic new emperor named Murzuphlus (after his bushy eyebrows). And shortly thereafter, no tears were shed when it was announced that while in prison, Alexius IV and his father had both mysteriously died of natural causes. While Alexius' death terminated any strict contractual right the Crusaders might have to the 200,000 marks the deceased prince had personally agreed to pay in exchange for placing him on the Byzantine throne, that was hardly the end of the matter. Neither the Venetians nor the Franks were prepared to forgo their promised rewards even if this required a full-scale reconquest of the Greek capital. It was at this point that the bishops accompanying the expedition came forward with a helpful bit of religious sophistry. A second assault was justified, they said, because by killing Alexius IV, Byzantium's rightful ruler, Murzuphlus had become a usurper whose crime disqualified him from ruling any Christian land, and by supporting the usurper, the Byzantine people themselves had become accomplices to murder. Thus, taking Constantinople from the Greeks was not only right and lawful, it had now become a Christian duty, in some ways equal to the Crusader obligation to deliver the Holy Land from Muslim infidels.[30]

The Franks and Venetians agreed to mount a joint amphibious attack against the same part of the harbor walls that had yielded to Venetian assault the previous July. Before doing so, however, the doge insisted that the parties stipulate in advance how spoils would be divided, how a new Latin emperor would be chosen, and what basic rules would govern Crusader conduct in the wake of a successful conquest. The resulting pact declared that the first use of all booty would be to make good on everything owed to the Republic under prior agreements, with the balance to be split evenly between the Frankish and Venetian Crusaders. The new emperor would be elected by a commission composed of six Franks and six Venetians. After bestowing one-fourth of the new Latin Empire, including a quarter of Constantinople, on the newly-elected emperor, the Venetians and the Franks would each receive a three-eighths share of all remaining imperial territory. Finally, no state at war with Venice would be allowed to trade within the Latin Empire; the Genoese and Pisans would be completely shut out except on terms dictated by Venice.[31]

On April 9, 1204, all was ready, and the second assault, manned by every available Venetian and Frank, was launched across the Golden Horn. On the Greek side, the new emperor Murzuphlus surveyed the coming battle from a red tent pitched on a hill directly opposite the point of attack. The new sovereign had already shown himself to be a far more able commander than his Angelus predecessors; for instance, he had raised the height of the harbor defenses by building large wooden ramparts above the existing stone walls and towers. This tactic plus an unexpected south wind blowing directly into the face of the assault prevented the Venetians from successfully inserting the Crusader infantry onto the walls through the flying gangplanks. After several furious attempts, the Westerners failed to gain a single foothold and were forced to retreat to their staging area across the Golden Horn. But when the attack was renewed three days later, a strong north wind blew the Venetian ships directly onto the ramparts, and Greek towers began to fall. After a day of hard fighting, some of the exhausted Franks resting just inside the walls began to worry about a Greek night attack launched from within the immense metropolis. To counter this danger, they started a third fire designed to burn inland but which instead moved southeast along the walls, devastating twenty-five acres of harbor property before reaching the edge of the immense burned-out region left by the second Crusader conflagration.[32]

No Greek night attack ever came and when April 13 dawned, the Crusaders were shocked to discover that the Byzantines, whose collective mass could still have easily overpowered the fragile Western hold on the city, had given up the fight. The desolation of their beautiful capital wrought by three devastating fires was undoubtedly a major reason for this collapse of Greek resistance. Although Emperor Murzuphlus attempted to rally his people, when they repeatedly ignored his calls to continue defending the city, he fled in a small fishing boat. The Franks, having spent an anxious night preparing for renewed combat with an enormous hostile population, suddenly found the metropolis at their mercy; in response, they immediately began the traditional three days of unrestrained savagery and plunder afforded a victorious medieval army. Although nothing could match the appalling architectural destruction Constantinople had already suffered from the three Crusader fires, the misery and loss heaped upon the Byzantine people during the next seventy-two hours would be extraordinary. For the first few frenzied hours, the Franks hacked, skewered, and decapitated virtually every Greek male they encountered and raped almost every female. After slaking their immediate thirst for rapine and slaughter, they turned to the collection of booty in the world's supreme storehouse of artistic treasure, an accumulation so vast that it would take months to discover it all. The Franks began by grabbing every portable item of conspicuous consumption in plain sight—gold, silver, jewels, ivories, enamels, furs, satins, silks, and ermines—the same precious objects their barbarian ancestors had seized when they first emerged from German forests to pillage Roman villas and cities. These compact luxury items were still at the heart of European feudal culture.[33]

When they finished looting the palaces, the Franks turned to vandalizing churches and monasteries. Rushing to fill their bulging spoils sacks, they accidentally smashed many of the fragile sardonyx goblets and painted glass bowls they found in ecclesiastical treasuries. But their overriding desire for small, portable loot, which was more easily concealed from fellow plunderers, also drove the Franks to deliberately shatter many large, complex art objects. For instance, they smashed the high altar of Haghia Sophia, a thirty-foot masterpiece of gold, silver, and precious gems, into its constituent materials, and broke many of the priceless relics and icons in the Great Church into formless piles of gold-embedded jewelry. While looting Justinian's church of the Holy Apostles, they broke into the great porphyry tombs containing the carefully preserved bodies of ancient Byzantine emperors to steal their burial treasure. They plundered the Greek monastery attached to the church of Saint John the Baptist of Studius (known as the Studion) near the juncture of the western land walls and the Sea of Marmara. The Studion had been a center of Greek spiritual, literary, and artistic culture since its founding in the middle of the fifth century, and its monks were renowned for their poetry, scholarship, and consummate skill in transcribing and illuminating ancient manuscripts. Fortunately, after seizing the Studion's most famous relic, the head of John the Baptist, the Franks lost interest in its precious intellectual treasures. Unfortunately, during their raids on other monasteries, they did destroy a large number of ancient manuscripts, some of which were the last extant versions of their texts. Seeing the agony this deliberate vandalism inflicted on the monks, the illiterate Franks mocked their educated victims by pretending to take a quill and copy out a book.[34]

Turning their attention to the city's pagan art treasures, the Franks melted down hundreds, if not thousands, of antique bronze statues, including many masterworks of Greco-Roman genius. Among the rarities the Franks rendered for their metal content were a bronze she-wolf that Constantine the Great had brought from Rome, a monumental statue of Hera which had miraculously survived the huge Crusader fire that destroyed the Forum of Constantine, Lysippus' colossal statue of Hercules, and hundreds of magnificent bronzes lining the racecourse in the Hippodrome.[35]

The total quantity of booty seized within the great metropolis was enormous. In addition to amassing a collective store worth 300,000 silver marks, individual Crusaders held back an estimated 500,000 marks of surreptitious loot.[36] Venetians certainly took their fair share of this huge cache, but they generally refused to join in acts of wanton destruction; to them, Constantinople was something more than one of the largest and wealthiest cities ever laid open to wholesale military pillage. Having lived in the ancient metropolis for centuries, Venetians understood that it was the last surviving link between classical Roman civilization and their own medieval world, that the fall of Constantinople was the final collapse of the Roman Empire. It might be a vastly reduced and weakened empire, but it still possessed unique living ties to early Christianity and the intellectual heritage of ancient Greece and Rome. Venetians knew the worth of what they had conquered, and while they had come to despise the Byzantines for their arrogance, they had never lost their awe of the Eastern Empire's ancient birthright. Far from desiring to annihilate Byzantine civilization, Venetians aspired to claim its antique mantle for themselves. To this end, they would spend the first half of the thirteenth century appropriating the physical splendor of Byzantine architectural monuments for their own, much smaller island city. Given the enormous quantity and quality of precious building spoil available to them in 1204, the prospects were truly breathtaking. As we shall see in the following chapter, this unique opportunity would have a profound effect on the Piazza San Marco.

CHAPTER SEVEN

An Imperial Dream (1205-1280)

Dandolo's Achievement

When Enrico Dandolo died in Constantinople in May 1205, Venetian Crusaders insisted on burying him in the imperial splendor of Haghia Sophia; in their minds, nothing else could possibly match what the Republic owed to her departed doge. In addition to his critical role as a military commander, he had performed indispensable services after the battle was won. Following the conquest of Constantinople, Doge Dandolo had made his headquarters in the Greek patriarch's elegant palace located on the southern flank of Haghia Sophia, and there, just north of the great Augusteum plaza (surrounded by the finest surviving monuments of Late Antiquity), he single-handedly founded a new Venetian empire. He began by assembling the Frankish war chiefs and engineering the selection of a Latin emperor who knew that he owed his office almost entirely to the doge's machinations. He then forced the new emperor, Count Baldwin of Flanders, to reaffirm the earlier Frankish commitment that no state at war with Venice would be permitted to trade within the Latin Empire. As long as this promise was honored, the Republic could always dictate the terms on which her competitors were granted access to Byzantine markets.[1]

Dandolo's extensive experience with the Eastern Empire proved to be extremely valuable to the Republic, particularly when the Franks and the Venetians began dividing up conquered Greek territory. The two parties had already agreed that if the attack were successful, each would receive three-eighths of Constantinople and an equal portion of all subjugated Greek lands outside the imperial capital, with the remaining quarter to go to the new Latin emperor. As the Venetian share of Constantinople, the doge chose a huge wedge-shaped area that ran from the central government precinct around the Augusteum (basically untouched by the invasion fires) north to the great trading emporiums along the banks of the Golden Horn. Outside the metropolis, the doge encouraged the Franks to lay claim to the empire's major land masses, knowing how difficult it would be to exact feudal tribute from resentful Greeks in such vast new holdings. For Venice, he requested only a chain of strategic naval bases located on the crucial trading routes linking the lagoon with the Aegean islands, Constantinople, the Black Sea, and the Middle East. But each of these new possessions—including Durazzo and Corfu along the eastern Adriatic coast, the ports of Modone and Corone on the southern shore of Greece, the principal Aegean island of Negropont, and the critically placed island of Crete—was shrewdly chosen to ensure Venetian domination of the eastern Mediterranean. And while the doge strongly supported the Frankish wish to impose traditional feudal relations within their own Eastern dominions, he successfully insisted that most imperial Venetian territories be kept free of such reactionary entanglements.[2]

The result was a Latin Empire of the Franks that for its entire fifty-seven-year history remained weak, divided, and beleaguered, and, hence, never a threat to Venetian exploitation of Christendom's largest and most profitable marketplace. At long last, Venice could look forward to enjoying the full commercial monopoly she had been trying to regain since her original trading privileges under the Golden Bull of 1082 began to be withdrawn in the 1120s. In addition to reclaiming her exclusive exemption from the ten percent customs tax imposed on every other European state permitted to do business in the empire, she expanded her trading domain to the lucrative ports of the Black Sea, from which her merchants had long been shut out by hostile Greek emperors. To ensure maximum profits from this long-awaited opportunity, the Venetian government itself now assumed the task of organizing commercial traffic between the lagoon and former Byzantine ports.[3]

The wealth and prestige that this new maritime empire transferred to Venice over the next half century were a direct result of the wisdom, foresight, and political skill of her elderly doge. From the first appearance of the Frankish envoys, Enrico Dandolo had been forced to make a series of critical choices on the basis of incomplete, highly speculative information. He had continually been faced with novel circumstances in which the facts were veiled, the future uncertain, and the need for immediate decision paramount. Being human, he had not always made the right decision, but even when his judgment had erred, he had kept his head and maintained a clear vision of what he wished to achieve. Over the course of a long, grueling campaign, he had repeatedly displayed reserves of physical and moral courage that would have been striking in a man half his age. And in the end, his conduct of affairs was so successful that many historians have seen him as a sinister genius who forced every other actor in the drama to fall in line with a preconceived Venetian plot. Although such a view is not supported by the historical record, the mere fact that such a narrative has become the conventional wisdom speaks volumes about the magnitude of Dandolo's achievements on behalf of the city he loved.[4]

A Wealth of Precious Stone

Dandolo also initiated something that had a major impact on the continuing Piazza San Marco project: the systematic delivery to Venice of precious building spoils from the conquered Byzantine capital. Of course, Venetian importation of rare and beautiful stone from Eastern ruins had been under way for over a century. It began no later than the dogate of Domenico Selvo (1071–1084), who had directed the Republic's overseas merchants to load valuable building material into the holds of their ships before returning to the lagoon. And ultimately, the city's tradition of relying on recycled architectural spoils went back to her earliest beginnings when, as refugees from the Roman mainland, the first Venetians returned to the continent to strip decorative stones from their abandoned homes. The first church of San Marco had incorporated into its fabric a collection of antique Roman columns and relief sculpture scavenged from mainland ruins. But the opportunity now before Venice was of a totally different order of magnitude. No longer would she be dependent on randomly discovered finds from miscellaneous sites. As the victor of the Fourth Crusade, Venice could methodically appropriate almost any architectural item or work of art that caught her fancy in the capital of the Eastern Roman Empire. And in spite of the significant damage Constantinople had suffered from the three Crusader fires and Frankish vandalism, in 1205, the bulk of the city's classical architectural heritage was still intact. Five-sixths of its surface had escaped the flames, and the Franks had concentrated their efforts on seizing portable booty and melting down freestanding bronze statues, not razing monumental buildings.[5]

To grasp the full significance of this unique Venetian opportunity, one needs to appreciate the impact of the great mass-production stone quarries that the Roman Empire operated for the first three centuries of its existence. From the reign of Augustus (27 B.C.– A.D. 14) to that of Constantine the Great (A.D. 306–337), the Roman Department of Marbles ran huge slave-labor quarries that extracted and finished enormous quantities of marble and other precious stone for delivery to classical building sites throughout the empire. As long as they remained open, these immense stone fabrication centers, located in the Aegean, Egypt, North Africa, Tuscany, and the Pyrenees, supplied the luxury building needs of the vast Roman world. But after the imperial quarries were permanently closed following the reign of Constantine, builders who needed a ready-made source of such precious material were left with only one available alternative: reusing the fabric of existing classical buildings and monuments. It was not only far cheaper and easier to extract ornate, finished stone from existing structures; in the case of certain types of material—porphyry, for instance—there was simply no more to be had from any other source. The Egyptian quarries that once supplied this rare material, used by Roman builders to symbolize the emperor's personal power, had long been exhausted. This was the general state of affairs when Constantine transferred the locus of imperial power to Constantinople and harvested the artistic and architectural treasures of the ancient world to enrich his new metropolis. Constantine's capital quickly became a repository for the most magnificent and sumptuous stonework produced by imperial Rome up to that time, a treasure house that, following the closure of the imperial quarries, no future sovereign could possibly hope to duplicate. And now this irreplaceable storehouse of rare monuments, most of which had survived Crusader destruction, was available to Venice for the taking.[6]

According to some Renaissance-era historians, one of the initial Venetian reactions to this architectural windfall was a proposal to move the capital from the northern Adriatic to the Bosporus, transforming Constantinople into the center of a new entirely Eastern Venetian maritime empire. If such a proposal was indeed ever seriously considered, it could not have found favor with Doge Dandolo, who had already begun to ship rare building spoils from the Byzantine capital to the Venetian lagoon. With his deep political insight, Dandolo would have instinctively understood the dangers inherent in such a radical change of physical environment. He would have been acutely attuned to the potential effect on her developing republican consciousness of a Venetian decision to transfer the seat of government to a huge ancient metropolis built to glorify and preserve the alien traditions of imperial Rome. In the end, Venice decided to follow the doge's lead by pursuing her own unique form of architectural grandeur at the head of the Adriatic. Consequently, except for the area immediately surrounding Haghia Sophia, neither the Venetians nor the Franks made any effort to repair or even maintain the physical infrastructure of the Byzantine capital. In particular, the Western victors did nothing to restore the homes of the 130,000 Greeks who, in the immediate aftermath of the three Crusader fires, were living in the smoldering ruins of their former dwellings. During the half century of Latin occupation, the city suffered four more major fires, and although most of its important monuments escaped destruction in the flames, many, including the Imperial Palace and the Hippodrome, were allowed to sink into dilapidation and ruin. Rather than institute a much-needed restoration campaign, the Venetians systematically mined Constantinople's surviving architectural treasures for transport back to the lagoon.[7]

Completing the Medieval Piazza San Marco

By the time of the Fourth Crusade, the builders of the Piazza San Marco had succeeded in carving out an elegant, spacious square within the most densely settled islands at the heart of the Venetian archipelago. The new Piazza was a rectangular opening in the urban fabric approximately 185 feet wide (north to south) and 570 feet long (east to west), whose creation more than doubled the length of public space directly in front of the Basilica San Marco *(Fig. 27)*. The builders had also created a second forum, approximately half the size of the Piazza, by filling in the harbor inlet that had formerly flowed up to the southern face of the Basilica. This smaller, trapezoidal public square, the Piazzetta, began as a wharf at the edge of the Venetian harbor and then ran north past the Ziani ducal palace before merging directly into the eastern end of the Piazza. Gone forever was the old impression of two separate, walled-off islands which had characterized the San Marco area for over four centuries. The Piazza and Piazzetta now formed a single continuous space in the shape of an inverted L, linked to each other by the shaft of the San Marco Campanile, which stood between them like a giant connecting rod.[8]

In the course of site preparation, virtually all the existing peripheral buildings (naturally excepting the Basilica, the Campanile, and the brand-new Ziani ducal palace) as well as the old Tribuno defensive wall that surrounded the two islands had been demolished. By the early thirteenth century, replacement buildings located above and behind light, elegant arcades were being erected around the Piazza, a process that lasted for the next half century, until the entire perimeter was lined with "troops of ordered arches...prolong[ed]... into ranged symmetry,"[9] in Ruskin's memorable phrase. To achieve this effect, builders employed a classically based design of fixed proportions and standardized detail borrowed from the wings of the late twelfth-century ducal palace. This architectural model employed a repetition of virtually identical columns, capitals, windows, and parapets along connected building fronts and placed two round-arched windows on the upper-story loggia over every semicircular arch on the ground-floor portico *(Fig. 28)*. This uniform design of the Piazza enclosure was also employed to construct the buildings that formed the Piazzetta's western boundary. On the opposite side of the Piazzetta was the western arm of the Ziani ducal palace, a mirror image of the palace's majestic southern wing with its superb views over the Venetian harbor. Round, high-stilted arches springing from delicate marble columns extended across the broad exteriors of both ducal palace façades. Many of the building façades around the Piazza and Piazzetta were faced with marble revetment or decorated with fresco inset with colored marble panels and roundels.[10]

Such uniformity of design across an entire building site, an ancient Roman and Greek practice borrowed, in this instance, from the Augusteum complex in Constantinople, was a striking novelty in the medieval West. It endowed the Piazza and Piazzetta with a genuine antique grandeur and a degree of classical regularity that would not be seen again, at least in such fully realized form, until the fifteenth-century career of Filippo Brunelleschi, the first great architect of the early Italian Renaissance. By 1280, both of these elegant Venetian forums had been paved with herringbone brick, and their arcaded perimeters were all but completed.[11]

The Role of the Procuracy of Saint Mark

The architectural coherence of the medieval Piazza complex, a century-long development spanning the terms of ten doges, was the direct product of continuous project management by a powerful new communal office: the Procuracy of Saint Mark. Before the twelfth century, major architectural undertakings in the San Marco area depended on the personal initiative and financial sponsorship of individual ducal leaders. For instance, architectural historians typically refer to the first, second, and third churches of San Marco

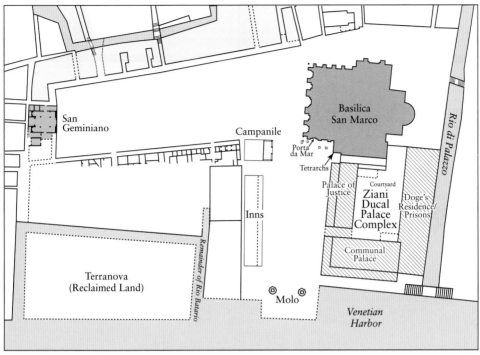

Fig. 27: Plan of the medieval Piazza and Piazzetta
(Thirteenth century)

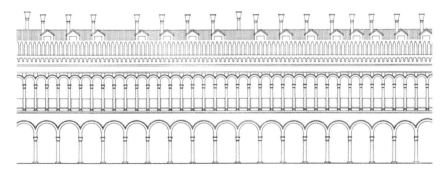

Fig. 28: Medieval Piazza perimeter

as the Participazio, Orseolo, and Contarini churches, respectively. But by the time of the Piazza San Marco project in the middle of the twelfth century, state power was passing from the hands of autocratic doges to newly constituted communal councils, and public architecture was not immune to this transformative process. By the final quarter of the twelfth century, the institution of the Procuracy, originally a single officeholder appointed by the doge to care for his private chapel, had become an independent communal office charged with long-term responsibility for major building efforts in the San Marco district like the massive new Piazza project.[12]

Election to the Procuracy was the second-highest distinction the Republic could confer, and procurators were chosen from the upper echelons of the merchant nobility. Appointment was for life, and the selection criteria included seniority, outstanding commercial success, and extensive state service in a variety of public posts. New doges were regularly chosen from the Procuracy, and its members were the only officeholders other than the doge who were supplied with official residences within the San Marco precinct. In addition to a token salary, the Republic provided each procurator with a spacious, rent-free apartment along the Piazza perimeter. Since the Procuracy owned and managed virtually the entire San Marco precinct, it could use the substantial rental income from completed portions of the square to subsidize ongoing project costs, including the expense of hiring a professional construction manager. When completed, most of the ground-floor arcades of the Piazza and Piazzetta were rented out as shops, and most of the upper-floor rooms not used as procuratorial apartment space were also leased by private tenants.[13]

Because its original role had been that of a ducal vicar appointed to care for the church of San Marco, it is hardly surprising that at some point during the creation of a large, magnificent square directly opposite the ducal chapel, the Procuracy would begin to take a fresh look at the face of the Basilica itself. By the early thirteenth century, what it found was hardly satisfactory; the Basilica's western facade, which faced the Piazza at an oblique angle, was extremely plain, and its unembellished brick surface was forty percent lower and twenty-five percent narrower than the building we see today. Prior to 1160, when the opportunity for viewing the church was severely hampered by its constricted island setting, such architectural modesty may have been acceptable. But when the viewing platform opposite the church was more than doubled, creating a splendid 570-foot vista whose focal point was San Marco's unadorned western front, expectations changed accordingly. It became imperative to find some means of integrating the Basilica into the ongoing Piazza project, to increase the size and grandeur of the church exterior to match its spacious new setting.

Presented with this challenge, Venice responded with an idea that had no precedent in classical Roman or Byzantine architectural practice, the two principal sources for the Piazza project up to this point. This was a decision to cover the Basilica exterior with the same type of exuberant decorative veneer that had already been applied to the church interior during the twelfth century. Up to this time, the Venetian use of polychrome marble had been closely tied to Byzantine architectural tradition, which consistently maintained a strict dichotomy between elaborately decorated interiors and plain, bare brick exteriors. This division between an ornate inner sanctum and a rude, unfinished outer surface even held true for magnificent imperial projects like the churches of Haghia Sophia in Constantinople and San Vitale in Ravenna *(Fig. 29)*. In a similar manner, classical Roman builders used different surface materials to distinguish inside from outside, reserving rare colored marbles for interior floors and walls and typically finishing their exteriors in bare brick or plaster, or if the project were a sufficiently important public building, an outer mantle of white marble, tufa or travertine, all common, easily obtainable materials. Even Hadrian's villa, a sumptuous imperial complex built by a passionate architectural experimenter with unlimited financial resources and a profound interest in Eastern building methods, observed this traditional Roman distinction; its interiors were decorated with polychrome marble veneer while its exterior walls were covered in travertine and tufa. No less an authority than Cicero declared that white was the proper color for temples, and the architect Vitruvius, author of the only antique Roman architectural treatise that has survived to our day, advised his contemporaries to finish their exteriors with plain tufa and travertine. Other classical Roman authors were even more severe, complaining that any use of colored marble, even in interior spaces, was a deplorable lapse from Roman order and decorum. Based on such classical dicta, when late medieval Florentines covered their Baptistery (which they erroneously believed to be an antique Roman building) with marble revetment, they limited themselves to simple geometrical designs in white and green. This same restriction was followed for the face of San Miniato al Monte, on the Badia facade in neighboring Fiesole, and in other examples of Tuscan Romanesque incrustation found in cities such as Pisa, Lucca and Pistoia.[14]

Fig. 29: Exterior of San Vitale, Ravenna

It is a striking fact that this radical thirteenth-century departure from antique precedent was carried out by the elderly members of the Procuracy of Saint Mark. In deciding to invest the Basilica exterior in a gorgeous polychrome blend of mosaics, rare ancient spoils, and precious marble sheathing, these seasoned magistrates seem to have been carried away by the same surge of triumphant exuberance felt by the conquering Venetian Crusaders themselves. Inspired by this vision, the procurators began to perceive the Piazza as a splendid theatrical vista, the ideal setting in which to celebrate the Basilica as the centerpiece of the city's collective identity. As the San Marco project moved forward, the Basilica and the Piazza progressively merged into a unified civic stage devoted to the founding legends of a new Venetian empire.

Reconstructing the Basilica

To prepare the Basilica for this innovative architectural program, a series of important structural changes had to be made to the eleventh-century Contarini church, the effects of which were to substantially increase the building's width, height, and bulk, particularly as seen from the Piazza *(Figs. 30, 31, 32)*.

First, in order to make the front of the western narthex strong enough to hold the tons of marble revetment and massed columns now planned for it, the five western entrance portals had to be significantly reinforced and deepened. When this work was completed, the impression created was that of five Roman triumphal arches, with the central arch noticeably wider and higher. This extension of the western façade toward the Piazza also created a roof terrace or loggia above the deepened portals.

Second, the barrel vault at the western end of the nave was brought forward over the narthex until it reached the rear edge of the new roof terrace; a century earlier, when the Contarini church had been completed, the vault stopped at the rear wall of the narthex. This massive extension not only furnished greater support for the western and central domes; as viewed from the Piazza, its forward juncture with the terrace created the effect of an upper-story, semicircular arch located immediately above (and therefore mirroring) the semicircular, ground-floor arch of the central narthex portal.

Third, northern and southern arms were added to the original western narthex, creating a continuous outer shell along three sides of the Basilica. Then, the western façade of the church was widened an additional forty feet (creating a total width of 170 feet) by adding tall, high-stilted ornamental arches beyond the corners of the narthex.

Fourth, second-story rooms were built above the three wings of the narthex, providing additional resistance to the lateral thrust of the domes. This upper story was finished off with a blind arcade that mirrored the arched portals below.

Fifth, the church's low profile was greatly heightened by installing a series of helmet-shaped lead cupolas over the original shallow Greek domes built in brick. The Venetians almost certainly borrowed this technique from Islamic architecture, where adding a tall outer shell over a mosque's relatively flat inner dome was a standard technique for creating a more commanding vertical impression.[15]

*Fig. 30: Model of the eleventh-century Contarini church of
San Marco without narthex (with the kind permission of
the Procuratoria di San Marco, Venice)*

*Fig. 31: Model of the Basilica San Marco showing early thirteenth-century
enlargement and reinforcement of the western façade (with the kind
permission of the Procuratoria di San Marco, Venice)*

Fig. 32: Model of the Basilica San Marco showing thirteenth century and later additions to the western façade (with the kind permission of the Procuratoria di San Marco, Venice)

Over this greatly enlarged surface, Venetians then applied a dazzling, multicolored coat of marble sheathing, mosaic painting, sculpted panels, high and low relief, ornamental columns, and antique capitals *(Fig. 33)*. Most of this decorative material came from carefully selected building sites in Constantinople, where the Republic's status as an occupying power allowed her to export whatever she wished virtually at will. As a result, the Basilica exterior is a fusion of many different sources and styles—classical Roman, Early Christian, Late Antique, Byzantine, Islamic, and medieval Italian. But the overall impression is one of organic unity, an artistic whole whose collective value transcends the effect of any particular component. It is a supreme example of the city's protean synthetic genius, the ability to create stunning compositions from the most disparate materials and periods. In this case, it was an assemblage designed to signal the Basilica's final transformation from private ducal chapel to majestic state sanctuary. But before we attempt a general understanding of this special Venetian gift for architectural integration, let us reverse the process and try to isolate some of the exterior's most prominent individual components.

As we stand in the Piazza gazing at the Basilica, one of the first things to capture our attention is the mantle of 160 gorgeous ornamental columns that line the western façade, most of which are classical spoils brought to Venice in the wake of the Fourth Crusade. As Ruskin observed, Venetian builders viewed these antique shafts as "nothing else than large jewels...[each] valued according to its size and brilliancy of color."[16] Just as a Byzantine gem artist might embed a ceremonial chalice or reliquary with rare emeralds and rubies, the Republic clothed her national church in rows of exquisite porphyry, verde antico, and breccia marble columns. However, even with her vast resources, Venice must have been hard-pressed to collect enough sufficiently beautiful matching pairs to cover the entire façade. Only her status as an occupying military power in Constantinople, the world's greatest repository of such classical spoils, made it possible for her to erect double rows of parallel shafts and capitals on both sides of each portal.[17]

A second prominent feature of the western façade is the series of relief sculptures that cover the concentric arches above the central portal *(Fig. 34)*. These reliefs present an extremely wide range of style and subject matter, from the highly expressive depiction of a primal world of violence and bestial behavior *(Fig. 35)* to a serene, classically derived sequence portraying Christian virtues and beatitudes. Other sections of this remarkable work are more realistic, such as the brilliant personification of the twelve months of the calendar and a fascinating visual catalog of the Republic's most popular trades and crafts. Taken as a whole, the ensemble displays a striking synthesis of classical Roman, Christian, Byzantine, Romanesque, and Gothic source elements carved by an anonymous artist whom Otto Demus has called one of the greatest medieval sculptors of northern Italy.[18]

However, as magnificently carved as these engaging portal images are, the major point they drive home is the relative paucity of sculptural decoration on the Basilica exterior (at least below the Gothic roof crest, which was not added until the early fifteenth century). Certainly, this is the unavoidable impression if one compares the façade of San Marco with other great medieval communal architecture such as the Gothic cathedrals of northern France. While the cathedrals and the Basilica were all national monuments built in response to similar groundswells of religious enthusiasm and patriotic feeling, their exterior surfaces could hardly be more different. True to its Byzantine architectural roots, sculpture plays a far less prominent role in the exterior decoration of the Venetian church, both in the total area given over to carved stone and in the size of the figures used in individual

Fig. 33: Western Facade of the Basilica San Marco,
watercolor triptych by Alberto Prosdocimi (with the kind
permission of the Procuratoria di San Marco, Venice)

Fig. 34: Basilica San Marco's central portal, western façade

Fig. 35: Sculptural detail, central portal, western façade,
Basilica San Marco

Fig. 36: Porta Sant'Alipio, northwest corner
of the Basilica San Marco

compositions. San Marco has nothing to match the great expanses of almost life-size portal sculpture and the profusion of monumental figures carved into the faces of Chartres, Notre Dame de Paris, and the cathedrals of Reims and Amiens. Given the enormous amount of exterior surface taken up by the Basilica's curtain of polychrome marble columns, there was relatively little space left over for the display of life-size statuary even if Venice had wished to produce it.[19]

And in fact, the thirteenth-century Procuracy of Saint Mark had no wish to commission large-scale sculptural works, for two principal reasons. First, the monumental Roman and Byzantine sculptures with which Venetians were familiar typically depicted imperial sovereigns and their families or other prominent members of the imperial hierarchy, and they often exalted these subjects by merging their likenesses with images of the classical gods. As we have seen, this type of personal glorification, this deification of the individual at the expense of republican communal life, was antithetical to the values that late medieval Venice wished to promote. Second, as we have also seen, by the thirteenth century, Venetian genius had developed its own distinctive aesthetic, a form of ensemble art that combined low-relief sculpture with mosaic and precious stone spoils to create a tightly unified artistic whole. This seamless integration of disparate components would have been much more difficult if not impossible to achieve if the builders of San Marco had introduced large, freestanding or semidetached sculpture into their compositions. Rather than blending easily with other constituent parts, such independent, large-scale figures would have demanded a generous expanse of surrounding space in which they could be the dominant element.

Perhaps the best way to appreciate the impression created by this new Venetian aesthetic is to focus our attention on a representative sample of the Basilica's complex, multifaceted exterior, like the leftmost portal of the western façade, known as the Porta Sant'Alipio *(Figs. 33, 36)*. The recessed curves that form the sides of the Sant'Alipio entrance contain two superimposed rows of ornamental columns, arranged so that they seem to support the triumphal arch that crowns the portal. Most of these recycled shafts are sumptuously veined Greek marble in shades of cream, yellow, red, and smoky blue, topped by capitals carved in various styles. Immediately below the portal arch is a concave lunette covered with a mosaic depicting the Basilica's brilliantly colored western front as it appeared around 1265, close to the completion point of the Piazza project. Below the lunette is a deeply cut ogival arch, a motif borrowed from Islamic architecture, and the surfaces immediately above and below this feature four widely different types of carved stone. There are floral and figurative reliefs on a gilded mosaic background, five delicately latticed stone window screens, small sculptural panels symbolizing the four Evangelists inserted into a green marble background, and an architrave or horizontal band composed of individual niche reliefs. Almost all of these elements appear to consist of recycled Byzantine and Early Christian spoils, perhaps combined with clever copying. Below the architrave is a thirteenth-century brass door that looks convincingly antique.[20]

Although the constituent parts of the Porta Sant'Alipio are extremely diverse in texture, color, style, and provenance, and although most of the ensemble is composed of recycled materials originally constructed to fit totally different settings, the overall effect is one of elegant, majestic harmony. No single feature dominates; each of the rich details contributes to an unbroken impression of luxuriant beauty. This is the special assemblage art of Venice, a talent for organizing unrelated objects into a new and unified whole. It is a complex artistic achievement requiring a number of rare and delicate skills. Chief among these are "a vigorous mind, steady and persevering attention, various powers of compensation and combination, and the resources of an understanding fruitful in expedients."[21] Venetians specialized in adapting and combining existing works and fragments and, where necessary, counterfeiting whatever parts they needed to complete an ensemble. Thus, one of the major Venetian workshops employed during the Basilica's thirteenth-century transformation was specifically devoted to restoring and copying antique spoil. The city's imitative skills were such that it is sometimes almost impossible to tell whether a particular item in a composition is an Early Christian or Late Antique original, reworked in the thirteenth century, or a medieval copy specifically created for the place it now occupies.[22]

The Use of Trophies

But not all of the spoils from the Fourth Crusade were displayed anonymously as part of a closely integrated artistic ensemble. In selected cases, the Venetians erected large individual works of recycled sculpture and architectural material in a manner that deliberately called attention to the objects' unique qualities. They treated such spoils as trophies, many of which were no doubt chosen for installation in a specific location within the San Marco precinct as part of a preconceived decorative plan. Some appear to be uncomplicated celebrations of Venetian triumph. For instance, where the corner of the Basilica juts out from its southern façade just opposite the ducal palace, there are two large unbroken wall surfaces covered in dazzling marble revetment and Byzantine relief panels *(Fig. 37)*. This exuberant display appears to be a direct expression of the pure Oedipal joy Venetians felt as they began to strip the architectural body of their defeated Eastern father. There was no attempt to disguise this act of artistic patricide; the stolen treasures were simply riveted to the underlying brick walls with large metal staples. Appropriately enough, the interior space behind this resplendent exterior belongs to the treasury of San Marco, where the Republic's share of portable booty from the sack of Constantinople is stored. Other openly triumphal displays of rare and precious stone revetment from the Fourth Crusade can be found on the interior walls of the church; there are, for instance, the rectangles of luxuriant marble that line the northern and southern aisles of the nave *(Fig. 16)*. These lavish stone inserts must have been installed in response to the removal of the overhead gallery floors, an action (only completed around 1230, according to the best authority) that flooded the once deeply shadowed aisles with natural light.[23]

Other trophies seem intended to convey a more defined message, for example, the porphyry statues of four Roman emperors *(Figs. 37, 38)* inserted into the same jutting southern corner of the Basilica described at the beginning of the preceding paragraph. These four figures represent the Tetrarchy of co-emperors that Diocletian established in 293 to rule an empire he had divided into four geographical regions. Diocletian was Constantine's immediate predecessor, and he appointed Constantine's father, Constantius, to be one of the Tetrarchy's original co-emperors. Although Constantine in turn ruthlessly eliminated his rivals and established himself as sole imperial sovereign, he wished for his heirs to rule the empire as a Tetrarchy in the manner that Diocletian had planned. To symbolize this posthumous intent, he installed these porphyry figures representing his four designated successors (three sons and a nephew shown in the act of embracing each other) on the shafts of two monumental columns. The pillars were located at an intersection known as the Philadelphion (place of brotherly love) along the great Mese thoroughfare in Constantinople. When the Republic inserted these four figures into the corner of the San Marco treasury, she undoubtedly meant to convey her strongly felt sense of historical connection to ancient Rome via the Byzantine East. Her action must also have been intended to signal

Fig. 37: Basilica San Marco treasury wall

*Fig. 38: Four Roman emperors carved in porphyry
(known as the Tetrarchs) inserted into the treasury walls
of the Basilica San Marco*

the overriding value medieval Venice placed on political arrangements where ultimate power was shared among theoretical coequals.[24]

One of thirteenth-century Venice's most prominent displays of a Crusader trophy was her installation of a gilded copper sculpture representing a four-horse chariot team or *quadriga* on the Basilica terrace directly above the central portal *(Fig. 39)*. This extraordinary work of art was reportedly first brought to Constantinople by Constantine himself, and virtually all scholars agree that the Venetian Crusaders found the quadriga installed in the Hippodrome above the starting gates at the northern end of the giant stadium. Some authorities have attributed the figures to an antique Greek master such as Phidias, Praxiteles, or Lysippus, while others have concluded that the group is probably a Roman work; the dates assigned to its creation and casting range over nine centuries, from the fifth century B.C. to the fourth century A.D.[25] But whatever its provenance, when seen at close range *(Fig. 40)*, the work is instantly revealed as a masterpiece of startling power and delicacy. (Fortunately, the original quadriga can still be seen in the museum on the second story of the Basilica, where the statues have been relocated to protect their delicate copper skins from air pollution; the four horses now installed on the western façade are copies.) The viewer is immediately impressed by the remarkable individuality and grace of the four figures, the empathy with which the head of each member of a pair turns toward its mate, the bright, expressive intelligence of the eyes, and the light prancing step of the lifted foreleg with its delicate curve. There is also a powerful realism in the strong, muscular rounding of the opened lower jaw and the flaring nostrils; the mouths almost seem to exude breath, and each head is finished off with the beautiful crested mane of a Greek warrior. Finally, one notices how the chest harnesses seem to lie weightless on the powerful bodies, capturing a supreme moment of effortless strength and cooperative intelligence.

In spite of his blindness, it was Doge Enrico Dandolo himself who chose the quadriga for transport back to Venice, and the work may very well have been specifically designated for installation in the center of San Marco's upper-story loggia even before it was removed from the Hippodrome. Its erection there in the middle of the thirteenth century (when the Basilica renovation project was finally completed or at least near completion) was intended to impart a number of powerful messages to contemporary medieval viewers. At the most overt level, the team of four spirited horses would have evoked images of victorious Roman emperors in horse-drawn chariots leading triumphal processions through the streets of the imperial capital. It was the perfect trophy to represent the Republic's new status as the conqueror of Byzantium and heir to three-eighths of the Eastern Roman Empire.[26]

But the quadriga also conveyed an important religious message, one that stressed the critical importance of Mark, the patron saint of Venice, to the triumph of Christianity within the Roman Empire. Medieval Europeans were generally familiar with a literary trope known as the *Quadriga Domini*, which envisioned Mark and his fellow Evangelists as a four-horse chariot team. This popular metaphor was commonly used to underscore the speed with which the four Gospel writers—the great communicators of Christ's life, death, and resurrection—had been able to spread his revolutionary vision to the distant corners of a hostile pagan world. To most men and women of the thirteenth century, the placement of a quadriga group above the central portal of the Venetian state church, a temple specifically dedicated to Saint Mark, would have constituted a clear reference to this well-known Christian symbol. And if this were not enough, it seems very probable that at the time the four horses were installed, the great arch immediately behind them was filled not with glass, as at present, but with relief panels depicting Christ and the four Evangelists, a repetition of the quadriga's symbolic content in unmistakably explicit form.[27]

Erecting the quadriga on the Basilica terrace also provided Venetians with a particularly vivid reminder of just how much the design of the San Marco complex was openly derived from Byzantine models. To anyone familiar with the Augusteum precinct in Constantinople, it would have been easy to recognize specific physical analogies. While installed in the Eastern capital, the quadriga had overlooked the *spina* or longitudinal axis of the Hippodrome; when reinstalled in Venice, it looked out over the length of the Piazza San Marco—another great, longitudinal enclosure with a similar mixture of public functions. The Hippodrome (to which admission was free) was the chief gathering place of the Greek populace; enormous crowds poured into the stadium to witness chariot races, religious spectacles, jousting tournaments, polo matches, imperial triumphs, and public executions or to take part in political demonstrations. It was here that the emperor, having entered his private viewing stand (the kathisma) by means of a special staircase connected to the Imperial Palace, showed himself to the assembled populace and tried to divine the city's shifting political winds. Often the first sign of impending trouble was the rustle of displeasure that swept over the multitude as the emperor took his seat in the arena.[28]

Fig. 39: Western façade of the Basilica San Marco

Fig. 40: Four-horse chariot team (quadriga) taken from the Hippodrome, Constantinople

Similarly, the Piazza San Marco was the site for popular participation in the Republic's most important political and religious rituals. It was here that the Venetian people gathered to lift up their newly elected doge and carry him into the Basilica. It was here that they thronged each April 25 to take part in the annual Saint Mark's Day ritual and then reassembled, a few weeks later, for the great Ascension Day festival which culminated in the reenactment of Venice's famous marriage to the sea. The Piazza complex was also the central stage for religious spectacles such as the annual Corpus Domini and Palm Sunday celebrations, as well as the setting for state receptions, victory parades, executions, the Venetian Carnival, jousting tournaments, guild processions, and public fairs. The best place to witness this flood of civic rituals, parades, festivals, and games was the loggia terrace of the Basilica *(Fig. 39)*, on either side of the newly installed quadriga. Accordingly, it was there that the doge and other members of the governing elite stood, watched, and presented themselves during important communal ceremonies. And just as the Byzantine emperor used a set of special palace stairs to reach his viewing stand in the Hippodrome, so the doge and other high officials had direct access to the Basilica viewing platform from the interior of the ducal palace.[29]

The Molo Pillars

Sometime during the thirteenth century, Venetian artisans transformed an assortment of miscellaneous spoils into a novel symbol of the city's maritime supremacy. To make this possible, builders first created an extended quay, called the Molo, along the Piazzetta's southern shore,[30] and here, just behind where harbor waters lapped against the freshly laid embankment, they erected two huge columns of reddish gray Egyptian granite, topped with tall Veneto-Byzantine capitals *(Fig 41)*. On top of one pillar, they installed a ten-foot-long bronze lion, which they gilded and then transformed into the Lion of Saint Mark by adding a large pair of outstretched wings *(Fig. 42)*. Scholarly opinion varies widely concerning the pre-Byzantine origins of this striking three-ton trophy from the Fourth Crusade; it has been called Etruscan, Persian, Assyrian, and even Chinese. But once installed atop its pillar as the Winged Lion of the Republic, it became the central emblem of Venice, the model for countless similar images throughout the city and every corner of Venetian territory, all testifying to the city's divinely ordained imperial dominion. On the other column, Venetians

*Fig. 41: View of Molo pillars against the Venetian harbor
by Ippolito Caffi*

Fig. 42: Bronze Lion of Saint Mark atop Molo pillar

mounted a composite statue of the Greek warrior Saint Theodore standing on the back of a dragon (which looks like a crocodile with the head of a dog). Theodore's Greek marble head sits on a second-century Roman torso, probably from the reign of Hadrian; the rest of the warrior-saint's body and halo, as well as his spear, sword, and shield and the dragon, were constructed from a hodgepodge of Fourth Crusade spoils joined to contemporary additions by a Venetian sculptor. The monumental columns themselves were very likely transported to Venice in 1172 in the ill-fated fleet of Doge Vitale Michiel II, which also carried the plague. The cargo holds of the returning Venetian ships carried three of these enormous stone shafts. During unloading, however, one of them toppled into the harbor just off the Molo, where it remains to this day.[31]

The Molo pillars ensemble is one of the most evocative examples of trophy reuse ever achieved by Venetian art. Framing a magnificent open-water vista over the southern lagoon, it was a direct expression of the medieval Republic's internationalist world view. It symbolized the confident projection of Venetian maritime power across the Adriatic and Mediterranean to the very heart of the Eastern Empire and the distant Middle East. Like the quadriga on the front of San Marco, it epitomized the lagoon dwellers' deep religious belief in Venetian exceptionalism, the unbridled future of their small, sea-girt nation. It is also a uniquely Venetian icon, one whose unbroken waterfront panorama would have been impossible in a city ringed with defensive walls.

Venice almost certainly borrowed the idea of erecting monumental columns at the end of her new quay, as well as the Molo pillars themselves, from Constantinople. Indeed, in the Eastern capital, as in Rome before it, the great imperial squares were dominated by massive freestanding stone pillars. But this characteristic Roman and Byzantine practice underwent a dramatic sea change in its translation to Venice. In Constantinople, monumental columns were typically crowned with statues of the emperors who had erected them or members of their families; like the other great monuments in the Eastern capital, they were designed to symbolize the Greek commitment to imperial absolutism. In erecting the Molo pillars, Venetians demonstrated a complete rejection of such political values. Rather than effigies of exalted ducal leaders, they crowned the Molo pillars with powerful communal symbols: Saint Theodore, their earliest protector when Venice was no more than a colony of beleaguered refugees, and a Winged Lion, the image of Mark the Evangelist, their patron saint, under whose banner they had now won an international empire.

Although she had recently been blessed with two of the greatest doges in her history, Sebastiano Ziani and Enrico Dandolo, the medieval Republic refused to permit the illustrious achievements of such men to be celebrated in the public space of San Marco.[32]

The Basilica Entrance Mosaics

The Winged Lion of Saint Mark crowning one of the Molo pillars did more than symbolize the Republic's far-reaching naval and commercial prowess. As the instantly recognizable emblem of Saint Mark as well as the first and most conspicuous work of art seen by travelers approaching the Molo from the Venetian harbor, it also served as a visual link to the iconography of the Basilica San Marco. After docking at the foot of the Molo pillars, medieval visitors enticed by the Basilica's splendidly enriched southern face would have crossed the Piazzetta to enter the church. There, they could either gain admittance through what was still the Basilica's primary entrance—a large, open, semicircular southern portal, the Porta da Mar or Sea Gate, which faced directly onto the Piazzetta[33]—or they could continue into the Piazza and enter through one of the portals of the elaborately embellished western façade. In either case, they would have been greeted by a carefully organized panorama of thirteenth-century mosaics illustrating the pivotal role God had assigned to Venice in the sweep of world history.

On the barrel vault immediately behind the great Sea Gate portal, visitors were confronted with a set of twelve mosaics depicting the life of Saint Mark. But unlike earlier Marcian cycles, the Porta da Mar series included a newly minted episode that we now refer to as the predestination legend (briefly described in the section titled "The Theft of Saint Mark" in Chapter Two). This late invention from the mythic imagination of medieval Venice recounts how during a missionary voyage across the lagoons of the upper Adriatic, the saint's boat was blown off course, leaving him stranded on the Venetian archipelago. At this point, an angel appears and tells Mark not to be alarmed; his predicament is only God's way of showing him where his body will one day be finally laid to rest. Long after his death, he will receive a spiritual reincarnation as the patron saint of Venice. The Porta da Mar mosaic cycle into which this predestination narrative was inserted ends with Mark's martyrdom and burial in Alexandria, events that occurred around A.D. 68. To see the fulfillment of the prophecy—that is, Mark's resurrection as the Republic's sacred protector—

thirteenth-century visitors had to walk around the corner of the church into the Piazza and stand in front of the lunettes installed over the Basilica's four lateral portals. The original mosaics in these entrance lunettes portrayed the Venetian theft of the saint's relics from the same Alexandrian tomb pictured on the barrel vault of the Sea Gate, their transport to the lagoon, and their reburial in the Basilica, actions that occurred in the year 828, seven and a half centuries after the legendary events of the predestination revelation.[34]

Having familiarized himself with the life of the Republic's divinely appointed New Testament guardian, a medieval traveler stepping into the vestibule of San Marco would have found himself surrounded by familiar pictures from pre-Christian Biblical history. Walking through the western narthex *(Fig. 18)*, he would have passed beneath low mosaic-clad vaults and domes filled with stories from the Book of Genesis ranging from the creation of the world and man *(Fig. 43)* through God's destruction of the human race except for Noah and his family. These images are among the best-known in the entire Old Testament, but a thirteenth-century visitor who had already absorbed the message of the Winged Lion atop the Molo pillar and the Marcian mosaics of the Sea Gate and western façade would not have missed one oft-repeated detail. In the narthex dome mosaics depicting God's creation of the beasts of the earth, the first animals to be formed are lions; when Adam is shown naming the animals, he first lays his hands on a pair of lions; and the first animals Noah takes into the ark and the first creatures to leave after the flood has ended are also lions. To a medieval Christian, who would have known that the lion was also the Old Testament symbol of the Jewish people, the message could not have been more clear. By the end of the thirteenth century, Venetians saw themselves as nothing less than another divinely chosen nation. By God's grace, they had been saved from the flood of barbarian destruction that swept away the Western Roman Empire while their fragile new society had been allowed to mature unmolested in its own watery fortress until it grew sufficiently powerful to inherit the Eastern Empire of Byzantium. Venetians had begun by imitating architectural models imported from a distant imperial mentor; as conquerors, they were now incorporating the very stones of Constantinople into their own state sanctuary.[35]

Yet the dominant tone of the narthex mosaics is not unrestrained triumphalism. For instance, if we look at the mosaics embodying the story of Noah located on the vaults to either side of the main entrance into the church interior, the images we encounter hardly suggest prideful conquest or naïve celebration. On the right-hand vault, Noah stands in the

Fig. 43: Genesis dome mosaics, western narthex, Basilica San Marco

window of the ark (which looks like a floating coffin) staring at a raven that is feasting on the corpse of a floating animal. Directly opposite is another mosaic of swirling flood waters filled with decomposing human bodies *(Fig. 44)*. On the left-hand vault, Noah is shown lying drunk and naked in his tent, an embodiment of gross sensuality *(Fig. 45)*. These vivid scenes of death and debauchery display a clear recognition of man's fallen state, of the inevitability of pain and loss as part of the human condition. They reveal that citizens of thirteenth-century Venice, chastened by the wisdom of the ancient Hebrew scriptures as well as Christian revelation, were capable of a dual vision. While they certainly saw themselves as imperial heirs and reveled in their newfound power and status, they also remembered the long, hard struggle that had brought them to this point. They saw themselves as a new, radically reborn society, whose recovery had been achieved against enormous odds.

Fig. 44: Mosaic of Genesis flood, western narthex,
Basilica San Marco

Fig. 45: Mosaic showing drunkenness of Noah,
western narthex, Basilica San Marco

Chapter Eight

A New Ducal Palace (1261-1348)

By the summer of 1261, Venetian builders were nearing completion of the magnificent, classically arcaded perimeter of the Piazza San Marco. A single elegant pattern, two upper-story, semicircular arches above each rounded, ground-floor arch, graced the building's façades on three sides of the long, rectangular courtyard. Like a superbly designed outdoor theater, the effect of this highly repetitive, tightly controlled enclosure was to focus attention on the Piazza's open eastern end, now dominated by the majestic western front of the Basilica San Marco. After a half century of labor, teams of highly skilled masons, sculptors, and mosaic artists had all but finished clothing the exterior in a gorgeous array of precious stone columns, mosaic tableaux, relief carving, exotic niches, and antique trophies. Within the next two decades, the entire plaza would be paved in herringbone brick. At its southeastern corner, the Piazza intersected with a smaller public square, the Piazzetta, whose north-south axis acted as a ceremonial forestage for visitors disembarking from the Venetian harbor. For grandeur and classical authenticity, the Piazza complex was unrivaled anywhere in medieval Europe and would not have a serious competitor for the next two hundred fifty years. Indeed, the Piazza San Marco was almost twice as long as the Forum of Trajan, the largest imperial square in ancient Rome, which, when it was built in the early second century, was considered one of the wonders of the classical world.[1]

Venetian Fortunes in the East

Venetians were fortunate that the Piazza project was approaching completion in 1261, because on July 25 of that year, a Byzantine general launched a successful surprise attack against the handful of Frankish knights still holding the old imperial capital of Constantinople. The Latin emperor Basil II saved himself by leaping aboard a Venetian ship just ahead of pursuing Greek soldiers. In that brief, inglorious instant, the Latin Empire of Constantinople ceased to exist, and with it vanished a number of critical advantages that Venice had enjoyed since the Crusader conquest of 1204. The Republic lost unfettered access to the most splendid store of classical sculpture and building material in the Mediterranean world, a vast treasure trove of architectural spoil that had been critical to the success of the medieval Piazza and Piazzetta building programs. She also lost the lucrative Eastern trading monopoly she had created for herself as the principal victor of the Fourth Crusade.[2]

When the Byzantine emperor Michael VIII Palæologus learned that one of his commanders had reconquered Constantinople, his first instinct was to expel the Venetians entirely. Accordingly, the Greeks torched the Republic's busy trading quarter, leaving thousands of frightened men, women, and children huddled on the shore of the Golden Horn until they were rescued by a Venetian relief fleet. The emperor then granted the city of Genoa, the Republic's chief rival for Eastern commercial supremacy, the same package of exclusive economic benefits that Venice had enjoyed for the past sixty years; in exchange, Genoa promised to help the Byzantines maintain their renewed hold on the empire. However, when the Genoese navy next encountered a Venetian war fleet off the coast of mainland Greece, the Genoese fled the battle after taking heavy casualties, and the Genoese merchants who flocked to Constantinople after the expulsion of the Republic were just as greedy and obnoxious as the Venetians had ever been. This led to a change in imperial strategy; rather than seek to impose a winner, the emperor decided to play the two implacable foes off against each other. Consequently, in 1268, the Venetians were once again admitted to the trading emporiums of the Greek Empire, but now they had to share those markets with the Genoese, whose Eastern commerce was rapidly expanding, particularly in Asia Minor and the Black Sea[3] (*see rear endpaper map*).

Venice and Genoa had been engaged in open warfare for Mediterranean naval supremacy since 1255. Although the population of Genoa totaled no more than half of the approximately 120,000 Venetians who made up the Republic, the Genoese were formidable adversaries—aggressive opportunists who had captured a large share of the trading profits created by the early Crusades. In the first stages of the struggle, Venice enjoyed clear naval superiority; she initiated most of the battles, and during periods of all-out belligerency where the two fleets tried to annihilate each other whenever they met, the result was usually a resounding Venetian triumph. However, between the end of the First Genoese War in 1270 and the next phase of open warfare, which began in 1295, Genoa took steps to fundamentally alter this strategic picture. It determined to improve Genoese naval prowess to the point that it could protect and even increase its greatly expanded trading hold on the Black Sea, where it had become the dominant commercial power. This vital trading preserve was also important to Venice, particularly after the fall of the Crusader city of Acre to the Sultan of Egypt in 1291. Acre had been a critical hub for transshipment to Europe of luxury goods the Republic imported from Central Asia by camel caravan. Venice needed a replacement port to carry on this immensely profitable business, and a major new Venetian outlet on the Black Sea would serve her purposes admirably. All that stood in the way was the Genoese navy, a force that had never been a serious impediment to past Venetian designs.[4]

Thus, when the Second Genoese War commenced, it no doubt came as a profound shock to the Republic's supremely confident seamen when they suffered a series of rapid defeats at the hands of a vastly improved Genoese navy. In one early contest, Venice lost twenty-five of her sixty-eight galleys, while in another, the Genoese totally annihilated the Republic's annual trading caravan. In the first major battle of the war, a huge naval engagement at Curzola pitting ninety-five Venetian vessels against a Genoese fleet of eighty, Venice lost almost seventy percent of her ships and suffered fourteen thousand men killed, wounded, or captured. But these grievous wounds to Venetian pride, men, and matériel did little to resolve the issue of who would dominate the Eastern Mediterranean and the Black Sea. After four years of all-out war, the economies of both states were so devastated that by 1299, both were anxious to pursue peace negotiations. Like Venice in the First War, Genoa was discovering how inconclusive and prohibitively expensive even an unbroken string of naval victories could be. In a war between rough equals, final victory required the winner to batter its opponent so badly that the losing side could never recover, and when the enemy in question was Venice, with her almost limitless powers of recuperation, this could seem like a hopeless quest. Moreover, it was a goal that became even more daunting in the early decades of the next century when the Venetian state quadrupled the size of the Arsenale shipyard (*Fig. 46*).[5]

The Venetian Political Constitution

Although by the end of the thirteenth century Genoa had achieved naval parity with Venice, the Republic still enjoyed one critical advantage over her ambitious rival. Unlike Venice, Genoa was continually riven by violent conflicts between the city's intensely

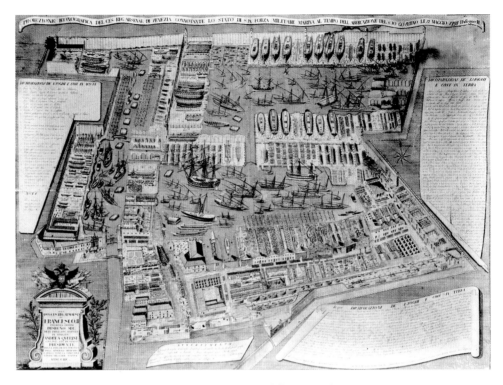

Fig. 46: Engraving of the Arsenale

partisan Guelf and Ghibelline factions. As a result, fourteenth-century Genoese politics was a bitter, winner-take-all struggle in which members of both camps knew that if they lost a critical military contest against the other party, they faced the prospect of immediate exile and loss of property if not summary execution. Worse still, once the habit of obliterating political opponents took root in a city, even a decisive win by one of the warring factions might not bring peace. Thus, in Florence in 1293, when the Guelf party (supporters of the pope) completely routed the Ghibelline faction (champions of the German emperor), the Guelfs themselves immediately split into two bitter factions, with the ultra-papal Guelf Blacks then defeating and banishing the more moderate Whites. One of the exiled Whites was Dante Alighieri (1265–1321), author of the *Divine Comedy*, the greatest literary work of the Middle Ages. In a show trial held while Dante was fortunately absent from the city, the poet was banished, his property confiscated, and he was condemned to be burned at the stake if he ever returned to Florence. Embittered exiles from cities such as Florence and Genoa were known as *fuorusciti*, that is, men driven beyond the protective embrace of their native walls. Believing that the only way to regain their homes was by promoting schemes of domestic treason and foreign military invasion, many fuorusciti devoted their lives to such conspiracies.[6]

Eventually there was a reaction against the chaos and carnage produced by such unceasing internal conflict, and people in the mainland cities began to prize peace and stability over all other political values. In almost every case, the means for achieving this end involved replacing the city's volatile communal government with a military dictatorship. During the thirteenth century, one after another of the nascent communes of northern Italy became transformed into a vigorous local tyranny, so that when the Republic of Venice looked west in 1300, what she saw was a series of entrenched family despotisms—the Visconti in Milan, the Scaligeri in Verona, the Carrara in Padua, the Este in Ferrara, and the Gonzaga in Mantua. Very quickly, these so-called *signori*, the uncontested lords of their domains, began to ape the manners of feudal monarchs in France, Germany, England, and Spain, where dynastic marriage and aggressive military campaigning were used to advance one's position in the ever-shifting board game of European politics.[7]

This entire system of government was anathema to medieval Venice, ensuring that when she had to transform her own existing communal arrangements to meet new political realities, she would move in a completely different direction. The core Venetian problem was that the conquest of Byzantium had created a large new class of wealthy merchant families which, from 1250 to 1300, contributed over half of the men elected to the Great Council, and this naturally created a good deal of friction with the old merchant nobility. In addition to the inevitable resentment an existing aristocracy typically feels for energetic newcomers, the policy views of the Venetian arrivistes were often quite different from those of the *case vecchie* or old families. In general, the new men supported concentrating as much power as possible in an oligarchy of wealthy nobles and favored an expansionist foreign policy, including the acquisition of Venetian territory on the Italian mainland. The established families were inclined to be more cautious about the danger and expense of mainland expansion, and some members of the old elite at least talked as if they wished to retain some political role for the populace at large. Over and above these ideological divisions, each wealthy merchant clan, whether old or new, had a large stake in ensuring that its individual family interests were adequately represented in the councils of the Republic.[8]

Membership in the Great Council, the central body in the city's early medieval constitutional arrangements, remained the indispensable stepping stone to participation in Venetian political life. The Council appointed virtually every public official in the state, and during the thirteenth century, it displaced the general assembly of the people as the Republic's fundamental legislative body. In certain cases, it chose to delegate some of its legislative power to two smaller bodies, the *Quarantia* or Court of Forty, which also served as a judicial court of appeals, and the *Pregadi* or Senate, which, over time, assumed primary responsibility for certain core matters such as commerce, navigation, foreign affairs, and national defense. Before 1297, members of the Great Council were restricted to one-year terms, and in spite of the large increase in the number of merchant families eligible for Council membership after 1204, the size of the Great Council actually decreased from 480 members in 1172 to no more than four hundred members in 1296. This unnatural compression despite an expanding base of eligible candidates and the frequent personal and policy conflicts between the city's wealthy new families and the old aristocracy gave rise to fears that Venetian politics might begin to display the same winner-take-all ferocity that had destroyed communal government in the mainland cities. Because members of each year's expiring Council chose the electors who would determine the makeup of next year's assembly, it was at least theoretically possible for a tightly organized faction to reelect itself in perpetuity. If this happened, those barred from membership might be forced to choose between virtual political exile and adopting extralegal measures to regain a place in the city's public life, including resort to outright violence.[9]

Understanding the problem she faced, Venice—unlike other Italian cities—determined to solve it by broadening, not shrinking, the membership of her communal governing class. In 1297, the Republic decided to amend its system so that virtually every male over twenty-five from an existing wealthy, influential family would be assured of an entry-level position at the bottom of the governmental pyramid. And she was prepared to implement this decision even if it meant, over time, more than quintupling the size of the Great Council. The actual method for carrying out this momentous reform was to have the Quarantia vote to confirm or reject each individual who had been a member of the Great Council during the preceding four years. Anyone who received at least twelve affirmative votes out of a possible forty—that is, ratification by a mere thirty percent—would receive a permanent seat in succeeding Councils. Although other Venetians could still be admitted to the Great Council if they were nominated by a special commission and confirmed by three-quarters of the Quarantia, in practice, this set of new confirmation procedures, known as the *Serrata*, created a closed caste of hereditary nobles (the patriciate). Such men would henceforth make Venetian politics one of their principal, if not exclusive, occupations. By eliminating all restrictions on the size of the Great Council, these amendments ended the potential exclusionary crisis that had threatened patrician solidarity; Great Council membership, which had been no more than four hundred in 1296, quickly rose to approximately eleven hundred in 1300.[10]

However, even after this radical enlargement of the Great Council, the Republic hardly constituted a democracy; the eleven hundred members of the Council, drawn from approximately two hundred families, constituted approximately one percent of the Venetian population. Compared to medieval Florence, where approximately six thousand men out of an estimated population of eighty-five thousand (that is, roughly seven percent of the populace) were eligible to hold public office and vote in political affairs, the Venetian political class appears relatively narrow. But statistics alone can be misleading. Thus, fifteenth-century Florentine history is a classic illustration of how a single family, the Medici, could completely undermine the reality of widely shared power while, at the same time, keeping the forms and institutions of communal government nominally intact. By periodically introducing seemingly minor, allegedly temporary exceptions to established constitutional procedures, this wealthy, ambitious clan gradually eroded the independence of the Florentine republic and prepared the way for a full-blown Medici dictatorship in the sixteenth century.[11]

In contrast, medieval Venice was serious—to the point of obsession—about doing everything she could to maintain as much political equality as possible among the one percent of her citizens who were members of the Great Council. Established constitutional safeguards were generally treated as sacrosanct, and nothing was left to chance. If it seemed likely that some fresh restriction could be of the slightest benefit in preventing the onset of violent factional politics or its attendant evil, the capture of the state by a military strongman, it was usually adopted, and even more important, it was strictly enforced. For instance, the Republic established a rule that no more than one member of any particular family could be represented on the Signoria (the six-man council of ducal advisers plus the doge and the three chiefs of the Quarantia) at any one time. Candidates for elective office were nominated by committees whose makeup was determined purely by chance through the drawing of names from an urn, and family members were not allowed to vote after a relative had been nominated. Elections were conducted almost immediately after nominations were closed so that campaigning by the selected candidates, which was banned in any case, would also be a practical impossibility. Men elected to a minor, unpaid position who refused to serve were fined and declared ineligible to hold more desirable offices. The cumulative effect of these techniques was to undercut the strength of party and family affiliation and to promote the random rotation of posts among a wide spectrum of the governing patriciate.[12]

The lengths to which the medieval Republic was prepared to go to eliminate every conceivable chance that dynastic or partisan politics would play a decisive role in her elections is perhaps best illustrated by the fantastic procedures Venetians adopted for choosing their highest public official, the doge:

- First, thirty members of the Great Council were chosen by lot;
- These thirty members were then reduced by lot to an initial nominating committee of nine;
- This first nominating committee chose another forty members of the Great Council;
- These forty members, when reduced by lot to twelve, became a second nominating committee that chose another twenty-five members of the Great Council;
- These twenty-five members, when reduced by lot to nine, became a third nominating committee that chose another forty-five members of the Great Council;
- These forty-five members, when reduced by lot to eleven, became a fourth nominating committee that chose another forty-one members of the Great Council to be the actual electoral college; and
- This electoral college was locked in a special room under armed guard, where it kept voting until a successful ducal candidate won twenty-five of its possible forty-one votes.[13]

The goal of promoting equality among members of the governing patriciate was also at work in the commercial sphere. Before the fourteenth century, Venetian overseas trade had largely been the province of individual entrepreneurs, freewheeling adventurers who were willing to take great risks for the sake of maximum personal gain. But after 1300, the Venetian state, controlled by an oligarchy that increasingly feared concentrated power in any form, began to view unfettered private enterprise, with its potential to create major financial winners and losers, as an unacceptable risk to social cohesion and political stability. To try to level the economic playing field, it quadrupled the size of the state shipbuilding facilities at the Arsenale (*Fig. 46*) and constructed a huge new public fleet of merchant galleys. It then organized a government monopoly of the most profitable trading routes to the Greek East, Cyprus, Syria, Egypt, and Western Europe. State convoys, sometimes consisting of as many as five hundred ships, departed the lagoon on precisely appointed dates and adhered to publicly announced sailing routes, all established by the Venetian Senate. Cargo space on state-owned galleys was auctioned to the highest bidders, and any private ship wishing to join a public convoy was forced to obey the same rules that governed the rest of the fleet. The government also established investment quotas restricting the amount of international trade an individual merchant could take part in, all based on a formula tied to the size of a man's officially declared wealth (i.e., the sum on which he could be forced to purchase state debt if the government wished to borrow money). Although this disqualified some would-be merchants whose property values fell below the required minimum, those who met the eligibility threshold could invest in foreign trade without being required to have the individual skill and major financial resources necessary to organize the voyage themselves.[14]

This ambitious program of state-run capitalism made medieval Venice the recognized European center for fast, efficient, scrupulously honest commercial transactions. Every trading day, Venetian bankers sat in their stalls under the portico of the church of San Giacomo in the Rialto market, recording complex debit and credit entries in the account books they maintained for their clientele of international merchants. Of course, the rapid accumulation of wealth registered in such ledgers was made considerably easier by the fact that income and ad valorem property taxation were prohibited by law. Even after the state budget was forced to absorb the costs of building a huge new Arsenale manned by sixteen thousand workers and an expanded civil service of government attorneys and accountants, fourteenth-century Venetian taxes were still restricted to a direct levy on everyday necessities such as food, salt, and wine, and the rich paid the same rate as the poor. When these funding sources were not sufficient, state expenditures were financed by compulsory loans imposed on all Venetians with property valued at three hundred ducats or more. But this was hardly a burden on the swelling bank accounts of prosperous Venetian merchants, since in return for the loans it extracted, the government issued bonds paying between twelve and twenty percent annually.[15]

This Venetian system of state-managed enterprise achieved its goal of ensuring widespread prosperity among members of the governing patriciate. Records show that in the fourteenth century, approximately one-eighth of all heads of household were classified as sufficiently rich to be obligated to buy the state's debt. In 1379, there were 2,128 such well-to-do heads of household, of which 1,211, or fifty-seven percent, were members of the patriciate (in fact, these 1,211 monied members of the merchant nobility must have amounted to virtually the entire patriciate), while the remaining forty-three percent were well-off commoners. Among such affluent heads of household, there were 117 truly wealthy men worth between ten thousand and one hundred fifty thousand ducats, of which ninety-one were members of the merchant nobility. Thus, within the governing class, even the accumulation of great wealth was spread over ninety-one individuals, and there were an additional 817 reasonably wealthy nobles with assets between three hundred and three thousand ducats.[16]

Creation of the Council of Ten

But even the most diligent efforts to promote economic equality and political harmony within a broad governing class are rarely proof against pure human folly. So it was that in 1310, a combination of ducal obstinacy and violent factional hatred resulted in an armed conspiracy by several of the city's oldest and most venerable aristocratic families to abolish the Venetian constitution and replace it with a narrow despotism. This blatant act of treason called for seizing the ducal palace, murdering Doge Pietro Gradenigo, and handing the reins of power over to a feckless adventurer from a distinguished Venetian family, one Bajamonte Tiepolo, who planned to establish himself as the lord of Venice. The precipitating event was a disastrous decision by Doge Gradenigo, representing the city's wealthy new families, to take the city to war with Pope Clement V over the issue of who would control the city of Ferrara. Clement reacted by excommunicating the Republic, an action that immediately terminated her commerce with the rest of Christendom and led to the seizure of Venetian property throughout Europe and much of Asia. When the Venetian garrison in Ferrara was stormed and overrun, the doge continued to defy the papal interdict even after the pope proposed a reasonable settlement offer. When political opponents from the old families accurately accused Doge Gradenigo of exercising his office in violation of Venetian law, the doge simply ignored such criticism, and when ordinary Venetians took to the streets to resist his stiff-necked intransigence, he suppressed public protest. It was in this lethal political environment, already close to the brink of open civil war, that the conspiracy was formed.[17]

Thanks to informants, Doge Gradenigo knew about the plot well in advance, and the assault on the ducal palace turned out to be a ludicrous failure; however, this brush with treason at the very heart of the city's governing elite made a deep and lasting impression on the leaders of the Republic. It led them to think carefully about how to deal with future threats, and from these deliberations emerged a remarkable addition to the Venetian constitutional fabric. Although known as the Council of Ten, its title is a misnomer. By design, this new body never functioned as a council of only ten members; it always met in conjunction with the doge and his six councilors, bringing its assembled strength to seventeen. It exercised two critical roles. Because it was small and capable of assembling quickly, it allowed the doge and his councilors to consult with a select body of seasoned officials whenever the need for rapid decision making or confidential deliberation argued against waiting for larger, less secure public bodies to convene. When functioning in this emergency mode, decisions by the seventeen men who comprised the Council of Ten had the same legitimacy as decrees by the Great Council itself. The Council of Ten was also given responsibility for ensuring the long-term safety of the Venetian state. To this end, it established an excellent intelligence service to track down the conspirators of 1310 who escaped immediate punishment and through assassination or other means, to eliminate such threats. Unlike the many embittered political refugees of Genoa, no disgruntled band of Venetian exiles, plotting its bloody return from a foreign port, ever became a serious problem.[18]

Looked at in isolation, the Council of Ten appears to have been granted extraordinary powers, yet it is important to understand that at the beginning of the fourteenth century, the Ten (just like every other public body in the Republic) was still very much a creature of the Great Council. It was the Great Council that determined the Ten's membership and closely monitored the exercise of its delegated authority, just as it did with the Quarantia and the Senate, those two other thirteenth-century offshoots of original Great Council jurisdiction. Primary legislative authority still belonged to the Great Council, and the principal role of the Quarantia (apart from its judicial function) was to prepare financial legislation for Great Council consideration. It is true that by the middle of the fourteenth century, the Great Council had voluntarily relinquished a substantial share of its legislative function to the Senate, an elite inner council of sixty members elected by the Great Council. However, many, if not most, critical political debates still took place in the larger body, and firm opposition to a particular matter by a Great Council majority was decisive, regardless of what might be said during Senate deliberations. If matters seemed to be getting out of hand, the Great Council could always, whenever it chose, dilute the power of the Senate by supplementing its ranks with a specially appointed commission, or if need be, transfer jurisdiction over a particular matter back to itself or another council.[19]

The Ducal Palace

At the opening of the fourteenth century, this intricate network of councils and commissions was housed in the Ziani ducal palace constructed at the end of the twelfth century. An elegant, symmetrical building, it consisted of two main wings, one facing south toward the harbor and another opening west onto the Piazzetta. Both were modeled on Late Antique Roman villa and palace architecture: an upper loggia set on top of a ground-floor portico, with each level composed of round, high-stilted arches springing from delicate marble columns. Each wing was flanked by tall corner towers and crowned with ornamental crenellation, and portions of the façades may well have been decorated with colored marble.[20]

However, after a century of use, the Ziani communal palace had begun to display a number of troubling deficiencies. Chief among these was the totally inadequate size of the Great Council chamber, a room occupying part of the upper story of the building's harbor wing. Built to hold a membership of 480, during the first four decades after the reforms of 1297, the Council hall had been forced to accommodate an expanded patriciate numbering between a thousand and twelve hundred. There were also serious problems of security and hygiene. The ground-floor entrance to the chamber was in the middle of a public way, a portion of which was often used for public gambling. Worse still, the hall sat immediately above the state prisons, some of which were so unsanitary that they could not be used during the summer months.[21]

Not surprisingly, from 1297 forward, there were intense discussions in the highest councils of state about the best way to remedy such glaring defects, with some arguing for a relatively inexpensive renovation and others proposing a major reconstruction or even a wholesale replacement of the existing palace. According to Ruskin, in 1301 the government arrived at a relatively rapid decision to build a new Great Council chamber along the eastern wing of the palace next to the Rio di Palazzo; however, according to more recent scholarship, no such consensus was ever reached, and inconclusive debate about the best way to proceed continued for more than four decades. In this latter view, it was not until December 28, 1340, that the Great Council finally took definitive action, electing to build an entirely new harbor wing on the site of the old palace, notwithstanding the enormous cost and physical disruption this would necessarily entail.[22] According to numerous early chronicles, including some that date from the early 1400s, the Council appointed Filippo Calendario, a local stonecutter, building contractor, and commercial stone dealer, to serve as project architect. Based on the testimony of these original sources, the Venetian government thought very highly of Calendario's architectural and sculptural skills and did not hesitate to name him to this important position.[23]

If the early chronicles are correct (as I believe they are), Calendario repaid the state's confidence with an ingeniously simple solution. To remedy the size problem, he proposed building a huge new two-story Council chamber capable of holding more than two thousand patricians; the new hall and its anteroom would be so large that their combined width would occupy the entire existing harbor front between the Piazzetta and the Rio di Palazzo. Then, to resolve any security concerns while at the same time avoiding the need to completely dismantle the existing Ziani palace before construction could begin, Calendario made a truly radical proposal. He recommended building this enormous meeting hall not from the ground floor up, but on top of the existing two-story ducal palace. This would leave the general populace free to come and go at will on the ground floor and second story while the Venetian patriciate enjoyed an entirely secure, enclosed assembly space raised well above such public areas. Calendario's Ducal Palace,[24] while only moderately wider than the harbor wing of the old palace, would be virtually twice as tall, making it appear massively larger when viewed from the Venetian harbor (*Fig. 47*). In Calendario's plan, the rounded arcades of the existing Ziani ground floor and second story would be replaced with Gothic arches and tracery, but the new building would retain the classical symmetry of the original façade. The Piazzetta wing, the interior courtyard, the entrance portals, and the eastern and northern precincts of the existing palace complex would be left largely intact.[25]

It was a brilliant conception, and as it took shape, Venetians would be impressed at the ease with which a huge forty-foot upper story was levitated above delicate trefoil Gothic arches without apparent strain or incongruity. Above all, they would marvel at the project's masterful synthesis of three great architectural traditions: Late Classical, French Gothic, and Islamic. It was this rare, protean ability to achieve a harmonious merger of apparent opposites that caused Ruskin to describe the completed Ducal Palace as "the central building of the world...the great and sudden invention of one man, instantly forming a national style, and becoming the model for the imitation of every architect in Venice for upwards of a century."[26]

The Building Process

In the summer of 1341, as Venetian patricians hurried to state councils in their robes of office, they would have been forced to pick their way through dusty piles of stone and brick, part of a large, busy construction site ranged around the Ziani palace. Beneath heavy wooden ladders and scaffolds which all but hid the palace façade, hundreds of artisans would have bustled about in their skullcaps, tunics and leather boots. The most numerous class of workers would have been the *taiapiera* or stonecutters who worked on site splitting and carving blocks of dense white stone imported from Istrian quarries at the head of the Adriatic. Somewhere in this maze of activity, there would have been an enclosed lodge where the architect and chief sculptor, Filippo Calendario, carved the large sculptural groups he had designed for the corners of the new Palace, as well as many of the superb capitals that would crown the muscular columns of the building's ground-floor portico. As master architect, it would also have been Calendario's job to draw an exact, life-size profile of each standard architectural element in the project, like the myriad units making up the fine stone tracery he designed for the second-story loggia (*Fig. 48*). Then

Fig. 47: Harbor face of Filippo Calendario's Ducal Palace

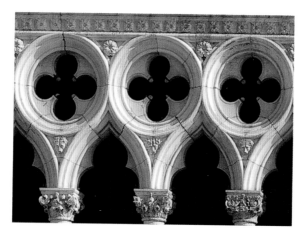

Fig. 48: Fine stone tracery, Ducal Palace
second-story loggia

someone using Calendario's outlines (possibly drawn on paper or parchment) would have created a wooden or metal template of each separate stone unit, and these durable forms (which were to be followed precisely) would have been handed out to journeymen stone-cutters sitting at open-air benches.[27]

This building site, one of the largest the city had ever seen, would also have been teeming with bricklayers, carpenters, and unskilled day laborers whose construction materials were manufactured in mainland brick factories and Dalmatian timber yards. Supplies of brick, wood, and stone were delivered to the Molo harbor landing by shallow-draft barges, including, no doubt, the fleet of such vessels owned by Filippo Calendario. Wheelbarrows were then used to transport small loads of lumber and brick from the water's edge to the front of the palace, where they were hoisted by block and tackle to the top of the scaffolding. Simple wooden barracks had been constructed around the borders of the construction site. These rude huts served the daytime needs of native workers but were round-the-clock sleeping and eating quarters for foreign artisans, including many highly skilled stonecutters drawn to Venice for the duration of the massive project. In addition to Calendario's overall responsibility for project design and sculptural decoration, the state may have also employed another highly experienced professional to act as an onsite construction manager.[28]

Ultimately, a major public building effort like the Ducal Palace, which was supported by the full resources of the Venetian state but not controlled by a specific communal body like the Procuracy of Saint Mark, was managed by the upper echelons of the Venetian government. This meant that overall project governance at any time tended to mirror the Republic's then prevailing political arrangements. Thus, the initial decision to appropriate ten thousand ducats to build a new Council chamber was made by the Great Council itself, but over the course of the fourteenth century, oversight of this complex undertaking tended to pass to the smaller and more cohesive Senate. However, at any point, if a particular project question were felt to be sufficiently important, its final resolution could be referred back to the Great Council. Such regular movement within the concentric circles of the Venetian government rarely caused major shifts in either foreign policy or architectural direction because many of the same influential patricians, drawn from the same prominent families, tended to rotate sequentially through all the important leadership posts within key political bodies. At its best, this intricate interconnectedness of the Venetian constitutional system ensured that political and architectural decisions alike were rarely made without being examined from a variety of perspectives and only after drawing on the judgment and taste of a large number of knowledgeable public officials.[29]

This was important because it helped late medieval Venice hold fast to a model of communal art and architecture that was rapidly disappearing in the rest of Italy. Elsewhere, rule by a single family—the lords of the city—had largely displaced communal arrangements as both the dominant form of government and the principal source of patronage for major architectural projects. Not surprisingly, these new signorial building programs were more narrow and egotistical in conception as well as more prone to ruthlessly destroy existing monuments capable of reminding the citizenry of a predecessor regime or an earlier communal period. From the fourteenth century on, Venice was almost unique in her ability to maintain and refine both her original communal form of government and the communal art and architectural traditions which it inspired. Within the Republic, public bodies commanding the accumulated wealth of the state continued to employ and direct the finest talents available, channeling their collective artistic genius into projects such as the Ducal Palace that embodied historic symbols of the entire nation.[30]

At the commencement of the project in 1341, it was estimated that the construction of an enlarged Great Council meeting hall would take approximately eight years. The first step was to extend the foundations for the new harbor wing past the corner towers of the Ziani palace. Then, the two existing stories of the harbor façade were braced with heavy timbers as temporary support for the massive new Council chamber (forty feet high, ninety feet deep, and 230 feet long) to be constructed directly above. Below, workers moving in incremental stages from right to left slowly demolished the rounded arches of the existing Ziani portico and loggia. However, even as they dismantled these elegant, classically derived structures, Venetians felt compelled to retain their two-to-one, upper-story to ground-floor symmetry. When completed, the new harbor front would present thirty-four loggia arches (of an extremely light and graceful Gothic design featuring trefoil arches rising between columns crowned with quatrefoil occuli) above seventeen heavy Gothic portico arches, flanked by another twelve identical loggia arches over six portico arches on the western side of the building facing the Piazzetta. These Gothic replacement elements were carved in gleaming white Istrian stone, and in the tradition of classical Greek and Roman architecture, the stonecutting was precisely uniform. Building components were so standardized and regular (*Fig. 49*) that they were interchangeable from bay to bay, an unusual accomplishment in a medieval building.[31]

Fig. 49: Precisely standardized building parts,
Ducal Palace portico and loggia

In early 1348, seven years into the project, most of the structural fabric of the new Great Council chamber (not including any finishing detail or interior and exterior decoration) had been completed, and roofing was about to begin. As to the rate of progress in dismantling and reconstructing the Ziani loggia and portico below the magnificent new hall, there is considerable scholarly debate. One prominent authority has concluded that the bulk of the work involved in carving and installing the Gothic arches and tracery on the lower half of the building was completed as early as 1344, but the weight of informed opinion holds that this part of the project was not finished until 1355 at the earliest, and perhaps not until the end of the century. Prior to that time, the freshly built Great Council chamber remained perched on wooden scaffolding left in place to reinforce the surviving remnants of the Ziani palace. As events unfolded, however, nothing that happened before 1348 would have any effect on the project's final completion date. The Republic, like virtually every other state in Europe, was about to be struck by one of the deadliest disasters in Western history, a biomedical catastrophe that would kill two out of every three Venetians, including an estimated quarter of the city's governing patriciate. Venice, at the height of her prosperity and supreme self-confidence, was about to suffer the equivalent of a nuclear holocaust.[32]

CHAPTER NINE

By the Skin of Her Teeth (1348–1423)

The Black Death

The devastation that struck Venice in 1348 was the indirect result of global climate change. Climate scientists now refer to the years 950 to 1250 as the Medieval Warm Period, a time span in which average temperatures rose by about two degrees Fahrenheit. In Europe, this led to longer growing seasons, plentiful food harvests, and a consequent doubling of population, the economic foundations for the cultural blossoming of the High Middle Ages that produced the magnificent Gothic cathedrals of northern Europe and the proto-Renaissance splendor of the Piazza San Marco. However, around 1300, as part of the Earth's natural climate cycle, temperatures began to fall, and the Medieval Warm Period was replaced by a period of markedly cooler weather now known as the Little Ice Age, which lasted for five centuries. As a result, European crops began to fail, and many peasants starved. In Asia, this major temperature shift was also accompanied by a number of violent atmospheric and seismic events—storms, floods, droughts, and earthquakes—that, among many other effects, caused a variety of rodents to migrate out of their highland burrows toward lower rural settlements and into more prolonged contact with humans. Among these displaced rodents were swarms of common black rats, and embedded in the fur of some of these rats was a flea carrying the bacterium *Yersinia pestis*, the source of bubonic plague, commonly referred to as the Black Death.[1]

The plague first took hold in central Asia, then spread west until it reached the Black Sea and ships owned by merchants from the bustling city-state of Genoa, which, for the preceding half century, had assumed the dominant commercial role in that region once played by Venice. When these Genoese vessels eventually arrived in Sicilian ports, the rats, carrying their tiny, lethal infestation, boarded other merchant ships, some of which, in early 1348, brought the disease to the Venetian lagoon. Meanwhile, from Sicily, the epidemic quickly spread to virtually every other Mediterranean port, almost all of which were also engaged in extensive trade with the Republic, so that within a short time every vessel that docked in Venetian waters was likely to be carrier. In a cruel reversal of fate, the city's unique lagoon environment, the very basis of her outstanding wealth, power, and security, now rendered her particularly vulnerable to this devastating new threat. Formed, as she was, by the consolidation of 117 partially submerged islands, her entire land surface was permeated by wharfs and piers that acted as ideal receiving platforms for the ship-borne rats. Once a vessel dropped anchor, the infected animals quickly scuttled down docking cables and moved inland in search of food. There they foraged through shops and houses, where the fleas embedded in their fur found warm human bodies to inhabit and bite. As a result, the contagion invaded virtually every Venetian neighborhood, pushing the city's death rate to a level almost twice that experienced in most of mainland Europe, where isolated, thinly settled villages were much more likely to escape the plague's worst effects. Over the next two years, the disease killed approximately sixty to seventy thousand Venetians out of a population of slightly over a hundred thousand; during the months of its greatest savagery, May through July of 1348, it produced an average of six hundred fresh corpses each day.[2]

Plague symptoms were extremely gruesome, so that in addition to excruciating physical agony, victims felt an intense self-loathing. According to a contemporary Venetian chronicle, an afflicted person watched helplessly as "glandular swellings...or poison-filled carbuncles" suddenly erupted across his body, particularly in the groin and armpits. These dark, egg-size pustules, called buboes (from which the plague took its name), exuded copious flows of blood and pus at the same time that the sufferer experienced acute headache, "unbearable burning fever," loss of motor control, and "unquenchable thirst." After three to five days of unrelenting pain, terror, and disgust, during which the victim's breath, perspiration, and blood gave off a loathsomely offensive smell, his internal organs generally failed, and he expired. Throughout the ordeal, the sufferer would have had no comprehension of what was causing his appalling condition—all he would know was that in the course of a day or less, his body had been transformed into a mass of decomposing flesh. The first Venetian cases were seen in March 1348, and by May, the pestilence "had burst all bounds, and the contagion raged, so that the [city's] fields, piazzas, tombs and all the graveyards were full of cadavers." Death was so plentiful that many corpses were simply "left to rot in their houses.... [and] the whole city was one great tomb."[3]

The disease attacked a Venetian populace swollen with mainland refugees from the famine of 1347. Carried in the stomach of the flea as well as in the bloodstream of the rat, the plague bacillus was injected into a victim as the result of his being bitten by either creature. Given the state of medieval medical knowledge, attempts to prevent the contagion or remedy its symptoms were completely useless. The hideous buboes seemed to appear on anyone who dared to have contact with a victim or even to touch an object that the sufferer might have used. According to one physician, it seemed as if a single contaminated person was capable of infecting the entire world. When asked to account for the mass mortality that had suddenly gripped all Europe, learned doctors opined that the devastation resulted from an unfortunate astrological conjunction which put Saturn in the House of Jupiter, causing evil vapors to corrupt the air. In an attempt to at least do something, the Venetian Great Council appointed a special plague commission, whose first priority was the construction of municipal burial ditches to handle the rapid accumulation of decomposing corpses. As soon as these "very wide and deep pits" were completed, bodies were tossed into them "in heaps," including some victims "who still drew breath;"[4] however, the speed of the pandemic left even these large new trenches filled to overflowing within a short time.[5]

Like the refugees of Giovanni Boccaccio's *Decameron* who left plague-ridden Florence for the Tuscan countryside,[6] many well-off Venetians abandoned their contaminated city for the relative safety of the mainland. In the rush to avoid what seemed like certain death, "fathers, sons, brothers, neighbors and friends deserted each other," and even "doctors not only visited no one, but [actually] fled from the sick" since "their arts were of no value, their herbs being useless."[7] Those left in the city, who suffered the highest death rates, tended to be younger, poorer, and female; pregnant women and newborn infants who were unable to leave almost invariably died. The general exodus of affluent Venetians included a number of governing patricians, whose ranks had been particularly hard hit in the opening weeks of the plague. As a result of this subsequent migration, the final mortality rate among the all-male patriciate seems to have been less than half of that experienced by the Venetian populace as a whole. An estimated twenty-five percent of the Great

Council membership died from the disease, compared to an almost inconceivable sixty to seventy percent of the population at large.[8]

What is impressive is that in such appalling circumstances there were a fair number of governing patricians who refused to abandon the city and died faithfully performing their official duties. However, at one point, so many nobles had died of the disease or fled to the mainland that several councils could not assemble for lack of members, and those who remained decided to delegate an increasing share of emergency authority to the Senate. Made responsible for combatting the plague's physical and psychological terrors as well as trying to salvage the Venetian economy, on the whole, this small, elite body seems to have performed quite well. Eschewing self-interest and class bias, it cut or eliminated patrician salaries, penalized nobles who abandoned their posts, and in an effort to repopulate the city, offered special immunities and tax concessions to new immigrants. Not surprisingly, given the fiscal nightmare that the state was facing in the summer of 1348, the Senate also temporarily suspended work on the Ducal Palace. Nineteen months later, in February 1350, a motion was made in the Great Council to cancel the project altogether on the grounds that its fundamental purpose had been to provide an enlarged Great Council assembly hall, a need which no longer existed given the large number of patricians who had already died in the plague. Supporters of the motion pointed out that many skilled craftsmen had also perished, inflating construction labor costs as much as fifty percent. However, in spite of such arguments, a majority of the Great Council voted to appropriate another large sum to complete the project.[9]

A few months later, in the summer of 1350, the plague finally began to release its death grip on the city. However, the disease's lingering effects continued to depress Venetian wealth, power, and population for some time to come, and the following three decades would prove to be one of the most hazardous periods in Venetian history. Because the contagion had killed so many skilled mariners, the city's critical naval strength was particularly slow in recovering; in the meantime, she was forced to fill her crews with mercenaries from Dalmatia and the eastern Mediterranean. This vulnerability would lead a host of foreign and domestic enemies to test Venetian social and political cohesion to the limit, and on one occasion, to almost extinguish her unique republican institutions. Almost as soon as the plague began to lift, Venice became embroiled in a third major war with Genoa for control of the Aegean and Black seas, a conflict in which Genoese admirals inflicted at least two major defeats on Venetian war fleets. The first came in 1352 at the Battle of the Bosporus, a frenzied struggle fought below the walls of Constantinople in a blinding winter snowstorm; as the struggle raged into the night, few prisoners were taken on either side, and the mutual slaughter intensified until Venetian ships withdrew from the conflict. A year later, the Genoese annihilated a large Venetian armada at Porto Longo on the southern coast of Greece; catching the Venetians unprepared, the Genoese captured the Republic's entire fleet of fifty-six ships and butchered 450 Venetian prisoners. Until combat was finally halted in 1355, Venetian and Genoese commerce in the eastern Mediterranean remained almost completely shut down, with both sides absorbing immense trading losses. The ensuing peace treaty left all the fundamental issues unresolved.[10]

Filippo Calendario

By 1355, Filippo Calendario had given ample demonstration of the Republic's wisdom in appointing him to be the architect of the Ducal Palace project. His design, a brilliantly conceived merger of Late Classical, French Gothic, and Islamic building traditions, had taken a sufficiently powerful hold on the Venetian imagination to be able to withstand the traumatic interruption of the plague years and a brutal war with Genoa. Calendario had also displayed his remarkable genius as a sculptor. It was his novel idea to erect groups of near life-size figures representing stories from the Old Testament, *The Drunkenness of Noah* (*Fig. 50*) and *The Fall of Man* (*Fig. 51*), at the lower corners of the Palace. Placing large-scale sculpted images in such prominent, eye-level locations on the corners (as opposed to the entranceways) of a monumental public building was a new concept that (except for the remounted Tetrarchs on the corner of the San Marco treasury) no Greek, Roman, or earlier medieval sculptor had attempted. Calendario also used an innovative storytelling device in both compositions, an idea he may have adapted from frescoes depicting the life of Christ that Giotto di Bondone (1266–1337), the great Florentine artist, had painted in the Arena Chapel in nearby Padua a half century earlier. The technique calls for imposing a radical narrative concision on the actions depicted in the work so that the story is told by means of a few carefully chosen human figures, each of whom is infused with his own distinctive character and emotion; as a result, the meaning of the overall composition becomes intelligible at a glance.[11]

Fig. 50: THE DRUNKENNESS OF NOAH
by Filippo Calendario

Fig. 51: The Fall of Man
by Filippo Calendario

Calendario's most original achievement in this vein is the sculptural group representing *The Drunkenness of Noah* located at the southeast corner of the Palace. As befits a composition installed only a few feet from a busy pedestrian bridge where the typical viewer has no more than a few seconds in which to grasp its narrative content, the work is a miracle of compression. As we take in Noah's heavy eyelids, bulging upper lip, and falling loincloth, as we watch his tall, thin body totter and sway, his left hand grasping and crushing fresh grapes even as he spills the wine cup he already holds in his right, we instantly absorb the story of the old patriarch's debauchery. A hand extended by one of Noah's sons from around the corner to shield his father from further humiliation links the two planes of the composition. In another strikingly original gesture, Calendario has built up the corner where these two halves of the composition converge with a sinuous grapevine whose muscular, projecting trunk and abundant foliage camouflage what would otherwise be a naked stone edge. This complex three-dimensional vine, which mirrors the Tree of Knowledge that Calendario carved along the corner of his *Fall of Man* composition at the southwest angle of the Palace, creates a strong visual connection between the two sculptural groups, as do the expressive hand gestures in both works. Medieval Venetians would have understood immediately that this visual linking was quite deliberate, that the artist intended them to see Noah as reenacting Adam's original fall. Together, the two works constitute a stern warning that human folly is an inherent, ever-present risk to even the most successful of nations.

Calendario also displayed remarkable skill with less somber themes. Examining the capitals of the Ducal Palace's ground-floor portico (*Fig. 52*), we are instantly charmed by his flair for capturing evanescent phenomena such as the delicate pleasures of youth. On the face of one young girl, we watch as a slow, curious smile appears to emerge from carved stone, while in another, gaiety and whim seem caught in mid-flight. It is this easy creative facility which Calendario had in such abundance, this rare protean ability to achieve greatly both as a master architect and a brilliant sculptor, that makes his tragic end so profoundly shocking. The facts are simply told.

In the middle of April 1355, reports began to filter in to Doge Marino Falier and his attending ducal council that some sort of plot to overthrow the Venetian Republic was under way. When the councilors began an investigation, they rapidly discovered that there was, in fact, an ongoing conspiracy, and that, incredibly, it was the doge himself who

Fig. 52: Youthful visages carved on Ducal Palace
ground-floor capitals by Filippo Calendario

seemed to lie at its malignant heart. At this point, inquiries were turned over to the Council of Ten, which quickly uncovered the entire fantastic scheme. The conspirators, who counted among their number a good many Venetian seamen and Arsenale workers, had agreed to put an end to the city's existing aristocratic government and to install Doge Falier as the crowned prince of Venice. Instead of the close-knit oligarchy that had governed the Republic for the past sixty years, where day-to-day power was concentrated in an effective Senate membership of one hundred nobles drawn from some thirty families, the plotters wanted to substitute a single, omnipotent lord modeled on the regimes of the Italian mainland. In early 1355, the disastrous Third War with Genoa was still under way, and some of the conspirators blamed the city's republican form of government for the shocking naval defeats Venice had recently suffered. To them, it appeared that if the city wished to survive in an age of despots, she needed to be ruled by a single master as well.[12]

The Council of Ten's investigation also quickly revealed that Filippo Calendario was one of the principal conspirators. His reasons for joining remain obscure; whatever they may have been, his son, his nephew, and two of his sons-in-law were also active in the scheme. He and a few other top leaders had each pledged to recruit twenty district chiefs to join the plot, with each district head to be responsible for finding forty additional men willing to follow orders and seize the Ducal Palace. Calendario seems to have focused his recruitment efforts on Venetian seamen and Arsenale workers, among whom dissatisfaction with the growing arrogance of senatorial government was at its height. However, many of those whom the conspirators sought to enlist not only refused to join but immediately reported having been approached to patrician friends who then notified Doge Falier and his councilors, thus commencing the investigation. Once it knew the facts, the Council of Ten acted with dispatch. Calendario, who had gone to work in the morning completely unaware that the plot had been discovered, was seized and carried away for immediate trial, very likely in the justice wing of the old Ziani ducal palace facing the Piazzetta, just behind the new Palace building site looking out on the harbor (*Fig. 53*). Following a swift conviction based on irrefutable direct testimony, Calendario was led out onto the second-story Ziani loggia, below which a large crowd had gathered. His arms were tied behind his back, an iron bit was shoved between his teeth, a noose was tightened around his neck, and he was thrown over the parapet to die an agonizing, humiliating death. Several days later, when Doge Falier was beheaded in the Ducal Palace courtyard, Calendario's corpse was still dangling from the Ziani loggia, only a few dozen yards from his half-completed masterpiece, the supreme symbol of the republican institutions he had plotted to destroy.[13]

Following this sacrifice to the demands of impartial justice, the government suspended work on the Ducal Palace for two years; then, just as progress was recommencing in 1357, a new crisis broke out. The king of Hungary demanded that Venice renounce her holdings in Dalmatia and moved to enforce his demand by invading northern Italy. Her treasury all but empty, Venice found herself too weak to halt the advancing Hungarian army before it overran virtually the entire lagoon shoreline, closing off the city's vital inland trading routes. Knowing he had the whip hand, the Hungarian king presented Venice with an ultimatum: surrender Dalmatia and keep the mainland or fight and probably lose both, with an attempted invasion of the city almost certain to follow. Feeling she had no choice but to capitulate, a humiliated Republic surrendered her claim to the entire eastern Adriatic below Istria, instantly losing her primary source of naval timber as well as access to the Dalmatian mercenaries who now made up most of her ship crews. When the city was also struck by a new plague outbreak, work on the Ducal Palace was suspended for the next five years. Once resumed, however, progress was rapid. Although the rough-brick exterior

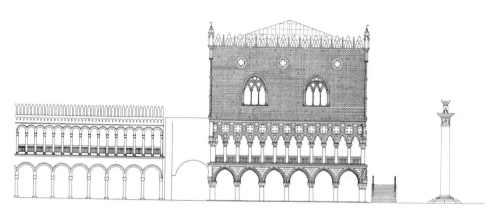

*Fig. 53: Piazzetta view of Calendario's Ducal Palace on the right
with the old Ziani palace of justice behind it to the left*

of the upper half of the Palace remained unfinished, by 1365 interior construction of the Great Council chamber was complete, and the Paduan fresco painter Guariento had been commissioned to cover the eastern wall with an enormous image of Paradise.[14]

The Fourth Genoese War

From the moment in 1355 when Venice and Genoa called a halt to their third all-out conflict, both sides knew that it was only a matter of time before the bitter rivalry once again erupted into fresh hostilities. Unfortunately, when warfare did reignite in 1378, the Republic was weaker than she had been at any time during the past 120 years. Her public debt had mushroomed sevenfold, from 423,000 ducats before the great plague outbreak of 1348 to a staggering three million ducats in 1378; consequently, Venice could no longer afford to build the great hundred-ship fleets she had routinely launched in the previous three wars. Nor, given her surrender of Dalmatia twenty years earlier, did she have access to the timber and naval personnel necessary to construct and man such an armada even if she could have paid for it. Worse still, Genoa would not be her only foe. For this climactic struggle, Genoa had allied itself with the Carrara despots of Padua and the king of Hungary (thus transforming Dalmatian lumber, foodstuffs, bases, and men into Genoese assets); each ally had pledged itself to the extinction of the Venetian Republic.[15]

Venice also had to contend with serious internal conflicts. Having received broad new powers to deal with the plague of 1348, the hundred or so wealthy nobles who habitually made up the Senate had grown increasingly fond of their expanded authority. To many outside this inner circle, the senators seemed to become more arrogant and resentful of popular criticism with each passing day, and nowhere was this view more deeply held than among the mariners of Venice, the very group on which the security of the Republic would now so heavily depend. Just how serious this social and political divide had become can be illustrated by a single revealing incident. One of the city's greatest naval commanders at this time was Vettor Pisani (*Fig. 54*), a patrician whose bold, direct style of leadership had made him a beloved figure to Venetian seamen. When Pisani was called as a witness in a routine court case involving an alleged infraction of Venetian shipping regulations, he politely asked that his firsthand account be accepted as conclusive evidence of the facts covered by his testimony. Hearing this, one of the patrician judges, Pietro Corner, the son of an extremely wealthy nobleman whose fortune was derived from Cyprian slave plantations, replied sarcastically that Pisani's word was hardly good enough to decide the matter.

Fig. 54: Statue of Vettor Pisani in church of Santi Giovanni e Paolo

When court adjourned, Pisani approached Corner and warned him to be armed the next time they met; later that evening, Pisani, dagger in hand, accosted the terrified aristocrat outside his palace but allowed him to escape unharmed. For this, Pisani was fined two hundred ducats and made to forfeit an office to which he had been recently elected.[16]

However, when war broke out, the government wisely ignored this episode and appointed Pisani to serve as captain general of a Venetian fleet of fourteen galleys dispatched to attack Genoese ships in their home waters. There, Pisani won a quick victory and returned to Venice with a large number of prisoners, including the Genoese fleet commander, before sailing to the Aegean on a new mission. During his absence, Genoa sent a second flotilla to cruise the Adriatic for targets of opportunity. In response, Pisani returned to the Adriatic, where, acutely aware that his men had been on constant sea patrol for six months, he asked that his tired crews and worn-out vessels be allowed to spend the winter recuperating in Venice. However, the Senate ignored his request and ordered Pisani to spend the cold weather months repairing his fleet as best he could in Pola, a small Adriatic port one hundred miles east of the lagoon. The decision cannot be explained rationally. Both Genoa and Venice routinely suspended naval operations during the winter, and clearly the best way to maximize the chances for a Venetian victory in the coming spring would have been to allow Pisani's homesick sailors to spend the interim with their families before reembarking in vessels refitted at the Arsenale. Then the Senate compounded its blunder. It ordered a second naval commander, Carlo Zeno, to take half the combat ships not holed up in Pola with Pisani on a distant mission far beyond the Adriatic, ensuring that in the event of an emergency, they would be unavailable to defend the city.[17]

The fruits of such folly were not long in coming. In May 1379, a large Genoese armada appeared at the mouth of Pola's harbor, where Pisani and his men had spent a miserable, sickly winter. Pisani, all too aware of the decrepit state of his fleet, at first sought to avoid battle, but when taunted by accusations of cowardice, responded by rashly ordering an attack. In the debacle that followed, hundreds of Venetian sailors were killed, only a handful of vessels escaped, and eight hundred mercenaries in Venetian service were captured and beheaded. Upon returning to Venice, Pisani, whose courageous leadership had enabled the few ships that did escape to fight their way out of the Genoese encirclement, was clapped in irons and accused of deserting his command in the face of the enemy. When the prosecutor asked for the death penalty, the doge intervened to prevent such madness, and Pisani was sentenced to six months in prison. Inexplicably, the Senate then ordered the city's last six war galleys to sail out of the Adriatic to join the fleet of Carlo Zeno, leaving the lagoon virtually stripped of naval protection.[18]

Seeing the extraordinary opportunity they had been offered, the Republic's enemies pounced. The Hungarian army closed in from the north, the Paduans blocked access to the lagoon from the west (*Fig. 1*), and the Genoese navy, in full control of the northern Adriatic, captured the critical city of Chioggia in the southern lagoon (*Fig. 5*). Sealed off from all external support, with her enemies tightening their grip and her granaries beginning to run low, Venice was faced with an existential threat even greater than Pepin's invasion of the lagoon five and a half centuries earlier. Then, the invaders had been a motley group of Frankish knights hazarding their first marine combat in a small flotilla of unwieldy boats. Now it was another nation of superbly skilled mariners moving in for the kill. Using powerful naval telescopes, Genoese admirals peered into the very heart of the city, where they could see anxious Venetian officials scurrying back and forth across the Piazzetta beneath the rough brick façade of the still unfinished Ducal Palace. Venice looked so temptingly near that one enemy commander bragged that he would soon place a Genoese bridle on the team of antique bronze horses gazing down from the Basilica San Marco.[19]

This boast might well have become a reality if the Venetian people had not forced their patrician governors back to their senses. Upon receiving the state's desperate call for universal military service, the city's soldiers and sailors replied that of course they were ready to risk their lives to preserve the Republic. They had only one, nonnegotiable demand: Vettor Pisani had to be released from prison and placed in charge of the city's defenses. At first the Senate hedged; it freed Pisani but appointed him to only a minor post; consequently, many draftees still refused to report for duty. But when the authorities finally relented and placed Pisani in the top command, the change was instantaneous. Volunteers poured in. Sullen disaffection was replaced by rapid, cheerful action, fear gave way to stern resolve, and Venetian confidence soared. Her eighty-year-old doge, Andrea Contarini, offered to personally lead the Republic into battle, and Pisani drew up an audacious battle plan designed to put Venice on the offensive and throw her adversaries into confusion. He proposed that before the Genoese could launch their final invasion of the lagoon, the Republic should sink barges in the channels leading from Chioggia to the Venetian harbor and from Chioggia into the open waters of the Adriatic. If this maneuver succeeded, the Genoese invaders in Chioggia would be trapped in place with all their entrances and exits blocked. They, and not the Venetians, would be transformed into besieged defenders, stranded and without adequate food supplies during the harsh winter months to come.[20]

This inspired strategy, born from deep knowledge of the city's unique marine environment, worked to perfection. Although a larger, superior Genoese armada continued to control the Adriatic, it could not relieve its starving countrymen on the other side of the lidi, nor could the desperate legions trapped there break out to the open sea. On June 24, 1380, the four thousand Genoese ensnared by Pisani's ingenious plan surrendered unconditionally. This almost miraculous deliverance touched off joyous victory celebrations in Venice, but the commander himself was not yet satisfied. As soon as Carlo Zeno's ships returned from the eastern Mediterranean, Pisani led the Venetian war fleet into the Adriatic in pursuit of the Genoese armada. In the crucial battle that followed, he was mortally wounded and died at sea, robbing the Republic of her greatest champion and her citizens of the hero's welcome they longed to bestow on a man they plainly loved. Certainly, few other Venetians were ever as deserving of such deep popular affection. Born leader, fierce patriot, and naval genius, Pisani refused to let personal abuse by the city's aristocratic governors cloud his judgment or alter his devotion to the common good. When the supreme moment arrived, he put aside the rancor he had every right to feel and applied his great talents precisely where they were most needed. By his heroism and selfless action, he saved his country.[21]

However, given the equal balance of opposing forces, no amount of valor or enterprise could have produced an absolute Venetian victory, and the Treaty of Turin, signed in 1381, left the two exhausted belligerents exactly where they had been before the conflict began. Although the Republic survived with her government, economy, and colonial empire essentially intact, three decades of plague, treason, and war had taken a severe toll. After another outbreak of the Black Death claimed an additional nineteen thousand victims in 1382, Venice would have to wait another century and a half before she regained her pre-plague population, and these devastating epidemics plus the wars with Genoa had been ruinously expensive. From 1348 to 1381, government expenditures swallowed up approximately thirty percent of the city's total wealth, and there was an almost twelve-fold increase in the public debt. Worse still, as holders of existing government bonds were forced to liquidate such securities to raise cash to meet new state levies, their market value plummeted. By the end of the Fourth Genoese War, the value of the Republic's securitized debt, known as the Monte Vecchio, had fallen from 92.5 to 18, and interest payments had been suspended.[22]

Venetian Recovery

Fortunately, the city's governing oligarchy, which had made so many nearly fatal mistakes during the final struggle with Genoa, appears to have returned to sanity in the postwar period. After the peace treaty of 1381, it added thirty new families to its ranks, so that by 1400, the patriciate numbered close to fifteen hundred, a sixty-seven percent increase over the 897 members of the Great Council who survived the plague epidemic of 1348–1350. Nor were commoners denied a means of participating in the city's revival. Although they were not allowed to play an overt political role, Venetian citizens-by-birth were eligible to hold important positions in the Ducal Chancery, the state bureaucracy that administered public affairs for the ruling nobility. And Venetian commoners could exert control over their personal economic fortunes through involvement in the city's powerful craft guilds (Venice was the first Italian city to offer full state recognition of such private trade groups). By easing class tensions within the body politic, these wise measures ensured that the Republic's recovery from the ordeals of the fourteenth century would be the most rapid of any state in Europe. In contrast, postwar Genoa was torn apart by bloody political infighting; it deposed ten ducal leaders in five years before transferring direction of its public affairs to a mentally deranged French monarch.[23]

By 1406, the Republic had incorporated the cities of Padua, Treviso, Bassano, Verona, and Vicenza into a fledgling mainland empire. She had restored her rule over the critical hinterland of Dalmatia, acquired Corfu and other key ports in the southern Adriatic, and won important new bases along the Greek coast and in the Aegean. In contrast to Florentine affairs, where plague-induced economic decline led many merchants to abandon trade for safer returns from state bonds and land, international Venetian commerce was enjoying a vigorous recovery at the dawn of the fifteenth century. With thirty-three hundred ships and thirty-six thousand seamen, the Republic was only a few short decades away from becoming the wealthiest state in Europe. The westward-marching Ottoman Turks, who had destroyed the Serbs at Kosovo in 1389 and smashed the French Crusaders at Nicopolis in 1396, were still a land-based military power which had not yet developed a naval force able to compete on equal terms with the fleets of Venice.[24]

Completion of the Ducal Palace

This Venetian political and economic resurgence intensified efforts to finish the much-delayed Ducal Palace project, so that by 1400, the massive façade of the nearly completed Palace (*Fig. 47*) rose in four almost equal tiers along the southern waterfront. Each tier was approximately twenty feet high. On each floor of the bottom two tiers, a sturdy ground-floor portico and an airy, graceful loggia, the bays were interchangeable, all having been carved to exacting precision in gleaming white Istrian stone. The top two tiers, forming the upper half of the building, constituted an enormous rough-brick, rectangular box forty feet high, 230 feet long, and ninety feet deep, which rested directly on top of the delicate second-tier loggia. The face of this huge, elongated upper half, which housed the new Great Council meeting hall and antechamber, was pierced by six large Gothic windows. The eastern wall of the Council chamber was decorated with an enormous fresco of Paradise by the Paduan master Guariento. The other three sides of the hall were lined with portraits of every doge who had held that office to date except Marino Falier, and the ceiling was painted a heavenly blue, sprinkled with stars.[25]

In 1404, Pierpaolo and Jacobello dalle Masegne installed an ornate Gothic window and balcony complex in the center of the Ducal Palace's upper-story wall. With its direct access from the floor of the Great Council chamber, the balcony provided members of the governing patriciate with a spectacular view of the Venetian harbor and the southern lagoon. Both sides of the window were framed by tall, slender piers extending well above the Palace roofline, and the composition was crowned with a stone canopy supporting the figure of Justice outlined against the Venetian sky. The lower niches of the composition contained sculpted images of the saints Mark, Peter, and Paul and the Byzantine warrior saints Theodore and George, each gilded to make it more visible to viewers standing below. The window's location at the centerpoint of the wall proved extremely valuable when workers began to overlay the Palace's unfinished upper surface with an ornamental covering. An interlocking diamond pattern (*Fig. 55*) created by the subtle alternation of white Istrian stone and red Verona marble bricks was laid down by separate teams of masons who began at the far left and far right edges of the building and worked inward toward the middle of the huge wall. The failure of this complex geometrical pattern to precisely mesh at the midpoint is cleverly concealed behind the Masegne window complex.[26]

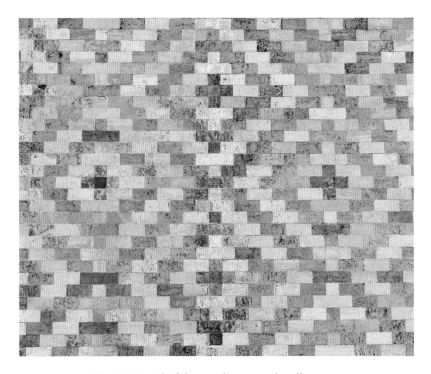

Fig. 55: Detail of diamond-patterned wall screen,
Ducal Palace harbor facade

The effect of this diamond-patterned wall screen has been compared to that of a huge bolt of cloth cut and stretched to fit over the top half of the Palace, a very useful metaphor because it successfully captures the impact on our visual imagination. This repetitive, slightly hypnotic design nullifies our sense of the enormous force that the Great Council chamber necessarily exerts on the slender Gothic arches and quatrefoil roundels directly below, so that, as viewers, we simply do not experience the upper story's tremendous bulk. To achieve this feat of altered perception, Venetians drew on what they had learned in their Eastern travels. From their firsthand encounters with geometrically patterned tiles on buildings in Persia and eastern Turkey, Venetians knew that one of the principal achievements of Islamic architecture was its ability to use surface decoration to dissolve the felt reality of building mass. This use of ornament to divert attention from the natural forces of load and stress was completely different from contemporary medieval architecture in Europe, where an open display of structural dynamics lay at the heart of the Gothic building style. Venetian builders also drew on the special qualities of Venetian light to make the lower stories of the Palace look more equal to the task of supporting the Great Council chamber perched above. When the arches of the portico and loggia are flooded with sunlight, the open spaces behind are cast into dense shadow, a visual effect that contributes to an enhanced sense of solidity and mass. Finally, the builders decided to erect a row of beautiful ornamental merlons along the crest of the Palace roofline. This parapet of exotic Islamic forms, inspired by the roofs of North African mosques and Syrian desert palaces, helps to dispel any residual sense of upper-story bulk.[27]

The Nature of the Architectural Achievement

When the Venetian patriciate assembled in the new Great Council hall (*Fig. 56*) for the first time in 1423, there was ample cause to celebrate. That the Republic had been able to complete a single consistent architectural design over more than a half century filled with war, plague, ducal treason, and near military extinction, was, by itself, sufficient cause for rejoicing, particularly given what had occurred in other Italian cities. In 1339, Siena had commissioned a magnificent enlargement of its cathedral designed to make it the largest church in Italy, but after the death of half its population in the plague of 1348, it abandoned the effort entirely. In Florence, where more than sixty percent of the population had died in the epidemic, the urban landscape was littered with abandoned monuments. Somehow Venice had managed to overcome the fear and turmoil which traumatized the rest of the peninsula, and in doing so she had restored her citizens to the peace, security, and wise republican government her resplendent new Ducal Palace now so perfectly symbolized. Its open, inviting form, complete with a spacious public courtyard, conveyed an entirely different message from that proclaimed by other medieval government palaces such as the Palazzo della Signoria (*Fig. 57*) in Florence. Three times as tall as any private Florentine residence, this enormous citadel was designed for a single purpose: to allow the current ruling faction to hold out as long as possible in the case of a popular revolt. With its huge defensive tower, massive stone walls, and barred windows and doors, it gazed over the rest of the city with a truculent, suspicious glare.[28]

*Fig. 56: View of Venetian patricians assembled in the
Great Council hall, by Francesco Guardi*

The Venetian Ducal Palace has been almost universally described as a masterpiece of Gothic workmanship—as, in fact, one of the world's premier examples of Gothic architecture. No less an authority than John Ruskin, after devoting an entire chapter of *The Stones of Venice* to the nature of Gothic, states that among the buildings of Venice, it is the Ducal Palace alone that "fully expresses the Gothic power."[29] Ordinarily, the weight of such opinion would be conclusive; however, in this case, I believe we would do well to attempt to rid ourselves of all preconceptions and examine the nature of this original Venetian achievement for ourselves.[30]

As an initial step toward clarity, let us make an inventory of the Palace's unmistakably Gothic elements. Almost everyone would agree that these are the relief sculptures on the

Fig. 57: Palazzo della Signoria (Palazzo Vecchio), Florence

capitals of the ground-floor portico, the pointed crests of the portico arches, the exquisitely carved French Gothic tracery of the second-story loggia, and the seven large windows—including the ornate Masegne window and balcony—that punctuate the upper story of the harbor façade. What we notice at once is that each of these features is purely ornamental. The Ducal Palace has almost none of the defining structural characteristics of Gothic architecture as it developed in medieval France and other northern European countries. There, major Gothic buildings—above all, the great cathedrals, but also private homes, town halls, market buildings, and other secular structures—displayed an architectural system of soaring verticality in which higher stories became thinner, lighter, and more ethereal as the eye moved upward from supporting pillars to overhead vaults. This often required the use of massive external buttressing to hold up fragile, membrane-thin walls, which Gothic architects seized every conceivable opportunity to fill with large expanses of brightly colored stained glass. It is significant that these distinctive aspects of Gothic architecture were not independent elements. On the contrary, each was part of a carefully wrought system, an ordered synthesis whose whole purpose was to permit the achievement of spectacular verticality and dazzling interior visual effects.[31]

The Ducal Palace is almost totally devoid of these distinguishing Gothic characteristics. How could it not be? The goal of its builders was to erect an enormous horizontal building mass forty feet in the air on top of thin supporting columns, with only minimal attention to interior illumination. Given such entirely different design requirements, it was impossible to show more than passing decorative conformity to the alien architectural system prescribed by standard Gothic construction. The wall of the Great Council chamber is twice as thick as the slender shafts on which it rests, a complete reversal of basic Gothic principles in which walls become thinner and lighter the higher they extend. Gothic builders showcased interior visual effects by expanding the wall space reserved for glass-filled windows in every direction, to the practical limits of medieval engineering. In contrast, the interior walls in the bottom half of the Palace are set back at least fifteen feet from the brilliant screen of portico and loggia arches that play such a vital role in the building's overall impression. Naturally, the price for this signature design feature is a substantial blocking of light into the lower floors. Nor does the visitor standing in the Great Council chamber, where only two of the walls are pierced by windows, have any sense of enveloping wall transparency. The openings there are designed to provide an acceptable minimum of internal illumination, not to focus attention on the divine, omnipresent source of all light, as in a Gothic interior. Rather than attempting to dramatize the effect of light in a contained interior space, the Ducal Palace encourages visitors to leave the building interior by stepping out onto the second-story loggia or the Masegne window balcony where they can enjoy the city's gorgeous exterior vistas in the lagoon's richly varied ambient light (*Fig. 58*).[32]

In *The Stones of Venice*, Ruskin himself provides a definition of Gothic architectural form that should make us cautious about attempting to place the Ducal Palace under such a heading. He draws a fundamental distinction between the external elements of Gothic architecture (which would include all of the structural and ornamental features previously discussed) and what he calls Gothic's internal characteristics (certain inherent tendencies derived from the psychological inclination of Gothic builders). According to Ruskin, unless a building complies with both parts of this definition (internal and external), we have no right to call it Gothic. He states that in testing for the presence of authentic Gothic architecture, the two most important subjective qualities to look for are Savageness and the Love of Change, that is, a strong bias against the production of precisely carved building units, which requires subjecting workmen to the drudgery of mechanical copying. In his mind, true Gothic stone carving always demonstrates a love of perpetual changefulness, and he contrasts this tendency with what he calls Greek or servile work where architectural parts are perfectly or nearly identical. To Ruskin, a process in which artisans are forced to turn out unit after unit from the same master pattern is a sure sign that the work is not Gothic. Yet, as we have seen, the architectural elements of the Palace were exceptionally standardized, coming very close to what we would expect to find in classical Roman or Greek construction.[33]

In sum, just because the Ducal Palace façade presents a number of clearly Gothic ornamental features does not mean that we should regard the building as an essentially Gothic edifice. Not only does the Palace not conform to several basic canons of Gothic form; viewed objectively, it is not a unitary structure of any kind, Gothic or otherwise. It is instead, as we have seen, a novel synthesis of three major building traditions: French Gothic, Islamic, and Late Antique. We have already discussed the Palace's Gothic and Islamic aspects. What remains to be emphasized is how much its essential character depends on the building's third vital ingredient: a controlling antique harmony consciously carried over from the old Ziani harbor wing. The Ducal Palace is much more regular and

Fig. 58: Vista from Ducal Palace second-story loggia

symmetrical, more counterbalanced between horizontal and vertical, than any purely
Gothic building. It is pervaded by the same respect for harmony, fixed proportion, and
standardized detail that characterized its predecessor and the other proto-Renaissance architecture of the medieval Piazza.[34]

Like the Basilica San Marco, the Ducal Palace is one of the great compositional
masterpieces of Venetian architectural genius. Its brilliant creator never tried to flaunt
his inventiveness. He simply took what he needed from a variety of sources to construct
the most elegant possible solution to the practical problems of size and security he had
been hired to address. Whether or not it is "the central building in the world," as Ruskin
claimed, it is certainly an extraordinary example of what Ruskin reminds us lies behind all
great architectural achievement: undiluted "mental power…pure, precious, majestic massy

intellect."[35] The Palace also illustrates what Ruskin called "the duty of...public edifices" to serve "as books of history."[36] Completed at great expense, it demonstrates, as nothing else could, the inherent strength of the Venetian communal ideal, the city's unmatched ability to rally and achieve architectural distinction while suffering through one of the most horrific periods in Western experience.

However, we should resist the pleasant illusion that the successive shocks of plague, treason, and near-suicidal warfare that buffeted Venice between 1348 and 1381 left no lasting scars. Over time, the Venetian psyche revealed the long-term trauma symptoms one would expect from such appalling events. By the mid-fifteenth century, these began to manifest themselves in a loss of collective self-confidence and a slackening of the zest for innovation and adventure that had propelled the Republic up to that point. Of course, such profound changes could not help but affect the deepest wellsprings of Venetian architectural genius. Thus, it is no accident that the Ducal Place, built to a master design from the early 1340s, would join only two earlier monuments—the eleventh-century Contarini church of San Marco (with its twelfth- and thirteenth-century marble investiture) and the twelfth- and thirteenth-century creation of the medieval Piazza and Piazzetta—in the final pantheon of truly great Venetian architecture. Brilliant and splendid as many later Venetian buildings would be, none would display the same level of stunning originality and compositional genius required to join this epic triad.

CHAPTER TEN

A Shift to the Mainland and the Renaissance Revolution (1423-1501)

Warning from a Dying Doge

According to John Ruskin, it was not until April 1423 that the enlarged Great Council chamber on which the Republic had labored for eight decades was finally put to its intended use. The occasion was a Council assembly presided over by Francesco Foscari (*Fig. 59*), the youthful, energetic, and ambitious procurator of Saint Mark who had just been elected the new doge of Venice against the passionate advice of his dying predecessor, Tommaso Mocenigo (*Fig. 60*) Speaking from his deathbed less than two weeks earlier, Mocenigo had delivered both a stern warning against Foscari's selection and a final report on the current state of the Republic. He catalogued an impressive list of Venetian commercial and military accomplishments since the dire days of the great plague of 1348–1350, the almost fatal war with Genoa that ended in 1381, and the economic depression and financial chaos which accompanied the entire period. By 1423, Venice had become one of the wealthiest nations in Europe; indeed, she would never surpass the relative prosperity she enjoyed in the fifteenth century. The city's merchant families controlled private commercial assets worth ten million ducats and were currently earning annual profits of twenty percent. The public revenues of the Venetian state were one and a half million ducats per year, considerably more than was flowing through the treasury of the king of France, whose domain was twenty times the size of the land mass governed by the Republic and contained ten times as many people. Thanks in part to a quadrupling of the size of the Arsenale in the previous century, the Venetian navy was a superb force of thirty-three hundred vessels manned by thirty-six thousand seamen whose dominance of Mediterranean waters, even against the

Fig. 59: Portrait of Doge Francesco Foscari
by Lazzaro Bastiani

Fig. 60: Tomb monument of Doge Tommaso Mocenigo
in the church of Santi Giovanni e Paolo

mighty Turkish Empire, was still almost uncontested. But, warned Mocenigo, virtually all of this unequaled wealth and success would be needlessly sacrificed if the patriciate were so unwise as to elect Francesco Foscari to be his successor.[1]

In the final legislative battle of his life, Doge Mocenigo had only barely succeeded in beating back an attempt by the city of Florence to pull Venice into a mutual defense pact intended to thwart the ambitions of the Visconti dictatorship that ruled Milan. In the Senate, where this momentous question was debated, the principal champion of the proposed Florentine alliance had been Foscari, who had led a large faction against the conservative position espoused by the eighty-year-old doge. Although Foscari was defeated in the Senate, Mocenigo knew that placing such a man in the ducal chair would constitute a clear repudiation of the earlier vote and signal that the Republic was now ready to adopt a more aggressive military policy on the Italian mainland. With his dying breath, the old doge did not hesitate to prophesy precisely what the consequences of such a reversal would be—perpetual warfare, resulting in the financial ruin of the Venetian state and the city's merchant nobility. In the most graphic language he could summon, Mocenigo told his countrymen that attempting to project Venetian power into the Visconti sphere of influence in northern Italy would make them slaves to their mercenary generals and, in the process, swallow up ninety percent of their existing wealth.[2]

Why, then, in the face of this grave forewarning from a highly respected leader did the patriciate raise his arch nemesis to the ducal chair at the age of only forty-nine (almost a quarter century younger than the election age of the average doge), where he presided over the Venetian government for the next thirty-four years? To Foscari's political enemies, the only reasons that made sense were voter corruption and brazen electoral trickery. As a procurator of Saint Mark, the traditional stepping stone to ducal office, Foscari had spent over thirty thousand ducats to buy the future votes of many poor patricians. Political opponents also charged that during the ducal election of 1423, Foscari supporters in the final electoral college seemed ready to cast their ballots for another, very unpopular candidate, causing many of the remaining electors (but not enough to clinch the result) to vote for Foscari. At this point, Foscari adherents switched back to their real candidate, taking the rest of the electors by surprise and sealing the result. Assuming the truth of this allegation, it demonstrates how even a process as obsessively complicated as the electoral procedure for the Venetian doge could be successfully gamed by men prepared to openly dishonor the antifactional values on which the Republic was constructed.[3]

But there was also an important foreign policy explanation for the decision to place Francesco Foscari in the ducal chair: fifteenth-century Venice had vital interests on the Italian mainland. She needed food for her growing population, timber for her huge merchant fleets, and a ready supply of other raw materials for the variety of manufactured goods such as glass and textiles that she was now beginning to produce in ever larger quantities. The Republic could not allow another Italian state to become so powerful that it could surround the lagoon and shut off her access to critical natural resources or close down her trade routes into the Italian interior, and from there to her extensive clientele in northern Europe. The grueling blockade she had endured during the dark winter of encirclement and near political extermination in her final war with Genoa had become etched into Venetian consciousness, and she was determined that it would never be repeated. In the minds of Foscari and his supporters, the most likely source of danger was Milan, the largest city in northern Italy, despotically governed by the cunning, unpredictable Visconti clan. Although the proposed Florentine alliance would increase the risk of a Milanese military reaction, it would also be a very useful defensive measure if Milan decided to initiate a first strike against Venetian interests, which she might very well do with or without provocation. In the end, the argument for preempting the Milanese threat won the day.[4]

The first five years of Foscari's bold new policy proved extremely successful, so much so that by 1428, Venice had extended her Italian terraferma empire to the city of Bergamo, deep within Lombard territory and three-quarters of the way to the walls of Milan itself. Together with Milan and Florence, she had become one of the three great land powers of the Italian peninsula. Unfortunately, having experienced such a rapid advance, she was then forced to spend the next quarter century in a state of almost constant warfare defending her new possessions against Milanese counterattack. The financial burden of this perpetual military conflict, conducted by mercenary captains whose interests in prolonged, inconclusive campaigns were clearly distinct from those of the Republic, seemed to increase with every passing year, and it was not until the 1450s that revenues from the Venetian mainland empire began to outpace expenses. However, some of the economic resentment this would normally have engendered was undercut by a new phenomenon: the growing desire of patrician families to secure their share of the government employment that accompanied the Republic's management of her subject Italian cities. Not only did such public salaries progressively become a greater share of patrician income, but the

city's noble families also began to diversify the sources of their wealth by investing in agricultural estates on the Venetian mainland.[5]

While Doge Mocenigo's effort to fix the course of Venetian foreign policy before his
death was an obvious failure, he was much more successful as an architectural catalyst. A
single act of his enlightened leadership initiated the city's most important fifteenth-century
building project. When the new southern wing of the Ducal Palace, under construction
along the city's harbor front since 1340, began to near completion after 1400, its size and
brilliance made a vivid contrast with the Piazzetta wing of the old Ziani palace to its immediate rear (*Fig. 53*). The visual clash between the new project—a stunningly original
merger of diverse building elements—and the old and dilapidated twelfth-century palace
(only half as tall) was particularly jarring where the two façades adjoined near the harbor
end of the Piazzetta. Venetians soon began to imagine how much more resplendent the
smaller square would appear if the new Palace's narrow western end (eighty feet in length)
could be extended another 165 feet north, absorbing and replacing the Ziani palace up
to its juncture with the southern face of the Basilica San Marco. The only real obstacle
to realizing such a vision was a self-imposed financial barrier. Sometime during the long,
costly process of completing the Palace harbor wing, the Venetian government had tried to
protect itself in advance from the expense of erecting the same magnificent design along the
eastern side of the Piazzetta. It had decreed that anyone who even made such a suggestion
would be fined one thousand ducats.[6]

There the matter rested until 1419, six years into Doge Mocenigo's term of office,
when a severe fire devastated the roof and cupolas of the Basilica and the adjoining Piazzetta wing of the Ziani palace, which housed the Venetian law courts. The doge responded
with a splendid public gesture; he had the thousand-ducat fine (drawn from his personal
funds) carried into the Great Council hall, where he offered a motion, which was soon adopted, to build a mirror image of the new Palace harbor front along the entire length of the
Piazzetta. Work on the new wing began in 1424, the year after Mocenigo's death; following demolition of the old palace, construction of a replacement building faithful in every
detail to the harbor front's original 1340 design lasted until 1438. Without Mocenigo's
addition, the Piazzetta as we know it today would be unrecognizable.[7]

During roughly the same period (1423–1438) that they were extending the Ducal
Palace along the Piazzetta, the governors of Venice also repaired the fire-damaged Basilica

and made two major changes to the church's fenestration. A Gothic rose window was inserted into the face of the southern transept vault, and a large expanse of bottle glass was installed in the great semicircular cavity where the western vault of the nave opened onto the second-story terrace, just behind the four antique gilded horses. As intended, both of these interventions brought much-needed sunlight into the interior, albeit at the expense of undermining the artistic integrity of the original Contarini church. However, another major addition to the Basilica made at this time was an unmixed success. The crest of the western façade was festooned with a line of sprightly Gothic sculpture, joyfully rising and falling along the tops of the five rounded arches comprising the church's upper-story profile (*Figs. 33, 39*). These semicircular forms were capped with ogee arches supporting a profusion of saints, prophets, and cabbage leaves, flanked by narrow Gothic tabernacles holding statues of the four Evangelists, the archangel Gabriel, and the Virgin Mary. The summit of the central ogee arch was crowned with a statue of Saint Mark, and the area directly below the Evangelist was covered with a mantle of piercing blue mosaic sprinkled with golden stars and a gilded image of the Winged Lion. The tops of the southern and northern façades were given similarly exuberant Gothic outlines. Most of the carving was done by Niccolò di Pietro Lamberti of Florence and Giovanni di Martino of Fiesole, the same sculptors who created Doge Tommaso Mocenigo's tomb monument, described in some detail in endnote seven of this chapter. Since these sculpted crests were meant to be seen against a deep blue Venetian sky, the ogee arches, the crowns of the tabernacles, and most of the roofline figures were originally gilded.[8] No one has improved on Ruskin's classic description of this delightful addition:

> [a] range of glittering pinnacles, mixed with white arches edged with scarlet flowers—a confusion of delight, amidst which the breasts of the Greek horses are seen blazing in their breadth of golden strength, and the St. Mark's Lion, lifted on a blue field covered with stars, until at last, as if in ecstasy, the crests of the arches break into a marble foam, and toss themselves far into the blue sky in flashes and wreathes of sculptured spray, as if the breakers on the Lido shore had been frost-bound before they fell....[9]

The Florentine Awakening

As it finally emerged in the early fifteenth century, the Basilica was one of the defining examples of Venetian communal art, a process characterized by the ability of successive teams of gifted artists to collaborate on large, multigenerational projects over very long time periods—in this case, over a span of six centuries. Like the city's other great monuments, San Marco is a brilliant composite formed from very different styles and traditions, a display of the special Venetian genius for merging diverse elements into a unique artistic whole. Meanwhile, at the same time that the Basilica was receiving this final major flourish as part of the complex assemblage art of Venice, one of the most distinctive personalities in the history of Western art was creating an entirely different type of architecture in the city of Florence.

Filippo Brunelleschi (1377–1446) began the public phase of his architectural career in 1418, at the age of forty-one, by entering the competition to design a gigantic dome large enough to cap the huge open drum at the top of the Florentine Cathedral of Santa Maria del Fiore (the Duomo) (*Fig. 61*). The son of a well-to-do civil servant and diplomat, Brunelleschi was short, bald, and irascible, a witty, secretive man with a deeply analytical mind and one of the most original and courageous intellects ever to design and construct public buildings. Ever fearful of having a competitor take credit for his inventions, this passionately learned autodidact refused to put his ideas on paper except in encoded form. His penchant for secrecy and total control of every project he undertook brought him into repeated conflict with the Florentine authorities. During his interview for the Cathedral dome commission, his evasive, quarrelsome responses so angered the judges that they had him carried out of the church and dumped into the public square. Decades later, at the height of his fame, he was arrested and imprisoned for refusing to pay his guild dues. He never married and was notorious for his dirty, unkempt appearance. But the brilliant, elegant buildings he produced were immediately recognized as nothing less than revolutionary—an astonishing succession of bold, harmonious visions from the inspired imagination of a solitary genius.[10]

One of the best ways to understand the vast distance that separated this new Florentine architecture from a great Venetian monument like the Basilica is to compare the experience of a visitor finding his way through the sanctuary of San Marco with that of

Fig. 61: Dome of the Florentine Cathedral
designed by Filippo Brunelleschi

someone who has just stepped into the interior of San Lorenzo in Florence, the earliest of Brunelleschi's church designs. The essential impression conveyed by San Marco (*Figs. 14, 18*) is that of a great treasure cave carved out of beaten gold and precious stone; wherever we look, we are profoundly acted upon by "beauty of surface, of tone, of detail, of things near enough to touch and kneel upon,"[11] in the words of Henry James. As sheaths of royal porphyry and slices of gorgeous veined marble in multifaceted shades of red, pink, orange, cream, blue, green, brown, and yellow vie for our attention, we are at the same time drawn forward to explore the mysteries of dark, shadowy aisles or to gaze up at the golden, flickering recesses of great hovering domes. Staggered by its profligate beauty, we become dazed wanderers through the Basilica's varied precincts. "Under foot and over head," we experience "a continual succession of crowded imagery, one picture passing into another, as in a dream."[12]

A visitor entering San Lorenzo (*Fig. 62*) undergoes an entirely different experience. No attempt is made to lure him into exploratory motion. Regardless of where he stands, he is confronted with an almost identical vision of fixed harmonies, a revelation of unchanging mathematical axioms; he feels that he is gazing upon the architectural incorporation of some permanent natural law. To this end, the emotional effects of color and surface texture have been kept to the barest minimum; except for the ceiling, the white and cream of the walls are varied only by the light gray stonework of the arcades, the fluted pilasters, and the other decorative trim. Nothing is allowed to interfere with the purely cerebral effect of rational, ordered harmony. The two mirror-perfect rows of identical columns and semicircular arches on Corinthian capitals with imposts, which make up the nave, look like an exercise in linear perspective, which is not surprising, since it was Brunelleschi who first worked out a series of practical mathematical procedures for creating this Renaissance visual effect. Nor is this highly rationalized design restricted to the nave; every component of the building is based on a precise mathematical calculation, all ultimately derived from the dimensions of the central spatial unit formed by the crossing of the nave and transept.[13]

During the decade and a half preceding the 1418 Florentine dome competition, Brunelleschi is believed to have lived in Rome for various periods, where he made a close study of the intact classical monuments he was able to unearth in the sadly decayed imperial capital. Based on these widely accepted biographical facts, it was once also commonly believed that many of Brunelleschi's subsequent accomplishments were based on his redis-

*Fig. 62: Interior of the church of San Lorenzo, Florence,
designed by Filippo Brunelleschi*

covery of lost classical building methods and prototypes. A number of influential commentators even claimed that his Roman excavations left Brunelleschi capable of imaginatively reconstructing the entire ancient city in his mind and that this provided him with a whole new repertoire of classical architectural models. Such views now seem naïve. To begin with, they ignore the lamentable condition of most of the Roman monuments whose secrets Brunelleschi was supposed to be deciphering. Ten centuries of fire, disintegration, and military conquest, of being buried in rubble or cannibalized for new construction, as well as the burning of enormous amounts of marble revetment in kilns to produce quicklime for wall plaster, had reduced most of classical Rome to formless mounds of rotting brick. In addition, a more critical examination of Brunelleschi's architecture has made it clear that there is very little correspondence between his own work and the actual forms and construction methods of ancient Roman building, even in structures such as the Pantheon that have been almost perfectly preserved. In fact, recent investigations of Brunelleschi's likely sources have emphasized his frequent borrowings from Byzantine, early Christian, Islamic, and Venetian architecture, as well as Tuscan pre-Romanesque and Romanesque buildings. Such corrective information helps us understand that what Brunelleschi gained from his visits to Rome was much more inspirational than technical—not detailed guidance as to how to build, but a vastly enlarged sense of what should be possible for men living in early fifteenth-century Italy. Fired by ambition, he returned to Florence with a burning desire to rival and even surpass the great architects of antiquity.[14]

As a testing ground for his expansive aspirations, Brunelleschi could not have found a better place than his native Florence at the time of his return around 1415. After successfully defending their national independence against repeated military incursions by the great Lombard power of Milan, the inhabitants of Florence, particularly its ardent humanist intellectuals, saw their city of forty thousand (less than half of the Venetian population of eighty-five to a hundred thousand) as a new Athens, the natural political and cultural leader of the Italian peninsula. Patriotic enthusiasm led Florentine propagandists to ignore the fact that their city's economic development had historically lagged behind that of Venice, Milan, Pisa, and Genoa, and that well in to the fifteenth-century, Venice remained the dominant Italian economic and military power. To the Florentines, such empirical data were irrelevant; they were convinced that now was the moment for Florence to assume its rightful place at the forefront of Italian intellectual, artistic, and architectural achievement (a status which, at least as to architecture, Venice had rightly claimed during the preceding three centuries). Nothing epitomized this Florentine self-confidence more clearly than the 1418 competition to choose an architect worthy of completing the municipal Cathedral, a massive work begun in 1294 whose domeless walls had sat uncovered, exposed to the elements, for the past half century. The winning architect would have to convince the selection committee that he knew how to erect a dome with a diameter of 143.5 feet, a foot and a half more than the span of the Pantheon in Rome (*Fig. 9*), and that he could do it without incurring enormous expense. It was the greatest architectural and engineering contest of its time. Here, at the very outset of his architectural career, was a challenge truly worthy of Brunelleschi's ambition to create monuments that would hold their own beside even the grandest works of antiquity.[15]

In many ways, the magnitude of the engineering obstacle that Brunelleschi faced in the Florentine dome competition reminds one of the architectural challenge that the architect of the Venetian Ducal Palace project successfully solved almost eighty years earlier. To justify his commission, Filippo Calendario had to devise a method of placing the weight of an enormous two-story rectangular box on top of slender Gothic tracery without making this reversal of normal constructive arrangements seem awkward, unstable, or even apparent. To eliminate his competitors, Brunelleschi had to discover a means of constructing the world's largest brick masonry dome without relying on prohibitively expensive wooden centering to hold the bricks in place until their mortar had fully cured. Interestingly, both men solved their dilemmas by seeking out and adapting Islamic building techniques which would have been familiar to traveling merchants from their native cities. Instead of turning to the ancient Roman model of the Pantheon, which employed massive concrete walls to support a shallow, rounded dome (*Fig. 63*), Brunelleschi used a very different octagonal, double-shelled, pointed dome design with an inner brick wall only seven feet thick at its base, a plan very likely based on a famous fourteenth-century mausoleum in Soltaniyeh, Persia. He also developed a system of interlocking herringbone brickwork, based on models found in Persian and Byzantine dome construction, to compensate for the absence of the wooden armature the Romans had relied upon when they cast the concrete vaults of the Pantheon.[16]

But the intriguing connections between Brunelleschi's creations and earlier Venetian architecture go well beyond an analogous use of Islamic building techniques. Central features of the Piazza San Marco complex very likely functioned as direct models for major building elements in the later work of the Florentine architect. An important example of this influence is Brunelleschi's frequent use of domes with pendentives over cubical spaces, an arrangement he repeated in his designs for the Old Sacristy in the church of San Lorenzo, the Pazzi Chapel (*Fig. 64*), and the nave crossing of the church of Santo Spirito. His rediscovery of the pendentive, a concave triangular form that permits circular domes to be erected over squares and rectangles, is not explained by his knowledge of ancient Roman architecture, which, as in the case of the Pantheon, consistently placed domes over circles, not squares. Instead, Brunelleschi found his inspiration for this ingenious transitional device in Late Antique and Byzantine architecture, whose chief Eastern examples were mag-

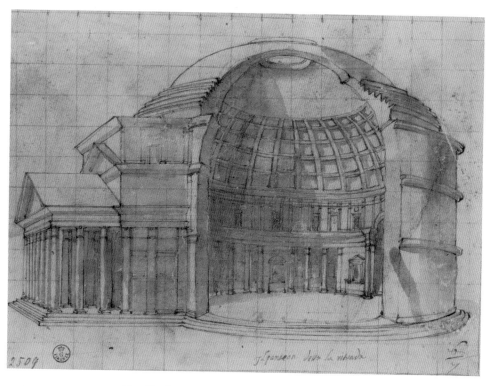

Fig. 63: Cutaway section of the Pantheon, Rome

nificent imperial churches such as Haghia Sophia and the Apostoleion in Constantinople. The latter, of course, was the model for the Basilica San Marco in Venice, which is permeated with dome and pendentive construction (*Figs. 12, 15, 19*), both in the sanctuary itself and in the western and northern arms of the adjoining narthex. The Venetian Basilica, the most authentic incorporation of Byzantine architectural principles ever imported to the West, was available to Brunelleschi even if he lacked direct, firsthand knowledge of original domed buildings in the Greek East.[17]

A second, almost certain example of direct Venetian influence was the effect of the symmetrical, classically derived porticoes that surrounded the medieval Piazza San Marco on Brunelleschi's creation of the arcaded portico of the Innocenti Hospital (*Fig. 65*). The

Fig. 64: Interior of the Pazzi Chapel, Florence,
designed by Filippo Brunelleschi

Fig. 65: Arcade of the Innocenti Hospital, Florence,
designed by Filippo Brunelleschi

Piazza, modeled on a functioning antique square in the ancient capital of Constantinople, was virtually the only sufficiently intact Western forum that could have served as a direct model for Brunelleschi's project. As he routinely did with original sources that stimulated his creative imagination, Brunelleschi took the pattern of rounded arches on columns and the use of repetitive antique detail which characterized the perimeter of the Venetian square and by subjecting it to greater mathematical rigor, restated it in a more elegant, purified form. However, unlike the builders of the Piazza San Marco, who were beneficiaries of the communal art ethos of Venice, it was difficult for an individual Florentine architect, even one with as commanding a personality as Brunelleschi, to project the powerful order and harmony of his designs onto a larger architectural context. It took until 1519, more than a half century after Brunelleschi's death, before Florentines carved out a piazza in front of Brunelleschi's original Innocenti portico. And it took almost another century after that to finally transform this emerging public space into an architecturally unified square by erecting a stylistically compatible arcade along its northern flank. There is no solid evidence of what Brunelleschi himself intended for the area in front of his Innocenti project, but if, as some have theorized, it truly was his idea to create what would ultimately, 140 years later, became the Piazza Santissima Annunziata, this was the most successful of his urban planning visions. A more typical example was his plan to orient the church of San Spirito toward the Arno and to construct a monumental public square stretching over three hundred feet to the bank of the river in front of the new building. This magnificent conception, which might have created a Florentine waterfront plaza worthy of being compared to the Piazza San Marco and the Piazzetta, was rejected as too expensive by his ecclesiastical clients. As a result, the church is located well inland with its back turned toward the river.[18]

The Renaissance and the Venetian Response to It

Supremely inventive genius though he was, the ideas for Brunelleschi's stunningly original buildings did not suddenly spring forth out of a cultural vacuum. They emerged from the sweeping reversal of values that we now call the Italian Renaissance. This phenomenon, whose ultimate expression was a fifteenth- and sixteenth-century explosion of talent and innovation in painting, sculpture, and architecture, began as a literary phenomenon concentrated in what we would today call the humanities—history, literature, languages, and philosophy. The new humanist outlook received its earliest memorable expression in the writings of the Italian poet and scholar Francesco Petrarca or Petrarch (1304–1374), who posited that there was a fundamental gulf between the world of the Middle Ages and that of classical antiquity. Profoundly stirred by his meditations on the vanished grandeur of ancient Rome, Petrarch's revolutionary perspective was to view the lost knowledge of the Greeks and Romans, much more than the teachings of the Christian Church, as the revealed light of truth. Under humanism's transforming lens, pagan emperors and magistrates who had presided over the martyrdom of early Christians were converted into conscientious rulers whose enlightened grasp of reality made them do everything in their power to hold back the dark tide of dissolution that threatened the civilized Mediterranean world. Primitive Christianity was again seen as a religion of the poor, the ignorant, and the gullible, and its eventual triumph over the sanctioned religions of the Roman state as a basic cultural collapse that ushered in a prolonged era of political chaos and artistic decay. In a search for this lost classical heritage, scholars devoted their lives to the recovery and emendation of ancient texts. Filled with dreams of piercing the black veil they believed had descended on Mediterranean culture after the fall of Rome, Petrarch and his successors quite literally looked forward to being born again in the radiance of the antique past.[19]

Within a short while, this enthralling sense of existential rebirth (*renaissance*, as it was called in French) was not only being used to describe what humanist scholars experienced as they rediscovered works of classical literature. It was also being employed to explain popular reaction to the frescoes of the Florentine painter Giotto di Bondone, who was extolled for his brilliantly conceived psychological portraits and realistic depictions of nature. By the early fifteenth century, the idea of a Renaissance in the fine arts had expanded to include sculpture, particularly the works of the great Florentine sculptor Donatello (1386–1446), who was hailed as an imitator of the ancients (having accompanied Brunelleschi to Rome, where they worked together to excavate the ruins of the imperial capital). Brunelleschi himself, of course, was seen as convincing proof that the Renaissance had spread to architecture. His buildings epitomized a core Renaissance belief that architectural merit depended on strict fidelity to certain universal mathematical truths which permeated the natural world. In Renaissance eyes, the microcosm of each man-made object should mirror the macrocosm of the revealed universe, which, to those who understood the true nature of reality, was imbued with a system of divinely ordained mathematical harmony. Not only was this guiding precept believed to underlie all classical architecture, it was argued that a Renaissance architect who followed this fundamental axiom could actually impart the proportions of cosmic order to his own individual creations. In time, this approach to architectural design, a fascinating merger of scientific method and religious aspiration, would be given written form, first in a famous *Treatise on Architecture* by Leone Battista Alberti (1404–1472) and later by a host of far more dogmatic sixteenth-century architectural theorists.[20]

In addition to teaching that the diligent study of classical architecture would allow the average intelligent builder to understand the mathematical interconnectedness of nature and so be capable of reproducing her divine harmony in his own constructions, the busy theorists of the Renaissance invented the antithetical idea of artistic genius. Brunelleschi was the first artist to receive this encomium when, at the time of his death in 1446, he was recognized as a "great ingenious man," a possessor of "divine genius."[21] Building on passages from Plato, Renaissance theorists portrayed artistic geniuses as beings set apart from the rest of humanity who underwent profoundly solitary experiences in which they were invaded—literally taken over—by creative inspiration. Having received this gift of divine seizure, these artists were then measured by their success in communicating such unique, isolated visions in virtually undiluted form. This conception is obviously very different from the earlier Renaissance idea that certain fundamental information (like the underlying mathematical harmony of the world) was available to any intelligent person who made a careful study of classical precedent. Increasingly, during the High Renaissance of the early sixteenth century, the lives of the most famous painters, sculptors, and architects (those viewed as the era's artistic geniuses) became transformed into cultural epics where the grandeur of artistic ambition frequently overshadowed candid evaluations of actual artistic achievement. Outstanding artists were looked upon as "mortal gods,"[22] and it became progressively less important whether their commissions were completed according to plan or even completed at all. It became fashionable to collect early conceptual drawings and preliminary sketches of unfinished projects.[23]

For many reasons, this constellation of Renaissance ideas and values found a much less receptive home in Venice. The fifteenth-century Republic was the product of an entirely different historical pattern than the one which had formed Renaissance Florence and Rome, and her citizens were far more resistant to sudden conversion and rebirth in the light of a freshly discovered antique past. Instead of fallen Rome, Venice traced her heritage back to Constantinople, the new imperial capital that Constantine the Great established at the juncture of Europe and Asia. Constantine's decision to export the power and culture of ancient Rome to the Greek East marked the very moment when what humanists viewed as "the dark ages" began to descend on the Western Roman Empire. As a result, Venice had the unusual experience of being born and nurtured in the artistic orbit of a vibrant, antique metropolis, still surrounded by unspoiled classical monuments every bit as magnificent as those which once graced the old Western capital. Venetians never felt like refugees from a lost classical heritage and never experienced the same deep longing for its recovery felt in other Italian cities. By the time of the early Italian Renaissance, Venice was the wealthiest state in Europe and had already completed her greatest architectural achievements. And she had accomplished these feats during a period that Renaissance intellectuals now looked down upon as an age of sad and contemptible degeneracy. The Republic could hardly be expected to agree that the epoch of her extraordinary rise to power had been nothing but a decadent, slumberous prelude to the Florentine awakening.[24]

But Venice's unique historical trajectory did more than prevent her from feeling the same profound spiritual yearning for antique culture which had overtaken the rest of Italy. It also insulated her from embracing abrupt cultural value reversals in general. As we have seen, in the fourteenth century, when Venice conceived of and built a new Ducal Palace, she was unwilling to replace the classical symmetry of her existing palace with an exclusive reliance on contemporary Gothic design. Correspondingly, a century later, she felt no urge to abandon the long-standing taste for mixed compositions which had produced her stunning new Palace and the brilliant façade of the Basilica San Marco in favor of a narrow, theoretical reliance on classical antiquity. In architecture as in so many other endeavors, she rarely chose to start over from radical new premises. Instead, she habitually reclothed historic monuments with additions created in the latest style, carefully merging and synthesizing each fresh object with its preexisting context. The aims and techniques of this traditional Venetian assemblage art, which delighted in creating beautifully integrated ensembles from disparate materials, periods, and traditions, were at the opposite extreme from the Renaissance ideal of abstract purity arrived at by refining the essence of Greco-Roman form. For instance, the Venetian love of profuse, melting color and the novel effects of mixed media, evident everywhere within the Basilica San Marco, contrasts sharply with the Renaissance dictum that church interiors should be painted a simple shade of white and contain a bare minimum of decorative ornament.[25]

Lastly, the social and political ethos of Renaissance humanism contradicted the communal approach to architectural and artistic production that continued to exert a forceful, if not exclusive, hold on the Venetian imagination into the fifteenth and sixteenth centuries. In the rest of Italy, where the lingering effects of entrenched feudalism made it much easier for a single lord or family to overturn existing communal arrangements, the princely despot and the Renaissance artist/architect turned out to be natural allies. Both were ambitious, socially mobile men on the make, and each needed what the other could provide. To legitimize their rule, parvenu lords eagerly sought out the symbols of learning and culture that Renaissance courtiers were believed to possess. And Renaissance artists and architects were delighted to appear as welcome guests at the courts of these wealthy new patrons even if such arrangements all too often produced inferior works of personal or family propaganda. This symbiotic relationship was accompanied and abetted by a radically heightened class consciousness that borrowed heavily from European feudal culture. The result was a new architectural elitism which demanded that municipal centers, once the focal point of medieval communal life, be refitted in classical Roman garb to better serve the needs of a single despotic individual or a narrow governing nobility.[26]

In the Republic, on the other hand, judgments about what and how to build were supposed to be, and normally were, made collectively by an extended network of interlocking councils, committees, and commissions whose members were chosen from the city's sizable merchant nobility. At the price of some unavoidable inefficiency, this complex process was intended to insulate Venetian political and artistic life from the unrestrained egotism which often blemished mainland architectural patronage. While it is true that, except for the procurators of Saint Mark (who enjoyed lifetime tenure), those elected to such magistracies generally served very short terms, this rapid turnover was offset by the fact that many of the most influential patricians from the same prominent families tended to rotate sequentially through the most important posts. It was hoped that such recurring patterns would impose a general consistency on daily decision making or, at the least, discourage frequent, precipitous shifts in architectural direction.

Of course, this is not to say that fifteenth-century Venice was entirely cut off from Renaissance energy and ideas. For instance, although the professional humanists who flocked to princely courts were much less of a force there, Petrarch himself, the greatest poet-humanist of the fourteenth century, lived in Venice at state expense between 1362 and 1368 and offered to leave his famous collection of ancient manuscripts as the nucleus of a Venetian public library. Both the city herself and neighboring Padua, an important part of the Venetian terraferma and home to one of Europe's oldest and most vital universities, contained extremely rich collections of classical sculpture, manuscripts, sarcophagi, medals, and coins. Connoisseurs who wished to buy their own personal specimens of classical antiquity made frequent trips to the lagoon and the Veneto. In addition, by the latter half of the fifteenth century, Venice, with her historic ties to the Byzantine East, had become the principal center of Greek scholarship in the West, particularly after the fall of Constantinople to the Ottoman Turks in 1453 and the flood of Byzantine refugees which this brought into the city. Renaissance Venice was also a leader in the tremendous diffusion of knowledge made possible by the invention of the printing press, a technological advance that caused a two-hundred-fold increase in the number of books in Europe during the last half of the fifteenth century. The Republic became the largest publishing center in Europe, producing an estimated 1,125,000 total volumes between 1480 and 1500. As the source of roughly one-quarter of all European books in print, Venice was a favorite destination for Renaissance intellectuals and theorists seeking to publish their own works or to buy the inexpensive Greek and Latin texts that the city's 150 printing houses, such as that of the great scholar-publisher Aldus Manutius, specialized in producing. In the sixteenth century, Venice took the lead in publishing important works on classical and Renaissance architectural theory and practice. For instance, the first illustrated scholarly edition of Vitruvius' *Ten Books on Architecture*, the only ancient Roman architectural treatise to survive from classical times and a work of enormous influence on all subsequent Renaissance architecture, was published in Venice in 1511.[27]

Given her firm policy against erecting personal effigies in important public areas like the Piazza San Marco, Venice is not generally known for her achievements in the field of heroic, freestanding sculpture. Therefore, it is all the more remarkable that the two finest equestrian statues produced in post-classical times were both authorized by the fifteenth-century Republic, in each case to honor a mercenary captain charged with protecting and enlarging her newly acquired terraferma empire. Donatello's mounted figure of Gattamelata, erected between 1445 and 1453 in the Piazza del Santo in Padua, and the equestrian monument to Bartolomeo Colleoni by Andrea del Verrocchio (1435–1488), installed at the end of the fifteenth century in the Campo Santi Giovanni e Paolo in the Castello district of Venice (*Fig. 66*), are among the greatest works of Renaissance sculpture ever created. As freestanding, larger-than-life, mounted figures cast in bronze, they exemplify what the ancients believed was one of the most difficult technical challenges any artist could undertake. Not surprisingly, then, both projects were entrusted to the finest sculptors of the age, both of whom were Florentine. The Gattamelata and Colleoni sculptures are striking portraits of individual will and power, images of the very type of mercenary commander whose assumption of one-man rule had often terminated republican government in other Italian states. Yet both received the Republic's blessing, suggesting that by the latter half of

*Fig. 66: Bronze equestrian statue of Bartolomeo Colleoni
by Andrea del Verrocchio*

the fifteenth century, the Venetian government had begun to reconsider some aspects of the ban on individual effigies, particularly where the person depicted was not a member of the governing patriciate and the work in question was installed some distance from the Piazza San Marco.[28]

Finally, there is the field of Renaissance painting where Venetian artists made a number of vital contributions, particularly in the substitution of oil painting on canvas for earlier media, a revolutionary change that became a hallmark of the Italian Renaissance. Medieval painters had two basic options. They could mix their pigments with egg yolk and water, producing a thin, quick-drying paste known as tempera that was then applied to wooden panels and dry walls. Or they could undertake the technically exacting art of *buon fresco* in which pigments ground in water were applied directly to a freshly plastered wall surface; as the lime plaster dried, the paint bonded to the wall through the chemical process of carbonization without the need for a binding agent such as egg yolk. In the 1420s, painters from Flanders and Holland became increasingly dissatisfied with the way in which tempera-based paints resisted a smooth, uninterrupted blending of colors and tonal values, thereby obstructing the realistic, three-dimensional pictorial effects these Low Country artists wished to achieve. To overcome this limitation, they began substituting oil for egg yolk and water, creating a much more slow-drying, flexible medium capable of producing a larger and continuous range of hues and shades.

It took another half century for these new techniques to reach Italy. One important breakthrough occurred in 1475 when the traveling Sicilian artist Antonello da Messina (c. 1430–1479) brought examples of his oil painting to Venice. The ingredients for a fundamental change in Venetian practice were already in place; the lagoon's moist, salt-drenched climate had always been a harsh environment for fresco, and the city's artists (who were usually eager to adopt genuine technical improvements) had previously experimented with oil-based paints. But now, as they were introduced to the realism and novel atmospheric effects achieved in Antonello's works in oil, they were dazzled by what they saw. His use of the medium opened up a whole new world of enhanced color effects, including the ability to depict the delicate play of light in near and deep space, something which had an intense appeal to the Venetian sensibility, fascinated as it was by the luminosity of the Basilica's golden mosaics and the city's unique aquatic environment (*Figs. 67, 68*). Venetian painters enthusiastically embraced the new Flemish techniques, while Renaissance artists in other Italian cities such as Florence continued to favor the use of fresco and tempera. This difference may be explained in part by the Florentine fascination with classical precedent and the fact that ancient Roman painters always remained firmly attached to the art of fresco and never experimented with an oil-based medium. Venetian artists, on the other hand, were unhampered by the idea that progress could only arise through building on classical methods. By the dawn of the sixteenth century, a Venetian master in oils such as Giovanni Bellini (c. 1438–1516) had so perfected the creation of radiant, atmospheric effects on canvas that he was universally regarded as one of the greatest painters in Europe. In 1479 he began to work on a series of ambitious state commissions originally given to his brother Gentile (c. 1435–1507). These called for replacing the faded frescoes in the Great Council chamber of the Ducal Palace with huge new oil canvases depicting famous events in Venetian history. To be able to carry out this assignment, Giovanni Bellini presided over what was probably the largest painting studio in Italy, with dozens of assistants. These acolytes are believed to have included the youthful Titian (c. 1490–1576), the greatest Renaissance painter of the next

Fig. 67: Madonna and Child Enthroned,
oil painting by Giovanni Bellini

Fig. 68 (opposite): The Baptism of Christ,
oil painting by Cima da Conegliano

generation, and Sebastiano del Piombo (1485–1547), who carried the intense colorism of his Venetian birthplace to Rome, where he is credited with introducing it to Raphael and other High Renaissance artists.[29]

Compared with her achievements in the fields of painting, publishing, Greek scholarship, and the collection of classical antiquities, the Republic's early Renaissance architectural projects were much more hesitant and, ultimately, far less successful. This was particularly the case with a program of ambitious state commissions authorized between 1438 and 1500 that included constructing a new ceremonial entrance to the Ducal Palace, rebuilding the Palace's eastern wing, and erecting a large clock tower in the Piazza San Marco. During this period of direct state patronage, well-designed, architecturally original buildings were all too often marred by inferior, inconsistent additions. With such projects, government officials often went to extraordinary lengths to curtail expense in the planning stage, only to overlook enormous cost overruns and blatant fraud during actual construction. Judged by the final architectural results of the period, the entire process of communal decision making, designed to yield works of the highest quality for which every option had been carefully considered, appears to have broken down. In addition to a slackening in quality, a number of doges were allowed to treat portions of the Ducal Palace as private monuments. Venetian state architecture began to display signs of the same unchecked narcissism that routinely debased mainland patronage.[30]

A New Ceremonial Entrance to the Ducal Palace

When the Piazzetta wing of the Ducal Palace was completed in 1438, its massive 245-foot flank ended only a short distance from the south wall of the Basilica San Marco; crammed into this brief interval directly opposite the San Marco Campanile was a low, meager doorway, one of the Palace's two existing land portals. The second opening, a narrow tunnel running from the ground-floor arcade of the Palace harbor front, was bordered on both sides by fetid prison cells. Not surprisingly, Venetian authorities felt an immediate wish to commission a much more architecturally distinguished entrance to their splendid new government center, and given its direct communication with the Piazzetta and Piazza, the slender passageway between the Palace and the Basilica was judged to be the superior site. The state chose the Venetian sculptors Giovanni (c. 1355–1443) and Bartolomeo Bon

(c. 1374–1467) to design and install the new portal, and a detailed contract was quickly signed. The Bon design (*Fig. 69*) drew heavily on the ornate window and balcony complex that the Masegne brothers had installed on the upper story of the Palace harbor wing three decades earlier. Of course, in the center of that enormous façade, the highly elaborate Masegne composition, located forty feet or more above eye level, functions as no more than a modest accent in a much larger architectural field. But placing such an ultra-refined work at ground level in an extremely constricted space creates an entirely different impression. Viewed close up, the new portal, known as the Porta della Carta, seems labored and precious, and its profusion of meticulous detail fails to harmonize with either of the two great building fronts between which it has been inserted. The Porta's cornices and string courses do not line up with the horizontal divisions of the Palace or the Basilica, and the simplicity and elegance which distinguish the quatrefoil tracery of the Palace loggia have, in the Gothic window of the Porta, degenerated into flimsy, insubstantial filigree (*Fig. 70*).[31]

The Porta della Carta also reveals the first troubling signs of ducal self-aggrandizement in San Marco district public architecture. While the Porta is crowned with the figure of Justice, and its side niches house representations of the virtues Temperance, Charity, Fortitude, and Prudence, the composition's central and most conspicuous feature is an extremely realistic, almost life-size statue of Doge Francesco Foscari (*Fig. 71*). Despite the fact that Foscari is shown kneeling before the Winged Lion of Saint Mark, the installation of this work immediately above the doorway was a clear violation of the rule forbidding ducal portraits outside the Ducal Palace. It ensured that each successor doge would have to pass directly under Foscari's effigy to reach the Palace courtyard where the final stage of his ducal coronation ceremony would be performed. The Foscari statue is not mentioned in the detailed project contract of 1438 and does not seems to have been part of the original Bon design. One can only surmise that at some later date, Foscari, one of the most imperious doges in Venetian history (just as Tommaso Mocenigo had feared he would be), forced his way into the ongoing project and began treating the Porta as a personal memorial. One commentator has even suggested that Foscari offered to build the Porta at his own expense, but there is no clear documentary evidence to substantiate this statement. What does seem certain is that Foscari, buoyed by the popular success of his expansionist policies on the Italian mainland, intentionally ignored existing state prohibitions against ducal self-glorification, and the rest of the Venetian government failed to check his arrogance.[32]

Fig. 69: Porta della Carta
by Giovanni and Bartolomeo Bon

Fig. 70: Detail of the Porta della Carta

Fig. 71: Effigy of Doge Francesco Foscari kneeling before the .
Winged Lion, above the doorway of the Porta della Carta

In 1440, work began on the second phase of Foscari's project, a stone passageway, twenty feet high, sixteen feet wide and eighty-four feet long, which would conduct visitors entering through the Porta della Carta (now nearing its construction midpoint) into the Ducal Palace courtyard. At the eastern end of this connecting tunnel, Doge Foscari and his successors in office spent the next four and a half decades erecting an eighty-foot-high, quasi-Gothic, quasi-classical, double-storied triumphal arch known as the Arco Foscari (*Fig. 72*). The Arco's central frame, a large rounded arch superimposed immediately above a handsome, semicircular portal, is a direct borrowing from the western façade of the Basilica, and its white and pink voussoirs of Istrian stone and Verona marble mirror the colors of the Ducal Palace. However, this architecturally distinguished core, carefully designed to harmonize with the public monuments of the Piazza and Piazzetta, is unfortunately flanked by and crowned with a variety of inferior additions in several incongruent styles. There is a huge disparity in the quality of the Arco's sculptural works, from Antonio Rizzo's magnificent bronze figures of Adam and Eve, inserted in niches just above eye level, to the insipid figures of Saint Mark and the Liberal Arts installed on spires at the top of the

Fig. 72: The Arco Foscari seen from the Giants' Staircase

composition. Etched into the Arco surface are the Foscari coat of arms and the heraldic symbols of two later doges, additional evidence that during the latter half of the fifteenth century, the old prohibitions against ducal self-aggrandizement in important public settings had ceased to be enforced.[33]

Rebuilding the Eastern Wing of the Ducal Palace

For most of the fifteenth century, the Arco Foscari was almost the sole note of architectural ornament in the Ducal Palace's otherwise plain, bare-brick courtyard, an enclosure that also served as the daily exercise yard for state prisoners held in surrounding ground-floor cells. Then, on September 14, 1483, a major fire severely damaged a large section of the Palace's eastern wing, including the doge's living quarters and many state council chambers located south of the ducal residence. The disaster could hardly have come at a worse time—territorial wars on the Italian mainland and the need to defend against constant Turkish attacks in the Eastern Mediterranean had already brought on a severe financial crisis. Yet, in spite of impending bankruptcy, the Republic immediately held an architectural competition to reconstruct the damaged building and allocated six thousand ducats to implement the winning proposal. The contract was awarded to Antonio Rizzo (c. 1430–1498 or 1499), a native of Verona whose essentially Renaissance design was chosen over other Gothic entries. It was an audacious decision; although Rizzo's earlier sculptural achievements on the Arco Foscari project were highly regarded, at this point his architectural experience was quite limited. One knowledgeable scholar has suggested that Rizzo's selection can be explained in part by his distinguished military service six years earlier; he had been wounded while courageously defending a Venetian outpost in Albania against Turkish assault. Whatever role such martial valor may have played in this initial decision, the state soon expanded Rizzo's commission to include the design and installation of a freestanding ceremonial staircase rising to the second story of the reconstructed eastern wing directly opposite the Arco Foscari. This addition would complete the entrance axis (from the Porta della Carta into the Palace courtyard) that the Republic had initiated over four decades earlier.[34]

Rizzo's undertaking began remarkably well, particularly his plan for embellishing the rear face of the eastern wing along the Rio di Palazzo. His design for this early phase of the project (*Fig. 73*) features a boldly rusticated base—a grid of sharply pointed diamonds in high relief—running two-thirds the length of the Palace just above the water line. Above this, the alternating square windows and panels of the mezzanine level and the tall, round-arched windows of the three identical loggia stages that make up the top half of the composition are framed with clear, simple moldings. The total impression, particularly at the lower levels, is vigorous, regular, and majestic, a striking merger of Gothic energy and Renaissance harmony. Ruskin called it the noblest work of the Venetian Renaissance and one of the world's finest examples of finished masonry. In fact, its artistry has led some scholars to suggest that the Rio façade was not designed by Rizzo at all, but rather by Mauro Codussi (c. 1440–1504), a Lombard stonemason who enjoyed a prolific architectural career in Venice after migrating there in the 1460s. In their view, Rizzo was merely the *proto* (short for *protomaestro*) or construction supervisor of a plan originally devised by Codussi, whom most experts agree was the greatest Venetian architect of the fifteenth century, in large part because his best work seems so close to the simplicity, clarity, and mathematical harmony of Brunelleschi, an acknowledged Renaissance genius.[35]

Fig. 73: The Ducal Palace facade along the Rio di Palazzo, designed by Antonio Rizzo

Inside the Palace courtyard, reconstruction commenced in the northeast corner, where the ducal apartments had been located. Here, the threshold issue was how much the disorderly array of interior walls and window openings that had survived the fire should be altered to support the construction of a new, stylistically consistent courtyard façade. Given the severe financial pressures of 1484–1485, the state opted for the cheaper, short-term solution of leaving the existing warren of walls and windows in place, a fateful decision that would plague later phases of the project. Rizzo tried to address this problem in part by running an arcaded portico and loggia across the two lower floors of the courtyard (*Fig. 74*), thereby masking the building's internal incoherence behind an orderly exterior, at least on the lower stories. Rizzo's handsome ground-floor portico, a series of sturdy semicircular arches resting on octagonal piers with a circular opening (an oculus) cut into the wall above each arch, conveys an impression of elegant but powerful Renaissance order. And while the second-floor loggia of pointed Gothic arches resting on stylistically incongruous double columns is not nearly as successful, it at least mirrors the strict regularity of the portico below. Together, the courtyard arcades (each a precise symmetrical pattern displaying twice as much shadowed opening as solid wall) recall the open, repetitive rhythms of the Palace's exterior facade.[36]

The freestanding ceremonial staircase that Rizzo built into the eastern wing of the Palace (*Fig. 75*) was designed to provide a raised platform for the climax of the ducal coronation ceremony. By the fifteenth century, this ritual opened with a religious service in the Basilica, followed by public festivities in the Piazza, and ended with the new doge mounting a landing in the Palace courtyard to receive the oath of office and be crowned with the ducal cap or *corno*. Rizzo's design, an assemblage of simple, pleasing shapes, is an impressive achievement, particularly when viewed head-on and framed by the arch of the Arco Foscari. The staircase is topped with a splendid stage surface twice the width of the stairs themselves, and the fact that the entire structure is restricted to the modest span of courtyard immediately opposite the Arco in no way defeats its impression of genuine Renaissance grandeur. Unfortunately, the project's decorative ornament is another matter entirely. While it is certainly grandiose—a cornucopia of imagery from the fabled Roman past, including torches, helmets, shields, tunics, and statues of winged victory—it bears almost no relation to the Republic's actual historical experience. This miscellaneous display of antique motifs was imported from the literary imagination of the Italian mainland,

Fig. 74: Arcaded portico and loggia, Ducal Palace courtyard,
designed by Antonio Rizzo

where, by the late fifteenth century, Venetian territorial acquisitions had become a major factor in the city's financial well-being. Erected purely for show (it was originally painted and gilded), its aesthetic qualities are decidedly inferior to the delightful figurative carving found on the capitals of the Palace exterior completed six decades earlier.[37]

The stairway decorative scheme also exemplified the blight of ducal self-glorification which plagued the fifteenth-century Ducal Palace program. The staircase was constructed during the dogate of Agostino Barbarigo (1486–1501), a proud, ambitious man (*Fig. 76*)

*Fig. 75: Freestanding ceremonial staircase (known as
the Giants' Staircase), Ducal Palace courtyard,
by Antonio Rizzo*

whose election to succeed his brother, Doge Marco Barbarigo, by itself violated one of the cardinal anti-dynastic principles of Venetian politics. Discovering that his fellow nobles were unwilling to enforce long-standing protections against ducal abuse, Barbarigo decided to abandon restraint altogether. He not only embellished the staircase with his family coat of arms; he defaced it with his carved portrait and a pompous Latin epigram that declared, "Agostino Barbarigo, Doge of Venice, had this work constructed." This was a deliberate reference to the famous inscription by the Roman general Agrippa engraved across the front of the Pantheon in Rome. Barbarigo's self-congratulatory gesture spoke volumes about the current health of the Republic's communal political life. Less than two generations after the death of Tommaso Mocenigo, a doge of Venice was using the iconography of the Ducal Palace courtyard, a site intended to be free from all displays of personal arrogance and egotism, to give himself the Venetian equivalent of a Roman military triumph.[38]

Fig. 76: Portrait of Doge Agostino Barbarigo
by Gentile Bellini

241

In the era of Tommaso Mocenigo, it is doubtful that such an obvious breach of Venetian ideals would ever have occurred, or if it had, it would quickly have been recognized for what it was—a clear warning of deeper systemic corruption. However, during the permissive age of Agostino Barbarigo, it seems to have been quite easy to hide evidence of gross criminal behavior. Thus, it took a prolonged two-year audit to discover that Antonio Rizzo had embezzled a total of twelve thousand ducats during the fourteen years he had served as proto of the courtyard rebuilding project. To put this in perspective, the amount Rizzo stole was almost six times his earned compensation during the same period. At the time of the state's investigation in 1498, the embezzled twelve thousand ducats represented fifteen percent of the eighty thousand ducats Venice had spent on the project to date, and the eighty-thousand-ducat total was more than thirteen times the original amount allocated to the project, which was only half finished. Nor did Venetians even enjoy the satisfaction of seeing Rizzo brought to justice. Upon being discovered, Rizzo fled to Foligno, beyond formal Venetian jurisdiction, where he is believed to have died shortly after his arrival. But the story does not end there. Three years later, a posthumous state inquiry based on the testimony of some two hundred witnesses revealed an equally appalling record of ducal corruption. Doge Barbarigo was found guilty of bribery, nepotism, sale of office, extortion, smuggling, and tax evasion, and his family was forced to repay thousands of ducats. Unfortunately, rather than being a completely isolated phenomenon, Barbarigo's criminality marked only the outer limits of a pronounced trend in the city's late fifteenth-century political culture. It was a period when improprieties and favoritism—a general tendency for patrician insiders to take advantage of their official positions to enrich themselves and their families and to look the other way when other nobles engaged in similar conduct—had become all too common. In this environment, an unscrupulous doge like Barbarigo was allowed to abuse his office in a manner that an earlier Republic would never have tolerated.[39]

By the time he fled Venice, Rizzo had completed the two lower floors of the eastern wing and all or most of the ceremonial staircase. The state replaced him with Pietro Lombardo (c. 1435–1515), the city's finest Renaissance relief sculptor. The new proto had already served as Rizzo's chief assistant, but his gift for architectural design was far less developed than that of his predecessor. Not surprisingly, then, Lombardo simply took the ultra-refined ornament of Rizzo's staircase and replicated it along the two upper floors of the eastern wing. However, before doing so, he made no attempt to systematize the many differently sized and randomly spaced window openings over which this huge swath of marble veneer was to be laid. As a result, in spite of being a virtuoso display of stone carving technique, Lombardo's upper-story addition remains a hopelessly confused mass of costly, incongruent detail (*Fig. 77*). On aesthetic as well as financial grounds, it would have been far wiser to eliminate the Lombardo phase of the project altogether, a judgment that even a momentary glance at the southern and western faces of the courtyard, where Rizzo's handsome, vigorous arcades are boldly contrasted with upper walls of unadorned brick, will confirm (*Fig. 78*).[40]

The Clock Tower

In 1495, the Senate and the Procuracy of Saint Mark jointly commissioned the construction of a Clock Tower along the northern boundary of the Piazza where the *Merceria*, the city's chief commercial street and the principal connection between San Marco and the Rialto market, entered the square. On general stylistic grounds, the Tower is widely believed to have been designed by Mauro Codussi, the leading architect of the early Venetian Renaissance. As with many of his works, Codussi's Tower seems to have been inspired by the architectural principles of Leone Battista Alberti, the humanist author of a widely influential treatise on classical architecture whose buildings Codussi knew even if he had not read Alberti's book. According to Alberti, to achieve classical correctness, a square tower should be built in tiers, with each stage displaying a different classical order, and the height of the stacked tiers should be at least four times their width. Codussi's Tower (*Fig. 79*) not only satisfied each of these Albertian criteria, its inventive form deliberately mirrored many of the Piazza's most salient features. For instance, the Tower's triumphal arch paralleled the western portals of the Basilica and harmonized perfectly with the round-arched bays and windows (derived from Late Antique architectural models) that lined the rest of the medieval Piazza. In addition, the Tower's conspicuous verticality (much more pronounced at that time since Codussi's shaft was almost twice as high as some of the buildings between which it was originally inserted) created an obvious reference to the Campanile. The blue enamel and gold leaf on the Tower face and the pink and gray marble of the Tower side panels were clearly intended to suggest the Basilica's chromatic richness. And the two bronze figures (known as the Moors) at the top of the Tower, when seen outlined against

*Fig. 77: Pietro Lombardo's Ducal Palace courtyard eastern
wing addition—a confused mass of costly detail*

the Venetian sky, evoked the Gothic roof sculptures of the Basilica and the statues of the Winged Lion and Saint Theodore that crowned the Molo pillars.[41]

Upon its completion in 1499, Codussi's Clock Tower was easily the most successful Renaissance addition to the San Marco precinct made during the fifteenth century. With the upper half of its imposing, four-tiered classical shaft clearly visible above its modest surroundings, it served as a grand vertical crescendo to the range of round-arched bays and windows making up the medieval Piazza. Unfortunately, between 1500 and 1506, the Tower's elegant classical profile was seriously disfigured by the addition of two bulky supporting wings from the hands of an unknown architect (*Fig. 80*). Codussi's solitary Tower was springy and graceful, brimming with tensile strength; the wing additions are pedestrian and ponderous, burdened with heavy ground-floor lintels that bear no relation to anything

*Fig. 78: Abutting eastern (left) and southern (right) faces
of the Ducal Palace courtyard*

else in the Piazza. The wings, twice as wide and almost as tall as Codussi's shaft, not only negate its dramatic verticality, their clumsy design destroyed the felt harmony between the Tower's triumphal arch and the arcades and windows of the medieval Piazza. Like Pietro Lombardo's incoherent completion of the eastern face of the Ducal Palace courtyard, the decision to add wings to Codussi's Tower was a serious artistic blunder. Both illustrate how a project begun in the most promising manner under an architect of true genius could be seriously compromised by entrusting a later design phase to a clearly inferior talent. All too often during the late fifteenth century and the first decade of the sixteenth century, the city's traditional method of communal decision making, which had produced the masterworks of the past, seems to have become dysfunctional or been discarded altogether.[42]

Fig. 79: Mauro Codussi's original Clock Tower

Fig. 80: Mauro Codussi's Clock Tower
with later wing additions

CHAPTER ELEVEN

Embattled Maturity (1502–1529)

Adopting Mainland Values

Venice would never surpass the relative power and prosperity she enjoyed during the fifteenth century. With a population of no more than one hundred to one hundred thirty thousand, she was a major European state, conducting international diplomacy on an equal footing with national monarchies such as France and England. Her maritime commerce thrived; the six precisely organized, five-hundred-ship trading convoys she typically launched each year connected Venetian markets with every major port in the eastern Mediterranean. And by the 1450s, she was beginning to receive a growing stream of income from a terraferma empire that stretched from the shores of the lagoon to within thirty miles of Milan. Yet, even at this zenith of commercial and military success, there were disturbing signs that all was not well. As we have seen, there was a general decline in the quality of state-sponsored architectural projects authorized between 1438 and 1500, a not insignificant phenomenon. Artistic choices, particularly those that shape the outcome of a collective enterprise like public architecture, involve a great deal more than pure aesthetic preference; over time, they reveal critical shifts in a society's morale and general world view.[1]

Was there something in the economic and social experience of the Republic that helps to explain this deterioration in the quality of state architectural commissions from the beginning to the end of the fifteenth century? Specifically, what could account for an achievement gap as large as that which separates the nobility of the Ducal Palace itself, built between 1340 and 1438, from the triviality of the upper floors of the eastern wing of the Palace courtyard, constructed after 1485? What could have attracted late-fifteenth-century Venetian patricians to such an empty parade of antique ornament?

In 1400, Venice remained what she had been for the past four centuries—an almost exclusively maritime republic. Instead of receiving their income from the passive ownership of land, her governing families were active participants in international commerce. This was the crucial difference that distinguished Venetian noblemen from the other aristocrats of Europe, whom the Florentine writer Niccolò Machiavelli termed proper "gentlemen...who live off the revenue from their [landed] properties in a state of idleness and luxury without paying any attention to the cultivation of land or to any other occupation necessary to make a living."[2] Well into the 1400s, the Republic channeled most of her energies into sustaining this distinctive maritime commercial identity. In the fourteenth century, she had doubled the size of the Arsenale not once but twice, producing a fifteenth-century Venetian navy of thirty-three hundred ships and thirty-six thousand seamen which had no rival and that even in small concentrations dominated the Mediterranean and its adjoining waters. For instance, in 1416, when fifteen Venetian galleys cruising the eastern Aegean were confronted by a Turkish war fleet of 112 ships, the small Venetian force decimated the Ottoman armada, capturing a large number of vessels and killing most of the enemy sailors who did not flee the battle.[3]

A century later, the situation had changed dramatically. By 1500, the Venetian annexation of a major land empire in northern Italy, initially a defensive move designed to ensure control of vital overland trade routes, had become an essential part of the city's economy. The state was no longer extracting a net profit from her maritime empire; overseas expenses of 200,000 ducats now exactly matched overseas revenues. However, the government's receipt of 330,000 ducats from its mainland territories now exceeded mainland expenses by 240,000 ducats, and state management of the terraferma supplied much coveted public jobs to approximately a third of the governing patriciate. The terraferma empire also enabled rich Venetian aristocrats to invest increasingly large portions of their wealth in mainland agriculture. By 1446, native Paduans were complaining that Venetians owned a third of all the land there, and a few generations later, the Venetian Senate had difficulty establishing a commission to review tax assessments in Padua because only fifteen of three hundred senators did not own landed property in Paduan territory. This same pattern was repeated in other parts of the Venetian terraferma such as Verona and Vicenza. At least initially, most Venetian landowners brought little, if any, sentimentality to the task of running their new agricultural estates; they were guided by the same tough entrepreneurial logic they had habitually applied to international trade. For anyone who could afford to buy arable land in the Veneto, there was a great deal of money to be made raising food for a large regional capital located within a land-starved lagoon. Landed property was viewed as a wise investment like any other, a prudent way to spread financial risk by diversifying the sources of family income.[4]

Over time, however, this shift toward landed investment had major effects far beyond the Venetian economy. When fifteenth- and sixteenth-century Venetian patricians transferred their capital to the Italian mainland, they did so in the midst of a general resurgence of European feudal values. As part of this cultural shift, successful Italian merchants and bankers began to dream of building powerful family dynasties based on inherited social position rather than leaving their family fortunes entirely dependent on the next generation's performance in the rough-and-tumble commercial world from which they themselves had risen. This attraction to a system of entrenched privilege based on blood was particularly powerful in the Veneto, where the Republic's agricultural investments were concentrated. Here, in cities such as Verona and Vicenza, local elites had long clung to feudal prerogatives such as the use of noble titles, and with the growing popularity of chivalric values throughout the rest of Europe, native aristocrats in the Veneto became even more contemptuous of active participation in non-noble pursuits like commercial enterprise. This strengthening of Italian feudal custom was bolstered by the simultaneous spread of Renaissance humanism throughout the peninsula, leading to the emergence of what the social historian Jacob Burckhardt has described as the Renaissance personality. According to Burckhardt, this was a type characterized by strong feelings of envy, a tendency toward despotism, a relentless desire for individual glory and a readiness to use any means, including extreme violence, to achieve personal fame, all traits that were very close to those at the heart of European feudalism.[5]

In this environment, the migration of Venetian patricians to the Italian terraferma, where they began to receive a mounting share of their income from land and reside at least part of the year among a local nobility whose values were strongly feudal and fiercely anti-business, became a transformative experience. Exposure to mainland traditions of class consciousness and Renaissance ideals based on conformity with an imagined version of antique Roman and Greek culture began to subvert the patriciate's sense of its unique maritime identity. It made Venetian aristocrats wish to be more like other European nobles, with the not very surprising result that Venetian architectural projects began to be increasingly influenced by works on the Italian mainland. There, Renaissance builders frequently employed classical pomp and splendor to glorify an individual prince or family without great concern over whether the new monument bore any relation to local architectural or historical traditions. Part of the difficulty, in Burckhardt's view, was that the "rapid progress of humanism...paralyzed native impulses. Henceforth, men looked only to antiquity for the solution of every problem, and consequently allowed [their works] to turn into mere quotation."[6] All too often, the result was a building or monument whose display of antique imagery was sheer idle fancy, part of an architecture that seemed hollow at the core. This is precisely what happened to the Republic's late-fifteenth-century effort to renovate the eastern courtyard of the Ducal Palace.

Nor was this the worst of it. In the case of another Venetian project carried out at this time, the state not only abandoned continuity with earlier monuments; it deliberately destroyed a vital part of the city's historical fabric: the grand ceremonial passageway into the Basilica San Marco known as the Porta da Mar or Sea Gate. Beginning in the eleventh century, this richly decorated southern portal had offered direct access to the interior from the waters of the Venetian harbor, and it continued to serve as one of the Basilica's principal entrances even after the harbor inlet which led directly up to it had been filled in to construct the Piazzetta. But in 1501 the Sea Gate's great semicircular opening was walled up (*Fig. 81*) to create a private chapel dedicated to the memory of Cardinal Giambattista Zen, the pope's nephew, who left a large bequest to the state on the condition that he be permitted to construct his tomb memorial in the Basilica. That the Republic would sacrifice this critical symbol of her seagoing heritage for cold, hard cash speaks volumes about Venetian morale and the eclipsed sense of maritime identity her patrician governors were feeling at the turn of the sixteenth century.[7]

A century earlier, many adolescent patricians had learned the basics of seamanship while serving as bowmen of the quarterdeck on ships of the Venetian navy. But now, few if any young noblemen took advantage of such apprenticeships, and it had become increasingly difficult to find competent naval commanders among the members of the Venetian aristocracy. This decline was part of a general pattern. In an era when the Ottoman Empire, the Republic's chief Eastern rival, had opened the top ranks of its administrative and military hierarchies to men of ability regardless of their social or religious origins, Renaissance

Fig. 81: Porta da Mar walled up to create the Zen Chapel

Venice was moving in the opposite direction by making her closed political system even more rigid and impervious to new blood. The fifteenth-century Republic sought to protect the privileged position of her existing aristocratic families by enacting strict new regulation of what constituted noble status. This included a law stating that in order to be officially recognized as noble, all patrician male infants had to be registered in the famous *Libro d'Oro* (Golden Book) within eight days of birth.[8]

The Turkish Vise and Other Calamities

Given such tendencies, it is not surprising that during the last three decades of the fifteenth century, Venice suffered a series of major defeats by the Ottoman Turks in the contest for Mediterranean naval supremacy. The Ottomans, who two centuries earlier had been an obscure tribe of Muslim holy warriors living on the eastern fringe of the Byzantine world, were in the midst of a remarkable power surge that would ultimately net them an empire of fourteen million subjects. After swallowing up the whole of Asia Minor and a large part of the Balkans, in 1453 they employed huge siege cannon to blast their way into the ancient Byzantine capital of Constantinople and put its Greek and Latin residents to the sword. Sultan Mehmet II (known as the Conquerer) next turned his enormous military and naval resources to the task of seizing Venetian outposts in the Aegean, and fleets of forty Venetian ships began to encounter hostile Turkish armadas of three hundred vessels. Although the city expanded the Arsenale until it was the largest manufacturing facility in Europe (its perimeter walls were three miles long), even this forceful response was unavailing. In 1470, using the assault tactics they had perfected at Constantinople, the Sultan's troops captured and sacked Negropont, the Republic's largest overseas colony and principal Aegean naval base. The commander of the Venetian rescue fleet ordered his ships to flee at the decisive moment of battle, and Turkish cavalry raids into the Veneto came so close to the lagoon that smoke from burning villages could be seen from the Campanile. In the ensuing peace negotiations, Venice renounced her claim to most of the Aegean and the Greek mainland and agreed to pay the Sultan an annual tribute of ten thousand ducats for the right to continue trading in what were now Turkish waters. The Republic's acceptance of such humiliating terms and utter failure to retard the pace of the Turkish juggernaut raised serious questions about her ability to protect the remainder of her maritime empire.[9]

The next major Turkish naval campaign did not begin until August, 1499, when an Ottoman fleet of 270 ships was sighted off the southwest coast of Greece. Unfortunately, the Venetian navy's performance in this action was no better than its conduct at the battle of Negropont three decades earlier. In a series of four quick contests, no more than a fraction of the 170 ships in the powerful Venetian fleet (including only a handful of its great war galleys) proved willing to engage the enemy. In each battle, a few Venetian vessels would charge into the thick of the Ottoman line and fight heroically while the bulk of the Venetian force, under the direction of aristocratic commanders with little naval competence and even less courage, held back and watched the Ottomans slaughter their countrymen. To make matters worse, the Venetian admiral, a rich businessman with almost no experience at sea, refused to discipline or even chastise his patrician officer corps for fear they might vote against him if he chose to run for doge. A hundred years earlier, the Republic had wisely entrusted her war fleets to charismatic sea dogs like Vettor Pisani, whose audacious brilliance and patriotic disdain for political intrigue made him able to defeat her enemies in the direst of circumstances. Now, in the wake of the city's latest naval debacle, Ottoman troops were once more making deep raids into the Veneto, and Venice was again compelled to accede to harsh Turkish peace terms. The Sultan stripped the Republic of virtually all her Greek coastal citadels, including the vital supply ports of Modone and Corone, which in her prime almost three centuries earlier she had wrested from the Byzantine Empire.[10]

At almost the same moment, that is, on September 9, 1499, the Portuguese navigator Vasco da Gama completed a direct all-water voyage between Lisbon and the spice markets of India by sailing around the Cape of Good Hope on the southern tip of Africa. In so doing, he demonstrated that it was both possible and extremely profitable to completely ignore the Mediterranean transportation system whose systematic exploitation had formed the basis of Venetian wealth and power for the past four centuries. Portuguese merchants could now bring precious Eastern spices directly to Europe without incurring the heavy customs duties and transit charges Venetians traders had to pay in Muslim ports such as Istanbul, Alexandria, and Antioch. For instance, to compensate Arab middlemen for the danger and expense of operating land caravans across Central Asia and the sands of Arabia, a hundred kilos of pepper that cost three ducats in Calcutta normally sold for one hundred ducats by the time it reached Egypt. Eliminating this land journey allowed

Portuguese traders, who were able to buy directly from Indian bazaars, to make profits of two hundred to three hundred percent, a rate of return Venetian merchants had not seen since their monopoly control of Greek markets immediately following the Fourth Crusade. In short, da Gama's feat transformed the entire Mediterranean into a secondary waterway. Europe's major trading highway for the importation of rare Eastern goods now led through the southern Atlantic and Indian Oceans, a new frontier that Venice was unwilling to enter, governed, as she was, by a timid, self-serving nobility no longer able to identify with the city's brilliant naval past. While the national monarchies of Europe embarked on an era of oceanic voyaging and discovery, Venice refused to step outside her historic comfort zone and never made a serious attempt to compete with transatlantic sea powers such as Spain, France, Holland, and England. Her governing patriciate seemed frozen in time, unable or unwilling to alter its established routines. Those who still earned a living as international merchants continued to plow the old Mediterranean trade routes, where the vast armadas of the Ottoman Turks now lay in wait.[11]

In establishing a terraferma empire, the city had made powerful enemies, including huge national and transnational states such as France, Spain, and the Habsburg Empire, all of whom had territorial designs on portions of Italy controlled by the Republic. In response to such threats, Venice hired a large mercenary army and hoped that this, plus the historic rivalries which normally divided her foreign antagonists, would be sufficient protection. And it was a successful strategy until the Venetian Senate made the fatal error of seizing territory in the papal state of Romagna, an action that enraged the new pope, Giuliano della Rovere, who upon election had taken the imperial sounding name of Julius II (*Fig. 82*). A towering, unbalanced egomaniac whose ungoverned outbursts and obsessive hatreds were the stuff of legend, Julius quickly formed the Republic's mainland adversaries into an alliance known as the League of Cambrai with the express goal of separating Venice from her terraferma possessions. He then excommunicated the entire Venetian populace and called on Christians everywhere to attack them and their property wherever they might be found. On May 15, 1509, the Republic's mercenary army and the collective forces of the League, both with around twenty thousand men, faced each other near a village called Agnadello, about twenty miles east of Milan. In the opening phase of the battle, a section of the Venetian army under a general named Alviano repulsed two French attacks, but when the senior commander, the count of Pitigliano, failed to support Alviano

Fig. 82: Pope Julius II (Giuliano della Rovere) by Raphael

with his main force, Venetian defenses crumbled, and her entire army was routed. Mass desertion quickly followed, and suddenly there was no organized military force between Milan and the shores of the lagoon capable of stopping the enemies of the Republic bent on her destruction. This set off an immediate chain reaction in which, one after another, the cities of the Venetian terraferma opened their gates to the league's victorious armies. Within the lagoon itself, residents were stunned to learn that in a matter of days, they had lost their entire mainland empire. Venetian bonds plummeted, losing as much as ninety percent of their value and impoverishing many members of the governing patriciate. To avert total ruin, the Republic was forced to accept the pope's draconian surrender terms, including a prescribed ordeal of public humiliation. Venetian peace envoys were required to remain kneeling on the steps of Saint Peter's for over an hour before Julius permitted them to crawl to the papal chair on their knees and kiss his foot.[12]

Then, seemingly having suffered total defeat, the Republic began to profit from the confusion of her enemies. Because the league had suddenly attained all of its goals in a single stroke, there was little reason for its members to remain united, and the alliance began to unravel; the pope and Spain turned against France, and France, in turn, joined with Venice against the pope and Spain. By acting opportunistically in the ensuing struggles, over time the city managed to reconstitute a great deal of her northern Italian empire. But despite this recovery of lost territory, the first two decades of the sixteenth century remained a period of severe economic crisis for Venice. Rich patricians were forced to shoulder an enormous tax burden to keep the government afloat, and when this proved inadequate, to subscribe to large involuntary loans despite the fact that interest on Venetian state debt had been suspended and revenue from the mainland had either stopped entirely or been drastically reduced.

The humiliation of Agnadello also remained a deep psychological wound to the city's collective consciousness even after most of its financial effects had passed. It marked a critical turning point, a defining moment when Venetians could no longer ignore the hard truth of their situation. Europe and the Mediterranean world were experiencing a massive acceleration in the scale and expense of both land and naval combat, and as a small republic with a population of no more than 200,000, Venice would never again be capable of matching the military power of the far larger states with which she was now contending. Although her sixteenth-century armadas would be four to five times larger than those with which she ruled the Mediterranean in the early fifteenth century, Venetian fleets would never again be equal to the Spanish or Turkish navies. Only states with populations numbering in the millions, like the kingdoms of France and Spain or the empires of the Habsburgs and the Ottoman Turks, could hope to meet the staggering costs of all-out warfare in the new imperial age. France had managed to become the richest state in Europe through consolidating its separate provinces into a single nation under the Valois dynasty. This concentration of resources not only financed French military aims, including the invasion of Italy under Charles VIII in 1494, it allowed monarchs such as Francois I (r. 1515–1547) to bring

Italian artists and architects such as Leonardo da Vinci to France. France's principal adversary in the struggle for European supremacy was the Habsburg Empire of Charles V, who by 1519 united in his person the titles of German emperor, Spanish king, and monarch of Austria and Holland. Commanding an empire that covered half a continent, he ruled on a scale not seen in Europe since Charlemagne the Great. Charles' lavish court was the focal point of renascent feudalism, and as the greatest Western art patron of the sixteenth century, his strong Renaissance cultural preferences exerted a powerful influence throughout the rest of Europe, including the city-states of Italy.[13]

Psychological Transformation and Protective Coloration

In the course of a single decade, Venice watched the Portuguese hijack her Eastern spice trade and witnessed the sudden collapse of her entire terraferma empire. These events, combined with a continuing failure to protect her Mediterranean strongholds from the advancing Ottoman Turks, struck hard at Venetian self-confidence. They shattered the Republic's long-held conviction that she enjoyed a special destiny, a providential insulation from the vicissitudes which affected the rest of Europe. Badly shaken, Venetian patricians remembered the jeers mainland aristocrats had often directed at their landless, mercantile origins. It was one thing to ignore being called a city of money-grubbing fishmongers during centuries of accelerating wealth and territorial expansion. But now, with their sense of divine ordination sapped by mounting reverses, it became much harder to disregard such coarse jibes. Disoriented and depressed, some Venetians even began to experience a hitherto submerged sense of inferiority when they compared their city with her larger and more powerful competitors. As they ceased to be capable of controlling their fate, their belief in Venetian exceptionalism (based on a series of brilliant achievements over a time span equaled only by that of the Roman Empire) began to waver. What emerged in its place was a feeling of continual apprehension and a fear of imminent loss, emotions that never entirely abated even during future periods of objective success.[14]

Once the city recovered her mainland territories, Venetian patricians returned to their estates in northern Italy. In fact, given the smaller profits available to seagoing merchants in a Turkish-dominated Mediterranean and the growing returns of mainland agriculture, the terraferma migration of Venetian capital began to accelerate. Naturally, this also hastened the transformation of Venetian identity begun in fifteenth century. There was an increasing disengagement from the city's maritime, commercial past and her historic reliance on Eastern architectural models, replaced by a growing embrace of the political and cultural orthodoxies that prevailed in the rest of Europe. In artistic and architectural terms, this meant conforming to the High Renaissance models patronized by the German, Spanish, and French courts and the Roman pontiff.[15]

With its political roots in resurgent European feudalism, sixteenth-century Renaissance thought stressed the importance of stringent class distinctions and linked this aristocratic sentiment to rigid ideas about acceptable forms of architecture. Its adherents argued that the only way to achieve architectural nobility was by strictly following classical Roman building models and resolutely scorning anything associated with commercial activity. In his treatise *Libro secondo*, the Renaissance architect and writer Sebastiano Serlio (1475–1554) spelled out exactly what this would mean for buildings like the existing monuments of the Piazza San Marco. He began by characterizing such architecture as mean and disorderly, appropriate only for use as shops and brothels by "citizens, lawyers, merchants, parasites and other similar persons." To remedy such blight, he recommended totally reconstructing the site to create "a decorous, orderly scene...entirely occupied by classical buildings."[16] This new all-Renaissance precinct should be set aside exclusively for members of the governing aristocracy, whom Serlio compared to great princes and kings, despite the fact that, in the case of Venetian patricians, their family fortunes were originally derived from the same mercantile pursuits the author held in such contempt.[17]

As Venetian vulnerabilities mounted, such ideas began to find a more receptive home within the Republic. If for no other reason than protective coloration—to project the aura, if not the reality, of national power—many influential Venetians concluded that the city needed to reclothe herself, at least partially, in the mantle of antique Roman authority adopted by France and the Habsburg Empire. Some even agreed with Serlio that the Republic should authorize an entirely new *all'antica* reconstruction of the Piazza area involving the wholesale replacement of its historic landmarks, but this was a minority view. Although clearly attracted by the international prestige of the Roman Renaissance, most patricians also remained loyal to the city's long-standing tradition of artistic synthesis rooted in the city's mercantile, non-Roman, nonfeudal, and primarily Eastern historical experience. The tension between these two perspectives, a radical all-classical revisionism and a judicious mediation between the old and the new based on the city's traditional assemblage art techniques, would dominate architectural initiatives in the San Marco district during the sixteenth century.

Reconstructing the Campanile and the North Face of the Piazza

In the decade following Agnadello, the Republic was engaged in almost continuous military strife to regain as much as she could of her lost mainland territories. Yet, as strained as this left her finances, between 1510 and 1513, the procurators de supra (the branch of the Procuracy of Saint Mark that retained responsibility for the architecture of the Piazza San Marco) commissioned two major replacement projects in response to natural disasters. These undertakings, reconstructions of the summit of the San Marco Campanile and the buildings making up the north face of the Piazza, were both placed in the hands of Bartolomeo Bon of Bergamo (c. 1450–1529), whose position as proto to the procurators combined the roles of architect and building supervisor. Begun in the late ninth century, the shaft of the Campanile did not attain its full height until the eleventh century, and its bell chamber was crowned with a gilded copper spire only at the end of the fourteenth. In 1489, the completed tower was struck by a bolt of lightning that destroyed its golden pinnacle and hurled its bells onto the bricks of the Piazza two hundred feet below; when Bon began reconstruction in 1510, the shattered chamber was covered with a squat wooden cap. The arcades of Bon's new pyramidal summit, finished in 1514, consist of tall, semicircular arches resting on slender columns, and the overall impression is one of simple, classical elegance. The total height of Bon's grand replacement crown—limestone bell chamber, brick attic, and copper-covered spire tipped with a gilded angel—is 160 feet. The vivid contrast between his white stone bell chamber and the red brick shaft below mirrors the colors of the nearby Ducal Palace.[18]

The second project begun during this period was even more ambitious. In 1513 the procurators de supra commissioned a total reconstruction of the north face of the Piazza after a series of fires destroyed substantial parts of that five-hundred-foot-long, classically arcaded medieval perimeter. Surprisingly for such a massive public contract, one that necessitated completely demolishing the existing structure above the foundations and transforming much of the Piazza into a dusty, crowded stoneyard for the better part of a decade, many important facts remain in doubt. For instance, we do not know who designed the Piazza's new façade or when the new building scheme was created, and opinion is split over the function this costly undertaking was intended to serve. Although Bon unquestionably supervised construction from 1513 to 1517, most scholars see the mark of Mauro Codussi, the finest Venetian architect of the fifteenth century, in the project's fundamental design. However, the ramifications of this are far from clear. Did Codussi, who almost certainly designed the adjoining Clock Tower around 1495, also take a direct hand in designing this new perimeter façade before he died in 1504, leaving Bon to simply carry out the master's directions from now lost plans or drawings? Or did Bon, having been influenced by Codussi over many years, himself conceive of an architectural plan which reminded everyone of the master? Some have even given credit to another, entirely different architect, and no one knows for sure. Just as puzzling is the fact that while most expert opinion holds that the project was commissioned to provide housing for the procurators themselves, one highly distinguished authority maintains that the procurators lived on the opposite or south side of the square and that all of the space in the new building was rented out to tenants. In any event, because the structure was commissioned, paid for, and owned by the procurators de supra, it has consistently been referred to as the Procuratie, and, since the waning years of the sixteenth century, as the Procuratie Vecchie (or old procuratorial apartments) to distinguish it from a later series of procuratorial residences built on the south side of the Piazza).[19]

But however shrouded in doubt its design process and original purpose may be, the architectural result is clear. If Mauro Codussi was the genius responsible for the design of the Procuratie Vecchie (*Fig. 83*), this has to rank as one of his finest efforts. If the scheme originated with Bon, then he deserves the supreme compliment of having produced an edifice whose blend of elegant classicism and creative innovation are truly worthy of being called Codussian. In part, such splendid qualities can be explained by the fact that the architect, whoever he was, based the form of the Procuratie Vecchie on the open, transparent, arcaded style of the medieval Veneto-Byzantine palace front he was asked to replace. To the harmony and proportion of this classically derived original with its roots in Late Antique Roman villa architecture, he added a number of contemporary Renaissance refinements and a few inspired novelties. After reinforcing the medieval foundations, three new stories were substituted for the two-story medieval palace, and two hundred slender, fluted

Fig. 83: North face of the Piazza San Marco known
as the Procuratie Vecchie

colonettes were added as decorative inserts on the two upper floors. Along the ground-floor arcade, the architect used square piers to replace the round columns on which the medieval arches had rested, thus conforming the new building to Alberti's dictum (based on antique precedent) that arches should always be supported on piers, and columns should carry only lintels. In addition, semicircular Renaissance arches were substituted for the more stilted Byzantine arches of the medieval palace, and the new façade, constructed in white Istrian stone, was outfitted with simple, unadorned moldings and entablatures in the style of Brunelleschi. Some of the Procuratie Vecchie's more inventive features are at its summit. For instance, the long horizontal line of its topmost frieze is perforated with one hundred occuli, one above each third-story arched window, and its rhythm of exuberant roof merlons (decorative stone jars alternating with what look like silhouettes of perfume bottles raised on pedestals) adds a crowning sense of architectural frolic.[20]

The Procuratie Vecchie is five hundred feet long, and each of its fifty bays conforms to a single, unvarying pattern from top to bottom, yet somehow this extreme repetitiveness never becomes tedious. Part of the explanation is that the façade is pierced with 350 major apertures, and these openings occupy a collective area which is nearly three times as great as the exterior solid wall surface. Consequently, like the portico of a Brunelleschi cloister from the previous century (with its emphasis on a two-dimensional outline rather than volumetric form), the façade of the new Procuratie lacks the built-up plastic surface and building mass of many sixteenth-century Renaissance buildings, which can weary the eye when replicated at great length. The generous semicircular openings of the ground-floor arcade also have an important scenic function; they permit visitors strolling along the Procuratie's covered walkway to enjoy a succession of framed panoramas of the Piazza, the Campanile, the Basilica, and the distant Ducal Palace.[21]

But for all their size and classically derived symmetry, the reconstructed Campanile summit and the Procuratie Vecchie did relatively little to alter an early sixteenth-century visitor's general impression of the Piazza and Piazzetta. More substantial change would have to wait until Venice made a more complete recovery from the economic and military calamities that followed her defeat at Agnadello. This did not occur until the pope and the German emperor signed a peace treaty in Bologna in 1529, inaugurating a long break in the European power wars that had devastated the city's mainland possessions for almost two decades. Of course, for such a major renovation effort to be truly successful, it would have to be directed by an architect who possessed both original genius and a sympathetic understanding of San Marco's existing historic monuments. Fortunately for the Republic, just such an individual was already near at hand.

CHAPTER TWELVE

The Roman Renaissance Comes to Venice (1527–1607)

The Arrival of Jacopo Sansovino

In 1527, when the forty-one-year-old sculptor and architect Jacopo Sansovino (1486–1570) fled to Venice to escape the horrors of the Sack of Rome, he had no idea that he would spend the rest of his life in the lagoon city (*Fig. 84*). He had already made one major resettlement, having left his native Florence for Rome at the age of twenty. Soon after his arrival in the papal city, the young Florentine was introduced by his fellow countryman, the architect Giuliano da Sangallo (1443–1516), to a trio of Renaissance geniuses: the architect Donato Bramante (1443–1514), the painter and architect Raphael (1483–1520), and Michelangelo Buonarroti (1475–1564), all of whom were working in the court of Pope Julius II. Despite his youth, Sansovino thrived in this highly competitive environment, working principally as a sculptor for most of the next decade; he became a particular friend of Bramante's and assisted him on two of his projects. His architectural career took a major leap forward in 1513 when the dying Julius II was succeeded by a Florentine pope, Leo X, the son of Lorenzo de' Medici. Within a few years, Sansovino was competing with Giuliano da Sangallo, Raphael, and Michelangelo to design a Renaissance façade for the Medici church of San Lorenzo in Florence. Even more impressively, he won the initial commission to build the Roman church of San Giovanni dei Fiorentini, intended to hold the growing colony of Florentines who had followed Leo X to the papal city. His proposal was chosen over designs submitted by Raphael, Baldassare Peruzzi (1481–1536), and Antonio da Sangallo the Younger (1484–1546). As his architectural reputation grew, he was invited for consultations in other Italian cities, including Venice, where in 1523 he met with the procurators de supra of Saint Mark to discuss a method for restoring and stabilizing the domes of the Basilica San Marco.[1]

*Fig. 84: Portrait of Jacopo Sansovino
as a young man by Tintoretto*

This promising early career came to an abrupt end in May 1527, when twenty thousand mutinous German and Spanish soldiers (originally commanded by the German emperor Charles V) marched to Rome, routed its defenders, and began an orgy of massacre, rape, and wholesale artistic plunder and destruction. Twelve thousand unresisting Romans were murdered in cold blood, thousands of bodies were dumped into the Tiber, and hundreds of palaces, churches, libraries, and archives were pillaged and burned. When the invaders departed after nine months (because food had run out and the plague had descended), the city was a reeking charnel house. Pope Clement VII weathered this ordeal from his fortress in the Castel Sant'Angelo, but the brilliant artists and architects whose collective genius had created the High Roman Renaissance had no such refuge; they fled for their lives. Ironically, it was the Renaissance popes themselves—above all, Julius II—who were the catalysts of this catastrophic destruction. Julius, a violent, unstable man, was ruled by a colossal narcissism that would have been remarkable even in a Roman emperor. For instance, he did not hesitate to demolish Constantine's historic fourth-century basilica of Saint Peter's and replace it with a new Renaissance structure whose dimensions he considered sufficiently grand to house his personal tomb monument. When this ruinously expensive building project rapidly outstripped Church revenues, Julius ordered a huge increase in the sale of papal indulgences. Papal agents called pardoners set up booths in every major market square in Europe, where they sold official forgiveness of any sin, including those not yet committed. Over time, this gross commercialization of Christianity's fundamental promise, the gift of eternal salvation, led to such revulsion against the established Church that it spawned the Protestant Reformation. In Germany, where the pope was regularly denounced as the Antichrist and Rome was portrayed as the Whore of Babylon, preachers like Martin Luther whipped antipapal zeal into a red-hot flame. German Lutherans formed a large part of the army that stormed the papal city in 1527, a fact which goes a long way to explain the shocking brutality of that attack, particularly the sadism directed against priests and nuns.[2]

Thus, by initiating a chain of events that dispersed Rome's accumulated artistic genius across the map of Europe, Julius II, one of the most remorseless enemies Venice ever faced, unwittingly furnished the city with her finest Renaissance architect. Of course, when he arrived in Venice in 1527, Sansovino came for only one specific purpose: to assist the procurators de supra in stabilizing and restoring the domes of the Basilica, the same task that had brought him to the lagoon four years earlier. His proposed solution, wrapping the drums of the precarious cupolas with large iron chains and installing a major buttress behind the eastern apse, was credited with preventing the collapse of the church presbytery. This competent intervention and Sansovino's energetic, persuasive manner impressed the procurators. When added to his reputation as one of a small circle of High Renaissance architectural experts chosen to work for the pope (men believed to understand the rules of true classical building then in such demand throughout Europe), it precipitated a decision. In 1529, upon the death of the incumbent, Bartolomeo Bon, the procurators asked Sansovino to become their proto. By accepting the offer, he would become the architect and building supervisor for all Piazza San Marco projects for the rest of his life, an amazing opportunity for someone whose list of completed architectural commissions at that point was actually quite modest. Before accepting the position, Sansovino no doubt compared his Venetian prospects with the likely shape of his architectural career if he returned to Rome, where, even if papal order and largesse were fully restored, he would be forced to compete with major figures such as Michelangelo, Peruzzi, and Sangallo the Younger. All indications are that he quickly embraced the procurators' offer and never regretted his decision. Over the course of forty-three remarkably productive years in Venice, he received repeated invitations to leave and work for a host of Europe's richest, most powerful patrons, including the kings of France, Spain, and England, but he refused them all. At one point, after almost two decades in Venice, he was asked by Pope Paul III to return to Rome to take charge of completing Bramante's huge new Saint Peter's, the most ambitious and expensive architectural project of the entire Renaissance era. When Sansovino declined the commission, the enormous undertaking was given to the seventy-seven-year-old Michelangelo.[3]

The procurators de supra provided Sansovino with an annual salary of 180 ducats and a house in the Procuratie Vecchie located just left of the Clock Tower. The new proto's first assignment was to complete the Procuratie Vecchie by continuing its elegant, three-story façade along the western end of the Piazza until it met the twelfth-century church of San Geminiano. While engaged in this task (not finished until 1538), Sansovino began to discuss an ambitious series of additional reconstruction projects for the Piazza area. In 1529, the pope and the German emperor had signed a peace treaty in Bologna ending two decades of warfare in northern Italy, and Venetian leaders such as Doge Andrea Gritti were anxious to use the ensuing period of economic recovery to convey the image of a confident, resurgent Republic. A new myth of Venice was in the air, one that sought to expunge the near-death experience of Agnadello by stressing the Republic's extraordinary political longevity and creating a direct link between the city's uniquely stable patrician government and the classical values of ancient Rome. In support of this program, Sansovino was expected to import a generous measure of High Renaissance architectural form to any future project in the Piazza or Piazzetta. But as he began to discuss his ideas with a wider circle of interested parties, he must also have become aware of the continuing strength of another, older Venetian self-image, one in clear conflict with the new architectural vision promoted by Doge Gritti and his Renaissance circle. This traditional narrative emphasized that the first Venetians were Christian exiles who, in the face of repeated barbarian invasions, chose to abandon their lives as Roman colonials. Against enormous odds, these refugees from the devastated Italian mainland created a unique maritime identity that did not look back to pagan Rome. Instead, they forged their animating cultural symbols over the course of a long relationship with the Greek capital of Constantinople and the eastern Mediterranean. In time, this enterprise proved to be such an enormous financial and political success that Venetians came to see themselves as a people set apart, neither fully Eastern nor Western. As Sansovino discovered, it was a view of Venetian exceptionalism still strongly embraced by many patricians, based as it was on a large amount of solid historical fact, and it encouraged a deep popular reverence for the great architectural monuments of the Piazza area: the Basilica, the Campanile, and the Ducal Palace.[4]

To someone as politically astute as Sansovino, it must quickly have become apparent that to succeed in his new role, he would have to be a skillful practitioner of the delicate art of mediation. While displaying complete mastery of the latest architectural currents from the High Roman Renaissance, he would have to adapt these imported forms to the demands of a highly venerated, existing environment. Although some parts of the square were frayed and in need of renovation after three centuries of continuous use, looked at as a whole, the Piazza ensemble of 1529 was still a well-defined, superbly organized architectural complex. In fact, up to this point, it had no equal anywhere in Europe, even in Rome, where every Renaissance scheme for creating an equally grand example of integrated urban design had either not been built at all or, like Bramante's projected Belvedere Court at the Vatican palace, had not been carried out in accordance with the architect's original intentions. Michelangelo, who visited Venice in 1529, had not even begun planning the magnificent three-sided Roman plaza he would construct on the crest of the Capitoline Hill; until the mid-1540s, that site remained a slippery, irregular mud bank occupied by a dilapidated medieval fortress.[5]

In contrast, the Piazza San Marco was a brick-paved, rectangular plaza, 570 feet long, 185 feet wide, and bordered on all sides by symmetrical, classically derived arcades. It had been designed to function as a unified public space with the adjoining Piazzetta, and together the two openings projected the authentic grandeur of an antique Roman forum (*Fig. 85 top*). The Piazza was bounded on the east by the Basilica, on the north by the Clock Tower and Procuratie Vecchie, on the west by a five-bay extension of the Procuratie Vecchie and the church of San Geminiano, and on the south and southwest by a series of multiple-story buildings featuring Gothic additions above original Veneto-Byzantine arcades. Thus, unless Sansovino were ready to propose the unthinkable—reconstruction of the front of the Basilica or demolition of costly recent additions like the Procuratie Vecchie—of the four faces of the Piazza, only the southern perimeter and the southern half of the western façade were available for renovation. And the same limitations applied to the Piazzetta. There could be no question of closing its southern end, which opened onto the harbor, or its northern end, which opened into the Piazza. And since its eastern boundary consisted of the Ducal Palace and the Porta della Carta, which were equally off-limits, the only part of the Piazzetta available to Sansovino was its western perimeter, which housed a line of decrepit thirteenth-century buildings whose original Veneto-Byzantine arcades were now obscured by a projecting row of lean-to stalls. Fortunately, the three façades that Sansovino was free to transform—the southern and southwestern faces of the Piazza and the western face of the Piazzetta (approximately forty percent of the collective perimeter created by medieval builders)—were contiguous. They formed an inverted L whose arms met at the Campanile; the tower's massive shaft was inserted like a giant spike into the angle where the two wings converged.[6]

The bold renovation plan devised by Sansovino not only outfitted the San Marco complex with the latest forms of Roman Renaissance architecture, it changed the basic shape of the Piazza. The medieval Piazzetta was already a slightly trapezoidal space whose oblique sight lines (viewed from the harbor) helped to enhance the Basilica's southern face. And there was a second trapezoidal space, formed by the angle between the western façade of the Basilica and the three bronze flagpole bases directly to its front, which reinforced the vista toward Codussi's Clock Tower. By transforming the Piazza itself from a rhomboid into a third, larger trapezoid (*Fig. 85 bottom*), Sansovino's plan called for producing this same optical effect in magnified form for the benefit of the Basilica. Although the plan was not implemented until after Sansovino's death, the Piazza's southern perimeter was eventually rebuilt seventy-five feet farther south, separated from the base of the Campanile by thirty feet. The result is a diverging perspective (viewed from the western end of the Piazza) that appears to shrink the distance between the viewer and the Basilica's majestic western façade. This new configuration also opened up additional sight lines from the Piazza into the Piazzetta, making it possible to see the Ducal Palace from almost any point in the great square. And by clearing away the welter of miscellaneous buildings that surrounded the Campanile, it unveiled the tower's sheer vertical power in all its uncluttered nobility.[7]

The other core component of Sansovino's master plan was his design and construction of a brilliant, two-story, classical façade along the western face of the Piazzetta (*Fig. 86*). This became the Marciana Library; through its planned interaction with the Molo pillars and the arcade and loggia of the Ducal Palace, it transformed the smaller square's north-south axis into a majestic ceremonial corridor running from the waterfront to the Basilica, the Campanile, and the Piazza beyond. But this was only the beginning of Sansovino's ultimate aim for this magnificent Renaissance elevation; he meant for it to be extended well beyond the Piazzetta. After forming the western side of the smaller plaza, it was to turn ninety degrees and run full length up the southern face of the Piazza before turning a second corner and running north until it reached the church of San Geminiano in the middle of the Piazza's western perimeter. Ironically, this enormously ambitious endeavor, a plan to alter the final appearance of both squares, began in a spasm of confused intentions.

When the Procuracy de supra first asked Sansovino to design a Renaissance elevation in July 1536, it was not in order to build the Marciana Library in the Piazzetta. The original commission was for a three-story residential building to be erected along the southern perimeter of the Piazza to house the nine procurators entitled to receive free state apartments in the great square. But not long after receiving the assignment, Sansovino relocated the apartment project to the Piazzetta, and in March of the following year, after construction had already begun, the procurators de supra decided to substitute a new library for the ongoing effort to replace their antiquated housing.[8] What could account for such a radical change of plans?

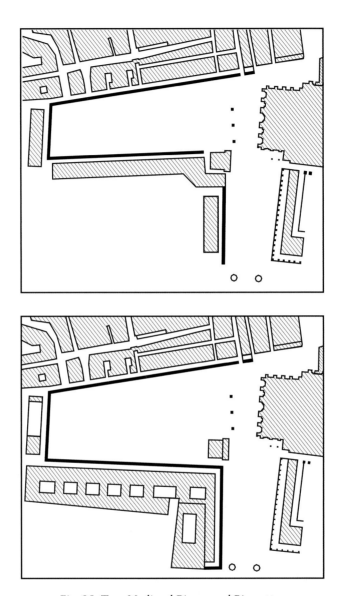

Fig. 85: Top: Medieval Piazza and Piazzetta

*Bottom: Sansovino's Renaissance conversion
of the medieval Piazza and Piazzetta*

Fig. 86: Façade of Sansovino's Marciana Library

Although many different reasons could no doubt be cited, at bottom the explanation was quite simple; it was guilt, the need to finally dispel a long, lingering sense of collective shame felt by the entire Venetian patriciate, that drove the Procuracy's decision. Seven decades earlier, that is, fifteen years after the Ottoman Turks had crushed the last remnants of Byzantine civilization in the old capital of Constantinople, Cardinal John Bessarion (formerly the Eastern archbishop of Nicaea, now a Greek refugee) had reached an important decision of his own. This erudite survivor of a displaced culture *(Fig. 87)* announced that he was leaving his personal library of over a thousand rare Greek and Latin codices to the

*Fig. 87: Portrait of Cardinal John Bessarion
by Joos van Gent*

Venetian Republic. He explained that he was "[c]onsumed with terror...after the destruction of Greece and the pitiful enslavement of Byzantium...lest all [his] wonderful books... should be brought to danger and destruction [or] dispersed and scattered after [his death]." He added that he felt certain Venice was the right place for his collection because his visits there had made him feel as though he were "entering another Byzantium." His sole condition was that the manuscripts "be preserved in a place that is both safe and accessible, for the general good of all readers,"[9] (i.e., a Venetian public library). The city readily agreed to these terms, and in 1469, the manuscripts were packed into crates, loaded onto the backs of fifteen mules, and carried north from the cardinal's villa on the outskirts of Rome over the Apennine Mountains to the lagoon. Unfortunately, as we have seen in Chapter Ten, the Republic that received the precious volumes was far from living up to Bessarion's high expectations. In the late fifteenth century, the state's chief architect successfully embezzled twelve thousand ducats, and the doge himself went unpunished while committing acts of bribery, extortion, smuggling, and tax evasion. Against this backdrop of systematic public corruption, ignoring the state's commitment to the cardinal must have seemed like a very minor affair. Upon their arrival in Venice, the codices were left unpacked and unsorted in the west wing of the Ducal Palace. Only once, in 1515, did the government even consider the question of building a suitable repository for the priceless collection. The Senate adopted a vague motion to house the volumes somewhere in the Piazza but then declined to adopt any funding for the project.[10]

Over time, these disgraceful facts began to look all the more embarrassing because they recalled aspects of the Republic's dismal experience with Petrarch (*Fig. 88*), the greatest European poet and humanist of his day, almost a century earlier. After moving from Padua to Venice in 1362, Petrarch offered to donate his books to the Republic as the foundation for a public library on the condition that the government furnish him with a rent-free house along the Venetian harbor. The city did supply the poet with the residence he requested; however, after living there for five years, Petrarch packed his volumes and returned to Padua, declaring that he had been insulted by certain Venetian patricians who questioned his merits as a scholar. A few years later, Francesco Carrara, the despot of Padua, gave the poet a villa in the surrounding Euganean Hills, where he died in 1374. According to most experts, Petrarch's collection was broken up and dispersed after his death, and the books were never retransported to Venice; however, one leading authority has stated that some of the missing volumes may have been returned to the city, where they were lost by negligent state officials.[11]

But the shame Venetian patricians were feeling in 1537 went beyond remorse over the Republic's failure to build a public library for the Bessarion manuscripts or the city's general reputation for careless handling of valuable literary documents. It tapped into a deeper sense of Venetian culpability for the final collapse of Greek civilization in the old Eastern Empire. It reminded Venetians of their failure to send effective aid to Constantinople before its conquest by the Turks in 1453. Whatever excuses the Republic might wish to offer, however unlikely a successful rescue may have seemed at the time, there was no denying that her efforts to save the last great metropolis of the late classical world had been halfhearted at best. By the time Venetian forces reached the city, the Ottomans had already butchered its Greek residents, and the Venetian ambassador had already been directed to begin trade negotiations with the victorious Sultan Mehmet II. While the pope and prominent Greek refugees like Bessarion preached the need for a crusade to retake the

Fig. 88: Portrait of Petrarch

ancient imperial capital, the Republic remained a reluctant participant. Although she dutifully enlisted in the cause, her merchants were not sad to see the effort fall apart after the pope's death in August 1464.[12]

But lurking beneath all this was an even deeper, keener guilt—the knowledge that the Byzantine Empire's true death stroke had been delivered not in 1453 but in 1204 when the doge of Venice had led an army of Frankish knights over the walls of Constantinople. The city's responsibility for the ultimate fate of Byzantium was immediately evident for anyone with eyes to see—the very stones of her temple cried out with it. Ravishing marble slabs and other rare architectural booty ripped from sacred shrines in the old Greek capital were spread over the San Marco precinct; the Basilica itself stood as an accusing witness not more than 120 feet from the site of Sansovino's new Library. Thus, Bessarion's manuscripts represented a double legacy. They were splendid survivors from the magnificent Greco-Roman heritage that had long found its most congenial home in the Byzantine Empire (from which Venice had drawn her own early aspirations), but they were also potent reminders of the crucial role the Republic had played in severing those cherished links to the past. To make amends, Venice was prepared to erect a building that would dazzle the contemporary Renaissance world.[13]

The Marciana Library

Born from this mixture of guilt and expiation, Sansovino's Marciana Library is a brilliant merger of orthodoxy and originality worthy of being measured against the finest public architecture of the Italian Renaissance. Sansovino combined careful, precise borrowing from antique and Renaissance models with a dazzling inventiveness that completes and enhances the building's classical features. Each floor of his two-story elevation is subdivided into twenty-one identical bays, each shaped around a semicircular, receding arch, and the entire façade is overlaid with a highly diverse mixture of architectural and sculptural motifs (*Fig. 89*). Everywhere, the wall plane virtually disappears behind a dense layer of projecting columns, piers, friezes, balconies, and bases interspersed with figurative carving in high relief. In describing the Library's effect on the viewer, Andrea Palladio (1508–1580), the greatest Renaissance architect of the next generation, called it "the richest, most ornate building since Antiquity."[14] Yet, despite its profusion of architectural and sculptural figures,

Fig. 89: Identical bays of Marciana Library

Sansovino's façade also conveys an impression of exquisite order, in large part because the architect has imposed a strong equilibrium of vertical and horizontal elements across the entire elevation. Each floor features a major entablature (frieze and cornice) supported by boldly protruding columns, all in gleaming white Istrian stone. Particularly when viewed in the angled light of early morning, these prominent, clearly defined lintel systems project an aura of calm, deliberate harmony. They also bear out Alberti's well-known dictum, first illustrated by Bramante in his design for the cloister of Santa Maria della Pace in Rome (1500), that building in the classical manner meant using columns to support entablatures, leaving arches to rest on piers. Of course, little weight is actually carried by any part of Sansovino's opulent Istrian stone surface. Like the marble façade of the nearby Basilica, it is only a decorative veneer applied over a load-bearing brick substructure.[15]

The Library's ground floor is distinguished by its highly accurate use of the severe Roman Doric order, a rigorously prescribed system of antique bases, columns, capitals, and entablature. The frieze (*Fig. 90*) displays the Doric order's obligatory alternation of triglyphs (Roman numeral IIIs) and metopes (square fields between triglyphs, often, as with the Library, filled with carved figures) plus a row of six guttae (small droplike projections) centered beneath each set of triglyphs. According to which scholar you consult, the model for Sansovino's Doric order was either an antique Roman monument such as the Colosseum, the Theater of Marcellus, or the Basilica Aemilia, or a seminal work of the High Roman Renaissance such as Bramante's Tempietto or Sangallo the Younger's Farnese Palace courtyard. However, none of these august sources could have supplied Sansovino with the solution to a famous architectural puzzle, one that had stumped each previous builder who elected to employ the Doric order. According to Vitruvius, the proper way to terminate a Doric frieze was to place a complete half metope at the end. Unfortunately, classical orthodoxy also dictated that the last set of triglyphs on a Doric frieze had to be centered above the last supporting column or pier, and following this obligatory step left no room for a full half metope. Sansovino solved this fifteen-hundred-year-old enigma by cleverly adding a small, indented extension to the final pier, thereby widening the superimposed frieze just enough to allow for a perfect half metope at the end of the building. After secretly resolving this ancient conundrum, Sansovino made a show of soliciting help from architects throughout the Italian peninsula. When no competing answer was forthcoming, he revealed his own masterly contrivance, a feat that enhanced his reputation for uncompromising classical accuracy and brilliant originality.[16]

The Library's second story is also a striking mixture of classical and Renaissance borrowing, and original genius. While for the most part, its columns, bases, capitals, and entablature are standard transcriptions of the classic Ionic order, the great exception is Sansovino's magnificently pagan frieze (*Fig. 91*). Although many architects working with the Ionic order elected to omit a decorative frieze entirely, Sansovino crowned his own Ionic story with a sumptuous, oversized relief whose rich, inventive air is all the more striking in juxtaposition to the ultra-orthodox austerity of the Doric frieze below. Between dark oval windows set in beautifully carved frames, light catches the limbs of joyful putti twirling and staggering under great swags of pendant fruit, and in the shadow of a deep, overhanging cornice, the heads of men and lions rise up from swollen garlands. Beneath this bacchanalian tableau, Sansovino inserted his own version of a Serliana window (a semicircular arch resting on colonettes slightly offset from broad flanking piers) into each of the floor's twenty-one bays. In composing this feature, Sansovino drew on illustrations in Sebastiano Serlio's influential treatise *Book IV, On the five styles of building*, published in Venice in 1537. Serlio, like Sansovino, had worked in Rome before immigrating to Venice and, while there, was famous for having immersed himself in the architecture of Bramante, Raphael, Peruzzi, and Sangallo the Younger. For his Venetian audience, Sansovino's incorporation of Serlio's ideas (based on Roman projects by Bramante and others) helped produce an overwhelming impression of classical authority and Renaissance authenticity.[17]

Sansovino filled the spandrels of each recessed arch on both floors with reclining nudes (sea and river gods and winged victories), whose highly muscular bodies recall Michelangelo's own carved and painted nudes. But the building's most original sculptural element (apart from its second-story Ionic frieze) is its crowning feature: a long row of freestanding antique gods and heroes elevated against the blue Venetian sky (*Fig. 92*). This marked the first time such a rooftop statuary composition had ever been used in a Renaissance building; earlier architects had capped their buildings with unadorned cornices. Michelangelo was so impressed by Sansovino's novel scheme that he copied it almost exactly when designing the roofline for the three palaces that form the outline of his Piazza del Campidoglio at the top of the Capitoline Hill (*Fig. 93*). It is the only major sculptural feature these otherwise very different Venetian and Roman façades have in common. This exuberant finishing touch, so important in balancing the horizontal momentum of Sansovino's long,

Fig. 90: Corner pier supporting the Doric frieze,
ground floor, Marciana Library

Fig. 91: Second-story frieze, Marciana Library

low elevation with an equally powerful vertical force, is clearly derived from the Republic's native architectural tradition. Although it required rare creative genius to translate this into a Renaissance idiom, the basic idea surely originated with Sansovino's exposure to the statues, pinnacles, and crenellations that line the crests of so many important Venetian monuments, particularly the neighboring Molo pillars, the Ducal Palace, and the Basilica. Forty feet or more above the ground (*Fig. 94*), the Library's classical nudes mingle with a flying lion, a Greek warrior-saint, a dragon that looks like a small crocodile, and a congregation of robed saints, apostles and archangels.[18]

Sansovino's Assimilation of the Assemblage Art Tradition

In designing the Library, Sansovino was supremely conscious of the great monuments surrounding his site, and the project's roofline sculptural group is only one example of his extraordinary ability to assimilate and merge his work with its architectural context. These skills enabled him to practice the assemblage art of Venice (that special genius for merging divergent elements into a novel artistic whole) on the largest possible scale in each of his major projects within the Piazza and Piazzetta. While his architectural vocabulary always remained entirely consistent with the High Renaissance style developed in Rome by Bramante and Raphael, he clearly designed his stylistically homogenous buildings with the overall Piazza setting in mind and consistently sought to make his distinctly Renaissance creations harmonize with and even enhance the square's earlier architectural achievements.

The clearest evidence that this was one of Sansovino's principal goals is the decisive manner in which he resisted every temptation to have the Marciana Library compete with the Ducal Palace on the opposite side of the Piazzetta. He refused to turn the Library project into a three-story building even though this made it impossible for him to display the last of the three principal antique orders—Doric, Ionic, and Corinthian—in the manner that classical orthodoxy was said to require. This three-story, three-order model had been given canonical blessing in ancient monuments such as the Colosseum, and Serlio had driven the point home in his authoritative architectural treatise published in Venice at the very time that Sansovino was designing the Library. To remove all doubt, Serlio's book illustrated the correct sequence of classical orders (from the simplest—the Doric—to the most ornate and decorative—the Corinthian) on a single page. But Sansovino steadfastly

*Fig. 92: Roof crown of freestanding gods
and heroes, Marciana Library*

*Fig. 93: Piazza del Campidoglio designed by Michelangelo,
Capitoline Hill, Rome*

Fig. 94: Sansovino's Marciana Library and Molo Pillar

ignored this scholarly consensus and did so despite the fact that an extra floor, which could have been leased to paying tenants, would have provided the Procuracy with badly needed rental income.[19]

Sansovino's resistance on this point is all the more remarkable if we recall that when the Procuracy originally authorized the project in 1536, it was commissioned as a three-story building, albeit one intended to be constructed on the southern side of the Piazza away from direct comparison with the Ducal Palace. One can only surmise that when the project was moved to the western side of the Piazzetta, Sansovino immediately recognized that within the smaller square, the Palace's dominant, iconic status was not something to be challenged or altered, but a supremely original achievement to be endorsed and, if possible, reinforced. Thus, although the stylistic vocabularies of the two buildings are completely different, Sansovino took the general pattern he found on the bottom half of the Palace (a second-story loggia on top of a ground-floor arcade) and imposed it on the Library façade. Omitting friezes and cornices, each floor of the Library is almost exactly the same height as the corresponding story of the Palace. And just as the Palace architect had done, Sansovino punctuated the face of his building with evenly spaced columns of precisely equal dimensions, ensuring that the two opposing façades would project the same strong impression of classical symmetry. He also meticulously adapted his building plan to its preexisting site, as illustrated by three quick examples. First, if one stands at the harbor end of the Library arcade and looks due east toward the Ducal Palace, the nearest Molo pillar (topped with Saint Theodore and the dragon) appears framed in the very center of the final arch. Second, to anyone standing on the Ducal Palace loggia or at the Campanile end of the Piazzetta, the Ionic cornice above Sansovino's great second-story frieze lines up almost exactly with the platforms at the top of the Molo columns. Third, Sansovino placed the Library entrance portal directly opposite the large circular relief or *tondo* depicting an allegory of Venetian power and justice that Filippo Calendario, the architect and chief sculptor of the Ducal Palace, carved on the Palace's western loggia sometime between 1341 and 1355.[20]

After the Library, the project that best exemplifies Sansovino's adoption of the Venetian assemblage art tradition is the Loggetta (*Fig. 95*), a small but resplendent Renaissance loggia in the shape of three triumphal arches which he began to construct at the foot of the Campanile in 1538. Viewed diagonally from the Basilica terrace, where Venetian governors would often have stood to watch public processions in the Piazza and Piazzetta, the Loggetta's three ground-floor arches appear like a natural extension of the Library's long classical arcade. To reinforce this connection, Sansovino decorated the Loggetta with the final and most refined of the classical orders, the Composite (a blend of Ionic and Corinthian), thereby completing the hierarchical sequence he had begun on the face of the Library, where he restricted himself to the Doric and Ionic orders. In fact, he may already have had the Loggetta project in mind when he exercised such self-restraint in the design of the Library elevation, a conjecture made more probable by the fact that, according to Serlio's 1537 treatise, the Composite order was particularly well-suited to projects such as the Loggetta that were meant to express a feeling of triumph. The Loggetta's ornate, deeply sculptural design, featuring a screen of eight rare Eastern columns protruding from a luxurious surface of red Verona and dark-green and gray-veined Carrara marbles, set below Istrian stone reliefs, also links it to the Basilica's highly plastic, polychrome facade.[21]

Fig. 95: Sansovino's Loggetta at the base of the San Marco Campanile

Sansovino also designed the Loggetta to function as a visual terminus for the east-west ceremonial axis formed by the construction of the Porta della Carta, the Arco Foscari, and Rizzo's freestanding staircase in the Ducal Palace courtyard. Thus, someone descending the stairway and continuing through the Arco corridor is exposed to a series of constantly expanding, perfectly framed views of the Loggetta seen through the Porta. Building on these connections, Sansovino used the Loggetta's sculptural program to introduce a new mythologized image of Venice, one that implicitly rebuked the examples of ducal narcissism found in the earlier portions of this ceremonial artery. In the Loggetta's ground-floor niches, Sansovino installed bronze statues of Minerva, Apollo, and Mercury, intended to represent the Republic's political wisdom, stability, and eloquence. The central attic relief portrays Venice as a goddess of Justice sitting between two river gods who symbolize the city's mainland empire. In the attic side panels, the Venetian maritime empire is personified by the figures of Jupiter and Venus, who in Roman mythology were the king and queen of the island of Cyprus, the city's most important remaining Mediterranean colony. Toward the end of his career, Sansovino completed this allegorical project by installing two larger-than-life marble nudes of Mars and Neptune (*Figs. 75, 96*), again symbolizing the Republic's terraferma and maritime empires, on the top landing of Rizzo's staircase (to be known forever afterward as the Giants' Staircase). While this extensive series of mythological abstractions bore almost no connection to the city's historical experience, its placement at both ends of the ritual axis that passed through the Porta and the Arco at least marked a return to celebrating the collective virtues and achievements of the Republic rather than glorifying individual Venetians.[22]

The Loggetta was finished in seven years, but completion of the Library, which nineteenth-century art and social historian Jacob Burckhardt called "the most splendid work of secular architecture in modern Europe,"[23] proved to be a much more torturous process. In 1545, eight years into the project, potential disaster struck when one of the ceiling vaults of the second-story reading room collapsed overnight, due to poor workmanship and the inherently precarious nature of vaulted (as opposed to wooden) ceilings in a city subject to constant subsidence. The Procuracy reacted severely. It had Sansovino arrested, terminated his 180-ducat annual salary, and ordered him to repay the thousand-ducat repair cost from his personal funds, a burden that took him twenty years to discharge. Because Sansovino displayed extraordinary grace and humility in submitting to these penalties, two years later, the procurators reinstated his wages, and he continued to work on the Library. By 1556, sixteen of the project's twenty-one bays had been constructed, as well as the second-story reading room and its vestibule. Seven artists including Paolo Veronese (1528-1588) painted twenty-one roundels on the reading room ceiling, Veronese and Jacopo Tintoretto (1519-1594) painted a series of oil canvases depicting great Western philosophers for the walls of the reading room (*Fig. 97*), and Titian produced an allegorical representation of Wisdom for the vestibule ceiling. Only in 1564, almost a century after Cardinal Bessarion had sent his precious codices over the mountains from Rome, were the volumes finally installed in their own splendid building.[24]

Fig. 96: Sansovino's statues of Neptune (left) and Mars (right) at the top
of the Giants' Staircase, looking toward the Arco Foscari

Fig. 97 (opposite): Reading room, Marciana Library, ceiling and walls
decorated with roundels and paintings by Veronese and Tintoretto

With near perfect eyesight and a youthful, energetic manner, Sansovino was able to work
until the very end of his life (*Fig. 98*). However, when he died in 1570 at age eighty-four,
construction of the last five bays of the Library had not yet begun, and the site continued
to house a popular meat market. Nor had Sansovino realized his goal of extending the
Library elevation into the Piazza and transforming that space into a trapezoid. Although
the Library's northeastern corner (where project construction had begun in 1538) was now
separated from the Campanile by an interval of thirty feet, no new vista into the western
end of the Piazza had yet been created. That view remained blocked by the walls of the

entury Orseolo hospice and a series of procuratorial apartments that still abutted the rear of the Campanile. Yet if Sansovino was unable to initiate this phase of his master plan before he died, he left little doubt about the degree to which he intended to integrate his original Piazzetta project with a renovated Piazza. One clear signal was the façade he designed in the 1550s for the church of San Geminiano, located midway along the western face of the Piazza (*Fig. 99*). Like the Library elevation in the Piazzetta, the church façade was a two-story scheme partially inspired by illustrations from Serlio's 1537 architectural treatise and like the Library, it was constructed of white Istrian stone. In addition, when the Piazzetta elevation was finally extended to the western end of the Piazza in the seventeenth century, certain prominent horizontal features of the Library design and the church were found to align. Sansovino also placed an image of the Winged Lion of Saint Mark on San Geminiano's small central pediment and flanked it with two Gothic roof tabernacles, thus making a playful reference to the Basilica's delightful Gothic crest at the opposite end of the Piazza. At his request, Sansovino was buried in San Geminiano, a later work for which he obviously felt a great deal of affection.[25]

Beyond the Piazza

The year of Sansovino's death, 1570, not only marked the beginning of an eighteen-year hiatus in completing the Library project; it was also the year that the Turkish sultan Selim II (known as Selim the Sot) ordered Venice to transfer the island of Cyprus, her principal remaining colonial possession, to the Ottoman Empire. When the Republic refused, Selim sent a 350-ship invasion force to crush the colony. After massacring most of the island's defenders, the Turks flayed the Venetian commander alive. But a year later, it was the Turks' turn to suffer a humiliating defeat. At the great naval battle of Lepanto, Venetian and Spanish ships smashed a huge Ottoman armada, destroying 240 enemy vessels and killing an estimated thirty thousand Turks (while suffering less than a quarter of the Ottoman losses). Unfortunately, this lopsided rout did little to deter the relentless Turkish juggernaut. That very winter, the sultan's shipyards in Istanbul (ancient Constantinople until its fall to the Turks in 1453) produced 150 new galleys and eight giant war galleasses, a feat the Venetian Arsenale, suffering from a serious lack of building timber, could no longer hope to match. Bowing to reality, three years later the Republic signed a peace treaty renouncing her claim

*Fig. 98: Portrait of Jacopo Sansovino near the end
of his life by Tintoretto*

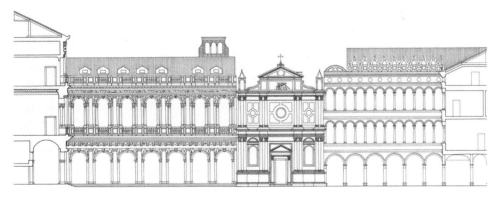

*Fig. 99: Sansovino's facade of San Geminiano in the middle of the
Piazza's western elevation (before Napoleonic destruction)*

to Cyprus and agreeing to pay the sultan 300,000 ducats. Then, before she could finish paying the extracted tribute, Venice was struck by a savage new plague outbreak which killed approximately thirty percent of the city's 190,000 residents; among the victims was the great Renaissance painter Titian, then age ninety-three.[26]

During the period from the Turkish conquest of Cyprus in 1570 through the lifting of the plague in 1577, Venetian maritime commerce suffered a precipitous decline; not surprisingly, this only accelerated the ongoing withdrawal of patrician capital from Mediterranean trade and its reinvestment in mainland agriculture. More efficient British cargo ships supplanted Venetian galleys in Mediterranean ports, and the Dutch, sailing around the horn of Africa, took control of the European spice trade. Given this reduced influence over foreign markets, the cost of feeding the city increased dramatically, including a doubling in the price of wheat. In such circumstances, it only made good business sense for patrician landowners to maximize the agricultural output of their nearby mainland estates. Venetians also began to reinvest their capital in new manufacturing enterprises, a development that transformed the city into one of the most important European centers for the production of woolen cloth. Thus, while fewer Venetians were making their fortunes in overseas commerce, the years 1550 to 1600 remained a period of outstanding prosperity for the Republic as a whole.[27]

As they shifted their assets from the risks of international commerce to the greater security and prestige of landed income, many patricians also withdrew from active participation in the Venetian government. Control of sixteenth-century state affairs became increasingly concentrated in a narrow aristocratic circle, so much so that by the 1580s, decisive power had become centralized in an expanded Council of Ten consisting of thirty-two members (ten ordinary members plus the doge and his six ducal councilors and a *zonta* of fifteen additional patricians). Within the council, some older, wealthier members had close ties to the papacy and were wary of offending the pope's ally, the Spanish Empire (ruled by the Habsburg princes of Germany) which dominated much of Italy and the rest of continental Europe. But there was also an influential group of younger patricians known appropriately enough as the *giovanni* that forcefully resisted attempts at Spanish coercion and denounced papal interference with traditional principles of Venetian religious independence. In their minds, it was an essential part of Venetian political liberty that Church property should be taxable, that bishops should not be permitted to hold political office, that clerics accused of criminal behavior should be tried in Venetian courts, and that priests should be elected by the local parish in which they served.[28]

The Venetian Career of Andrea Palladio

It was no coincidence that 1570, the year that Sansovino died, was also the year that Andrea Palladio finally came to live in Venice. Born to a Paduan mill worker and married to a carpenter's daughter, Palladio began as a stonemason before transforming himself into one of the most celebrated architects in Western history. During the early decades of his career (1540–1560), he lived in Vicenza, and most of his projects were urban palazzos and country villas built for wealthy private clients. But the work that truly established his reputation was his first major public project, the design of a Renaissance building screen to encase Vicenza's aging Gothic senate house (*Fig. 100*). Adopting ancient Roman practice, Palladio referred to the building as a basilica because it also housed the municipal law court. He received the commission in 1546, when he was a relatively unknown local architect of thirty-eight, following a lengthy competition against older, established masters such as Sansovino, Serlio, Michele Sanmicheli (c. 1484–1559) and Giulio Romano (1492–1546). Upon obtaining the award, Palladio made numerous trips to Venice, and some notable features of his final conception, like using the severe Doric order for the ground-floor arcade and adding a rooftop crest of freestanding classical nudes, appear to be direct transcriptions from Sansovino's Marciana Library. In other cases, even where we can identify an element that the two buildings have in common, what strikes us most forcefully is Palladio's splendid originality. For instance, while Sansovino employs the Serliana motif (a semicircular arch supported by colonettes and flanking piers) as no more than a bit of decorative background, Palladio's novel use of this feature is the pivotal aspect of his entire design. Palladio's fundamental challenge was to preserve the existing fabric of the basilica and still be able to fit symmetrical Renaissance loggias to the irregular bays of the old Gothic building. To do this, he used the Serliana motif as his basic compositional unit, keeping the central arches of the Serliana units completely uniform while subtly adjusting the distance between the colonettes and flanking piers to match the varying widths of the Gothic bays.[29]

Palladio's innovative basilica scheme demonstrates that when forced to do so, he could adapt his ideas to an existing context with the same tact and skill that Sansovino repeatedly displayed in Venice. Over the course of a long career, however, Palladio rarely displayed such dexterity in the face of architectural givens; instead of taking cues from their particular sites, his buildings usually turned out to be isolated, self-referential creations whose forms were derived from abstract principles. For Palladio not only shared Alberti's intellectualized approach to architecture, he was even more rigorous in turning his theories into actual buildings. He believed that God had manifested His design of the cosmos in a system of complex numerical ratios and that it was incumbent on a true architect to ensure that his work revealed the same divine order which pervaded every other aspect of the universe. The result was an architecture that emphasized a precise hierarchical ordering of parts, a tight correspondence between exterior and interior space, and the rigorous subjection of every element to the principles of mathematical proportion. When the project was an agrarian villa to be constructed in an unobstructed rural landscape, implementing such an approach was relatively simple, but in a crowded municipal setting, the result could easily be a beautiful but abstract architectural microcosm almost completely divorced from its surroundings.[30]

It was this autonomous, highly theoretical form of architecture that Palladio attempted to impose on several Venetian public projects in the mid-1550s. Although his proposals were eagerly supported by a small circle of aristocratic humanists with close ties to the papacy—members of the Barbaro, Foscari, Corner, Emo, Grimani, and Pisano families, whose leader was Daniele Barbaro, the patriarch of Aquileia and an authority on Vitruvius—a majority of the patriciate found them unacceptable. Thus, Palladio lost the 1554 competition to become proto to the Salt Office, which would have made him responsible for most of the city's public buildings, including the Ducal Palace (but not the rest of the Piazza San Marco complex, which was controlled by the Procuracy of Saint Mark). Another building committee also rejected his highly impractical proposal for reconstructing the Rialto bridge as a classical portico joined at both ends to large public forums. In addition to severely constricting water and foot traffic at this critical commercial intersection, Palladio's plan would have eliminated an irreplaceable historical structure: the little fifth-century church of San Giacomo di Rialto, the oldest in Venice. Palladio's claim for total architectural autonomy was completely at odds with the Venetian system of interlocking magistracies and commissions which, while keenly appreciative of artistic skill and conceptual genius, stressed the need for works of continuity and balance rather than isolated centers of abstruse brilliance.[31]

*Fig. 100: Andrea Palladio's Basilica in Vicenza, a Renaissance
building screen encasing the old Gothic Senate house*

Thus, although Palladio constructed rural villas for a number of Venetian nobles in the 1550s, it was only after 1560 that he was commissioned to build within the lagoon itself. And even then, none of his Venetian projects was sited within the city's central core, much less within the San Marco precinct itself, and only one was commissioned by the Venetian state. Each of these awards required Palladio to construct a religious edifice—a sanctuary, a church façade, a refectory, or a cloister—around the periphery of the city. In 1562, the Grimani family chose Palladio to create a façade for San Francesco della Vigna, a church on the northeastern outskirts whose underlying structure had been designed and built by Sansovino, who had also furnished an unbuilt façade design. Palladio used this victory over his venerable older rival to solve an architectural puzzle whose complete resolution had resisted the efforts of earlier Renaissance masters such as Alberti, Bramante, and Peruzzi. The dilemma was how to create the convincing impression of a symmetrical classical temple front over the entrance to a Christian basilica, an incompatible structure characterized by the juncture of a high nave with low flanking aisles. Palladio's answer was to use two simulated temple fronts: a large central one in strong relief (matching the height and shape of the nave) superimposed over a smaller, flatter front (whose central mass is merely implied) covering the side aisles. Once he had successfully employed this solution at San Francesco, he designed refined variations for the façades of two later churches built in more prominent locations. The first of these was San Giorgio Maggiore (*Fig. 101*), commissioned by the Benedictine monastic order around 1565, and the second was the Redentore, a work of communal expiation that the Senate vowed to build in 1576 at the height of a devastating plague epidemic which ultimately killed over fifty thousand Venetians. San Giorgio was constructed on a small harbor island directly opposite the Ducal Palace, and the Senate elected to build the Redentore on the northern edge of Giudecca island, facing the San Marco precinct. Thus, to someone standing at the edge of the Molo gazing over the waters of the Venetian harbor, the two churches lie on the horizon like brilliant abstractions, unassailable geometrical propositions realized in gleaming white stone (*Fig. 102*). They are distant images of what might have been if Palladio's splendid intellectual solutions and demand for absolute autonomy had not been in radical conflict with preservation of the city's historic building sites.[32]

The potential destructiveness of Palladio's uncompromising vision is best illustrated by what happened after a devastating fire consumed the upper floors of the Ducal Palace in

*Fig. 101: Façade of the church of San Giorgio Maggiore
by Andrea Palladio*

December 1577. The Great Council chamber, which filled the harbor wing of the Palace, and the halls of justice, which occupied the Piazzetta wing, were both gutted, leaving the existing building a burnt-out shell. Palladio was one of twelve experts consulted on whether the Palace should be restored to its original form or totally reconstructed as a Renaissance edifice. Eleven of the architects agreed that it should be restored as it was; Palladio alone urged tearing down the existing structure and replacing it with a new classical building. In his report, he stated that the old Palace's "inverted form," with its huge upper hall balanced on slender Gothic arches, was fundamentally unsound and "offend[ed] all natural principles."[33] Supports must not only be sufficient to bear their assigned load, he declared, they must also appear to be completely adequate. Therefore, he concluded, the only acceptable solution was to substitute a new Renaissance palace based on the "natural" rules of classical architecture for the faulty, untutored handiwork of the Palace's medieval builder, and he contributed an initial design for just such a project.[34]

Palladio's response tells us more about his own conceptual limitations than it does about the intrinsic flaws of the building he was prepared to destroy. Venice is not and never has been a "natural" place in the sense intended by Palladio. In the natural course of events, you do not build a city on water. Nor, as a medieval state, do you bestow ultimate state sovereignty on a two-thousand-member legislative council with an equally oversized architectural requirement. Yet, the Venetians did both of these things, and in the context of their unique history, each made perfect sense and was an outstanding success. It is this long saga of Venetian exceptionalism, so skillfully reflected in great monuments like the Ducal Palace, that makes the city so fascinating. Unfortunately, for all his genius, this novel Venetian reality was totally lost on Palladio.

Of course, if the existing Ducal Palace had been pulled down, there would have been no physical requirement to make the replacement building conform to the footprint or the general dimensions of the demolished edifice. And according to evidence uncovered by the English scholar Howard Burns, it was just such a basic change that Palladio seems to have intended. Burns has identified an elevation drawing in the British Chatsworth collection (*Fig. 103*) as a sketch of Palladio's proposed new ducal palace, and several prominent scholars have concurred in this analysis. The Chatsworth drawing depicts a classical façade of three equal stories, which, if constructed, would have been some thirty-five feet narrower than the existing Palace harbor wing, making it totally at odds with the internal layout of the medieval Palace. Thus, if Burns' identification is correct, Palladio must have intended to alter the Palace's interior arrangements, including, very likely, reducing the size of the Great Council chamber. Why would anyone want to do this? Well, for one thing, we know that Palladio's aristocratic patrons, the same men who enthusiastically endorsed his Renaissance palace replacement project, belonged to an ultra-elitist patrician minority which strongly supported the continuing transfer of political power from the Great Council and the Senate to the Council of Ten. What better way to promote such a change than by reconstructing the governing Palace's interior layout to reflect this desired outcome? When the medieval Palace was designed and built, membership in the patriciate was expanding and eagerly sought after, requiring a vastly expanded Great Council meeting hall. But by 1577, Venice was emerging from a savage plague epidemic that had killed one quarter of the Council's estimated twenty-five hundred members, and interest in public service was declining rapidly. The number of patricians eligible to attend Great Council meetings never again exceeded eighty percent of that pre-plague figure, and the number of actual attendees was far below that, fluctuating between forty and sixty percent, with a quorum set at only six hundred members. Of those who did attend, many were poor nobles whose presence in the Council chamber was solely to ensure that they or their relatives were elected to a salaried government job. Likewise in the Senate, which had taken over most of the Great Council's legislative functions, only about sixty percent of that body's three hundred members typically attended meetings, and the quorum requirement was set at a mere seventy members. To Palladio and his supporters, the Ducal Palace fire of 1577 must have seemed like a heaven-sent opportunity to eliminate a building they viewed as a Gothic deformity and to reestablish Venetian architecture and politics on a sound classical and elitist basis. Fortunately, this outlook remained a minority view within the Senate, where the final decision was made. The essential layout of the Ducal Palace interior was preserved, and the exterior was rebuilt to look precisely as it had before the conflagration.[35]

Palladio's Successor

The death of Palladio in 1580 was a severe blow to the circle of Venetian nobles centered around Daniele Barbaro which had backed the great architect's abstract, unyielding classicism for three decades. However, even the passing of their longtime champion did not deter

Fig. 102: Andrea Palladio's church of San Giorgio Maggiore
seen across the Venetian harbor

Fig. 103: Elevation drawing for a new Renaissance ducal palace
in Venice by Andrea Palladio

this small group of determined men. Having lost Palladio and the battle to build a Renaissance ducal palace, they quickly found another state project where they believed they could install a sympathetic architectural collaborator. This was the long-delayed effort to complete Sansovino's Library and extend the same Renaissance elevation along a new southern Piazza perimeter offset from the Campanile, as Sansovino had recommended. Circumstances appeared promising. Marcantonio Barbaro, a procurator of Saint Mark who was also the brother of Daniele Barbaro and an active participant in his pro-Palladian circle, had recently been elected chief project commissioner, and in 1582, the building committee chose Vincenzo Scamozzi to serve as project architect. While angling for the post, Scamozzi, an ambitious thirty-two-year-old native of Vicenza, had left nothing to chance. He had moved to Rome to study classical ruins, written a book on the subject as well as a treatise on perspective, and arranged to have these volumes circulated among the members of the Barbaro coterie in Venice. He had energetically promoted himself as Palladio's leading disciple, having completed the deceased master's famous Villa Rotonda on the outskirts of Vicenza, and, last but certainly not least, he had carefully studied and dutifully annotated Daniele Barbaro's 1567 edition of Vitruvius.[36]

But for all his posturing and public relations, Scamozzi quickly demonstrated that he was no second Palladio (in fact, he harbored deep-seated feelings of jealousy and resentment against the great architect). While some of his early work is genuinely impressive, upon arriving in Venice, Scamozzi unfortunately began to reveal the intellectual limitations of a rigid academic theorist, perhaps because he thought such antiquarianism would endear him to Palladio's former patrons. He declared that architecture was a "science" whose "demonstrations are certain and indisputable"[37] and that the difference between an architect who understood the mathematically based truths that governed the universe and a builder who lacked such knowledge was akin to the distinction between a nobleman and his house servants. When he incorporated these elitist concepts into his treatise *L'idea dell'architettura universale*, he produced a book so ponderous and pedantic, it resembled a piece of medieval scholasticism more than a work of the early seventeenth century. And when he attempted to put such ideas into practice by designing a Venetian church for the Celestine nuns, his clients were so dissatisfied with the result (they called it an architectural monster) that they halted the project in mid-construction and had it demolished before beginning over with a different architect.[38]

Immediately after his appointment to complete the Marciana Library, Scamozzi seems to have been careful to refer to Sansovino with the respect he believed his new employers would expect of him. But within six months, he had begun to suggest that Sansovino's two-story design was a blatant error that needed to be corrected, not only if it were to be extended into the Piazza but within the Piazzetta as well. According to Scamozzi, Sansovino's decision to forgo a Library third story (a deliberate choice made to prevent the project from competing with the Ducal Palace) demonstrated a shocking gap in his predecessor's classical knowledge. He advised that the correct solution was to destroy Sansovino's magnificent second-story Ionic frieze and erect a third Corinthian level across the entire Piazzetta façade. This massive intervention would allow the new elevation to contain the complete sequence of classical orders dictated by antique precedent, the paramount consideration to a mind like Scamozzi's, whose antiquarian ambitions were soaring at this point; he had also begun trying to convince Venetian leaders to sponsor a wholesale classical correction of the entire harbor front. It is worth recalling that Scamozzi's criticism of Sansovino's Library design contrasted sharply with Palladio's view. Palladio had praised Sansovino's two-story Library façade (with its joyous Ionic frieze) as the richest and most ornate building constructed since ancient times, and he drew on it liberally in designing his own early masterpiece, the elegant two-story loggia he designed for the Vicentine basilica.[39]

Scamozzi's proposal to radically revise Sansovino's Library façade was forcefully opposed by a group of procurators allied with the giovanni (antipapist, anti-Spanish) camp within the patriciate. As a result, the issue of raising the Library to three stories remained unresolved until the Senate intervened in 1588 and ordered Scamozzi to complete the last five bays of the Library according to Sansovino's original Piazzetta design. As a consolation, Scamozzi was awarded a new commission for which his genuine classical erudition was much better suited: the interior design of the Library vestibule, which would house the Grimani family's highly prized antique statuary collection. But even as work proceeded on the last five bays of the Library, Scamozzi and his supporters were unwilling to give up their comprehensive architectural vision: a Renaissance face-lift of the harbor front plus a three-story reconstruction of the Library and its extension into the Piazza. This provoked a vigorous counterreaction in the Senate, where a group of anti-Romanist patricians tried to cancel the Piazza extension altogether rather than see Scamozzi's dogmatic model superimposed on Sansovino's original design. Only in 1596 was a compromise finally reached.

In the Piazzetta, Sansovino's two-floor Library elevation would remain unchanged, but Scamozzi would be allowed to add a third Corinthian story when extending it along the southern boundary of the Piazza. There would be no wholesale classical reconstruction of the harbor front.[40]

Before his death, in 1616, Scamozzi managed to complete at least ten bays of his three-story Piazza extension (set back thirty feet from the edge of the Campanile, as Sansovino had wished), leaving his successor, Baldassare Longhena (1598–1682), to complete the project. The result is an unusually long, thirty-five bay structure ending at the southwest corner of the Piazza; it is known as the Procuratie Nuove (*Fig. 104*) because its two upper stories originally housed spacious apartments for the procurators of Saint Mark. Scamozzi did an unbelievably poor job of joining his three-story Procuratie to the existing two-story Library (*Fig. 105*). Rather than inserting a bay of neutral design between the two elevations, Scamozzi elected to run his own dramatically inconsistent Ionic entablature directly into Sansovino's Ionic frieze—his second-story cornice smashes headlong into the face of Sansovino's final frolicking angel. But even apart from this glaring incongruity, Scamozzi's third story has often been criticized as a generally inferior addition. Yet those who would censure Scamozzi for having the temerity to add a third floor to the Piazza façade (apart from the manner in which he performed the task) must themselves confront certain inherent difficulties. Sansovino's refined, two-story design, which appears to such majestic effect in the Piazzetta, would have created a very different impression if its lesser height and mass had been repeated along the much greater length of the entire Piazza. As Ruskin correctly pointed out, there is no perfect answer to this vexing architectural issue.[41]

One of Her Finest Hours

For all the erosion of her military strength and occasional failure of political will following her sudden, shocking defeat in 1509 at the hands of Pope Julius II and his League of Cambrai, late-sixteenth-century Venice, when viewed in the round, remained a very viable concern. She was still the chief port in the Adriatic and one of the most active harbors in the entire Mediterranean region. Although her shipbuilding and merchant marine sectors were in sad decay, the general Venetian economy was on the upswing. Commerce and manufacturing were both expanding, and even the city's Mediterranean spice trade was

Fig. 104: Façade of Scamozzi's Procuratie Nuove

*Fig. 105: Juncture of Scamozzi's Procuratie Nuove
and Sansovino's Marciana Library*

on the mend. On major public architectural issues, communal decision making (which referred to the three-hundred-member Senate such questions as the final appearance of the Piazza and Piazzetta or whether Palladio's votive Redentore church should be sited in the city or on an offshore island) was alive and well and, on the whole, producing intelligent outcomes. In addition to successfully opposing inflexible classical building schemes in the Piazza district, the group of younger nobles known as the giovanni worked to hinder papal intrusion into the city's religious life and to reverse the flow of political authority from the broader-based Senate to the narrower Council of Ten. For many years, the leader of the giovanni had been Leonardo Dona, an eloquent statesman who had acquitted himself with distinction in a variety of public posts. Dona had played an important role in preventing Scamozzi from imposing his rigid classical views on Sansovino's Library, a battle that in Dona's mind was closely linked with the continuing need to resist Roman interference with Venetian political and intellectual freedoms. Thus, in 1596, when Pope Clement VIII released a new index of proscribed writings that the city's printers could not publish and Venetian bookshops could not sell, Dona once again led the opposition. The pope, he argued, was acting like a parochial Roman; his real intent was to damage the flourishing Venetian book industry. In response, the Senate refused to allow the ban to be enforced in Venice, and the pope, realizing he could not reverse this decision, quickly relented and granted special permission for the city to print and sell the proscribed works.[42]

This contest over the papal index was swiftly resolved in the Republic's favor because Pope Clement was a political realist. However, in her next major clash with the papacy, Venice would find herself face-to-face with a very different type of opponent. Camillo Borghese, who in 1605 became Pope Paul V (*Fig. 106*), was raised in a middle-class family in Siena and practiced law in Perugia and Bologna before his father purchased a place for him in the Church hierarchy. Although stolid and fleshy in appearance, inwardly he seethed with the religious conviction of a true zealot and the prickly defensiveness of a born despot. When he declared that the earth was the unmoving center of the universe and that the sun dutifully revolved around it, the issue was settled as far as he was concerned. If anyone, such as the Polish astronomer Copernicus or the Italian physicist Galileo Galilei, had the temerity to question the pope's authority in scientific matters, the solution was to crush such skeptics. Paul also made his papacy synonymous with princely wealth and lavish artistic patronage, and not surprisingly, he maintained the same policy of personal egotism and infallibility in his architectural undertakings. In 1606, he decided to complete the destruction of the old basilica of Saint Peter's begun a century earlier by another colossal narcissist, Pope Julius II. In short order, the roof was dismantled (including a marble cross placed there by the emperor Constantine himself), the nave was razed, and almost thirteen hundred years of Christian history were summarily erased. Having obliterated the old church, Paul rejected the Greek-cross replacement structure insisted on by both Bramante and Michelangelo. Instead, he commissioned an inferior talent named Carlo Maderno (1555–1629) to connect Michelangelo's magnificent Renaissance dome to an elongated nave. At the pope's direction, Maderno then added an oversized, badly designed entrance façade to the front of the church and carved Paul's name across the top in five-foot-high letters.[43]

This was the dogmatic, hypersensitive adversary the Republic faced in 1605 when she arrested two alleged clerics for crimes over which the pope claimed exclusive ecclesiastical jurisdiction and adopted a decree restricting further Church acquisition of Venetian realty. In Venetian eyes, the city was only exercising her traditional religious freedoms, but to Pope Paul, who fancied himself an expert on canon law, such assertions of independence were seen as nothing less than pointed insults to his personal authority. He ordered the city to rescind both actions and threatened that if she refused, he would place her under an immediate papal interdict banning all Church services within Venetian territory. At this point, the old doge died, and Leonardo Dona, the leader of the giovanni, was elected to lead the city through the impending crisis. The Senate, realizing that in addition to a raw power struggle, the city would soon be engaged in a fierce battle for European public opinion, sent for a certain fifty-three-year-old Venetian friar from the Servite order. This was Paolo Sarpi (*Fig. 107*), an intellectual prodigy with an international reputation who, besides being thoroughly versed in theology and canon law, was an accomplished political philosopher, scientist, and mathematician. He was credited with discovering the circulation of the blood and had been thanked by Galileo for helping the great scientist (while he was a professor at the nearby University of Padua) construct his famous telescope. In fact, Galileo called Sarpi his father and master, and both men, as well as Doge Dona himself, belonged to a small group of intellectuals who often met at the Morosini palace in Venice to discuss current religious, political, and scientific topics.[44]

Fig. 106: Bust of Pope Paul V (Camillo Borghese)
by Gianlorenzo Bernini

Fig. 107: Statue of Paolo Sarpi
by Emilio Marsili

When the interdict became effective in the spring of 1606, Venice, having prepared herself for all-out political and ideological warfare, weighed into the fray with every resource at her command. To the pope's charge that the Republic was now governed by Calvinists, Doge Dona responded "What is a Calvinist? We are Christians, as good as the pope himself, and Christians we shall die, whether others like it or not." On Sarpi's advice, Dona banished the Jesuit order from Venetian territory, and the rest of the clergy was put on notice that all religious observances, especially the Mass, would be performed as though the pope had never spoken. In the war of ideas, Sarpi began to produce a stream of briefs and letters dismantling Paul's contention that he had a legal and spiritual right to interfere in the city's domestic affairs, and thanks to the brilliance of Sarpi's argument, the controversy quickly caught the attention of the educated West. Realizing that she was becoming an advocate for many post-Reformation Catholics throughout Europe, the Republic's messages to Rome began to exhibit a sharper edge. How long did His Holiness wish to continue the contest, she inquired. And if the conflict were prolonged, what would happen if other nations began to follow the Venetian example? These were telling questions, since it was becoming clearer with each passing day that the interdict had failed in its basic purpose: to engender such fear of papal retribution (both in this life and the next) that resistance would simply collapse. The result was a widespread loss of respect for a pope who had tried to wield his power so unsuccessfully. Naturally, it was very difficult for a man like Paul to accept such public failure, but over time, he was left with no other choice and eventually agreed to a French offer of mediation. In April 1607, the interdict was lifted and formal relations were restored—on Venetian terms. The Republic would not apologize; the original offending actions would not be reversed; the ban on Jesuits would remain in force; and Sarpi, who had personally embarrassed the pope, would continue to be honored as a Venetian hero. It was the last interdict the Church would ever attempt.[45]

The struggle over and the battle won, Sarpi retired to his monastic cell, where he again disappeared behind a pile of scholarly books and papers. No doubt still intrigued by the arguments that had so occupied his mind for the previous year, he began work on a history of the Council of Trent, the Catholic Church's most sustained effort to come to terms with the issues raised by the Protestant Reformation. But he also continued to work for the Venetian state, and one afternoon in October 1607, while crossing a bridge upon his return from the Ducal Palace, he was set upon and nearly killed by assassins who repeatedly stabbed him in the head and neck before leaving him for dead. One of the knives was driven home with such force that the blade remained embedded in his cheekbone. Upon regaining consciousness and being shown the weapon, Sarpi replied that he recognized the papal *stile* (style) of the affair, making a witty pun on the Italian word *stiletto* for dagger. Meanwhile, his would-be murderers fled to Rome, where, despite making no effort to hide their crime, they were never arrested or charged. In Venice, the Republic offered Sarpi a more secure residence in the Piazza, but he declined to leave his home in the monastery of Santa Maria dei Servi in the city's remote northwestern precincts (where he hung the assassins' dagger in the church). As a result, he suffered two more assassination attempts before completing his historical opus and dying peacefully in bed in 1623. One of the last of the great Venetians, he survived the worst his mortal enemies could do and won a splendid victory on behalf of European religious liberty. His dying words were a prayer that the city he loved might endure forever.[46]

The interdict struggle was a battle of clashing ideas, the type of intellectual debate more often associated with Florentine political theorists such as Machiavelli than with citizens of the Republic. It also exemplified the courage and conviction the city had often demonstrated in earlier conflicts. Threatened by a powerful, aggressive enemy, Doge Dona and Paolo Sarpi summoned up the same fierce patriotism, the same unshakeable belief in Venetian exceptionalism that inspired Vettor Pisani and his countrymen to counterattack against a superior, encircling foe at the end of the fourteenth century when resistance seemed almost hopeless. In both cases, the roots of action were the same: a passionate certainty that the Republic's brilliant achievements were far too valuable to surrender without a fight.

CHAPTER THIRTEEN

Challenging a Fundamental Paradigm

A fair and accurate evaluation of the architecture of the Piazza San Marco complex raises basic critical issues because it challenges a fundamental artistic paradigm. Since the time of the Italian Renaissance, Western art criticism has generally subscribed to a belief in the sovereign individual artist as the ultimate creative force. From then to now, most authors have explicitly maintained or implicitly assumed that in order to reach the highest level of artistic achievement, it is necessary to unleash the uncompromised force of solitary, individual genius.

The quality of genius was first attributed to an Italian artist when the Florentines publicly recognized the architect Filippo Brunelleschi as "a great ingenious man," as, in fact, "a divine genius,"[1] at the time of his death in 1446. Prior to that, even a supreme creator like the fourteenth-century painter and architect Giotto di Bondone was viewed by his contemporaries as nothing more than a "skilled and famous man" and "a great master."[2] However, Renaissance writers, building on passages from Plato's dialogues, theorized that as men of genius, some artists were essentially different from the rest of humankind. In the exercise of their genius, they underwent profoundly solitary experiences in which they were invaded, literally taken over, by divine inspiration. Having received this gift of divine seizure, the artist's perfection was measured by his ability to communicate its unique, individual content in virtually undiluted form. This emphasis on novelty and the vital contribution of the individual artist led to the idea that a genuine work of art is one that necessarily alters existing standards and must therefore be evaluated by its own self-sufficient criteria. In this view, artists of genius create autonomous works of art that respond to their own internal rules, not to external environments or reference points. The inherent solipsism of such a process gave rise to the kindred notion that genius is often associated with feelings of alienation from the world of ordinary mortals. By the publication of Giorgio Vasari's influential sixteenth-century work *Lives of the Artists*, such conceptions seem to have become firmly established. The attribution of individual genius to an architect, painter, or sculptor had become the supreme encomium. When Vasari referred to Michelangelo, Leonardo, and Raphael as "divinely inspired spirits" and "mortal gods,"[3] he intended to offer these artists both the highest possible praise and a convincing explanation of what were viewed as their unparalleled achievements.[4]

In their fully developed High Renaissance form, such ideas amounted to a belief that pairing the resources of a single all-powerful patron (emperor or pope) with a solitary, divinely inspired individual (a Michelangelo or a Bramante) was the obligatory formula for supreme cultural achievement. But as the narrative chapters of this book have repeatedly shown, the architectural ensemble of the Piazza San Marco, an artistic production of the highest order, is the result of an entirely different model of creation.

Western Communal Art

The Piazza complex is one of the great examples of Western communal art. During its general ascendancy from the eleventh through the fourteenth centuries, communal art's defining characteristic was the ability of successive teams of gifted but often anonymous architects, artists, and artisans to collaborate at a very high level of creativity and technical skill on large, multigenerational projects. According to James Ackerman, the demise of communal art and its replacement with the theory of individual genius explains why there are so few Renaissance monuments which display the same profound integration of architecture and sculpture that we find in a great work of the Middle Ages such as Chartres Cathedral. The Renaissance cult of personality, with its emphasis on individuality and the creative genius of a few specific artists, broke the spell of anonymity in which medieval artists had flourished. It destroyed the climate of mutual support and commitment that made masterworks of collaboration possible even over extended project periods lasting a hundred years or more and replaced it with a focus on well-publicized rivalries among a handful of artistic titans. The highest products of medieval communal art, such as the Piazza San Marco ensemble or the Gothic cathedrals of eleventh- and twelfth-century France, were national monuments, whose enormous costs, willingly borne across all social classes, provided unmistakable evidence of the religious ardor and patriotic zeal animating a re-vived Western Europe. As part of the natural climatic phenomenon known as the Medieval Warm Period (950–1250), temperatures rose, leading to increased agricultural production and a doubling of population across the continent. Venetian, Genoese, and Pisan merchant ships began to ply ancient Mediterranean trade routes, Christian believers increasingly made pilgrimages to sacred Middle Eastern sites, and a united Church led crusades to rid the Holy Land of Islamic rule. In medieval Italy in particular, cities were growing rapidly, commerce and manufacturing were thriving, and a burgeoning middle class was seeking a more prominent public role for its restless energies. Rooted as it was in such urban dy-namism, it is not surprising that communal art also flourished in this Italian setting; even religious projects such as cathedrals and baptisteries were frequently sponsored and man-aged by communal bodies rather than by Church officials.[5]

Italian communal governments (whether characterized as oligarchies or republics) reached political consensus after a vigorous discussion of important public issues by the city's leading citizens. Constitutional arrangements, designed to disperse political power among a large, representative group, were interlaced with restrictions on the formation of permanent factions or the usurpation of authority by a single individual or family. Instead, decisions were made through an interlocking network of councils and committees whose members were selected by lot and who usually served for brief, strictly limited periods. The governing ideal was collaboration among equals performed by men chosen from the upper ranks of the city's financial and civic hierarchy. While far from being democratic in any modern sense, such communal governments were, in fact, broadly representative of collective municipal interests. In many ways, the Italian communes were, and certainly saw themselves as, medieval legatees of the ancient Greek and Roman city-states. Arising out of the bloody chaos of feudal Europe, their founding recreated "a spot on earth where the largest possible proportion of the inhabitants [were] citizens in the fullest sense of the word,"[6] to quote Jacob Burckhardt. Religious and civic icons were virtually indistinguish-able within a medieval commune, so that the image of a city's patron saint would typically be emblazoned on its military banners. This strong communal ethos caused most citizens to frown on attempts to glorify a particular person in public art and architecture. For instance, Florentine medieval tradition prohibited placing the image of an individual on church exteriors, and it was not until after the Florentine republic was finally extinguished by a Medici tyranny in the 1530s that the statue of an individual ruler was erected in the public square.[7]

Within such Italian communes, public architecture was typically managed by a citizen building committee (known as an *opera*) that functioned as a municipal office of the works, a practice whose roots went back to ancient Greek city-states. A typical opera was a representative body whose membership could be expected to fluctuate dramatically during the long construction period required to complete a major project. The sometimes staggering cost of such enterprises was commonly paid from public sources, including municipal taxes, a circumstance that acted to diffuse responsibility and concern for the quality of the final result well beyond members of the building committee. In Italy, an opera was typically established, either by the commune itself or by a prominent trade guild or confraternity, to oversee the construction of a particular major undertaking. If the building committee were also responsible for financing the project, it could find itself transformed into a semiautonomous body possessing its own independent funding sources. In such a case, it might retain its existence after project completion in order to administer and care for the new building and perhaps to draw on its accumulated experience by undertaking other large projects on different sites. Such permanent, self-sufficient building committees were particularly common in Venice and Florence. For instance, the Opera del Duomo, the office of the works for the Florentine Cathedral, also managed construction of the Florentine town hall (the Palazzo della Signoria) and the square in which it sat (the Piazza della Signoria), located six blocks from the church. If charged with responsibility for the ongoing operation, maintenance, and repair of one or more important buildings, the opera's members, who typically met no more than once a week, would need to hire a staff of building professionals. This would include a *capomaestro* or master builder and a master of the works, who would handle day-to-day financial and administrative duties. With the exception of the Procuracy of Saint Mark in Venice, almost all Italian building committees experienced fairly rapid turnover; their three to six members were usually appointed to terms of no more than one year. Whenever it wished to do so, a communal government could take over the decision-making process and impose its will on an opera whose members it had appointed.[8]

The Rise of the Procuracy of Saint Mark

For the first 350 years after a new Venetian government was established on the Rialtine islands at the beginning of the ninth century, architectural projects in the San Marco area remained dependent on the personal initiative and financial sponsorship of individual doges, who ruled as monarchs of relatively unrestricted power. In recognition of this fact, historians usually refer to the first, second, and third churches of San Marco as the Participazio, Orseolo, and Contarini churches, respectively, and to the new ducal palace built after the burning of the ducal center in 976 as the Orseolo palace. During this early period, the church of San Marco functioned as an exclusively ducal chapel, and the ducal palace remained a grim, fortified castle guarded by a ducal garrison. Both buildings sat on a small island crisscrossed by intersecting dirt paths, within an area enclosed by Pietro Tribuno's dilapidated brick wall and split into two halves by an intersecting canal. However, by 1160, Venice had taken the first serious steps to transform herself from a state ruled by quasi-regal doges into an oligarchical republic where governance was shared among members of a large and powerful merchant nobility. As this occurred, the cramped dirt field in front of the ducal chapel began to seem completely inadequate. The city felt the need for a grand new public space where the enlarged communal government of the Venetian Republic could assemble and view itself as a collective enterprise. The result was a century-long building initiative that more than doubled the size of the square fronting the church and marked the beginning of communal architecture in Venice. From 1160 to 1280, the city created the Piazza and Piazzetta (collectively, the largest and most splendid public space in medieval Europe), enlarged and embellished the Basilica San Marco following the conquest of Constantinople in 1204, and built a new governmental palace to serve as both a ducal residence and a meeting hall for new communal councils and commissions.[9]

Not surprisingly, during an era when political power was gravitating from the doge to communal magistracies, responsibility for a huge architectural undertaking like the Piazza complex also slipped out of ducal hands into those of a new communal body, the Procuracy of Saint Mark (introduced to the reader in Chapters Five and Seven). This important institution, at first a single nobleman appointed by the doge, probably originated about the time of the consecration of the Contarini Basilica in 1094, although the earliest verifiable record of its existence dates from 1152. The Procuracy's initial responsibilities were limited to the maintenance, rebuilding, and decoration of the Basilica, but sometime during the dogate of Vitale Michiel II (1156–1172) while initial site clearance for the Piazza development project was under way, it began to assume a new oversight and management role for this monumental undertaking. When Vitale Michiel II was assassinated in 1172, his rich and brilliant successor, Doge Sebastiano Ziani, no doubt had a critical influence on the original design of the Piazza complex, although the brief span of his dogate (1172–1178) meant that no more than a small portion of the project was actually built during his term of office. But by the early 1200s, the ability of an individual doge to affect the Piazza project was considerably reduced. The power to appoint procurators had been transferred from the doge to the Great Council, and the Procuracy had been charged with long-term responsibility for supervising the development of the Piazza and most of the buildings around its perimeter. By 1268, there were four procurators, two of whom (known as the procurators de supra) were specifically charged with overseeing the architectural condition of the Basilica and the newly built Piazza. This, as much as any other factor, accounts for the remarkable architectural coherence of the completed medieval Piazza. Not only was the Venetian square based on a clear classical model (the Augusteum, a functioning antique forum in the imperial Byzantine capital of Constantinople), most of its development (a process spanning the terms of ten separate doges) was controlled by a single quasi-governmental body.[10]

By 1422, there were three procurators de supra, as well as six other procurators divided into two sections, *de citra* and *de ultra*, who served as the state's principal fiduciaries for the administration of wills, trusts, and estates. By virtue of their ownership and management of virtually the entire Piazza area and other large real estate holdings, the procurators de supra also possessed considerable financial power. Selection by the Great Council as a procurator of Saint Mark was the second-highest distinction the Republic could confer on a member of the merchant nobility. Appointment was for life, and the criteria for election included seniority, business acumen, and extensive prior service in a variety of official posts. New doges were very often selected from the ranks of the procurators, and they were the only public officials other than the doge who were eligible for state-provided housing in the San Marco precinct. In addition to a token salary, the Republic supplied each procurator with a spacious, rent-free apartment along the Piazza perimeter. However, although procurators enjoyed an exalted status near the pinnacle of the Venetian political hierarchy, the Procuracy was not intended to function as an integral part of the government itself. By design, it was a special, insulated public body whose members, in light of their concentrated financial power, were discouraged from taking an active role in the city's daily governance. On Sunday afternoon, when all the other members of the patriciate were summoned to the Doge's Palace to attend the weekly session of the Great Council, the procurators remained outside, often gathering in the loggia at the foot of the Campanile. As a result of their separation from the actual business of the state, the procurators often had to be briefed on current affairs by the doge and his advisers.[11]

The procurators de supra were able to finance their architectural responsibilities on an independent, self-supporting basis. They collected a large rental income from their extensive real property holdings, not only in the Piazza and Piazzetta but throughout the city and the Republic's mainland possessions. In the Piazza, most of the space behind the ground-floor arcades was leased to merchants, and many of the upper-story rooms not used as procuratorial office and living space were also let to private renters. Additional revenue flowed to the Procuracy from Venetian trading colonies abroad, including income from the churches the city's merchant communities established and attended in overseas ports. To finance important building projects, the Procuracy was also empowered to borrow against its treasury holdings. Given such ample financial resources, it was also occasionally called upon to loan money to the state to meet critical nonarchitectural needs, as it did, for example, in the late 1530s to help defray the massive cost of defending the Republic's embattled Mediterranean empire against Turkish aggression.[12]

The procurators de supra were able to hire a proto or master builder (the Venetian equivalent of a capomaestro) to provide them with the professional advice they needed to carry out their duties. As a permanently salaried employee responsible for coordinating all the various building crafts, the proto also typically functioned as the designing architect for procuratorial projects. The Procuracy was an extremely demanding patron. In spite of his illustrious reputation as a master of the Roman Renaissance style, Jacopo Sansovino (proto to the Procuracy from 1529 to 1570) was required to busy himself continuously with his employers' personal architectural requirements. The procurators exercised total control over their proto and could be extremely harsh and unforgiving when he failed to live up to their exacting expectations. As we have seen, when a small portion of the Marciana Library's vaulted ceiling collapsed in the winter of 1545, the Procuracy had Sansovino thrown in jail and ordered him to personally repay the one-thousand-ducat repair cost. Yet, in spite of such treatment, Sansovino fully appreciated the extraordinary architectural opportunities afforded by his position and willingly submitted to procuratorial authority. Over the course of a forty-one-year career as proto, he turned down lucrative competing offers from the pope and several European monarchs.[13]

When the Great Council transferred communal control of the Piazza complex (with the significant exception of the Ducal Palace) to the Procuracy, it did so with certain expectations. It believed that, on the whole, this self-governing body of senior public officials, backed by major independent financial resources, would display a consistent, long-term perspective and bring a high degree of disinterested public concern to the performance of its duties. And in general, prior to the middle of the sixteenth century, the hopes embodied in this liberal grant of power and financial autonomy seem to have been realized. For example, in 1536, the procurators de supra commissioned Sansovino to construct new apartments for their own use along the southern side of the Piazza, but when Sansovino responded by producing a design of astonishing classical elegance, the procurators did not hesitate to put the public interest ahead of their personal needs. They quickly altered the purpose of the commission, decreeing that Sansovino's brilliant new edifice would now be constructed along the western side of the Piazzetta to achieve an entirely different purpose: a long-delayed municipal library to house Cardinal John Bessarion's invaluable classical manuscript collection. When presented with an architectural design they deemed worthy of such an undertaking, the procurators readily subordinated their own ease and comfort to the city's greater good.[14]

State Architectural Patronage in Venice

As previously explained, although the Procuracy of Saint Mark was located near the apex of the Venetian political pyramid, it was not part of the government per se. Accordingly, although the procurators de supra were responsible for the maintenance and development of the city's most important and venerable architectural site, their proto was not the state architect of Venice. That distinction belonged to the proto of the *Magistrato al Sal* or Salt Commission, one of the Venetian government's principal administrative bureaus. Aside from its architectural functions, the Salt Commission was both a regulatory agency responsible for licensing and taxing the production and sale of salt within Venetian territory and a public instrument for purchasing salt from areas outside the Republic's control. This government monopoly over a necessity like salt generated a huge revenue stream equal to ten percent of the total income of the Venetian state. As proof of its commitment to public architecture, the government dedicated this massive flow of money to the support of state building projects throughout the city, with special priority given to the Ducal Palace.[15]

In its fully developed form, the decision-making apparatus for direct state architectural patronage outside the Procuracy was a flexible, overlapping network of councils, commissions, and magistracies manned by short-term officeholders elected from the city's merchant aristocracy. Each of the Republic's two thousand to twenty-five hundred male aristocrats over the age of twenty-five (one to two percent of the population), belonged to the Great Council, making them eligible for election to a brief term on one of the public bodies that supervised state architecture in Venice. But within this large pool of candidates were one to two hundred men who, by repeatedly holding a few dozen key positions at the helm of critical institutions like the Senate and the Council of Ten, constituted a governing circle at the center of Venetian public affairs. The Salt Commission stood near the bottom, not the summit, of this governmental hierarchy. Rather than exercising real independent authority, its six commissioners, who served terms of sixteen months, acted as administrative agents of the most powerful policy-making bodies in the Venetian constitutional pyramid. If the Great Council, the Senate, or the Council of Ten wished to initiate a building project, it would typically delegate to the Salt Commission such tasks as entering into the required architectural contract, supervising construction, and paying the bills. The best way to illustrate the extremely adaptable manner in which this basic structure could operate over time is to describe several centuries of architectural decision making in connection with the Ducal Palace, the major building in the Piazza complex for which the state itself (rather than the Procuracy) had primary responsibility.[16]

In the early part of the fourteenth century, the doge still lived and the Republic's communal councils still met in the Ziani governmental palace, a Veneto-Byzantine building constructed at the personal initiative of Doge Sebastiano Ziani in the latter part of the twelfth century. But in December, 1340, the Venetian government, responding to serious problems of size, security, and hygiene, decided to replace the Ziani palace with a new Ducal Palace whose principal feature would be a much enlarged Great Council chamber at the top of a newly constructed wing facing the Venetian harbor. In light of the enormous cost and physical disruption such a project would entail, the decision to proceed was made by the Great Council itself. Thereafter, to the degree that direction of the Ducal Palace project remained with the Great Council, a smaller body known as the Signoria (consisting of the doge, his six ducal councilors, and the three chiefs of the Quarantia, the city's supreme criminal court) acted as an intermediary between the Council and the Salt Commission. In general during the fourteenth century, however, the Great Council's role in architectural decision making, as in financial and military questions, began to pass to the Senate. The Republic believed that by centralizing the resolution of such critical issues among the thirty or so families making up the city's senatorial oligarchy, she could impose a greater consistency on public policy decisions. In the architectural arena, this gave Venice the confidence to undertake and complete enormous projects like the medieval Ducal Palace, even over a prolonged construction period in which she was repeatedly buffeted by plague epidemics, treason plots, and military defeats. As ultimate control of the Ducal Palace project passed to the Senate, the full *Collegio* (a body composed of sixteen members elected by the Senate plus the Signoria and which set the agenda for the Senate) became the chief contact with the Salt Commission.[17]

In 1422, when a decision was made to duplicate the harbor wing of the Ducal Palace along the eastern face of the Piazzetta, it was made at the initiative of Doge Tommaso Mocenigo, who personally paid the thousand-ducat fine that the law levied on anyone who even suggested such an extravagant proposal. But the actual vote directing the Salt Commission to allocate funds for the Palace extension was made by the Great Council, as was the decision not to cancel the massive project outright as a result of the devastating plague of 1348–1350. Thereafter, state records indicate that active supervision of Ducal Palace architectural efforts was typically supplied by the Senate, the Collegio, and the Signoria, with an occasional major decision being referred to the Great Council. As we have seen in Chapter Ten, some fifteenth-century additions to the Palace, particularly sculptural commissions for the Porta della Carta, the Arco Foscari, and the ceremonial staircase and eastern wing of the Palace courtyard, became occasions for ducal self-promotion. Consequently, in the 1480s and 1490s, when evidence of such corrupt behavior began to gain widespread attention (particularly after it was revealed that the Palace proto, Antonio Rizzo, had been allowed to embezzle twelve thousand ducats), the Council of Ten began to play a larger role in project oversight.[18]

In short, at any given point in time, the pattern of architectural decision making and management for a major state project like the Doge's Palace tended to mirror the general political structure of the Venetian constitution. During the fourteenth through sixteenth centuries, there was a tendency for basic decisions (which, early on, were made by the Great Council) to gravitate to smaller, more efficient bodies like the Senate and the Collegio, and if even greater accountability seemed desirable, to the still smaller Council of Ten. However, if at any time, a particular matter were felt to be sufficiently important to warrant such action, its resolution could be pulled back toward the base of the constitutional pyramid, including removal to the Great Council itself, the ultimate repository of public authority in republican Venice. Such centrifugal and centripetal movement within the interconnected circles of the Venetian political system only rarely caused a significant shift in policy, since the many of the same key officials drawn from the same cluster of prominent families tended to occupy leadership posts at each separate level of government.

Joint Projects and Border Disputes

Although the procurators de supra were intended to function as autonomous guardians of the city's most venerable architectural site and to finance their responsibilities on an independent, self-supporting basis, they still had many interactions with the official organs of the Venetian state. Looking closely, we find the same pattern of elastic borders and frequent consultation that guided the conduct of Venetian public affairs in general. For instance, although caring for the Basilica San Marco treasury was one of the Procuracy's most fundamental responsibilities, the doge and his councilors still had to approve any proposed sale or transfer of such assets, even when the proceeds were to be used for another core procuratorial function such as reconstruction of the church building itself. Conversely, in 1280, the Republic entrusted the job of renting ground-floor rooms in the Ziani ducal palace to the Procuracy, a prerogative that had formerly belonged exclusively to the doge.[19]

More often, collaboration between the Procuracy and the regular machinery of the Venetian government occurred as the result of a joint building effort, particularly where improvements to one building, such as the Ducal Palace, might affect the appearance of a neighboring structure like the church of San Marco. Ruskin recounts an instance in 1355 when the Procuracy paid for a gilded stone lion to be placed over the gate of the old Ziani ducal palace near where the palace joined the Basilica. Similarly, in the next century, when the Great Council decided to extend a copy of the Palace's new harbor wing along the eastern edge of the Piazzetta, the project was supervised by the Procuracy despite the fact that the money for this state initiated enterprise came from the Salt Commission. A few years later, the Procuracy also managed the Porta della Carta project even though the Salt Commission funded the work and contracted with the Bon family for its design and installation. In 1495, the Senate and the Procuracy jointly commissioned the construction of Mauro Codussi's stately Clock Tower near the northeast corner of the Piazza. Although such an undertaking would normally have been the sole responsibility of the Procuracy, the state paid for this edifice from Salt Commission revenues, and both the Senate and the Signoria remained closely involved in project supervision. In 1554, when the Marciana Library façade was extended to incorporate the entrance to the neighboring Mint, there was a need for cooperation between the Procuracy and the special commission that administered the Mint under the direct control of the Council of Ten. Collaboration was facilitated to a certain extent by the fact that the Procuracy and the Mint had appointed the same architect, Jacopo Sansovino, to design and construct both buildings. Nevertheless, a conflict did erupt when the Procuracy was asked to relinquish a portion of its rent-producing harbor property to accommodate Sansovino's design for the Mint's advancing footprint. The dispute was finally settled in 1558, but only through the intervention of a special tribunal of twenty-five senators appointed by the Council of Ten.[20]

Thus, even when it had to accommodate an autonomous, *sui generis* entity like the Procuracy, the framework of public architectural direction in Venice was sufficiently firm in principle and fluid in practice to handle a variety of potentially troublesome issues. When operating as it was designed to function, such overlapping authority ensured that decisions were rarely made without being examined from a multitude of perspectives incorporating the judgment and taste of a substantial number of seasoned public officials. Government by committee it certainly was, but the results were usually successful and often superb.

Procuratorial Misconduct

In addition to resolving relatively routine matters like architectural boundary disputes, the state could also take more fundamental action when that seemed to be required. For instance, the Great Council, which appointed the procurators de supra to their life terms, could, at any time, alter the scope of their delegated authority. In 1556, the Council enlarged the powers of the Procuracy by allowing it to manage its own budget without ducal supervision; then, in 1569, it revoked this freedom and appointed a special commission to examine procuratorial finances. When the investigation revealed that for the previous ten years, more than half of the procurators' total expenditures had been for repairs to their own properties, particularly their own state-supplied residences, the offenders were ordered to make restitution to the Republic. This pattern was repeated in 1578, when it again became necessary for the Senate to audit the procurators' spending patterns and to issue detailed new regulations setting out exactly what the state considered acceptable procuratorial conduct. But in spite of such reform efforts, a degree of corruption and financial irregularity continued to tarnish procuratorial affairs for the remainder of the sixteenth century. Due to a loss of public confidence in the Procuracy during this period, the Senate stepped forward to become the final decision maker for critical issues in the ongoing reorganization of the Piazza and Piazzetta begun by Sansovino's Library project. Arguments for and against competing proposals continued to be heard by the Procuracy, but final debate and resolution were removed to the Senate. In September 1588, it was the Senate that intervened and ordered Scamozzi to complete the last five bays of the Library according to the existing Sansovinian model. Again, in 1596, it was the Senate that debated and decided on a final compromise for extending Sansovino's Library elevation (with the addition of a third story) along the southern wing of the Piazza.[21]

Such self-centered procuratorial behavior was a far cry from the communal spirit displayed a few decades earlier, when the procurators willingly sacrificed their personal interests to make the long-deferred idea of a Venetian public library an immediate reality. Still, even in the face of such embarrassing financial misconduct, two points should be kept in mind. First, however corrupt their actions may have been during any particular period, the consistent, long-term vision that the procurators de supra typically brought to the development of public architecture in the Piazza was a huge advance over the chaotic methods by which projects were initiated and guided in the rest of sixteenth-century Italy. For instance, the stability and continuity provided by the Procuracy stands in vivid contrast to the inconsistent, egotistical patronage practiced by a succession of popes during the design and construction of the new Renaissance Saint Peter's in Rome. Over the course of 161 years, this enormous project passed through the hands of twenty-two popes and thirteen architects. New popes threw out their predecessors' plans and substituted their own novel ideas, with the result that original designs by masters such as Bramante and Michelangelo were abandoned in mid-construction. Second, even where procuratorial malfeasance might arguably have affected architectural quality, the Venetian system was capable of adjustment and correction. When circumstances warranted, the Procuracy's charter could be amended, its independence could be curtailed, and parts of its role in the public building process could be transferred to the Senate or another more accountable body. This ready ability to shift functions within the intricate web of Venetian constitutional arrangements, to remain true to fundamental principles while adapting to particular circumstances, was one of the Republic's special strengths.[22]

The Persistence of Communal Ideals

During the centuries when it was at the apogee of its power, the merchant aristocracy that governed Venice and directed public architecture in the Piazza San Marco precinct generally placed an extremely high value on communal decision making and feared rule by a single individual or dominant faction. At its best, it was a system that valued anonymity, balance, consensus, and tradition and was continually on the alert for signs of arrogance and ostentation among members of its ruling patriciate. From the twelfth to the sixteenth centuries, the Venetian governing class devoted enormous energies to designing a set of constitutional constraints that it hoped would promote collective ideals and impede the display of individual egotism. The goal was to transform the inevitable struggle for power and public office into an open contest where the constant jostling for position by a large number of competing candidates would protect the state from the ambitious designs of any particular individual or family. To achieve this, the Republic believed that she had to create a set of stringent regulations and to insist that they be rigorously enforced. And since the Venetian aristocracy clearly understood the powerful influence that works of art and architecture exert on human ideas and behavior, one of its basic rules was that no individual, whatever the merits of his service or value to the state, could be honored with a purely personal effigy in the public areas of the San Marco complex. Instead, the city's public architecture and iconography were supposed to represent the Venetian state in its idealized essence and to encourage a standard of aristocratic behavior that put communal values before personal advantage.[23]

Of course, the Republic did not always live up to such lofty, impersonal standards. But even during the fifteenth century, when projects such as the Porta della Carta, the Arco Foscari, and the eastern wing of the Ducal Palace courtyard displayed blatant ducal self-aggrandizement, the rule against individual effigies in the San Marco precinct was only bent, not broken, and the prohibition appears to have been fully reestablished by the early 1500s. The depth of feeling behind this restriction is perhaps best illustrated by a famous episode in Venetian art history. In 1475, the Republic discovered that she was a contingent beneficiary in the will of the illustrious *condottiere* Bartolomeo Colleoni, one of the greatest mercenary generals of his age. For a quarter century, Venetians had paid huge sums to Colleoni to defend their Italian mainland possessions, and the shrewd old Bergamese soldier had shown himself to be an excellent businessman. When he died, his estate was valued at more than 600,000 ducats; the cash portion alone was comparable to the wealth of Cosimo de' Medici, the richest banker in Italy. Colleoni bequeathed the entire sum to Venice on one condition—the Republic must erect an equestrian statue of the general in the Piazza San Marco.[24]

In 1475, Venice desperately needed the financial relief this huge bequest would provide. Having recently fought an unsuccessful battle to halt Turkish seizure of her maritime empire, the Republic was nearly bankrupt. Just five years earlier, she had lost the island of Negropont to the Ottomans, and many Venetians feared that the struggle would not end until the city had been stripped of all her Mediterranean trading ports. Despite this, no serious thought was ever given to executing Colleoni's wish in the Piazza. Of course, the episode is best known for what happened after the Republic refused to carry out the general's explicit request. Venice successfully argued that she had found a way of coming close enough to the terms of the will that she should be allowed to keep the money. A famous Florentine sculptor was commissioned to design and cast what is arguably the finest equestrian bronze statue since the age of the ancient Romans (*Fig. 66*), and the Republic ordered this masterwork erected several hundred yards from the Piazza in front of the Scuola Grande de San Marco rather than the Basilica San Marco. Of course, if the Colleoni bronze, with its extremely high base, had been installed in the Piazza, it would have looked ridiculously oversized and out-of-place without the huge brick church of Santi Giovanni e Paolo to serve as a backdrop. But apart from such aesthetic considerations, the point is that even under extreme financial and military stress, late-fifteenth-century Venice decided that the rule against personal effigies in the San Marco area could not be violated in such a blatant manner.[25]

This tradition of communal art and architecture involving the employment and direction of exceptional talent by a network of public bodies commanding the full resources of the state enjoyed an unusually long life in Venice. It persisted there from the middle of the twelfth century until well into the seventeenth century, a span of over five hundred years, whereas by the middle of the fifteenth century, it had been eclipsed or was waning throughout most of the rest of Italy. In Rome, the reigning pope and his chosen architect (plus a handful of wealthy cardinals who hoped one day to buy the papal chair for themselves) dictated architectural form. Elsewhere in the peninsula, military despots had largely replaced communal governments, so that in cities like Milan, Verona, Mantua, Ferrara, Rimini, and Urbino, new-made lords exercised absolute control over matters of state and public architecture. These upstart tyrants were only too eager to set aside communal traditions that paid homage to earlier political symbols. Lacking any historical claim to political legitimacy, they felt an urgent need to establish their credentials by the most effective means available, including artistic and architectural propaganda. And Renaissance humanists, with their carefully cultivated reputations for learning, literature, and art, all rooted in the prestige of antique culture, were in an excellent position to assist such anxious rulers. In exchange for at least some temporary financial support, perhaps even a permanent place at court, they willingly glorified their princely patrons, portraying their reigns as the natural embodiment of classical history and myth. For instance, artists working for Francesco Carrara, the despot lord of Padua, decorated the main hall of his palace with the portraits of thirty-six heroes of the Roman republic, all based on research performed by Petrarch.[26]

In the Republic, on the other hand, even a genius like Sansovino, who had been specifically recruited from Rome to export the new High Renaissance style to Venice, was obligated to work under strict communal supervision. During his entire forty-one-year career as proto to the Procuracy, Sansovino worked within a corporate framework in which extensive collaboration with public magistracies and assiduous attention to the city's preexisting architectural fabric were prerequisites to success. In Venice alone in the late sixteenth and early seventeenth centuries, would a large deliberative body such as the three-hundred-member Senate be the entity which commissioned, debated, and determined the design and location of two huge votive churches, Palladio's 1576 Redentore church and Longhena's Santa Maria della Salute in 1630.[27]

324

CHAPTER FOURTEEN

The Special Genius of Venice

A Vanguard State

In the surge of urban wealth and communal identity that swept over Europe in the late Middle Ages, Venice was a vanguard state. Having begun her existence as a collection of traumatized survivors from the vandalized Italian mainland, by the eleventh century, she had become one of the Mediterranean's chief naval powers. By 1204, she had conquered Constantinople, the capital of the fabled Byzantine Empire, her historical mentor. She had transformed herself into a world power with a population of at least one hundred thousand, three times that of Florence and twice that of Paris. By the end of the fourteenth century, she had eliminated effective competition from her longtime mercantile rival, the republic of Genoa, and asserted her commercial domination of the lucrative trade routes linking Mediterranean harbors with the ports of northern Europe. In the fifteenth century, she began to balance her overseas hegemony with an expanding mainland empire of sub-ject northern Italian cities.

Throughout this long period of mounting success, Venetian public architecture often displayed a type of artistic synthesis rooted in her maritime, nonfeudal, and nonwestern historical experience. Before the sixteenth century, when they borrowed artistic forms, Venetians typically looked not to Rome but to the Byzantine and Islamic East, where, as international traders, they often spent a decade or more of their early careers. These strong commercial and artistic ties to what had once been the ancient Roman Empire of the East provided Venetians with both the wealth and the classical models to experience an architectural proto-Renaissance as early as the twelfth century. Other burgeoning Ital-ian communes typically had to shoulder the huge cost of building and rebuilding an ever-expanding circuit of defensive walls and cope with bitter quasi-feudal quarrels within their own gates. In Venice, the natural defenses of her lagoon environment and the exceptional political cohesion of her merchant aristocracy enabled the Republic to concentrate communal resources on a single, all-encompassing public building project.

Thus, in the period 1160–1280, the city created the Piazza San Marco, the largest and most splendid public square in Western Europe, a century ahead of even remotely comparable efforts in other parts of the Italian peninsula. By way of comparison, when the principal Florentine square, the Piazza della Signoria, took its initial form in 1268, its shape was a pure accident, an irregular hole carved out of a dense urban fabric by the destruction of a sprawling medieval tower complex belonging to an exiled political clan. The medieval Piazza San Marco, on the other hand, was a stunning, highly deliberate achievement. It was twice the length of the great court in the Forum of Trajan, the largest imperial Roman plaza built in the West. However, instead of having a direct Roman source, the Piazza was consciously modeled on the Augusteum, the enormous public forum in Constantinople where the imperial palace and adjoining state church created a single magnificent setting for enactment of the city's most important public rituals. For Venice, it was an extraordinarily ambitious undertaking, the recreation on a scale befitting a small island state of the most resplendent classical space in the most brilliant city in Christendom, a thriving medieval metropolis which still remained the "beating heart of antiquity."[1] The Piazza's size, splendor, and fidelity to its ancient archetype ensured that it would serve as a model and provide inspiration for later Renaissance squares.[2]

A Rare Synthetic Talent

But it was not merely its precocity which set the Piazza San Marco complex apart from its successors. Its chief distinguishing feature has always been its unrivaled synthesis of major styles—the deliberate creation of an artistic whole that transcends the value of any single component. According to Ruskin, it was this Venetian merger of artistic opposites that accounted for the city's exceptional architectural energy and beauty. Thus, if we examine a so-called "Gothic" masterpiece such as the Ducal Palace, what we actually find is a brilliant fusion of Gothic, Islamic, and Late Antique (Veneto-Byzantine) architectural features. In Ruskin's view, it is the fact that the architect of the Ducal Palace found a way to unify these three distinct elements that makes it "the central building of the world."[3]

There is also the example of the Basilica San Marco, whose builders, in the first half of the thirteenth century, added an exuberant, uniquely Venetian marble investiture to the plain brick exterior of an eleventh-century Byzantine church, and then, at the beginning of the fifteenth century, crowned the façade with a triumphant crest of Gothic sculpture. Intriguingly, this ensemble effect is even more pronounced if we examine the Basilica surface in greater detail. Virtually every expanse of wall, both inside and out, is an exquisite amalgam of sculptural relief, glimmering mosaic, and precious stone spoil in shades ranging from pink, orange, and green to smoky cream and blue. Although the materials making up such wall compositions are extremely diverse in texture, color, style, and provenance, and most were originally constructed to fit totally different settings, the overall impression is one of majestic, balanced harmony. No one feature dominates. Instead, all contribute to a deeply sensuous, liberating beauty—the enchanting assemblage art of Venice. Nor is this special Venetian artistry at combining disparate elements restricted to individual monuments. It is the Piazza San Marco ensemble as a whole, conceived of as a single complex artifact composed of multiple buildings in several different basic styles erected over a span of centuries, that is the supreme example of Venetian genius.[4]

Before the death in 1570 of Jacopo Sansovino (the last great Venetian architect in this ensemble tradition), with a few notable exceptions, when Venetians added a structure to the Piazza's existing fabric, they were intensely conscious of the delicacy of their task. They understood that their actions were being measured against a very exacting standard—whether the new combination they were creating was truly an improvement to the already superbly achieved context in which the latest addition would take its place. They were masters of the long view extolled by the eighteenth-century aesthetic and political philosopher Edmund Burke. Using an architectural metaphor that makes his remarks so apposite to the development of the Piazza complex over seven centuries, Burke exalted a process in which

> the useful parts of an old establishment are kept, and what is superadded is to be fitted to what is retained....One advantage is as little as possible sacrificed to another. We compensate, we reconcile, we balance. We are enabled to unite into a consistent whole...various anomalies and contending principles....From thence arises, not an excellence in simplicity, but one far superior, an excellence in composition.[5]

While Renaissance theorists preached that the only form of architectural excellence worth pursuing was a rigorous simplicity based on certain unassailable principles of hierarchy and mathematical order, the majority of Venetians remained unpersuaded. Their preferred model emphasized the value of contending principles. The aesthetic response they continued to call for was one of compensation, reconciliation, and balance, with the goal of creating an excellence in composition—a deliberate interplay of constituent parts requiring the subordination of each individual component to the strength and impression of the whole. These were the governing ideals of Venetian political and artistic practice during the long era of her ascendancy and dominance. Masterworks of the past were perceived as existing equally and simultaneously in time with new works, a viewpoint later made famous in the early twentieth century by T. S. Eliot. Rather than a deliberate devaluation of traditional monuments, as Renaissance theory often demanded, the Venetian conception of architectural achievement called for synthesizing each newly made object with the city's preexisting context.

A Longstanding Bias

All too often, the difference between the Venetian ideal of an excellence in composition and the governing Renaissance concept of an excellence in simplicity has been reduced to a tired, misleading formula. Far too many art historians have been comfortable repeating the cliche that Venetian art and architecture have suffered from being controlled by members of a patrician elite who were artistic and political reactionaries. As we have seen, this simply does not square with the actions of the Venetian patriciate in creating the medieval Piazza San Marco, a public space whose size, antique grandeur, and classically derived syntax would remain unequaled in Europe for at least 250 years. The Piazza's proto-Renaissance features caused it to serve as a standard, if not a direct model, for High Renaissance works such as Michelangelo's Piazza del Campidoglio on the crest of the Capitoline Hill in Rome, undertaken sometime in the late 1530s or 1540s. There is also good reason to believe that in creating some of his early Renaissance masterworks, Brunelleschi drew on important features from the Piazza San Marco complex. Brunelleschi's reputation as the creator of a new architectural style (allegedly based on rediscovered classical models) derives in large part from his introduction of a design vocabulary based on rounded arches, piers and columns of fixed proportions, and a stripped-down building order of standardized dimensions. What is important to note is that it was just such features, particularly the repetitive use of semicircular arches and a standardized order (base, column, capital, and entablature) in projects such as the Innocenti Hospital and the churches of San Lorenzo and San Spirito, that were the distinguishing characteristics of the medieval Piazza San Marco. The Piazza's regularity, symmetry, and uniformity of detail across an entire building site, an ancient Roman and Greek concept borrowed by Venice from the imperial Augusteum square in Constantinople, supplied an extremely valuable prototype to Brunelleschi and Michelangelo. In light of the Venetian square's almost inescapable influence on such Renaissance masters, describing the men who commissioned and directed its construction as architectural reactionaries would appear to be highly questionable.[6]

It seems much closer to the mark to view the medieval architecture of the Piazza San Marco as a proto-Renaissance time capsule in which authentic antique elements, embodiments of an intact Eastern classical tradition, were held in suspension in Venice until their rediscovery by the rest of Italy during the Renaissance of the fifteenth and sixteenth centuries. Consider, for example, the Renaissance revival of interest in the placement of domes over squares, a building feature central to the design of several of Brunelleschi's most important works: the Pazzi Chapel (*Fig. 64*) and the Old Sacristy in the church of San Lorenzo, as well as to Bramante's plan for the new Basilica of Saint Peter's. If they had turned to classical Rome for models, Renaissance architects would have found few, if any, usable precedents for the dome architecture they wished to build. When they constructed domes, ancient Roman architects preferred to place them over circles, as at the Pantheon (*Fig. 9*). On the other hand, a dome resting on four pendentives (concave triangular spandrels), which permitted an overhead cupola to merge seamlessly with a square ground-floor space, was a prominent feature of Byzantine architecture. After its repeated use in the sixth-century churches of the Byzantine emperor Justinian (*Fig. 10*), the dome-on-pendentives form was imported to the Venetian lagoon, where it pervaded the design of the Basilica San Marco (*Figs. 12, 15, 19*) and from there became available to Brunelleschi, Bramante, and the Italian Renaissance in general. The architectural historian Richard Krautheimer identifies this as a case of Venetian architecture continuing to observe Late Antique building principles as part of a natural, continuous process. But in the West beyond Venice, where reliance on classical prototypes died out relatively early, such models had to be consciously revived in a sudden burst of rediscovery during the fifteenth century.[7]

Notwithstanding such facts, the effort to portray Venice as a creative backwater, particularly in architecture, has a lengthy history. In large measure, it is part of the long-standing effort to project Florence as the natural birthplace of the greatest achievements in Italian art. Beginning in the late fourteenth century, Florentines launched a powerful propaganda campaign designed to convince the world that their city was the center of Italian cultural life and that all new "forms tend to originate in and emanate from Florence."[8] Then, in the middle of the sixteenth century, Giorgio Vasari, the father of art history, placed this myth at the center of his highly influential work *Lives of the Artists*. Vasari devoted ten times as much space to Florentine painters, sculptors, and architects as he did to those with any connection to Venice. He also explicitly declared that it was because "Florence is the seat of art as Athens was of science," that the "Almighty Creator," observing this superiority of artists born in Tuscany, and particularly in Florence, "decreed that Michelangelo, the greatest artist of all time, should be born there." As an astute public relations agent, Vasari understood that to exalt the reputation of Florence, it was necessary to diminish the fame of her fiercest competitor, which he was fully prepared to do. Thus, Vasari tells his readers that when Michelangelo visited Venice as a young man in 1494, the Venetians were so blind to his creative genius that he could not find work there. For good measure, he adds that when the great Florentine artist returned to Venice in 1529, he came away with "a poor opinion [of the Venetians'] judgment in artistic matters." Of course, given the fact that Michelangelo almost certainly drew inspiration for his greatest architectural work, the Piazza del Campidoglio in Rome, from his exposure to the Piazza San Marco in Venice, Vasari's tale seems highly suspect. In the same vein, Vasari wrote that if Titian, whom he regarded as the greatest artist who ever worked in Venice, had only possessed the wisdom to move to Florence or even Rome, where he could have immersed himself in "the antique," he could "have equaled Michelangelo" and Raphael "in design—the great foundation of all art." According to Vasari, when Titian did make short visits to these centers of artistic innovation, he was "amazed at the sight of the fine works" he found there. Amazingly, Vasari (generally regarded as a second-rate painter at best) was so consumed by anti-Venetian bias that it caused him to condescend to Titian. He informs his readers that Titian, inspired by his visit to Florence, offered to do a portrait of the reigning Medici duke, Cosimo I, but the prince, surrounded, as he was, by an abundance of native talent (that is, by Vasari and his studio of obsequious propagandists), simply ignored Titian's offer, "not giving himself much trouble in the matter."[9] Vasari offers this story without the least apology, seemingly oblivious to its devastating picture of Cosimo's tasteless provincialism. He does this despite the fact that he has previously informed the reader that Titian completed several portraits of much more powerful sovereigns with far superior artistic judgment, including the German emperor Charles V (who refused to be painted by anyone other than Titian) and King Philip of Spain (who offered Titian a lifetime position at court).[10]

This same basic thesis, much more coherently expressed, also lies at the heart of Jacob Burckhardt's influential classic *The Civilization of the Renaissance in Italy*, published in 1860. Burckhardt emphasizes the dichotomy between "Florence, the city of incessant movement," whose "wondrous…spirit, at once keenly critical and artistically creative," promoted "the most varied forms of human development" and "Venice, the city of apparent stagnation" and "intellectual backwardness." To him, "no contrast can be stronger than that which is offered by these two" states. In Florence, "the growth of the new individualism" and the rediscovery of classical antiquity combined to support a resurgence of artistic creativity and innovation. While in Venice, "even the art of the Renaissance was imported into the city from without, and it was not before the end of the fifteenth century that she learned to move in this field with independent freedom and strength."[11]

Having attained classic expression in Burckhardt, it is not surprising that this same anti-Venetian prejudice is frequently encountered in the work of modern Renaissance scholars, particularly in connection with architecture. These specialists often seem to address Venetian building projects of the fifteenth and sixteenth centuries almost solely as occasions for making unfavorable comparisons with concurrent achievements in Florence and Rome. Several representative examples of this tendency can be found in Frederick Hartt's otherwise excellent *History of Italian Renaissance Art*. Hartt's point of departure is the announcement of a new birth of creative genius in fifteenth-century Florence:

> In the early Quattrocento in Florence, we can trace the development of a new art dedicated to human potential and human standards and informed by forms and ideas drawn from the civilization of Greek and Roman antiquity in which these human standards had been raised to a high level of expression.[12]

He then shifts the setting to sixteenth-century Rome where the pace of creative activity only accelerates:

> The Roman period of the High Renaissance is distinct from its Florentine prede-cessor—grander in scope, freer in its dynamism—and it developed with rapidity from phase to more majestic phase….Such was the grandeur of [Pope] Julius [II]'s undertakings that Italian art, even in Venice, could never again return to its for-mer, more modest self.[13]

And finally, there is poor, stagnant Venice:

> In its entire history, Venice produced few architects of importance. Venetian build-ers, [who were] for the most part imported from other regions, [either restricted themselves to] the Byzantine tradition [or employed other foreign styles such as] the Flamboyant Gothic style from France and Germany. [The] first timid appearance of the Renaissance in Venetian architecture [is] in structures built almost exclusively by Lombard masters.[14]

The similarity of the architectural ideas expressed by Vasari, Burckhardt, and Hartt, writing centuries apart, is striking; they all seem to be based on the same unexamined as-sumptions. These are that Renaissance buildings are superior to anything produced during earlier communal periods; that this superiority is based, in major part, on the Renais-sance recovery of original classical knowledge achieved through the direct study of an-cient Roman buildings; and that by her reactionary allegiance to pre-Renaissance monu-ments, Venice deliberately stunted her architectural development. Only biases such as these would seem to explain certain otherwise puzzling passages in these writers' works—for instance, Hartt's description of Brunelleschi's Innocenti Hospital project in Florence (*Fig. 65*). Hartt tells how the façade of Brunelleschi's fifteenth-century hospital, together with two "matching loggias" by later architects, finished in 1525 and 1601 opposite and adja-cent to Brunelleschi's building, created the Piazza Santissima Annunziata. Hartt then calls this plaza "the first of the great unified squares of modern design" and suggests that "this harmonious series of arcades was probably planned [by Brunelleschi] from the first."[15]

XIV • THE SPECIAL GENIUS OF VENICE

Nowhere is there any mention of the creation of the Piazza San Marco as a larger, more unified classically derived square three centuries before the completion of the Florentine enclosure, or the effect of the Piazza's round arches and standardized classical detail on Brunelleschi's original design of the Innocenti. Hartt acknowledges none of this although if his thesis is correct and Brunelleschi did intend a unified square from the beginning, his conception must have been powerfully influenced by the Piazza San Marco, the only functioning Western forum that could have served as a working model for such a grand, symmetrical public space.[16]

Hartt also goes out of his way to convey the message that Venetian architecture is a largely imported phenomenon. After stating that "[i]n its entire history, Venice produced few architects of importance," he adds that it is a fact that "not one of [the Grand Canal's] Renaissance palaces was built by an architect born in Venice."[17] This emphasis on place of birth is very important to Hartt's argument. It allows him to create the false impression that Mauro Codussi should be seen as a Lombard architect and that Jacopo Sansovino was somehow a Florentine master, despite the fact that both men immigrated to Venice very early in their architectural development and spent all but a tiny fraction of their long careers designing buildings for the city's unique lagoon environment. In evaluating Sansovino's architectural achievements, how relevant is it that he was born in Florence, since he built virtually nothing there and relatively little in Rome before arriving in Venice in 1527? After forty-three years of working exclusively in Venice and repeatedly turning down lucrative offers to emigrate to Rome or any one of several major European courts, in what meaningful sense is Sansovino not a Venetian architect? But what truly reveals the biases shaping Hartt's work is his completely different treatment of Rome. At the same time that he attempts to characterize Codussi and Sansovino as non-Venetian, he refers without qualification to "[t]he Roman period of the High Renaissance."[18] At no point does he acknowledge the well-known fact that none of the great masters who brought the High Renaissance to Rome was born or trained there, that they all immigrated to the papal city later in life. For instance, Bramante, born near Urbino, was fifty-five when he finally arrived in Rome after a long career in Lombardy, principally Milan.[19]

Such misleading characterizations are no accident; they are an established feature of the literary tradition to which Hartt's book belongs. For instance, we read in Vasari that Giotto was born in Vespignano, fourteen miles outside Florence, where he was taken by the painter Cimabue when he was ten years old. Giotto, who only became a Florentine citizen at the end of his life, spent a large part of his long career executing commissions outside Florence. He worked for extended periods in the rest of Tuscany as well as in other parts of northern Italy and the Kingdom of Naples, and may even have visited the papal court at Avignon in southern France. His greatest creation, the frescoes he applied to the walls of the Arena Chapel in Padua, are located only a short distance from Venice. Yet Vasari's chapter title refers to him as "Giotto, Painter, Sculptor and Architect, of Florence." Contrast this with the author's treatment of Titian, who was born in Cadore at the foot of the Dolomites north of Venice. At the age of eight, Titian was sent to Venice, where he spent his youth studying with Giovanni Bellini and Giorgione, the greatest Venetian painters of their day. Although he occasionally visited other Italian cities and the German imperial court in Augsburg to carry out specific commissions, Titian spent his entire, astonishingly long artistic life as a citizen of Venice, overseeing a large staff of painting assistants in a busy studio next to his home on the city's northern shore. Vasari's chapter title refers to him as "Titian, Painter, of Cadore."[20]

The Quality of Mind of the Venetian Patriciate

It should go without saying that nothing I have written is intended to disparage the brilliant achievements of Renaissance architecture in Florence and Rome; my sole purpose is to encourage a fair and impartial evaluation of Venetian accomplishments. Specifically, I want to challenge the oft-repeated view that in architectural matters, the Venetian habit of mind was reactionary, that is, closed to the prospect of future change and improvement. Such a statement is simply not supported by the facts. On the other hand, it is quite true that Venetian patricians were deeply conservative in one critically important sense—they were not easily stampeded by claims of architectural fashion divorced from a profound regard for the Republic's historic building monuments. Nor is this surprising. As inhabitants of a city whose very foundations were located immediately above the course of a flowing tidal current, Venetians were always conscious that they lived in a fragile, precariously perched environment, and this made them acutely aware of context, of the necessary balance that every new thing, in order to be truly valuable, must establish with the preexisting order of things. Venetians would have readily agreed with Edmund Burke that it is impossible to judge "anything which relates to human actions and human concerns as it stands stripped of every relation, in all the nakedness and solitude of metaphysical abstraction."[21] Like Burke, they would have believed that it is considerably easier to display originality in architecture, as in any other field, after first clearing the site of all earlier structures. On the other hand,

> at once to preserve and reform is quite another thing. When the useful parts of an old establishment are kept, and what is superadded is to be fitted to what is retained, a vigorous mind, steady, persevering attention, various powers of comparison and combination, and the resources of an understanding fruitful in expedients is to be exercised...in a continued conflict with the combined force of opposite[s].[22]

Venetian architectural practice in the Piazza San Marco area was almost always guided by a deep commitment to this positive aesthetic. A priori architectural theorists with slight regard for a city's historic building fabric might find a receptive home in papal Rome or at the court of a Renaissance prince. But they were much less highly regarded in Venice, not because the patricians of the Republic were blindly conservative, but because they subscribed to a different theory of architectural value.

Venetians esteemed what they considered to be a more "delicate and complicated" architectural skill demanding "a vigorous mind, steady and persevering attention, various powers of comparison and combination, and the resources of an understanding fruitful in expedients." In their minds, this led to an "excellence in composition"[23] which was not only superior to the brilliant rationalism of a Bramante or a Palladio, it was the supreme architectural virtue, requiring a concentrated application of what Ruskin has described as "pure, precious, majestic, massy intellect."[24] In their view, the results could not have been more clear. An unbroken commitment to this alternative architectural conception over many centuries had created and preserved the Piazza San Marco ensemble as one of the most majestic and delightful man-made spaces in the world.

Nor were Venetians alone in their adherence to this more conservative architectural perspective even during the Renaissance. According to the distinguished Harvard architectural historian James Ackerman, in virtually every one of Michelangelo's major architectural projects, he was forced to deal with some unalterable given embedded in the site, and these inherent restrictions acted as a spur to his highest creative powers. For instance, Ackerman cites the presence of preexisting building structures that could not be removed as important factors in the architect's brilliantly original designs for the Laurentian Library in Florence and the Piazza del Campidoglio on the Capitoline Hill in Rome. He even speculates that Michelangelo may have looked for such immovables in his architectural commissions, just as he allowed a process of musing on a seemingly unyielding block of marble to trigger his sculptural imagination.[25] The early Renaissance master Alberti also subscribed to a version of the Venetian excellence-in-composition theory. In his *Ten Books on Architecture*, written in the middle of the fifteenth century, he recommended a judicious blending of old and new whenever a Renaissance architect was asked to complete an earlier, pre-Renaissance structure. He warned that an egotistical architect or patron

> who, because of ambition feels the overwhelming desire to add new parts to what is already there [may] ruin buildings that others began well. I believe it is necessary to be faithful to the intentions of the [original] author, which surely was the result of long deliberation and intent reflection, which we, with attentive and prolonged study and more precise judgment, may be able to discover.[26]

Accordingly, Alberti advised a skillful restoration rather than a wholesale rebuilding of Constantine's old Saint Peter's, and he consistently followed such strictures in his own architectural practice. For instance, in his design of a new façade for the church of Santa Maria Novella in Florence, he was so successful in merging his additions with the existing Gothic building fabric that until recently, scholars were unable to identify with certainty whether some portions were from Alberti's hand or whether he inherited them.

The Tangible Presence of the Past

It has often been asserted that the rediscovery of lost classical prototypes lies at the heart of the sudden efflorescence of architectural genius in Renaissance Florence and Rome. The corollary is that since fifteenth- and sixteenth-century Venice did not participate as actively as other Italian cities in this accelerated recovery of antique Roman building methods and models, her architectural development was severely handicapped. Vasari's unsophisticated conception of this phenomenon, summarized in his chapter on Brunelleschi, has remained influential. He writes that because Brunelleschi's goal was "to restore classic architecture," he repeatedly measured ancient Roman buildings and took care "to follow the classical rules and orders and the correct architectural proportions." In Vasari's mind, the explanation for Brunelleschi's great accomplishments was that through diligent study, "he became capable of reconstructing the city entirely, and, in his imagination, beheld Rome as she was before her ruin."[27] This belief that the Renaissance revival depended on a freshly revealed repertoire of classical building models just waiting to be unearthed and copied is also implicit in the works of Burckhardt and Hartt.

In its unqualified form, this view now seems outdated. To begin with, it ignores the wretched physical state of most of the Roman monuments whose secrets Brunelleschi and other Renaissance artists were supposed to be actively uncovering and deciphering. A millennium of fire and disintegration as well as being cannibalized for the construction of new buildings had reduced most of classical Rome to bare mounds of decomposing brick. I am much more impressed by Erwin Panofsky's astute perception that what truly characterized the minds of Renaissance architects and intellectuals was a continuing realization of the profound gulf that separated them from the ancient world. Finding relatively few intact monuments amid a mass of crumbling, truncated structures, many Renaissance figures were unavoidably aware that they looked upon classical Rome from a forbidding distance.[28] Alberti, one of the most brilliant voices of the early Renaissance, could not have been clearer on this point. As a practicing fifteenth-century Italian architect, he complained that

> it was less difficult for the Ancients—because they had models to imitate and from which they could learn—to come to a knowledge of supreme arts which today are most difficult for us. Our fame ought to be much greater, then, if we discover unheard-of and never-before-seen arts and sciences without teachers and without any models whatsoever.[29]

What Alberti's candor underscores is that, at its heart, the Renaissance recovery of antiquity was essentially a literary phenomenon whose roots go back to Petrarch's scholarly labors in the thirteenth century. Ancient Roman texts were of far more importance in forming Renaissance ideas about Roman architecture than the handful of buildings preserved from classical times. Unfortunately, as Alberti's statement clearly implies, in designing the types of buildings they were actually hired to construct, Renaissance builders found no more practical help in Latin literature than they did from examining Roman ruins. The public buildings typically described in the texts of ancient Roman writers—baths, sports arenas, aqueducts, and pagan temples—were almost completely irrelevant to the desires of Renaissance patrons. And the same was true of many intact classical buildings; they simply were not useful guides for the projects Renaissance architects were called upon to build.[30] Take the challenge that Brunelleschi faced in designing a dome for the Florentine Cathedral (*Fig. 61*). The huge horizontal span of 143.5 feet that the dome had to cover and the enormous cost and delay that would result from the use of wooden scaffolding to support the cupola during construction were the fundamental dilemmas to which Brunelleschi had to find solutions. According to Vasari, Bruenelleschi solved these problems and won the project competition of 1418 by drawing on his extensive knowledge of the dome of the Pantheon, which "he was forever pondering"[31] during his sojourns in Rome.

We now know that Vasari's description of Brunelleschi's architectural sources is almost entirely erroneous. No doubt, the dome of the Pantheon, which spans a diameter of 142 feet (a foot and a half less than the project specifications for the Florentine vault), did serve as a kind of general inspiration for Brunelleschi simply by demonstrating that a dome of such dimensions could be built at all. But neither the Pantheon nor any other Roman building he might have studied could have provided Brunelleschi with the techniques he needed to design and build the Florentine cupola. The main problem faced by the architect of the Pantheon dome was lateral stress, and to overcome it, he used poured concrete and wooden molds to erect massive wall abutments twenty-three feet thick at the base (*Fig. 63*). In contrast, Brunelleschi's dome could not use concrete as a building material and, as a consequence, is only seven feet thick at its base. Instead of concrete, which was far too heavy to be supported by the already completed Cathedral walls and drum that Brunelleschi inherited in 1418, he chose to construct the Florentine dome out of brick. His basic task boiled down to discovering a technique that would permit the construction of the world's largest masonry dome without resorting to the prohibitively expensive use of wooden scaffolding to hold the bricks in place until the mortar used as a permanent adhesive had fully cured. Having no useful Roman models to draw on, Brunelleschi did what Venetian architects had often done—he sought out and adapted methods commonly employed by Islamic and Byzantine builders. Instead of constructing huge concrete walls to support a rounded, shallow dome, as the Romans had, Brunelleschi used an octagonal, double-shelled, pointed dome design, a plan very likely based on a famous fourteenth-century mausoleum in Soltaniyeh, Persia. And to compensate for the thinness of the cupola walls and the absence of a wooden armature to keep the partially built dome from collapsing before the mortar had dried, he developed a system of interlocking herringbone brickwork derived from Persian and Byzantine building models.[32]

As Alberti's declaration and the example of Brunelleschi's dome clearly illustrate, rather than basking in the comfort of a rediscovered antiquity that supplied ready-made answers to their practical dilemmas, Renaissance architects and humanists faced the undeniable fact of a deeply broken connection with the classical past. Consequently, they often experienced feelings of anxiety and sharp discontinuity when they compared their own era, the "deplorable"[33] present, as Petrarch called it, to the time of the ancient Romans. For many, the realization that the antique world was truly a lost civilization called forth a passionate desire to somehow bridge this impassable gulf, to find a way to emerge from the darkness of contemporary life into the light of classical grace. The emotional force behind this longing for redemptive transformation was genuinely religious in its intensity, and it is no accident that in describing the period and its struggle to revive classical culture, the French word *renaissance*, meaning rebirth, was borrowed from the vocabulary of the Christian New Testament. In architecture, such otherworldly aspirations eventually gave rise to a reactionary belief that the worthiest new buildings were those which most precisely mirrored the form, proportions, and detail of the few unspoiled classical structures available to Renaissance architects. Second-rate talents such as Scamozzi and Vasari confidently declared that architecture should be regarded as an abstract science in which the highest achievements resulted from the inflexible duplication of classical archetypes. As men who had made a systematic study of antique models and who believed that by so doing, they had gained an unvarying formula for architectural excellence, such antiquarian theorists did not scruple to condescend to past masters such as Giotto and Sansovino. Naturally, they were hostile to almost every aspect of the medieval building environments with which they were surrounded.[34]

In contrast, Venetians always felt much more comfortable with their own cultural inheritance. Indeed, it would be strange if they did not, since that historical legacy was immediately available to them on a daily, tangible basis. Not, as in Rome, in mounds of decaying brick whose original splendor they could barely begin to imagine, but in the well-preserved form of their most magnificent public square and its monuments, an ensemble of mesmerizing beauty that incorporated every successive facet of Venetian communal life from the ninth century to the present. Chief among these was the Basilica San Marco, a temple believed to contain the very body of the Apostle who had been the city's spiritual guide and symbol of collective identity for eight centuries, built of stones that had once helped form the capital of the Eastern Roman Empire. It was this heritage of Late Antique and Byzantine culture, derived from only slightly older antique Roman models, to which Venetians saw themselves as legitimate heirs. With such visible proof of their unbroken connection to this ancient tradition constantly before their eyes, it was difficult for Venetians to look at Roman ruins with the same keen sense of longing felt by humanist intellectuals in Florence and Rome. In what sense was it even possible for Venice to experience a renaissance, that is, a conversion or overpowering rebirth of enthusiasm for antique architecture, when such classically derived forms had never ceased to have a central place in the city's most revered public buildings? The attitude toward antiquity of a typical Venetian aristocrat was much closer to the view adopted by the greatest architects of the Renaissance, men such as Brunelleschi, Alberti, Michelangelo, and Sansovino. Far from viewing the classical past as the incarnation of revealed perfection to be approached with academic solemnity and acts of ritual piety, these masters embraced the general adoption of antique forms as a means for expressing their own architectural ideas. As in the long-standing Venetian assemblage art tradition, part of the special genius of an Alberti, a Michelangelo, or a Sansovino lay in his special gift for integrating the architect's new vision, expressed in carefully selected and enhanced classical motifs, with a preexisting architectural context.[35]

CHAPTER FIFTEEN

An Apparent Enigma

As we have seen, collective direction of Venetian public architecture was exercised by an interlocking network of councils and commissions whose members were elected from the Republic's large merchant aristocracy. Most of these patrician officeholders served relatively short terms of no more than six months to a year. And members of the one architectural body composed of lifetime appointees, the procurators de supra, were almost always chosen for this position late in life after long careers in commerce and public life, with an eye to selecting men who might be suitable candidates for later election as doge. As such, they were chosen for their political and business skills rather than any particular aesthetic expertise, although, as men of wealth, some were no doubt experienced art patrons as well. This Venetian system, so different from artistic patronage in the rest of Renaissance Italy, presents a clear challenge to our modern ideas about artistic creation, about what conditions are most likely to produce the highest level of artistic performance. The essential question comes down to this: how can the Piazza San Marco ensemble, one of the noblest and most delightful architectural creations in the history of art, be the result of an unending round of committee meetings? Could anything be more at odds with the Renaissance paradigm of sovereign artistic creation by uniquely gifted individuals? How could what is arguably the largest and most splendid square in Italy have been created by subjecting architectural genius to collective control by non-artists?

Let us begin by recalling that the beauty and wonder of the Piazza complex are products of the special assemblage art tradition of Venice, a process whose distinguishing characteristic has always been its synthesis of major styles—the deliberate creation of an artistic whole transcending the value of any single component. We are then in a position to ask ourselves what we know about the nature of individual artistic talent and its general reaction to such a tradition. I believe that most of our experience teaches us that, in general, men and women who possess unusual artistic gifts do not naturally gravitate toward that "excellence in composition"[1] which was the hallmark of communal art creation in Venice. Someone whose special talent is creating brilliant, beautiful objects is usually not overly concerned with balancing and reconciling his new creation with the preexisting order of built things. Artists generally feel that their particular mission is to produce the most strikingly original new works of which they are capable, and, possessed by this single-minded focus, they typically leave it to others to worry about preserving and protecting the existing context in which their art must find its proper place. As Plato explained in *The Republic*, each art has no other interest than "its own greatest possible perfection."[2] This basic psychological truth has been brilliantly explicated by the political philosopher Hannah Arendt, who points out that while the ancient Greeks and Romans revered beauty, they also harbored a deep distrust of the artists who fabricated the beautiful objects they so admired. Indeed, the classical Greek word for a philistine, that is, a man of an exclusively utilitarian turn of mind who cannot judge a thing apart from its specific function, was derived from the term for artists and artisans. Philistinism was a defect most likely to be found in artists because a fabricator of the beautiful cannot help looking at everything he touches as a means to his particular end. This gives rise to the irony that the greatest threat to the continued existence of any finished work of art is the very type of fabricator mentality that brought it into being in the first place. Alberti was acutely aware of this danger when he warned against projects whose chief inspiration was the thirst for individual glory, where personal ambition wedded to power and wealth could easily spell ruin for architectural monuments of the past.[3]

This classical view of the risks inherent in commissioning fresh works of art was, of course, studiously ignored by Renaissance propagandists for the new status of artists. While such authors typically treated classical texts as revealed truth, this particular piece of antique wisdom was deliberately ignored because it undermined a basic Renaissance goal: convincing rich patrons to hire certain contemporary artists for their reputed ability to produce one-of-a-kind creations. Wealthy purchasers needed to be persuaded that an elite group of painters, architects, and sculptors possessed such invaluable specialized knowledge that only their productions could be considered true works of art. Obviously then, it was totally against self-interest to hint that there might be a danger in ceding too much control to an individual fabricator. On the contrary, it was necessary to convince patrons that they should abandon active supervision of their commissions altogether and become mere consumers of art objects whose value they would be taught to appreciate by the producers themselves. Fabricators who could do this stood to dramatically increase their social and financial status.[4]

As we have seen, such ideas were diametrically opposed to the Venetian tradition, which called for active participation by Venetian aristocrats in the creation of communal art. Because the patriciate valued the historical results of such power sharing, it resisted yielding increased control to the artist fabricators it commissioned. As a result, the city was shielded for a time from the deliberate manipulations of taste and fashion which were a significant aspect of Renaissance art production in other Italian states. As we have seen, after a devastating fire in 1577 destroyed large parts of the Ducal Palace, an overwhelming majority of the Senate voted to restore the building to its pure pre-conflagration state rather than commission a more "modern" classical design from the hands of a Renaissance master, Andrea Palladio. To these patrician governors, the Palace's fourteenth-century façade had come to represent the history and longevity of the Republic herself, and they saw themselves as caretakers of this world of cherished objects and communal institutions which appeared to have no value in a Renaissance consumer culture. For instance, they had watched popes and cardinals with reputations as great champions of classical architecture tear down ancient Roman buildings and use the rubble to construct lavish new churches and palaces for their own glorification and comfort. And these Renaissance patrons had been aided by some of the greatest artists of the age, who proved only too ready to plunder antique monuments to feed their masters' uncurbed building appetites.[5]

Unbridled Egotism

Nothing better illustrates this destructive process than Pope Julius II's famous initiative to build a new Renaissance church of Saint Peter's on the Vatican Hill in Rome. Although this massive architectural endeavor, the largest and most expensive of the entire Renaissance period, has been alluded to in earlier chapters, to understand Venetian fears about what could result from the narcissistic patronage of a man like Julius, we now need to describe this undertaking in greater detail. As we have seen, Julius was an unstable egomaniac with a ferocious temper. He carried a heavy cudgel, which he used on the backs and limbs of those who did not immediately carry out his irascible demands. When he turned this savage hostility on Venice, he handed her the worst military defeat in her long history. Then, a half year later, he performed a complete about-face, cast himself as the city's savior, and launched a campaign to free Italy from the foreign invaders he had invited into the peninsula to crush the Republic. Julius was equally mercurial as an architectural patron. When he initially summoned the thirty-one-year-old Michelangelo to Rome in 1505, he had no intention of building a new Saint Peter's to replace the emperor Constantine's original fourth-century basilica. Instead, the project he had in mind was a huge personal monument to be installed on the floor of the old church directly opposite the tomb of the first Apostle. This memorial was originally envisioned as a freestanding, three-story monolith to be covered with forty larger-than-life marble statues, including, at its apex, a ten-foot effigy of Julius being carried into Paradise wearing the papal tiara. However, having commissioned the most ambitious sculptural project of his age, the pope's megalomania then caused him to believe that Constantine's ancient basilica was insufficiently grand to accommodate such an imposing addition. Thus, in 1506 he decided to demolish the old church and construct a much larger building in the latest Renaissance style. Soon after this, Julius' enthusiasm for his mausoleum project evaporated entirely, and he decided that the huge replacement church he had just authorized would itself serve as his personal memorial. In the meantime, Michelangelo had transported ninety wagons of Carrara marble to the square in front of old Saint Peter's and was just beginning to carve the first of forty proposed statues when he was informed that his commission had been canceled. Julius, faced with the cost of constructing a mammoth new church, refused to reimburse Michelangelo for his heavy outlays in buying the marble blocks and carting them to Rome.[6]

Having transferred his restless narcissism from the original tomb project to a new church building, Julius determined that his replacement Saint Peter's would display a true Caesarian grandeur. He commissioned a design from Donato Bramante, a sixty-two-year-old architectural genius whose volatility and monumental self-regard almost matched that of his papal patron. Bramante's scheme called for erecting a huge hemispherical dome above a spacious Greek-cross floor plan, an undertaking he described as placing the Pantheon on top of the Basilica of Maxentius in the Roman Forum. To prepare the site for their new colossus, the pope and his architect began to pull Constantine's old church to the ground. When this elicited a protest from Michelangelo, Bramante replied that there was nothing in the world he would not tear down if he could build something he considered more beautiful in its place. This shameless egotism (as pure an expression of the fabricator mentality as was ever uttered) underscored the mutual character flaw that prevented Bramante and Julius from being able to see the inherent problem with their ambitious building program. A project of such immense size would necessarily require the length of many papacies to complete, and during the brief tenure each pope could expect to enjoy, he and his chosen architect would undoubtedly be just as determined as their predecessors to impose their own personal vision on the undertaking. Hence, the odds of sustaining any original building design were quite small, and indeed, this is precisely what happened with Julius' project. Julius died seven years after its commencement, and Bramante followed him a year later, leaving the building effort in such a confused state that succeeding generations, even if they had wished to be faithful to the original plan, would have found it almost impossible to discern precisely what was intended. From Bramante to Bernini (1506–1667), the project consumed 161 years and was subjected to the vagaries of twenty-two successive popes and thirteen different architects. As a result, Bramante's original design is only dimly recognizable in the completed church.[7]

But there was ample opportunity for the final result to be much worse than it is. For instance, only the death of Antonio da Sangallo the Younger in 1546 allowed Michelangelo to succeed him as papal architect just in time to avert complete disaster. Sangallo was preparing to almost double the size of the already enormous project by encasing Bramante's Greek-cross plan in a bulging ambulatory to which he then planned to add an obese dome and a pair of ten-story flanking towers (*Fig. 108*). If Sangallo had lived another eighteen years, he and Michelangelo would both have died in 1564, and the century's greatest architect would never have been given an opportunity to replace Sangallo's bloated vision with his own simplified, muscular design, one compatible with Bramante's original Greek-cross conception. However, even this brilliant reprieve did not survive unaltered. A half century later, an arrogant new pope, Paul V, ordered his architect, Carlo Maderno, to finish the building by ignoring Michelangelo's centralized plan. Maderno obliged by constructing the final eastern arm as an elongated nave and connecting it to an outsized, top-heavy entrance façade that obstructs the view of Michelangelo's magnificent dome (*Fig. 109*). To improve the proportions of Maderno's ungainly building front, in 1638 the Baroque genius Gianlorenzo Bernini (1598–1680) attempted to construct a huge bell tower at each end of

*Fig. 108: Antonio da Sangallo the Younger's
proposed redesign of Saint Peter's in Rome*

the facade only to watch the first of these gigantic shafts buckle and crack due to the weakness of Maderno's foundations. As a result, the effort to erect the towers was abandoned.[8]

Papal Vandalism

But the architectural confusion that the fabricator mentality could bring to a vast, multigenerational undertaking like the new Renaissance Saint Peter's was only part of the story. With their deep conservationist ethic, Venetians would have been equally concerned over

*Fig. 109: Entrance façade of Saint Peter's in Rome
designed by Carlo Maderno*

what had to be destroyed to make way for such a project. If there had never been a Renaissance replacement project, what would a sixteenth-century traveler have seen during a visit to the original basilica constructed by Constantine the Great?

Fortunately, we know the answer to this question with some specificity (*Fig. 110*). After making his way through the welter of narrow streets making up the surrounding Borgo neighborhood, a visitor would have emerged into a modest plaza that abutted a broad stone platform preceded by five flights of stairs. At the summit of this imposing marble stage, there was a façade of handsome two- and three-story medieval buildings of varying

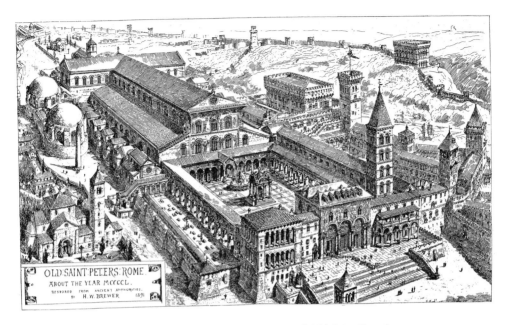

*Fig. 110: Reconstruction drawing of Old Saint Peter's
by H. W. Brewer*

designs, most with graceful loggias and porticoes and one with a tall, elegant campanile. In the middle of this heterogeneous facade were three arched portals leading into a magnificent classical atrium surrounded by colonnades. The courtyard contained two running fountains, the larger of which displayed a gilded tabernacle above a giant bronze pine cone and was adorned with peacocks and four water-spouting bronze dolphins. One of Giotto's finest mosaics, known as the Navicella (showing Christ with Saint Peter and the other disciples on the Sea of Galilee), was installed above the atrium entrance. At the far end of the courtyard was the church itself, its outer wall covered with splendid mosaics of Christ enthroned between Saints Peter and Paul. Upon entering the basilica, the visitor would have found himself standing in a vast rectangular space lined with four rows of gigantic antique columns that rested on aisle floors built five steps above the nave. The columns supported an enormous classical entablature, and above this were wall portraits of every pope since Peter and scenes from the Old and New Testaments, portions of which had been frescoed by Giotto. The nave floor was a mixture of gleaming colored marbles and recumbent papal tombstones. The interior glittered with light from thousands of wax candles.[9]

Looking toward the far end of the nave, our visitor would have seen a large triumphal arch framing the original shrine built over Saint Peter's tomb. Inscribed in mosaic at the top of the arch was Constantine's personal homage to the Christian God he believed had made him sole ruler of the Roman world; it read: "Because under your leadership, the triumphant universe has reached to the farthest stars, victorious Constantine dedicates this church to you."[10] This message marked one of the most consequential transformations in world history, the point at which the Emperor of the Roman Empire ceased being Christianity's most implacable enemy and became its unwavering supporter. Four and a half centuries later, Constantine's church was the scene of another epochal change in the relationship between Christianity and the secular world. On Christmas Day in 800, Charlemagne, the leader of the Frankish Empire, who had just conquered much of Western Europe, knelt in front of Peter's burial shrine. As a reward for faithfully defending the papacy against barbarian raiders and rebellious Roman subjects, the pope crowned Charlemagne as Constantine's heir and successor, appointing him Caesar Augustus, Holy Roman Emperor of the West. Charlemagne and the pope then vowed to treat each other as sovereign powers within their respective realms, and for the next seven centuries, the same ritual was celebrated on the same spot by almost every Western emperor. Before its obliteration by Julius, old Saint Peter's was unquestionably the most extraordinary "book of history"[11] the Western world has ever known, to use Ruskin's superb phrase.[12]

Yet, as appalling as it was, it is important to understand that this act of deliberate papal vandalism was hardly an unprecedented event. It was only a particularly egregious example of a larger destructive process, one that over time eradicated all but a few remnants of the vast architectural heritage bequeathed to succeeding ages by ancient and Early Christian Rome. Constantine's basilica was destroyed by the same relentless forces that stripped Emperor Septimus Severus' massive Palatine Hill residence, a building 490 feet long, 390 feet wide, and 160 feet high, of every piece of marble that once covered its floors and walls, leaving "only a few pieces of crumbling [brick]…here and there against the cliff." Septimus' palace succumbed to the same powers that caused 250,000 running feet of marble to disappear from the giant athletic stadium known as the Circus Maximus located just below the Palatine cliff, leaving nothing but a grassy depression where huge stone bleachers had once seated 150,000 spectators. As Rodolfo Lanciani, a leading authority on the subject, has asked, "Who broke up and removed, bit by bit, that mountain of masonry? Who overthrew the giant? Was it age, the elements, the hand of barbarians, or some other irresistible force the action of which has escaped observation?" The answer is not what we have been taught to expect. The barbarians and other foreign armies that invaded and sacked Rome through the centuries bear very little responsibility for such wholesale architectural destruction.[13] Absent rare circumstances, conquering warriors, hot for blood, rape, and portable loot, are not inclined to undertake the immense physical effort (often spanning weeks or months) necessary to reduce a huge stone building to its constituent elements and then haul the rubble away to a distant site. Who, then, would have had the time and incentive to perform such arduous labors?

It was anyone (mostly wealthy builders and their architects) who wished to construct a stone structure in Rome after the middle of the fourth century. Before that time, the Roman imperial government operated a Department of Marbles which ran mass-production quarries throughout the Mediterranean world. Capable of supplying the demand for stone building material throughout the Roman Empire, these slave-operated assembly lines turned out a huge quantity and variety of standardized items, from architectural components to classical sculpture. But when the Western Empire began to falter, the great quarries were closed, and emperors and lords who wished to finish their new projects in stone were forced to begin living off the accumulated supply contained in existing Roman buildings and monuments. Architectural scavenging continued through the medieval period but accelerated sharply during the Renaissance when the idea of building on a scale to rival or surpass the ancients began to seize the imagination of popes and other Italian princes.[14] Assessing the condition of Roman monuments at the end of the Middle Ages, before Renaissance architectural ambitions began to have their effect, Burckhardt states that

> far more was left than we now find, and probably many of the remains still had their marble incrustation, their pillared entrances, and their other ornaments, where we now [as a result of Renaissance plunder] see nothing but the skeleton of the brickwork.[15]

According to Lanciani, the general practice of Renaissance building patrons and their architects was first to "secure the possession of a *petraia*, that is, an ancient structure or part of a structure, from which they could obtain materials of construction, lime and ornamental marbles." From the fifteenth century on, "[t]here [was] no edifice in Rome... the erection of which did not simultaneously carry with it the destruction or mutilation of some ancient structure." Classical "temples, baths, theatres and palaces" were demolished and to the extent the stone rubble was not integrated into new buildings, "their marble ornaments were broken to pieces and thrown into the lime-kilns" to make the rich plaster used on the walls and ceilings of Renaissance palaces.[16] Raphael, who witnessed this process firsthand, summed it up by stating that "[t]he new Rome which we now see standing in all its beauty and grandeur...is built throughout with the lime obtained from ancient marbles."[17] Buildings selected for demolition or reduction included Rome's greatest classical monuments, and Renaissance popes were among the chief plunderers. A great deal of this cannibalization was directed toward the rebuilding of Saint Peter's; almost half of the Colosseum vanished to become part of the new Renaissance church. In one year alone, Pope Nicholas V removed twenty-five hundred cartloads of marble from the Colosseum, and, not surprisingly, Julius II was known for his many pillaging expeditions. During a succession of later papacies, a huge amount of marble from the Roman Senate building, the Temple of Jupiter Best and Greatest atop the Capitoline Hill, the Basilica Julia, the Forum of Julius Caesar, the Temple of Venus and Rome, and the Baths of Diocletian was also recycled into the fabric of Saint Peter's. In their attempts to complete the massive project, Renaissance popes turned their architects and artisans into organized looting crews.[18]

What puzzles us, with our modern preservationist sensibility, is how Renaissance popes could have felt a genuine admiration for classical buildings (which there seems to be little cause to doubt) and, at the same time, have continued to obliterate the very monuments they esteemed so highly. While the notion of a divided mind is hardly new or strange to us, cognitive dissonance of this magnitude seems hard to explain. What prevented such an obvious conflict from continually emerging into consciousness? While it is probably impossible to fully answer such a question, Erwin Panofsky has at least provided us with an intriguing clue by observing that in their passionate investigation of the classical Roman past, Renaissance humanists often created a profound divide between themselves and the antique artifacts to which they devoted their studies. To such men, the world of the ancient Romans ceased to seem like an actual, tangible reality and became transformed into an abstract idea capable of being reconstructed only in their artistic and architectural imaginations. For Renaissance patrons and their architects, building anew on a colossal scale was their attempt to reproduce a more believable version of the revered Roman past. Their feelings of distance and alienation were so acute that to find relief, they were prepared to sacrifice most of the material Roman heritage which had actually survived into their own deplorable present. In contrast, the inhabitants of medieval Rome typically felt much more comfortable with classical buildings and were content to construct their own modest dwellings within the shelter of ancient monuments.[19]

The Florentine Example

The example of Julius II and other Renaissance popes left Venetian aristocrats convinced of the harm to historical treasures that could result from placing public architecture in the hands of a single egotistical prince. But it was the example of sixteenth-century Florence that made them fully appreciate another serious risk of such arrangements—that they might well produce decidedly inferior work. During its long communal period when Florentine public architecture was generally commissioned and directed by municipal building committees, the city erected the municipal Cathedral known as the Duomo (including Brunelleschi's magnificent dome), Giotto's bell tower, the inimitable Palazzo della Signoria, the majestic Loggia dei Lanzi , the spacious Franciscan church of Santa Croce, and a host of other brilliantly innovative buildings by Brunelleschi. The Florentine masters Donatello and Verrochio produced the finest freestanding bronze equestrian statues since classical times, and Michelangelo carved his great marble statue of David, seen by everyone as a powerful symbol of Florentine political liberty. In painting, it was the age of Giotto, Masaccio, Masolino, Fra Angelico, Fra Filippo Lippi, Paolo Uccello, Sandro Botticelli, Domenico Ghirlandaio, Leonardo da Vinci, and Raphael. Throughout much of this period, approximately twenty-five hundred to three thousand male citizens were eligible to hold public office (although the ruling elite was usually restricted to a few hundred influential families), and even during the period of the Medici oligarchy (1434–1494), great care was paid to preserving at least the external forms of communal government. When the Medici were overthrown in 1494, Florence adopted a truly republican constitution that concentrated political power in a council of more than three thousand members consciously modeled on the Venetian Great Council.[20]

Communal control of Florentine public architecture over such a prolonged period was not without its problems. There was considerable tension between the city's municipal building committees and some of the master artists and architects they employed, particularly in the early Renaissance period. In the first half of the fifteenth century, Brunelleschi frequently found himself at odds with the Opera del Duomo, the committee of the works in charge of the Florentine Cathedral. During the quarter century he worked to design and construct the Cathedral's monumental dome, Brunelleschi constantly struggled to control every detail of the massive project, an effort that the Opera often deliberately stymied. To demonstrate its power, the Opera made Brunelleschi share the title of capomaestro with three other architects, including two of his most bitter rivals. At one point, it cut his salary in half, and at every major stage of the undertaking, it forced him to engage in a fresh competition to retain his position as chief architectural adviser. It was only after his death in 1446 that the city fathers expressed public recognition of their great architect's "divine genius." In Brunelleschi's own mind, his Duomo experience was a running battle with a group of ignorant nonprofessionals whose protracted authority over the details of the project was misguided at best.[21]

A century later, all such friction was a relic of the communal past. In 1512, Pope Julius II, supported by a Spanish army, crushed the Florentine republic and placed a Medici puppet government in power. When Julius died, his successor, Pope Leo X, the son of Lorenzo de' Medici, occupied the city and turned the Great Council chamber into a military barracks. After a new republican government again took control of Florence in 1527, another Medici pope, Clement VII, used Spanish troops to starve the city into surrender (the siege killed one third of the population) and install a hereditary Medici dukedom. When the first duke, the twenty-year-old illegitimate son of a Medici servant girl in Rome, was stabbed to death by his psychotic kinsman, he was replaced by another Medici youth who, as Duke Cosimo I, would rule the city for the next twenty-seven years. After installing a large occupying army and a network of spies, Cosimo, whose temperament was cold, gloomy, and secretive, ran Florence as an undisguised police state. Assembling in public without government approval was a capital offense, and the duke's command was enough to have a man murdered or thrown into one of the regime's gruesome prisons. The largest building project undertaken during this period was a mammoth fortress and political prison, the Fortezza da Basso, built north of the city by the forced labor of three thousand workers. Apart from hunting and fishing, Cosimo's one great love was his family, particularly his wife, Eleanora di Toledo, the wealthy, temperamental daughter of the Spanish viceroy to Naples. When she died in 1562, twelve years before his own demise, the duke was inconsolable. In his final years, he often gave way to childish rage and uncontrollable sobbing.[22]

True to the pattern of earlier Italian despots, one of the ways the duke sought to demonstrate his legitimacy was by establishing an image of the Medici family as generous art and architectural patrons (*Fig. 111*). To this end, he commissioned an extensive program of interior redecoration in the Palazzo della Signoria (known today as the Palazzo Vecchio) which had formerly housed the executive and legislative councils of republican Florence. His professional collaborator in this transformation of the communal palace into a princely residence was the architect, painter and author Giorgio Vasari (1511–1574), whose public relations genius was perfectly suited to the task. Vasari's invention of an idealized past for the Medici family and his energetic attempts to fill the rooms of Cosimo's palace with convincing symbols of antique grandeur were critically important for a small, recently invented dukedom with aspirations for acceptance by the royal families of Europe. In carrying out this huge promotional effort, Vasari was given a free hand to do whatever he wished. Among other things, he converted the Salon of the Five Hundred, once the legislative chamber of the Florentine republic, into a grandiose ducal reception hall.[23]

Cosimo also enhanced state security by constructing a large office building known as the Uffizi. By bringing government agencies and major trade guilds under one roof, it became much easier to keep influential Florentines under close surveillance. The design for this project, a long, slender, U-shaped building arranged around an extremely narrow courtyard, is generally attributed to Vasari, but the plan seems to have received major assistance from a talented sculptor and architect named Bartolomeo Ammannati (1511–1592). Most of the architectural motifs displayed on the Uffizi's handsome exterior are borrowed directly from the vestibule and reading room of Michelangelo's Laurentian Library at the church of San Lorenzo, a project that Ammannati was in the process of finishing when work began on the Uffizi. Cosimo's other major architectural conception was the Chapel of the Princes, a huge family mausoleum not fully completed until the eighteenth century. Tacked on to the rear of San Lorenzo like an enormous, oversized egg, its tastelessness and

Fig. 111: Duke Cosimo and His Artists
by Giorgio Vasari

poverty of imagination are truly breathtaking. The interior is a garish miscellany of slick, multicolored stone slabs (marble, coral, jasper, agate, mother-of-pearl, and lapis lazuli) thrown together to impress the viewer with their sheer costliness. Possessing the wealth to commission whatever he wished, Cosimo chose to authorize this vulgar family shrine but casually dismissed Titian's offer to paint his portrait. He seems to have genuinely preferred the large cartoonlike works produced by Vasari and his studio because they could cover huge amounts of surface area (like the interior of Brunelleschi's dome (*Fig. 112*)) in record time. Realizing that a patron as provincial as the duke would spell death to their aspirations, the finest Florentine artists and architects fled the city and could not be persuaded to return.[24]

Culture and Politics

The merchant nobility that directed Venetian public patronage clearly understood the architectural pitfalls exemplified by the new Renaissance Saint Peter's and the repressive regime of the Medici dukes. It seemed obvious that if left unchanneled, the search for unfettered personal expression could easily endanger the existing world of highly valued objects, and that despotic patronage often led to a serious decline in artistic quality. Because the fabricator mentality was a real danger, it needed to be opposed by a potent counterforce. While, as individuals, the patrician governors of Venice might possess no special qualifications for such a task, they did believe that as members of a tightly connected communal network, they were better equipped to play this critical role than any other part of society. This had long been their historic function, and they felt they had to exert it forcefully if architectural ensembles like the Piazza San Marco complex were to be enhanced and preserved.

Insight into the role of the Venetian patriciate in directing public architecture can be gleaned from a fascinating essay by Hannah Arendt. The author points out that in classical Western philosophy from Aristotle to Kant, the capacity to make discerning artistic judgments has consistently been viewed as a specifically political skill. That is, the ability to make sound choices about public art and architecture is premised on the same type of enlarged mentality that enables a person to make well-balanced political decisions. To perform either function well, the judging person must first orient himself in the public realm, the world of common sense and action that is open to all intelligent, fair-minded individuals. Just as in the art of political persuasion, in making and defending aesthetic judgments, all that a person can do is attempt to woo the assent of those around him and simply hope that in the end, some of them will agree with at least a portion of his views. As a starting point, he must acknowledge that in matters of politics and culture, a claim to possess certain a priori knowledge or absolute truth is almost false by definition. Rather than matters of knowledge and truth, politics and culture are arenas of judgment and preference; they are activities best carried on through robust debate about the nature of the common world the citizens of a particular community wish to inhabit. In this respect, the realms of politics and culture are at the opposite extreme from the specialized sphere in which the individual artist lives and works. In the purely isolated world of the fabricator, it is always

Fig. 112: THE LAST JUDGEMENT *by Giorgio Vasari,*
dome of the Florentine Cathedral

the particular degree of talent possessed by a given artist and the quality of the things that he can produce which are determinative.[25]

As strange as it may sound to modern ears, it is this political aspect of cultural judgment—the requirement for observing a wider, deeper standard of value beyond mere personal advantage or current fashion—that explains the long-term success of artistic decision making in communal Venice. For much of its history, political choices and the commissioning and direction of public architecture were determined by a single process: one of compromise and consensus building worked out in a seemingly endless succession of interlocking councils and commissions. The undeniable benefits of that system in the realm of politics—the unparalleled cohesion and consistency produced by Venetian constitutional arrangements over many centuries—were once hailed as established facts throughout Europe. Hopefully, we can now see that these same institutions and qualities of mind also explain her remarkable ability, over the course of half a millennium, to create the Piazza San Marco complex as one of the supreme achievements of Western architecture. Properly understood, the two accomplishments are inseparable.

NOTES

Notes to Chapter One

1. F. C. Hodgson, *The Early History of Venice from the Foundations to the Conquest of Constantinople A.D. 1204* (London: George Allen, 1901), 7–8, 11; Giorgio Geromet, *Aquileia, La Grande Metropoli Romana* (Aquileia: Fondazione Societa per la Conservazione della Basilica di Aquileia, 1996), 29–30, 41–43, 57–58; Peter Kidson, "Rome," *Great Architecture of the World*, ed. John Julius Norwich (New York: Random House, 1975), 73; John Julius Norwich, *A History of Venice* (New York: Alfred A. Knopf, 1982), 4.
2. Frederic C. Lane, *Venice: A Maritime Republic* (Baltimore and London: The Johns Hopkins University Press, 1973), 2.
3. Geromet, 20-21, 186–90; Norwich, *A History of Venice*, 4–6, 10–11.
4. Geromet, 17, 21, 35, 146–48; Hodgson, 10–16; Norwich, *A History of Venice*, 5.
5. Justine Davis Randers-Pehrson, *Barbarians and Romans: The Birth Struggle of Europe, A.D. 400–700* (Norman and London: University of Oklahoma Press, 1983), 40–42; John Julius Norwich, *A Short History of Byzantium* (New York: Alfred A. Knopf, 1997), 47.
6. Norwich, *A Short History of Byzantium*, 3.
7. Edward Gibbon, *The Decline and Fall of the Roman Empire*, abridged by Dero A. Saunders (New York: Penguin Books, 1981), 314, 317; Michael Grant, *The Roman Emperors* (New York: Charles Scribner's Sons, 1985), 208.
8. Richard Krautheimer, *Rome: Profile of a City* (Princeton, N.J.: Princeton University Press, 2000), 24.
9. Charles Freeman, *The Horses of St Mark* (London: Little, Brown, 2004), 21.
   Constantine's removal of the seat of Roman power to the East permanently confirmed the actions of his predecessor Diocletian (285–313), the first emperor to fix his everyday residence in a distant eastern province thousands of miles from Rome during a time of peace. Like Constantine, Diocletian was born outside Italy and felt a provincial's distaste for the old capital and what he believed were its arrogant, dissolute inhabitants. He felt no allegiance to its once hallowed institutions, including the Roman Senate, whose traditional prerogatives he openly ignored from his imperial residence in Nicomedia, south of the Black Sea and very near the ancient city of Byzantium, the future site of Constantine's imperial capital. For the sake of form, Diocletian did rebuild the Senate House in the Roman Forum after it was destroyed by fire in 283; in fact, it is Diocletian's restoration that is still standing today. But he never considered restoring the Senate itself to any true political power. Unlike Constantine, Diocletian was the author of the most ruthless and bloody Roman persecution ever launched against the fledgling Christian sect. Gibbon, 327–29; Grant, *The Roman Emperors*, 208.

10. Krautheimer, *Rome: Profile of a City*, 33, 35–37, 39, 46; Gibbon, 276–77, 278, 290–91.

11. Krautheimer, *Rome: Profile of a City*, 33; Gibbon, 591.

12. Randers-Pehrson, 211.

13. Norwich, *A History of Venice*, 10.

14. *The Stones of Venice: The Works of John Ruskin*, 3 vols. (London and New York: The Chesterfield Society), 2:6, 8–9.

15. Norwich, *A History of Venice*, 10, 12, 17; Otto Demus, *The Church of San Marco in Venice* (Washington, D.C.: Dumbarton Oaks Research Library, 1960), 19–20; Donald M. Nicol, *Byzantium and Venice: A Study in Diplomatic and Cultural Relations* (Cambridge: Cambridge University Press, 1988), 9–11.

16. Hodgson, 20-22.

17. Ibid., 36; Demus, *The Church of San Marco in Venice*, 20; Elizabeth Crouzet-Pavan, *Venice Triumphant* (Baltimore and London: The Johns Hopkins University Press, 2002), 196; Horatio F. Brown, *Venice, an Historical Sketch of the Republic* (London: Rivington, Percival & Co., 1895), 18, 23; Giuseppe Cappelletti, *Relazione storica sulle magistrature venete* (Venice: Filippi Editore, 1992), 10, 12; Charles Diehl, *La République de Venise* (Paris: Flammarion, 1985), 31–32; Norwich, *A History of Venice*, 10–11.

18. Horatio F. Brown, *Venice, Its Individual Growth from the Earliest Beginnings to the Fall of the Republic* (Chicago: A. C. McClurg & Co., 1906), 12, 19–20; Norwich, *A History of Venice*, 17, 19; Brown, *Venice, an Historical Sketch*, 23, 27, 31–32, 34; Nicol, 11–14.

19. Norwich, *A History of Venice*, 20–21; Nicol, 14–16.

20. Juergen Schulz, "Urbanism in Medieval Venice," *City States in Classical Antiquity and Medieval Italy*, eds. Anthony Molho, Kurt Raaflaub and Julia Emlen (Ann Arbor: University of Michigan Press, 1991), 425 (fn. 14); Hodgson, 29–30.

    To appreciate the dimensions of the enormous long-term reclamation project the Venetians undertook when they decided to relocate to the Rialtine islands, it is important to understand that in the year 811, the total above-the-waterline land mass of the archipelago was no more than fifty percent of the city's present surface area, not counting the huge area presently taken up by the car park, train yards, and shipping dock built just off the nineteenth-century causeway that connects Venice to the mainland. Alvise Zorzi, *Venice: the Golden Age 697–1979* (New York: Abbeville Press, 1980), 76–77.

Notes to Chapter Two

1. Ruskin compared this verdant island field to the little piazza on abandoned Torcello. *The Stones of Venice*, 2:58.

2. Ibid. Within a short time, Doge Agnello and his sons would impart their family name to this small stream which became known as the Rio Batario or Canal of the Badoers. In Venetian dialect, the word Badoer is a shortened form of the surname Participazio. During the twelfth century, most of the Rio Batario was filled in to create the medieval Piazza San Marco, but modern visitors can still see a portion of it running in the same north-south direction that formerly split the original site in two. This can be accomplished by strolling

into the Napoleonic Gardens that front the harbor basin just west of the Zecca or Mint designed by Jacopo Sansovino, then walking over to the small canal which forms the park's right-hand boundary. Now called the Rio di Zecca, this foreshortened stem is what remains of the stream that greeted Doge Agnello Participazio in 810.

3. Support for the view that Justinian's sixth-century general was the Narses who built San Teodoro can be found in Deborah Howard, *The Architectural History of Venice* (New Haven: Yale University Press, 2002), 3; Deborah Howard, *Jacopo Sansovino: Architecture and Patronage in Renaissance Venice* (New Haven: Yale University Press, 1975), 77; Ennio Concina, "San Marco, Constantinopoli e il primo Rinascimento veneziano: traditio magnificientiae,"*Storia dell'arte marciana: l'architettura*, ed. Renato Polacco (Venezia: Marsilio Editori, 1997), 26, 31; Peter Lauritzen, *Venice: A Thousand Years of Culture and Civilization* (New York: Atheneum, 1978), 26; John Warren, "La prima chiesa di san marco evangelista a venezia," *Storia dell'arte marciana: l'architettura*, 188; Brown, *Venice, an Historical Sketch of the Republic*, 12-13.

4. Demus, *The Church of San Marco in Venice*, 21; Norwich, *A History of Venice*, 8, 12, 18; Ennio Concina, *A History of Venetian Architecture* (Cambridge: Cambridge University Press, 1998), 9–10.

5. Support for the view that Narses also built San Geminiano e Mena can be found in the sources cited in note 3 above in connection with the construction of San Teodoro. Narses is said to have erected the two churches to express gratitude for Venetian naval assistance in 539 and 551 in connection with his retaking of Ravenna from the Goths.

6. Richard Goy, *Venice: The City and Its Architecture* (London: Phaidon Press, 1997), 60–61. Some sense of the feudal interior of this first ducal castle is still available today. If, upon entering the Doge's Palace, you proceed to the ground-floor room at the southwest corner, then walk into the second room north of that, you will discover what may very well be a large interior remnant of the original ducal fortress. Noticeably different from the brick building fabric of the other ground-floor walls, the northern wall of this third room is composed of large, thick, rough-faced stone blocks. The wall is about eighteen feet high and four feet thick and is pierced by a low, narrow passageway about two feet wide. It comes as a shock to encounter this primitive, fortresslike relic within the Gothic and Renaissance environments of the Palace. It is a vivid reminder of just how much protection from a hostile outside world it must have taken to calm the minds of the Participazi, the Candiani, the Orseoli, and the other early doges of the ninth and tenth centuries.

7. Warren, "La prima chiesa," 189–190; John Warren, "The First Church of San Marco in Venice," *Antiquaries Journal*, LXX (1990), Part II, 342. Warren makes a convincing case that the original ninth-century church and convent of San Zaccaria were built only a few dozen yards north of the ducal fortress and just east of San Teodoro, on land donated for that purpose by the Participazio family, rather than on the site of the present San Zaccaria several hundred yards farther east of the Doge's Palace. In Warren's view, San Zaccaria was rebuilt in its present location only after its destruction in the great fire of 976, which gutted all of the principal buildings in the San Marco area. This conflagration, deliberately set to end the reign of Doge Pietro Candiano IV, is described in detail at the end of this chapter.

8. Demus, *The Church of San Marco in Venice*, 10–11; Otto Demus, *The Mosaic Decoration of San Marco, Venice* (Chicago and London: University of Chicago Press, 1988), 2.

9. Patrick J. Geary, *Furta Sacra, Thefts of Relics in the Central Middle Ages* (Princeton, N.J.: Princeton University Press, 1978), 20, 32, 35, 40, 45, 47, 53, 135.

10. As shown in *Fig. 7*, this episode of the customs search is wonderfully illustrated in a seventeenth-century mosaic covering the lunette at the top of the far right-hand portal on the western or main façade of Saint Mark's Basilica.

11. This predestination legend, codified in the abridged Latin inscription held in the Lion's paw (an image that recurs everywhere in Venice), took its earliest written form in Martino da Canale's *Estoires de venise* (1275). Vittore Carpaccio's painting, signed in 1516 *(Fig. 8)*, now hangs in the Sala Grimani of the ducal apartments, located in the east wing of the Doge's Palace.

12. Goy, *Venice: The City and Its Architecture*, 67, 70, 110; Demus, *The Church of San Marco in Venice*, 45-48, 55; Richard A. Goldthwaite, *The Building of Renaissance Florence* (Baltimore and London: The Johns Hopkins University Press, 1980), 2; Schulz, "Urbanism in Medieval Venice," 436.

13. Prominent examples of early basilica-plan churches built in or around the Adriatic lagoons can still be seen in Ravenna and nearby Classe (Sant'Apollinare Nuovo, San Giovanni Evangelista, and Sant'Apollinare in Classe), Aquileia (the Basilica), and the lagoon communities of Grado (Sant'Eufemia and Santa Maria delle Grazie) and Torcello (Santa Maria Assunta).

14. Warren, "La prima chiesa," 189; Warren, "The First Church," 335, 342, 344, 356; Demus, *The Church of San Marco in Venice*, 67, 45-48, 55; Richard Krautheimer, *Early Christian and Byzantine Architecture* (New Haven: Yale University Press, 1986), 407; Ferdinando Forlati, *La basilica di San Marco attraverso i suoi restauri* (Trieste: Edizioni LINT, 1975), 58; Goy, *Venice: The City and its Architecture*, 149.

15. Constantine's fourth-century church of the Holy Apostles is not directly relevant to the architectural history of San Marco, since that original structure was replaced in its entirety by Justinian's sixth-century building, which alone served as the model for the Venetian church. However, the monument that Constantine carefully designed as his final resting place does offer a wealth of insight into the mind of the man whose actions constitute a major part of the historical background for the first half of this book.

   Constantine's enormous Greek-cross mausoleum was built just within the walls of his capital to take advantage of one of the city's finest sites. The emperor's tomb was placed under a canopy near the altar in the exact center of the building. The enclosed area containing the imperial sarcophagus was surrounded by twelve other sarcophagi, collectively representing the twelve Apostles from which the church derived its name, and Constantine left specific directions that the Mass be performed over his tomb. Thus, at a minimum, Constantine meant for later Christians to see him as an apostolic equal, the thirteenth of Christ's disciples. But the central position he gave his own shrine clearly suggests that he intended something much more radical. The emperor placed his own corpse where an image of Christ would normally be found. While this revelation of the imperial mind must have been profoundly shocking to his Christian contemporaries, it expressed to perfection

NOTES TO CHAPTERS 2 & 3

the emperor's own view of his proper role in Christian worship. Richard Krautheimer, a profound scholar, has written that Constantine saw himself as nothing less than Christ's earthly double. *Three Christian Capitals, Topography and Politics* (Berkeley: University of California Press, 1983), 58–60, 64, 66–67.

As part of his complete reconstruction of the Apostoleion, the Emperor Justinian removed the Constantinian remains to a new mausoleum of circular design that functioned as a separate appendage to Justinian's new church, thereby eliminating what was by then widely viewed as a scandalously heretical and sacrilegious architectural arrangement.

16. Demus, *The Church of San Marco in Venice*, 67; Warren, "The First Church," 349; Forlati, 58.
17. Demus, *The Church of San Marco in Venice*, 49, 90–94.
18. Ibid., 97–98.
19. Warren, "La prima chiesa," 196–97; Warren, "The First Church," 340; Demus, *The Church of San Marco in Venice*, 65–66; Robert Cecchi, *La basilica di San Marco* (Venezia: Marsilio Editori, 2003), 30; Forlati, 51, 58–59; Goy, *Venice: The City and Its Architecture*, 49.
20. Warren, "La prima chiesa," 191; Warren, "The First Church," 337-38.
21. Warren, "La prima chiesa," 190; Demus, *The Church of San Marco in Venice*, 68; Cecchi, 116; Ettore Vio, "The Crypt," *The Basilica of St. Mark in Venice*, ed. Ettore Vio (New York: Scale/Riverside, 1999), 142.
22. Gregorio Gattinoni, *Il Campanile di San Marco* (Venezia: Giovanni Fabbris, 1910), 2–8; Lauritzen, *Venice: A Thousand Years*, 28; Norwich, *A History of Venice*, 37–38.
23. Norwich, *A History of Venice*, 39–43, Laura M. Ragg, *Crises in Venetian History* (New York: E. P. Dutton, 1928), 19–21, and Diehl, *La République de Venise*, 32–33, are the sources for the history of Pietro Candiano IV that follows.

Notes to Chapter Three

1. Norwich, *A History of Venice*, 44–45; Ragg, 21; Lauritzen, *Venice: A Thousand Years*, 29; Lane, 89–91; Thomas F. Madden, *Enrico Dandolo and the Rise of Venice* (Baltimore: The Johns Hopkins Univesity Press, 2003), 54, 56-57, 75, 79–80, 90, 93–95.
2. Norwich, *A History of Venice*, 44. Norwich states that the corpus of the doge's personal contribution was large enough to yield eight thousand ducats annually for eighty years.
3. Ragg, 33; Madden, *Enrico Dandolo*, 2; Demus, *The Church of San Marco in Venice*, 55. This political change and the very different form of ducal palace that resulted from it in the late twelfth century are described in detail at the end of Chapter Five in the section "The Piazza Project in the Twelfth Century."
4. Demus, *The Church of San Marco in Venice*, 21–22, 69–70; Cecchi, 32, 123–24; Forlati, 66–68; Gattinoni, 7; Lauritzen, *Venice: A Thousand Years*, 29, 35; Warren, "La prima chiesa," 189–90.
5. *The Stones of Venice*, 2:60–61.
6. Norwich, *A History of Venice*, 74; Ragg, 21; Goy, *Venice: The City and Its Architecture*, 152; Cecchi, 33.

7. Vio, "The Crypt," *The Basilica of St. Mark in Venice*, 143; Ettore Vio, "L'architecture," *La Basilique Saint-Marc de Venise*, ed. Ettore Vio (Paris: Citadelles & Mazenod, 2001), 128, 134, 140; Ettore Vio, "Ritrovamenti strutturali nella fabbrica marciana," *Storia dell'arte marciana: l'architettura*, 101.

8. Norwich, *A History of Venice*, 44–45.

9. Ibid., 46–48.

10. Ibid., 49–50.

11. Zorzi, *Venice: The Golden Age*, 93.

12. Ragg, 29.

13. Goy, Venice: *The City and Its Architecture*, 22; Madden, *Enrico Dandolo*, 7; Christopher Hibbert, *Florence: The Biography of a City* (New York: Penguin Books, 1993), 13; Wladimiro Dorigo, "Venetia Before Venice: From Grado to San Marco," *Venice Art and Architecture*, ed. Giandomenico Romanelli, 2 vols. (Cologne: Konemann, 1997), 75; Crouzet-Pavan, 13–14; Howard, *The Architectural History of Venice*, 4.

14. Jack Lindsay, *The Normans and Their World* (New York: St. Martin's Press, 1974), 49.

15. John Julius Norwich, *The Other Conquest* (New York and Evanston: Harper & Row, 1967), 39–40, 68, 71–72, 76–77, 92–93, 124–25; Lindsay, 113–14.

16. Norwich, *The Other Conquest*, 168–73, 175–85, 200, 220–21; Norwich, *A Short History of Byzantium*, 236–42, 250–51; Norwich, *A History of Venice*, 70; Lindsay, 266; Charles Diehl, *Byzantium: Greatness and Decline*, trans. Naomi Walford (New Brunswick, N. J.: Rutgers University Press, 1957), 114, 120–21.

17. Norwich, *The Other Conquest*, 220–21, 228–29; Lindsay, 268; Norwich, *A Short History of Byzantium*, 236; Norwich, *A History of Venice*, 70; Lane, 28.

18. Norwich, *The Other Conquest*, 228–33, 235–44; Norwich, *A History of Venice*, 70–73; Lane, 28; Norwich, *A Short History of Byzantium*, 253–54.

19. Norwich, *The Other Conquest*, 244–45; Norwich, *A Short History of Byzantium*, 254; Norwich, *A History of Venice*, 72–73.

20. Norwich, *A History of Venice*, 73; Diehl, *La République de Venise*, 49, 52; Nicol, 76, 81; Horatio F. Brown, "The Venetians and the Venetian Quarter in Constantinople to the Close of the Twelfth Century," *Journal of Hellenic Studies* 40 (1920), 72; Michael Maclagan, *The City of Constantinople* (London: Thames and Hudson, 1968), 104; Demus, *The Church of San Marco in Venice*, 23; Zorzi, 94–97.

21. Demus, *The Church of San Marco in Venice*, 12, 35–36, 71–72, 97; Norwich, *A History of Venice*, 62; Concina, *A History of Venetian Architecture*, 22; Ennio Concina, "St. Mark's Triumphant: Piety and Magnificence," *St. Mark's: The Art and Architecture of Church and State in Venice*, ed. Ettore Vio (New York: Riverside Book Company, Inc., 2003), 90; Cecchi, 33–34, 124; Warren, "La prima chiesa," 190–98.

22. As the foremost apostles' church in Christendom, the sixth-century church of the Holy Apostles in Constantinople served as the model for later apostles' churches in northern Italy and Asia Minor. Although Mark, Luke, and John were not among the twelve original disciples of Christ, as Evangelists, they were traditionally included among the apostles, particularly in the East. Saint Paul, Christianity's greatest missionary and the author of over half of the New Testament, was also referred to as an apostle. An apostles' church

was not required to possess relics of more than a handful of apostles, since all were thought to be represented by the few whose bodily remains were collected in any particular location. Thus, the Apostoleion, whose full name was the church of the Holy Twelve Apostles, contained the relics of only Andrew, Luke, and Timothy. Curiously, although Venetians have made little effort to publicize the fact, San Marco possesses relics attributed to Peter, Paul, and nine other apostles in addition to those of Saint Mark himself. Demus, *The Church of San Marco in Venice*, 6–8, 16–18.

23. Ibid., 90, 97–98, 100. Some scholars believe that Doge Contarini imported more than one master Byzantine architect to guide his project (Ennio Concina, "St. Mark's Triumphant: Piety and Magnificence," 92), and Otto Demus refers to both "the architect" and "the architects" of the Contarini church on the same page (Demus, *The Church of San Marco in Venice*, 90, 98). Since there is no definitive evidence regarding how many Greek architects were responsible for the church's redesign and reconstruction, in the interests of simplicity, I have decided to refer to a single architect.

24. Demus, *The Church of San Marco in Venice*, 73, 93; Warren, "La prima chiesa," 194–97; Warren, "The First Church," 338; Cecchi, 16, 33–34, 55; Howard, *The Architectural History of Venice*, 19, 61.

25. Demus, *The Church of San Marco in Venice*, 91–92.

26. Ibid., 71, 74; Goy, *Venice: The City and Its Architecture*, 49; Warren, "La prima chiesa," 195; Crouzet-Pavan, 37.

27. Warren, "La prima chiesa," 192–93; Vio, "L'architecture," *La Basilique Saint-Marc de Venise*, 140; Demus, *The Church of San Marco in Venice*, 85, 88, 93.

28. Warren, "La prima chiesa," 190, 196; Warren, "The First Church," 336; Vio, "L'architecture," *La Basilique Saint-Marc de Venise*, 130, 140, 142; Demus, *The Church of San Marco in Venice*, 21–22, 73, 76, 97.

Renovations have revealed two barred windows beneath the marble cladding of the wall separating the northern arm of San Marco from the Chapel of S. Isidore. It seems almost certain that this interior wall was once part of the southern exterior wall of the ancient church of San Teodoro. In fact, it is probable that all of the rooms and chapels appended to the northern arm of the Basilica San Marco were once a part of San Teodoro. Demus, *The Church of San Marco in Venice*, 73, 76.

29. Demus, *The Church of San Marco in Venice*, 81–82.

30. Warren, "La prima chiesa," 196; Giulio Lorenzetti, *Venice and Its Lagoon*, trans. John Guthrie (Trieste: Edizioni Lint, 1975), 162.

As shown in *Fig. 11*, the incorporated portal relic from the Participazio guardhouse still serves as the central entrance from the narthex into the church. The interior stairway to the right of this main entrance now conveys visitors to the museum on the second floor.

31. Demus, *The Mosaic Decoration of San Marco, Venice*, 87.

32. Demus, *The Church of San Marco in Venice*, 88, 92–94, 97; Vio, "L'architecture," *La Basilique Saint-Marc de Venise*, 140, 142.

33. Demus, *The Church of San Marco in Venice*, 88, 93, 97–99; Giuseppe Samona et al., *Piazza San Marco: l'architettura, la storia, le funzioni* (Padua: Marsilio Editore, 1970), illustration 18.

34. Demus, *The Church of San Marco in Venice*, 86–88; Hugh Honour, *The Companion Guide to Venice*, 4th ed. (Woodbridge, England: Companion Guides, 1965), 39.

35. Demus, *The Church of San Marco in Venice*, 73, 88; Krautheimer, *Early Christian and Byzantine Architecture*, 407; Norwich, *A History of Venice*, 68, 72–74; Goy, *Venice: The City and Its Architecture*, 152.

36. Demus, *The Church of San Marco in Venice*, 14.

37. Ibid., 12–15.

   The *apparitio* (like Saint Mark's predestination legend or *prædestinatio*, which is briefly described in the last paragraph of the section "The Theft of Saint Mark" in Chapter Two), appeared in Martino da Canale's *Estoires de venise*, published in 1275. Neither legend appears in earlier chronicles, since both were late inventions that "grew out of the new and proud nationalism of the Venetians of the thirteenth century, a nationalism that led to a rewriting of Venetian history as the story of a chosen people." Demus, *The Church of San Marco in Venice*, 13–14.

   Demus also proposes that just as the Apostoleion in Constantinople served as the architectural model for the Contarini church, it may also have suggested the germ of an idea that grew into the apparitio legend. According to Eastern tradition, the relics of the saints Andrew, Luke, and Timothy were found buried on the site during the Emperor Justinian's rebuilding of the church of the Holy Apostles in the sixth century. Venice may have decided to go the Greeks one better and transform the Byzantine story of a fortunate discovery into a Venetian myth of divine and saintly revelation. *The Church of San Marco in Venice*, 12–13.

   Visitors to San Marco can find the very pier whose crumbling surface is supposed to have revealed Saint Mark's protruding arm. It is located at the northeastern (left-hand) opening of the Chapel of Saint Leonard on the eastern side of the southern transept. For many years, June 25, the anniversary of the miracle, was celebrated as one of the major Venetian feast days. Priests would sprinkle the pier and the congregation with rosewater to commemorate the strong scent of roses that streamed forth when the masonry fell open. Just across the southern transept on the western wall, visitors can also view two thirteenth-century mosaics depicting the events of the miraculous apparition.

   Following their reappearance, Saint Mark's relics were reburied in the crypt in a marble sarcophagus, where they remained until 1836, when they were relocated to the apse, just under the main altar, in part, to protect them from serious flooding in the subterranean regions of the church.

38. Geary, 133, 137–38.

39. Demus, *The Church of San Marco in Venice*, 80, 82; Samona et al., illustration 18.

40. Demus, *The Church of San Marco in Venice*, 53, 98; Krautheimer, *Early Christian and Byzantine Architecture*, 407–11. Large expanses of the Basilica's original eleventh-century brick surface can still be seen on the exterior lunette-shaped walls just below the southern and eastern domes; Concina, "St. Mark's Triumphant: Piety and Magnificence," 92.

41. Krautheimer, *Early Christian and Byzantine Architecture*, 408; Howard, *The Architectural History of Venice*, 13.

Notes to Chapter Four

1. Lauro Martines, *Power and Imagination: City-States in Renaissance Italy* (New York: Vintage Books, 1980), 32–33, 35–36; Mary McCarthy, *The Stones of Florence* (New York: Harcourt, Brace, 1963), 71; Christopher Hibbert, *Florence: The Biography of a City* (New York: Penguin Books, 1993), 13–14; Richard A. Goldthwaite, *The Building of Renaissance Florence: An Economic and Social History* (Baltimore: Johns Hopkins University Press, 1980), 1, 31.

2. Martines, 32–33, 35; McCarthy, *The Stones of Florence*, 70–71.

3. R.W.B. Lewis, *The City of Florence* (New York: Henry Holt, 1995), 24–27; Goldthwaite, *The Building of Renaissance Florence*, 3; McCarthy, *The Stones of Florence*, 69, 71; Martines, 32, 37; John Larner, *Culture and Society in Italy 1290–1420* (New York: Charles Scribner's Sons, 1971), 87; Eve Borsook, *The Companion Guide to Florence* (Englewood Cliffs, N. J.: Prentice-Hall, 1979), 60–61.

4. Richard A. Goldthwaite, *Wealth and the Demand for Art in Italy 1300–1600* (Baltimore: The Johns Hopkins University Press, 1993), 180; Lewis, 29; Nicolai Rubenstein, *The Palazzo Vecchio* 1298–1532 (Oxford: Clarendon Press, 1995), 1.

5. Juergen Schulz, "La piazza medievale di San Marco," *Annali di architettura*, IV (1992), 134–35, 144; Larner, 76; Juergen Schulz, "Urbanism in Medieval Venice," 435–38; Michela Agazzi, *Platea Sancti Marci: luoghi marciania dall'XI al XIII secolo e la formazione della piazza* (Venezia: Commune di Venezia, 1991), 146-48.

6. Christopher Hibbert, *Rome: The Biography of a City* (New York: W. W. Norton, 1985), 89–90, 93; Krautheimer, *Rome: Profile of a City*, 152–56, 231; Norwich, *A History of Venice*, 102.

7. Hibbert, *Rome*, 92–94, 342; Krautheimer, *Rome: Profile of a City*, 197, 206–207, 286–87; James S. Ackerman, *The Architecture of Michelangelo*, 2nd ed. (Chicago: University of Chicago Press, 1986), 143–44; Rodolfo Amedeo Lanciani, *The Destruction of Ancient Rome* (London: MacMillan, 1901), 180–88.

8. Diehl, *Byzantium*, 191–92; Norwich, *A History of Venice*, 100; Maclagan, 103; Donald E. Queller and Thomas F. Madden, *The Fourth Crusade: The Conquest of Constantinople* (Philadelphia: University of Pennsylvania Press, 1997), 108; Charles Diehl, *Constantinople* (Paris: Librarie Renouard, 1924), 28; Tamara Talbot Rice, *Everyday Life in Byzantium* (New York: Dorset Press, 1967), 144; James Barter, *A Travel Guide to Medieval Constantinople* (San Diego: Lucent Books, 2003), 8; Philip Sherrard, *Byzantium* (Amsterdam: Time-Life Books, 1966), 37; F. A. Hayek, *The Fatal Conceit* (Chicago: University of Chicago Press, 1988), 29, 90-91.

Madden, *Enrico Dandolo*, 105, states that the lagoon population was one hundred thousand in the late twelfth century. Lewis, 24, gives a population figure of thirty thousand for Florence in 1175, and various sources estimate a Paris population of between twenty-five thousand and fifty thousand at this time. In his article "The Venetians and the Venetian Quarter in Constantinople to the Close of the Twelfth Century," 82–83, Horatio Brown says that there were twenty thousand Venetians in the Byzantine Empire at a relatively low point in their immigration to that area. Elsewhere, Brown states that as many as 200,000 Venetians reportedly lived in the Venetian quarter of Constantinople in the middle of the twelfth century (Brown, *Venice, an Historical Sketch*, 100). Brown's second, much higher estimate is repeated by J. G. Links, *Venice for Pleasure*, 4th ed. (Mount Kisco, New York and London: Moyer Bell, 1984), 58.

9. Schulz, "Urbanism in Medieval Venice," 422; Goy, *Venice: The City and Its Architecture*, 21–22; Zorzi, *Venice: The Golden Age*, 76–77; Paolo Maretto, *Venezia* (Genova: Vitali e Ghianda, 1969), 13; Brown, *Venice, an Historical Sketch*, 93; Norwich, *A History of Venice*, 91.

10. Over time, the term Rialto (from the Latin *Rivus altus*), which had originally signified the entire archipelago of 117 islets when the Rialtine islands had become the new capital of the lagoon in 811, took on a more localized meaning. The name specifically attached itself to the area of the international trading market situated on the northwestern or *de ultra* side of the Grand Canal.

11. Wladimiro Dorigo, "Venetia Before Venice: From Grado to San Marco," 76; Schulz, "Urbanism in Medieval Venice," 425–28; Goy, *Venice: The City and Its Architecture*, 94–95; Maretto, 16.

12. Dorigo, "Venetia Before Venice: From Grado to San Marco," 76–77; Schulz, "Urbanism in Medieval Venice," 428–32; Goy, *Venice: The City and Its Architecture*, 74; Maretto, 16.

13. Lane, 90, 95; Madden, *Enrico Dandolo*, 93, 105; Norwich, *A History of Venice*, 109; Brown, *Venice, an Historical Sketch*, 102; Crouzet-Pavan, 196.

14. Madden, *Enrico Dandolo*, 4, 20–21, 93; Lane, 90; Brown, *Venice, an Historical Sketch*, 102.

15. Madden, *Enrico Dandolo*, 21, 94; Lane, 91.

16. Norwich, *A History of Venice*, 105-106; Madden, *Enrico Dandolo*, 53-56, 79, 95.

17. Madden, *Enrico Dandolo*, 57–58, 79, 95; Lane, 92.

18. Norwich, *A History of Venice*, 109–10; Brown, *Venice, an Historical Sketch*, 104.

19. Madden, Enrico Dandolo, 95–98.

20. Ettore Vio, "The Interior of the Basilica" and Renato Polacco, "The Tessellated Floor of St. Mark's," *The Basilica of St. Mark in Venice*, 93, 134; Howard, *The Architectural History of Venice*, 26–27; Krautheimer, *Early Christian and Byzantine Architecture*, 407–408; Lauritzen, *Venice: a Thousand Years*, 39, 42–43; Concina, "St. Mark's Triumphant: Piety and Magnificence," *St. Mark's, the Art and Architecture of Church and State in Venice*, 90; Lorenzetti, 182, 197.

21. Polacco, "The Tessellated Floor of St. Mark's," *The Basilica of St. Mark in Venice*, 134–40; Paul Hills, *Venetian Color, Marble, Mosaic, Painting and Glass 1250-1550* (New Haven and London: Yale University Press, 1999), 32–39.

22. Concina, "St. Mark's Triumphant: Piety and Magnificence," *St. Mark's, the Art and Architecture of Church and State in Venice*, 90; Ruskin, *The Stones of Venice*, 2:76, 2:89; Krautheimer, *Early Christian and Byzantine Architecture*, 407–408.

23. Demus, *The Mosaic Decoration of San Marco*, 98; *Henry James on Italy, Selections from Italian Hours* (New York: Weidenfeld & Nicolson, 1988), 16.

24. Demus, *The Mosaic Decoration of San Marco*, 13, 192, 200–201; *Knopf Guide to Venice* (New York: Alfred A. Knopf, 1993), 66–67; Hills, 50–55.

25. Demus, *The Mosaic Decoration of San Marco*, 86–88, 98, 188–89, 192; Krautheimer, *Early Christian and Byzantine Architecture*, 337–38, 352, 365–67, 393; Lauritzen, *Venice: A Thousand Years*, 43; Lorenzetti, 197.

26. Demus, *The Mosaic Decoration of San Marco*, 5–6, 98, 189–93, 200, 202; Wladimiro Dorigo, "The Medieval Mosaics of San Marco in the History of the Basilica," *Patriarchal Basilica in Venice, San Marco: the Mosaics, the History, the Lighting*, ed. Ettore Vio (Milan, 1990), 48–51; Hills, 47.

27. Demus, *The Church of San Marco in Venice*, 83, 85–88; Honour, 39; Demus, *The Mosaic Decoration of San Marco*, 14, 193.

Notes to Chapter Five

1. Zoe Oldenbourg, *The Crusades* (New York: Pantheon Books, 1966), 56-57; Norwich, *A Short History of Byzantium*, 255-256.

2. Norwich, *A Short History of Byzantium*, 256–57; Diehl, *Byzantium*, 206–207; Jonathan Phillips, *The Fourth Crusade* (New York: Viking, 2004), 13, 20–22, 52, 74–75.

3. Diehl, *Byzantium*, 16, 27–29.

4. Oldenbourg, 55, 497.

5. Ibid., 73; Diehl, *Byzantium*, 181.

6. Nicol, 69–70; Oldenbourg, 308; Norwich, *A History of Venice*, 83, 88; Madden, *Enrico Dandolo*, 10, 14–16.

7. Madden, *Enrico Dandolo*, 16; Norwich, *A History of Venice*, 83, 89–90; Brown, *Venice, an Historical Sketch*, 87; Diehl, *La République de Venise*, 50, 53–54; Phillips, 22, 25; Barbara Tuchman, *A Distant Mirror* (New York: Alfred A. Knopf, 1978), 10; Oldenbourg, 583–84.

8. Nicol, 60, 64, 70, 75–76, 77–81; Lane, 23–24, 34, 90; Madden, *Enrico Mandolo*, 14–17; Norwich, *A History of Venice*, 88; Brown, *Venice, an Historical Sketch*, 89.

9. Nicol, vi-vii, 78; Madden, *Enrico Dandolo*, 9.

10. Norwich, *A Short History of Byzantium,* 217–44; Diehl, *Byzantium*, 128; Diehl, *Constantinople*, 27.

11. Norwich, *A Short History of Byzantium*, 265; Diehl, *Byzantium*, 27–29, 181–83; Madden, 50–51; Brown, "The Venetians and the Venetian Quarter in Constantinople," 84; Nicol, 85–87.

12. Norwich, *A History of Venice*, 97; Nicol, 93–97; Diehl, *Byzantium*, 181–83; Madden, *Enrico Dandolo*, 50–51.

13. Nicol, 97, 100, 104, 106; Norwich, *A Short History of Byzantium*, 288; Norwich, *A History of Venice*, 104; Brown, "The Venetians and the Venetian Quarter in Constantinople," 82, 85.

14. Nicol, 99-100; Norwich, *A History of Venice*, 105–106; Norwich, *A Short History of Byzantium*, 288; Diehl, *Byzantium*, 182–83.

15. Nicol, 106–10, 112–19; Madden, *Enrico Dandolo*, 82–83, 112–13; Norwich, *A Short History of Byzantium*, 287, 292–95; Oldenbourg, 441; John Freely and Ahmet S. Cakmak, *Byzantine Monuments of Istanbul* (Cambridge: Cambridge University Press, 2004), 234; Norwich, *A History of Venice*, 97, 121, 125; Brown, "The Venetians and the Venetian Quarter in Constantinople," 88.

16. Diehl, *La République de Venise*, 54; Concina, "St. Mark's Triumphant: Piety and Magnificence," *St. Mark's, the Art and Architecture of Church and State in Venice*, 92.

17. Madden, *Enrico Dandolo*, 21, 94; Lane 91.

18. Schulz, "Urbanism in Medieval Venice," 433; Madden, *Enrico Dandolo*, 2; Schulz, "La piazza medievale di San Marco," 134; Schulz, "Urbanism in Medieval Venice," 432–33; Norwich, *A History of Venice*, 82–83.

   Ruskin compared the pastoral appearance of the little campo of San Marco before its medieval transformation to the small, grassy field in front of Santa Fosca on the abandoned island of Torcello. *The Stones of Venice*, 2:58.

19. Schulz, "Urbanism in Medieval Venice," 432, 437; John McAndrew, *Venetian Architecture of the Early Renaissance* (Cambridge, Mass.: MIT Press, 1980), 403.

20. Schulz, "Urbanism in Medieval Venice," 434; Schulz, "La piazza medievale di San Marco," 142–43; Demus, *The Church of San Marco in Venice*, 53; Richard J. Goy, *Building Renaissance Venice, Patrons, Architects and Builders c. 1430–1500* (New Haven and London: Yale University Press, 2006), 33; Reinhold C. Mueller, "The Procurators of San Marco in the Thirteenth and Fourteenth Centuries," *Studi Veneziani*, XIII (1971), 108–10.

21. Nicol, 97; Norwich, *A History of Venice*, 104; Brown, "The Venetians and the Venetian Quarter in Constantinople," 74–75, 82–83, 85; Warren, "The First Church," 350.

   The Venetian quarter in medieval Constantinople was a narrow (eighteen-hundred-foot-wide) strip located just above the modern Galata Bridge that transports the citizens of Istanbul to the northern shore of the Golden Horn. John Freely, *The Companion Guide to Istanbul and Around the Marmara* (Woodbridge, England: Companion Guides, 2000), 18–19.

22. Krautheimer, *Early Christian and Byzantine Architecture*, 350; Schulz, "Urbanism in Medieval Venice," 438–39; Schulz, "La piazza medievale di San Marco," 146; McAndrew, 403; Lanciani, 180–88; Hibbert, *Rome*, 92; Krautheimer, *Rome: Profile of a City*, 231; Maclagan, 103; Queller and Madden, *The Fourth Crusade*, 108; Diehl, *Constantinople*, 28; Rice, 144; Barter, 9; Sherrard, 37.

23. Pierre Gilles, *The Antiquities of Constantinople*, trans. John Ball (New York: Italica Press, 1988), 16–19; Sherrard, 37–38; Rice, 145; Krautheimer, *Three Christian Capitals*, 47–55; Freely and Cakmak, *Byzantine Monuments of Istanbul*, 30.

24. Krautheimer, *Three Christian Capitals*, 49–52; A. G. Paspates and William Metcalfe, *The Great Palace of Constantinople* (London: Alexander Gardner, 1893), 99–100, 107; Maclagan, 23, 44, 71; Freely and Cakmak, *Byzantine Monuments of Istanbul*, 14; Schulz, "Urbanism in Medieval Venice," 438–39; Schulz, "La piazza medievale di San Marco," 146; Samona et al., illustration 18; Krautheimer, *Early Christian and Byzantine Architecture*, 68–69, 90, 103–105, 202.

25. Sherrard, 37–38, 43; Diehl, *Constantinople*, 36–37, Krautheimer, *Three Christian Capitals*, 49–55; Paspates and Metcalfe, 62–63, 77–78; Freely and Cakmak, *Byzantine Monuments of Istanbul*, 14, 32, 73; Stephen Turnbull, *The Walls of Constantinople AD 324–1453* (Oxford: Osprey, 2004), 8; Schulz, "Urbanism in Medieval Venice," 439; Rice, 42; Sherrard, 38, 48–49; Barter, 45, 51; Glanville Downey, *Constantinople in the Age of Justinian* (New York: Dorset Press, 1991), 5.

26. Sherrard, 38; Diehl, *Constantinople*, 23–24; Maclagan, 65–66, 71, 105; Paspates and Metcalfe, 33, 60, 70, 73, 100, 105–106, 111–15, 146; Queller and Madden, 137; Schulz, "La piazza medievale di San Marco," 146.

27. Schulz, "Urbanism in Medieval Venice," 436–39; Schulz, "La piazza medievale di San Marco," 145–46, 154 (fn. 82); Goy, *Venice: The City and Its Architecture*, 67, 70; Goldthwaite, *The Building of Renaissance Florence*, 2; McAndrew, 378, 403; Samona et al., illustration 18; Maclagan, 71; Paspates and Metcalfe, 99–100;

28. Krautheimer, *Early Christian and Byzantine Architecture*, 39; Diehl, *Byzantium*, 27, 34.

29. Diehl, *Byzantium*, 27; Schulz, "La piazza medievale di San Marco," 147.

30. Schulz, "La piazza medievale di San Marco," 135–36, 150 (fn. 14); Schulz, "Urbanism in Medieval Venice," 433; Gattinoni, 9–10; Lewis, 23-26; Martines, 34; Goldthwaite, *The Building of Renaissance Florence*, 3; Agazzi, 79-81, 83–86, 135.

31. The dimensions of the Piazza today are very close to those of the medieval square begun in the twelfth century: 570 feet east to west from the Basilica to the Napoleonic Wing and 265 feet south to north from the Campanile corner of the Sansovino Library to the façade of the Procuratie Vecchie. McAndrew, 378; Samona, illustration 18. See also Goy, *Venice: The City and Its Architecture*, 61.

32. Modern visitors can still see a portion of the Rio Batario that formerly separated the two islands making up the original San Marco district by following the directions in note 2 to Chapter Two.

33. Schulz, "La piazza medievale di San Marco," 142–44; Schulz, "Urbanism in Medieval Venice," 434; Borsook, 32, 34.

34. Goy, *Venice: The City and Its Architecture*, 61–62; Lauritzen, *Venice: A Thousand Years*, 40–41; Schulz, "Urbanism in Medieval Venice," 432–34, 439–40; Schulz, "La piazza medievale di San Marco," 134–36, 138–39, 141–42, 145–49; Goy, *Building Renaissance Venice*, 33; Mueller, "The Procurators of San Marco in the Thirteenth and Fourteenth Centuries," 113; Agazzi, 83-86, 133-35.

35. Ziani had become so rich so quickly that the phenomenon spawned a number of legendary explanations for the source of his wealth. One told of an early Ziani ancestor who returned to the family estate on the mainland after the barbarian invasions and, while digging in his cellar, unearthed a golden cow.

36. Schulz, "Urbanism in Medieval Venice," 432; Schulz, "La piazza medievale di San Marco," 134–43; Agazzi, 84-85, 120, 133.

37. Deborah Howard, "Civic and Religious Architecture in Gothic Venice," *Venice Art and Architecture*, 1:122; Agazzi, 84, 135-37.

38. Lauritzen, *Venice: A Thousand Years*, 40–41; Goy, *Venice: The City and Its Architecture*, 61; Schulz, "La piazza medievale di San Marco," 137, 151 (fn. 29); Umberto Franzoi, "Per

la storia del Palazzo: origini e sviluppi," *Palazzo Ducale storia e restauri*, ed. Giandomenico Romanelli (Verona: Arsenale Editrice, 2004), 81–82; Howard, "Civic and Religious Architecture in Gothic Venice," 122; Agazzi, 140-41.

39. Peter Lauritzen and Alexander Zielcke, *Palaces of Venice* (London: Dorset Press, 1978), 34–35; Lauritzen, *Venice: A Thousand Years*, 41; Goy, *Venice: The City and Its Architecture*, 61; Howard, *The Architectural History of Venice*, 34; James. S. Ackerman, *Distance Points: Essays in Theory and Renaissance Art and Architecture* (Cambridge, Mass.: MIT Press, 1994), 310–16; James S. Ackerman, *Palladio* (Baltimore: Penguin Books, 1966), 45; Dorigo, "Venetia Before Venice," 78; Alvise Zorzi, *Venetian Palaces* (New York: Rizzoli, 1989), 42; Agazzi, 84.

40. Krautheimer, *Early Christian and Byzantine Architecture, 347–48*; Maclagan, 44–46; Diehl, *Constantinople*, 39–40; Freely, *The Companion Guide to Istanbul*, 94–95; Robert S. Nelson, *Hagia Sophia, 1850–1950* (Chicago and London: University of Chicago Press, 2004), 2, which contains a reconstruction drawing of the Bucoleon Place and the entire Augusteum complex done in 1934 by Charles Vogt. The drawing is taken from Albert Vogt's *Le livre des ceremonies*, vol. 1, pt. 2 (Paris, 1967); Sherrard, 42–43, 52; Barter, 49.

Although the Blachernae Palace in the northwestern corner of the capital replaced the Bucoleon Palace and the larger Imperial Palace complex as the emperor's chief residence after 1081, the Bucoleon was evidently still in good physical shape as late as 1204. After the conquest of Constantinople by the warriors of the Fourth Crusade in April of that year, Boniface of Montferrat, a leader of the Crusade, who could have had his pick of the magnificent accommodations then available to the victorious Franks, immediately seized the Bucoleon as his own living quarters in the expectation that he would soon be elected emperor of the new Latin Empire of Byzantium. Although Boniface was disappointed in his imperial ambitions, only a month later, the Bucoleon did become the departure point for Baldwin of Flanders' imperial coronation procession to Haghia Sophia, as well as the site of the post-coronation banquet. Phillips, xi, 258, 274. We also know that from 1204 to 1261, the Crusader emperors of Constantinople made the Bucoleon Palace their principal residence. However, according to the Greeks who reconquered the city in 1261, the palace was practically in ruins at this point. Freely and Cakmak, *Byzantine Monuments of Istanbul*, 248, 251–52.

Notes to Chapter Six

1. Following the almost universal practice of those who write histories about medieval Europe, in this book, the noun Frank and the adjective Frankish will be used to refer collectively to Crusader knights and common soldiers from France, Flanders, Italy, the German Empire, and other parts of Western Europe.

2. Queller and Madden, 6–9; Phillips, 55, 57–58; Oldenbourg, 3, 16.

3. Phillips, 1–3, 13, 21, 52–54; Madden, *Enrico Dandolo*, 119; Oldenbourg, 464–68, 616-617; Queller and Madden, 4–7, 52; Diehl, *Byzantium*, 191–92.

After Saladin's Saracen army took Jerusalem in 1187, the chivalry he displayed to its Christian inhabitants threw into conspicuous relief the brutal murder of virtually every Muslim and Jew in the Holy City perpetrated by the soldiers of the First Crusade almost a century earlier. In addition, after taking Acre during the Third Crusade, Richard I of England (known as the Lionhearted), in haste to arrive at Jerusalem, directed the methodical butchery of three thousand unarmed Muslim warriors in front of the city walls.

4. Geoffrey de Villehardouin, *The Conquest of Constantinople*, trans. Margaret Shaw (London: Penguin Books, 1963), 32–33; Queller and Madden, 9–11, 14–17, 70; Phillips, 58–62, 65; Madden, *Enrico Dandolo*, 122–24, 127, 131.

Villehardouin's chronicle of the events of the Fourth Crusade is one of the principal firsthand sources on which our knowledge of this episode is based. It is a clear, unself-conscious account by a military chieftain from one of the leading centers of Crusader enthusiasm and, as such, offers an almost perfectly transparent view into the mental and emotional processes of Frankish chivalry at the beginning of the thirteenth century.

5. Oldenbourg, 609–10; Queller and Madden, 4–7, 16, 33, 37, 42–43, 46; Madden, *Enrico Dandolo*, 121–22; Phillips, 1–3, 10–12, 66.

6. Villehardouin, 33–35; Madden, *Enrico Dandolo*, 125–27; Queller and Madden, 1, 16–17, 20, 44; Phillips, 62–66, 76.

7. Madden, *Enrico Dandolo*, 78, 111–13, 117–18, 123, 128–30; Queller and Madden, 11, 17, 56–59, 73, 78; Phillips, 61–62, 66, 70–72, 111; Lane, 24, 37, 60, 62–65.

8. Lane, 37; Queller and Madden, 22, 56-59, 73, 78; Madden, *Enrico Dandolo*, 16, 111-113, 128-29, 135, 142.

9. Madden, *Enrico Dandolo*, 131; Queller and Madden, 23, 25–26, 46–52; Phillips, 66, 78–81, 99, 106, 108.

10. Phillips, 48, 67; Marc Bloch, F*eudal Society*, vols. 1 and 2, trans. L. A. Manyon (Chicago: University of Chicago Press, 1974), 73–75, 293–94, 443.

11 Tuchman, *A Distant Mirror*, 16.

12. Oldenbourg, 33, 36; Bloch, 293–95, 311; Lane, 37.

13. Queller and Madden, 17, 44, 58–61, 68–70; Madden, *Enrico Dandolo*, 130, 136–37, 141, 244–45 (fn. 70), 248 (fn. 47); Phillips, 75–76, 106.

14. Queller and Madden, 28–30, 33–36, 46, 64, 82–83, 227; Madden, *Enrico Dandolo*, 142, 146–48; Phillips, 82–85, 90–91, 127–29; Villehardouin, 50.

The religious rupture between the Greek East and the Roman West, which had widened in the ninth to twelfth centuries, had several principal causes, but at its heart was a refusal by the Eastern Church to agree that the pope in Rome had unilateral authority to resolve important doctrinal disputes. The intense emotions felt by the warring theological factions, which often turned on the precise metaphysical relation of Christ to God the Father, was particularly strong in the Byzantine East. To the Greeks, therefore, it was absurd to allow such fundamental issues to be determined by the accident of which Italian prelate happened to be the Bishop of Rome at any given moment.

The Greeks believed that conflicts among the faithful were too important to be settled by anything less than a full council of leading clerics from every part of Christendom, where the pope would be, at most, a first among equals. As precedent, they pointed to the early history of Christianity. Beginning in the fourth century, when such controversies arose (usually as a result of theological speculation originating in the East), they had generally been settled by ecumenical councils convened by a Roman emperor ruling from an Eastern city.

For instance, the First Ecumenical Council of 325 was called by Emperor Constantine the Great at Nicæa in northern Asia Minor to deal with the Arian heresy, a monotheist view that refused to accept the full divinity of Christ. A subsequent convocation, the Fourth Ecumenical Council, held in 451 in Chalcedon (just across the Bosporus from Constantinople), reestablished doctrinal consistency regarding the nature of Christ within the two halves of the old Roman Empire and bestowed the title of Patriarch on the Bishop of Constantinople, thereby expressly rejecting the supremacy of the pope in doctrinal matters within the Eastern Empire. These early councils were more heavily attended by Eastern than Western bishops, since at this time and for many centuries to come, Italy was desperately trying to defend itself from repeated barbarian invasions.

In the midst of this Western power vacuum, the sixth-century Roman emperor Justinian declared the Eastern Church in Constantinople to be superior to all other Christian sees, including Rome. When Justinian's generals finally conquered Gothic Italy after several bloody campaigns, he and his successors for the next two centuries made certain that the Bishop of Rome understood that he was now nothing more than an imperial subject. Popes who did not willingly submit were hounded, imprisoned, deported, and occasionally placed under a threat of death.

However, all of this changed when Byzantine power in Italy waned in the eighth century. Popes not only reasserted their spiritual authority within Western Europe, they began to exercise temporal rule over former Byzantine possessions in Italy and to look for opportunities to project their power into Eastern religious quarrels. Naturally, such new political realities were poorly received in the East. To the Greeks, a medieval pope was a rebel against lawful authority who had treacherously seized lands belonging to his master, the Greek emperor. Diehl, *Byzantium*, 214. In 1054, resistance by the Patriarch of Constantinople to continued papal intrusions in Eastern religious affairs finally led to an open break. Papal legates seized the pulpit of Haghia Sophia to deliver a formal Bull of Excommunication against the Eastern Church, and the Greek hierarchy responded with its own spiritual banishment of Rome.

This open hostility only increased when Westerners and Greeks began to find themselves in physical contact with each other during the Crusades of the late eleventh and twelfth centuries (see the section "Western Crusaders Arrive in Constantinople" at the beginning of Chapter Five). The mutual aversion felt by the two cultures was deepened by the alien architectural and liturgical environment Latin Crusaders and pilgrims discovered when they attempted to worship in Greek churches. At home, they would have taken their place among a crowd of joyous worshippers filling the long nave of a Western cathedral. In Constantinople, they were crammed into side aisles and distant galleries, from which they watched strange ceremonies performed by a professional priesthood speaking the incomprehensible Greek language and claiming the entire church center as their exclusive prerogative. What they witnessed was not only baffling; to many, its alien forms seemed to smack of heresy. Norwich, *A Short History of Byzantium*, 259.

15. Queller and Madden, 73, 77, 95–96; Phillips, 70, 116–20; Madden, *Enrico Dandolo*, 142, 150, 158.

16. Diehl, *La République de Venise*, 54; Norwich, *A History of Venice*, 125; Queller and Madden, 84–85, 87–89, 92–93, 97–99, 106; Madden, *Enrico Dandolo*, 148–49, 112–16; Phillips, 132–35, 139.

17. Queller and Madden, 65–67, 74–76, 80–81, 86–92, 105–106; Madden, *Enrico Dandolo*, 143–45; Phillips, 116, 124.

18. Queller and Madden, 85–87, 89–92, 95–99; Colin Thubron, *The Venetians* (Alexandria, Va.: Time-Life Books, 1980), 38; Madden, *Enrico Dandolo*, 156; Phillips, 139–40.

19. Norwich, *A Short History of Byzantium*, 65–66; Maclagan, 52–62, 103; Freely, *Companion Guide to Istanbul*, 28; Villehardouin, 59; Oldenbourg, 497; Downey, 5.

20. Queller and Madden, 36, 106–108; Madden, *Enrico Dandolo*, 148; Maclagan, 76–79, 81, 93; Phillips, 158–59; John Thomson, "Castles," *Great Architecture of the World*, 109.

21. Queller and Madden, 110–14; Villehardouin, 64–65; Madden, *Enrico Dandolo*, 159.

22. In the lateen sail rigging that characterized Venetian ships, the cross-spars were attached to the mast in a very flexible manner so that a yardarm with an unfurled sail typically hung down diagonally.

23. Queller and Madden, 116–19, 122; Phillips, 168–74; Freely, *Companion Guide to Istanbul*, 219.

24. Queller and Madden, 116–18, 120–21; Phillips, 40–41, 166–71; Tuchman, *A Distant Mirror*, 65; Freely, *Companion Guide to Istanbul*, 214, 217; Downey, 6; Freely and Cakmak, *Byzantine Monuments of Istanbul*, 73–74, 231; Turnbull, 8, 50–51.

    The tower of Isaac II Angelus (a projecting structure with three windows whose roofline rises a modest distance above the surrounding walls) has survived and can still be seen today approximately 850 feet south of the Golden Horn.

25. Queller and Madden, 122–25; Phillips, 172–76; Madden, *Enrico Dandolo*, 160–62; Thomas F. Madden, "The Fires of the Fourth Crusade in Constantinople, 1203–1204: A Damage Assessment," *Byzantinische Zeitschrift* 84/85 (1992): 73–74.

26. Queller and Madden, 114, 122–28; Phillips, 172–81; Madden, *Enrico Dandolo*, 160–62.

27. Queller and Madden, 128–34, 136; Phillips, 180–84.

28. Queller and Madden, 140–42, 144–46; Phillips, 200–203, 206–208, 214; Madden, *Enrico Dandolo*, 164; Madden, "The Fires of the Fourth Crusade," 74–89, 93.

29. Queller and Madden, 146, 185; Phillips, 208–10; Madden, *Enrico Dandolo*, 164; Paspates and Metcalfe, 32–43; Madden, "The Fires of the Fourth Crusade," 83–89; Christopher Hibbert, *London, the Biography of a City* (Harmondsworth, England: Penguin Books Ltd, 1969), 68.

30. Queller and Madden, 152–58, 163–65, 168–70, 173–75; Phillips, 216–19, 223–25, 227, 233–34; Madden, *Enrico Dandolo*, 164–68; Jan Morris, *The Venetian Empire: A Sea Voyage* (New York and London: Harcourt Brace Jovanovich, 1980), 43; Madden, "The Fires of the Fourth Crusade," 84.

31. Queller and Madden, 175–76; Phillips, 238–40; Madden, *Enrico Dandolo*, 169–71.

32. Queller and Madden, 177–85; Phillips, 236–37, 242–55; Madden, *Enrico Dandolo*, 171–72; Madden, "The Fires of the Fourth Crusade," 84–85, 93; Freely and Cakmak, *Byzantine Monuments of Istanbul*.

33. Queller and Madden, 185–92, 196, 198–99; Phillips, 255–57, 267; Madden, *Enrico Dandolo*, 173; Madden, "The Fires of the Fourth Crusade," 88; Nicol, 143; Freely and Cakmak, *Byzantine Monuments of Istanbul*, 247; Villehardouin, 92; Goldthwaite, *Wealth and the Demand for Art in Italy*, 151–55; Phillips, 258–59.

34. Queller and Madden, 193–95, 198, 291 (fn. 19); Phillips, 259–63, 279; Madden, *Enrico Dandolo*, 273; Freely and Cakmak, *Byzantine Monuments of Istanbul*, 32–35, 38, 41, 66–67, 146, 247; *Eyewitness Travel Guides, Istanbul*, 116.

35. Queller and Madden, 195–96; Phillips, 279–80; Madden, *Enrico Dandolo*, 173.

36. Queller and Madden, 108, 199–200; Phillips, 268; Madden, *Enrico Dandolo*, 173; Nicol, 183.

Notes to Chapter Seven

1. Madden, *Enrico Dandolo*, 174–78, 193–94, 259 (fn. 12), 266 (fn. 145); Nelson, 3; Queller and Madden, 201–203; Phillips, 270–74; Norwich, *A History of Venice*, 140–42; Nicol, 144–45; Freely and Cakmak, *Byzantine Monuments of Istanbul*, 249.

   Dandolo's tomb was probably located in Haghia Sophia's south gallery, near the spot where a small, light-brown floor stone (perhaps part of a sarcophagus lid) bearing his name in Latin can be seen by modern visitors. The tomb remained in place until the conquest of Constantinople by the Ottoman Turks in 1453 when Haghia Sophia became a mosque; the Turks no doubt unceremoniously disposed of whatever they found buried in the tomb. In spite of all he accomplished on behalf of the Republic, Dandolo was never honored with a major monument within the city of Venice.

2. Madden, *Enrico Dandolo*, 188–89; Norwich, *A History of Venice*, 140–42, 148; Nicol, 141-42, 149–50, 163; Freely and Cakmak, *Byzantine Monuments of Istanbul*, 249.

3. Lane, 68–69.

4. Madden, *Enrico Dandolo*, 193–94; Norwich, *A History of Venice*, 141–42; Demus, *The Church of San Marco in Venice*, 19.

5. Madden, *Enrico Dandolo*, 173–74; Nicol, 184.

6. Goldthwaite, *The Building of Renaissance Florence*, 212–14, 216, 218; Lanciani, 33–34; Freely and Cakmak, *Byzantine Monuments of Istanbul*, 112.

7. Madden, *Enrico Dandolo*, 196; Norwich, *A History of Venice*, 149–50; Nicol, 153; Freely and Cakmak, *Byzantine Monuments of Istanbul*, 251–52; Madden, "The Fires of the Fourth Crusade," 78, 80, 82, 88, 90–92.

   Although the Venetians and Franks made little, if any, effort to maintain the portions of Constantinople that survived the three Crusader fires, relatively few buildings seem to have been deliberately destroyed during the Latin occupation, as is often alleged. The Franks had no interest in erecting new architecture in the Greek capital and, thus, no incentive to cannibalize existing structures for that purpose. Moreover, the work of demolishing a stone building was a hard, physically exhausting task, something that feudal warriors were not likely to undertake unless there was an immediate financial payoff. It is also relevant that the number of Franks in Constantinople fell dramatically after the conquest as thousands of Latin knights and soldiers returned home to Europe. Consequently, the Latin Empire of the East, perpetually short of even the minimum amount of manpower required to hold onto its territorial conquests, was hardly inclined to engage in strenuous feats of motiveless demolition.

As for the Venetians, when they mined Constantinople for architectural stone, they concentrated their efforts not on wholesale destruction but on selecting and removing the very finest specimens for reuse within the confines of Venice, principally in the Piazza San Marco.

Still, it is undeniable that Constantinople lost an enormous amount of ancient architecture after 1204, including the almost total elimination aboveground of great monuments such as the Imperial Palace and the adjoining Hippodrome, both of which we know survived the Crusader invasion fires essentially intact. Rather than deliberate destruction by the Crusaders, two factors seem to have been at work: (1) the natural effects of gravity and decay when allowed to work on large unmaintained structures, compounded by the destructive force of earthquakes and the four additional fires that occurred during the half century of Latin occupation, and (2) the demolition of buildings and reuse of architectural materials by the Ottoman Turks after their conquest of Constantinople in 1453. Unlike the Franks, the Ottomans were major builders with an enormous need for architectural spoil, and it only makes sense that they would have helped themselves to the antique building materials that remained.

For instance, the Turks demolished Justinan's great Apostoleion church and used its building fragments as material for the construction of the mosque complex of Mehmet the Conqueror. In addition, the antique columns that surround the courtyard of the great Suleymaniye Mosque built between 1550 and 1557 for Sultan Suleyman I by the brilliant Turkish architect Sinan are said to have been taken from the Byzantine emperor's royal box (the *kathisma*) in the Hippodrome. It is also almost certain that stone from the Hippodrome and the Imperial Palace were used to construct the adjoining Blue Mosque of Sultan Ahmet I, a magnificent temple built by the imperial architect Mehmet Aga between 1609 and 1616. There must have also been many other undocumented acts of Ottoman architectural cannibalization. In fact, it was only Mehmet the Conqueror's immediate transformation of Haghia Sophia into a mosque which prevented that magnificent edifice from suffering the fate of other imperial monuments. Freely, *The Companion Guide to Istanbul*, 147; Gilles, 51–52, 67–68, 83–84, 95–97; Paspates and Metcalfe, 56, 70, 106; Freely and Cakmak, *Byzantine Monuments of Istanbul*, 30, 54, 151, 296–98; Maclagan, 125, 136; *Eyewitness Travel Guides, Istanbul* (New York: DK Publishing, Inc., 2004), 78–79, 90–91.

8. Schulz, "La piazza medievale di San Marco," 137–38, 150 (fn. 14); Schulz, "Urbanism in Medieval Venice," 421, 432; McAndrew, 378; Samona et al., illustration 18; Norwich, *A History of Venice*, 114; Concina, *A History of Venetian Architecture*, 47–48; Madden, "The Fires of the Fourth Crusade," 75.

9. Ruskin, *The Stones of Venice*, 2:67.

10. Schulz, "Urbanism in Medieval Venice," 432–33, 439–41; Schulz, "La piazza medievale di San Marco," 136–39, 141–42; Ruskin, *The Stones of Venice*, 2:67, 2:142, 2:233; Umberto Franzoi, "Per la storia del Palazzo: origini e sviluppi," 81–82; Howard, "Civic and Religious Architecture in Gothic Venice," 122; Agazzi, 84, 120, 123, 135-37.

11. Goldthwaite, *Wealth and the Demand for Art in Italy*, 180; Schulz, "La piazza medievale di San Marco," 136, 138–39, 141–42, 145; Schulz, "Urbanism in Medieval Venice," 434; Agazzi, 137.

Filippo Brunelleschi (1377–1446), one of the greatest architects who ever lived, was a Florentine whose most famous achievement was the design and construction of the great dome of the Florentine Cathedral. His other masterpieces, such as the Innocenti foundling hospital, the churches of San Lorenzo and San Spirito, and the Pazzi chapel, all in Florence, exhibit a precise symmetrical order based on mathematically proportioned spatial units and his own personal repertoire of classically derived architectural forms.

12. Schulz, "Urbanism in Medieval Venice," 432, 434; Lane, 90; Schulz, "La piazza medievale di San Marco," 142–43; Demus, *The Church of San Marco in Venice*, 53; Goy, *Building Renaissance Venice*, 33; Agazzi, 85-86.

13. Mueller, "The Procurators of San Marco in the Thirteenth and Fourteenth Centuries," 108, 113; Schulz, "Urbanism in Medieval Venice," 436; Schulz, "La piazza medievale di San Marco," 138, 140–41, 145; Richard J. Goy, *The House of Gold* (Cambridge: Cambridge University Press, 1992), 32.

14. Lorenzo Lazzarini, "Le pietre e i marmi colorati della basilica di san marco a venezia," *Storia dell'arte marciana: l'architettura*, 312–13; Irene Favaretto, Ettore Vio, Simonetta Minguzzi, and Maria Da Villa Urbani, eds., *Marmi della Basilica di San Marco* (Venezia: Rizzoli, 2000), 77; Giorgio Ortolani, "Lavorazione di pietre e marmi nel mondo antico," *Marmi antichi*, ed. Gabriele Borghini (Roma: Edizioni De Luca, 1998), 31–32; Patrizio Pensabene, "Amministrazione dei marmi e sistema distributive nel mondo romano," *Marmi antichi*, 43; Rice, 217–18, 221; Michael Grant, *The Art and Life of Pompeii and Herculaneum* (New York: Newsweek, 1979), 15, 152; Anna Maria Librati and Fabio Bourbon, *Ancient Rome, History of a Civilization that Ruled the World* (New York: Barnes & Noble Books, 2004), 164, 211, 241, 246–47; Lauritzen, *Venice: A Thousand Years*, 81; Rudolf Wittkower, *Architectural Principles in the Age of Humanism* (New York and London: W. W. Norton, 1971), 9.

15. Warren, "The First Church," 337; Krautheimer, *Early Christian and Byzantine Architecture*, 407; George Mitchell, ed., *Architecture of the Islamic World* (London: Thames & Hudson, 1978), 143; Ross King, *Brunelleschi's Dome: How a Renaissance Genius Reinvented Architecture* (New York: Walker, 2000), 10; Samona et al., illustration 18.

Visitors to the museum on the second story of the Basilica will find fascinating, extremely informative wooden models of the various stages of the church's architectural transformation, including its thirteenth-century widening and heightening. Photographs of these models can be found in Ettore Vio's "Il cantiere marciano: Tradizione e techniche," *Scienza e Technica del Restauro della Basilica di San Marco*, eds. Ettore Vio and Anthony Lepschy (Venezia: Instituto Veneto di Scienze, Lettere ed Arti, 1999), 101, 104–105, 522–26.

16. *The Stones of Venice*, 2:83.

17. Demus, *The Church of San Marco in Venice*, 54; Lazzarini, "Le pietre e i marmi colorati della basilica di san marco a venezia," *Storia dell'arte marciana: l'architettura*, 314; Simonetta Minguzzi, "Aspetti della decorazione marmorea e architettonica della basilica di San Marco," *Marmi della Basilica di San Marco*, 31, 33.

18. Demus, *The Church of San Marco in Venice*, 148–63, 165.

19. Demus, *The Church of San Marco in Venice*, 149-150; H. W. Janson, *History of Art* (Englewood Cliffs, N. J.: Prentice-Hall, Inc., 1982), 298; Rice, 217–18, 221.

20. Demus, *The Church of San Marco in Venice*, 114, 140–43, 168–70; Giovanni Lorenzoni, "Byzantine Heritage, Classicism, and the Contribution of the West in the Thirteenth and Fourteenth Centuries," *Venice Art and Architecture*, 1:103.

21. Edmund Burke, *Reflections on the Revolution in France* (New York: Library of America, 1955), 196–97.

22. Demus, *The Church of San Marco in Venice*, 147, 155, 163–66, 177, 179, 181.

23. Michael Jacoff, *The Horses of San Marco and the Quadriga of the Lord* (Princeton, N.J.: Princeton University Press, 1993), 6–9; Demus, *The Church of San Marco in Venice*, 83–85.

24. Jacoff, 79–82; Schulz, "Urbanism in Medieval Venice," 439; Freely and Cakmak, *Byzantine Monuments of Istanbul*, 27.

25. Diehl, *Constantinople*, 44; Jacoff, 5–6; Freely and Cakmak, *Byzantine Monuments of Istanbul*, 16; Vittorio Galliazzo, *I Cavalli di San Marco* (Treviso: Edizioni Canova), 68–69; Licia Vlad Borrelli, "The Horses of St. Mark's," *The Basilica of St. Mark in Venice*, 70–75; Michael Jacoff, "The Horses of St. Mark's," *St. Mark's: The Art and Architecture of Church and State in Venice*, 108–109; Freeman, 8, 10, 59–60.

26. Jacoff, 6–9, 11, 99; Demus, *The Church of San Marco in Venice*, 114; Nicol, 183–84; Madden, *Enrico Dandolo*, 173; Freeman, 89, 175, 184, 263.

27. Jacoff, 12–22, 4–35, 48, 75, 109; Freeman, 99–101.

28. Jacoff, 98–99; Rice, 146; Krautheimer, *Three Christian Capitals*, 49–50; Barter, 75–79; Diehl, *Constantinople*, 45; Downey, 38–40.

29. Goy, *Venice: The City and Its Architecture*, 70–72; Schulz, "Urbanism in Medieval Venice," 434–35; McAndrew, 403; Norwich, *A History of Venice*, 158; Jacoff, 98–99.

30. There are at least three distinct opinions about when the new Molo quay was added to the Piazzetta. According to the most recent scholarship, it was constructed shortly after 1280, and the two Molo columns and the Winged Lion were in place by 1283. Schulz, "La piazza medievale di San Marco," 137–38, 152 (fns. 33 and 36); Agazzi, 137. Others have traced this important alteration to the middle of the thirteenth century. Jacoff, 92–9. The traditional view has been that the project commenced in the 1170s under Doge Sebastiano Ziani. Goy, *Venice: The City and Its Architecture*, 61–62; Lauritzen, *Venice: A Thousand Years*, 40; Concina, *A History of Venetian Architecture*, 47–48.

31. Brown, *Venice & Antiquity*, 18–19; Schulz, "La piazza medievale di San Marco," 146; Schulz, "Urbanism in Medieval Venice," 433–34; *Knopf Guide to Venice*, 251; Lorenzetti, 150; Debra Pincus, *The Arco Foscari: The Building of a Triumphal Gateway in Fifteenth Century Venice* (New York and London: Garland Publishing, Inc., 1976), 385–89; Norwich, *A History of Venice*, 118. The story of Doge Michiel's decision to lead the shattered, plague-ridden Venetian fleet back to the lagoon after failing to free the Venetian hostages held by Emperor Manuel Comnenus is recounted in Chapter Five in the section "The Collapsing Byzantine Alliance."

    The statue of Saint Theodore now in place at the top of the Molo pillar is a copy. The original is available for close inspection along the northern wall of the Ducal Palace courtyard.

32. Maclagan, 65; Diehl, *Constantinople*, 23; Schulz, "Urbanism in Medieval Venice," 438–39; Lane, 233; Norwich, *A History of Venice*, 355.

33. The Sea Gate functioned as the main entrance to the Basilica until its grand portal was closed off in 1501 to create a private chapel dedicated to Cardinal Giovanni Battista Zen, the pope's nephew.

34. Demus, *The Church of San Marco in Venice*, 14, 56; Demus, *The Mosaic Decoration of San Marco, Venice*, 30, 179–81; Jacoff, 43–45; Antonio Niero, "St. Mark: A Biographical Profile," *The Basilica of St. Mark in Venice*, 18.

    The præstinatio or predestination legend took its earliest written form in Martino da Canale's *Estoires de venise* (1275). Its codification in a handful of Latin words inscribed on the pages of an open book held by the Winged Lion of Venice, a symbol copied thousands of times throughout the city, is explained in Chapter Two at the end of the section "The Theft of Saint Mark". The image of the Winged Lion has been memorably captured in a famous painting by Vittore Carpaccio *(Fig. 8)* that is now in the Sala Grimani of the ducal apartments located in the east wing of the Ducal Palace.

    Only one of the original thirteenth-century mosaic paintings installed over the Basilica's five western portals has survived. The far left portal of Sant'Alipio, which contains a vividly colored, strikingly realistic depiction of the western front of San Marco as it appeared around 1265, has remained intact from that date to the present. To understand how the other western portal mosaics appeared in the thirteenth century, one must visit Gentile Bellini's great 1496 oil painting *The Corpus Domini Procession in Piazza San Marco* in the Accademia picture gallery.

35. Antonio Niero, "The Genesis Mosaics in the Narthex," *Saint Mark's: The Art and Architecture of Church and State in Venice*, 258–59, 262–63, 270–74, 278; Demus, *The Church of San Marco in Venice*, 179.

    The mosaics of the western narthex described in the last two paragraphs of Chapter Seven are still in place and available to the modern visitor.

Notes to Chapter Eight

1. Schulz, "La piazza medievale di San Marco," 136; Schulz, "Urbanism in Medieval Venice," 434; Georgina Masson, *The Companion Guide to Rome* (Bury St. Edmunds, England: St. Edmundsbury Press, 1998), 307; McAndrew, 378, 403.

2. Norwich, *A History of Venice*, 155, 159–60, 164–66; Norwich, *A Short History of Byzantium*, 316–17; Nicol, 163, 177–79, 182; Lane, 68–70.

3. Norwich, *A Short History of Byzantium*, 316, 318–19; Norwich, *A History of Venice*, 160–63; Nicol, 177–82, 188–93; Charles Diehl, "La Colonie Venitienne à Constantinople," *Etudes Byzantines* (New York: Burt Franklin, 1963), 243–45; Lane, 76–79, 127.

4. Lane, 73, 76–79, 82–83; Norwich, *A History of Venice*, 160–62, 175–76.

5. Lane, 83–85, 129, 163; Norwich, *A History of Venice*, 176–77, 179–80, 202.

    Among the five thousand Venetian prisoners from the battle of Curzola, there was one who spent his year in a Genoese cell dictating a work that would come to be known as the

Travels of Marco Polo; it recounted the writer's adventures as a much younger man when he had traveled extensively through thirteenth-century China. Polo had been seventeen when he left Venice as a companion to his father and uncle, merchant adventurers who had agreed to undertake a papal mission to the great Mongol ruler Kublai Khan. It took the Venetians four years to make the three-thousand-mile trip over high mountains and vast deserts before reaching the Mongol capital of Peking. After spending a quarter century in Khan's service, during which Marco, at least, toured much of the Mongol Empire, the three Polos were finally allowed to return to Venice, where their descriptions of Khan's wealth and the Mongols' advanced knowledge of certain arts and sciences were at first received as patent fabrications. Lane, 79–82; Norwich, *A History of Venice*, 177–79.

6. Lane, 84–85; Paul Johnson, *The Renaissance: A Short History* (New York: Modern Library, 2000), 27–28; John Ciardi, Introduction to his translation of *Dante's Inferno* (New Brunswick, N. J.: Rutgers University Press, 1954), xix–xx; Hibbert, *Florence*, 30–34; Lewis, 29; John Julius Norwich, *The Middle Sea* (New York: Doubleday, 2006), 196; McCarthy, *The Stones of Florence*, 64–65.

   In the *Paradisio*, the third book of his *Divine Comedy*, Dante reflects on the final nineteenth years of his life as a Florentine exile by reminding his readers "how salty tastes another man's bread, and how hard a path it is to go up and down another's stairs." Ciardi, Introduction to his translation of the *Inferno*, xx.

7. Lane, 104; Norwich, *A History of Venice*, 181–82; Norwich, *The Middle Sea*, 195–96, 219–21; Tuchman, *A Distant Mirror*, 64.

8. Crouzet-Pavan, 212; Norwich, *A History of Venice*, 164–65, 173–74, 186–89; Lane, 114.

9. Lane, 96, 100, 114, 208; Crouzet-Pavan, 203–204; Norwich, *A History of Venice*, 109, 164–65, 184; Gerhard Rosch, "The Serrata of the Great Council and Venetian Society, 1286–1323," *Venice Reconsidered, the History and Civilization of an Italian State 1297–1797*, eds. John Martin and Dennis Romano (Baltimore and London: The Johns Hopkins University Press, 2000), 72, 78–79; Umberto Franzoi, "Per la storia del Palazzo: origini e sviluppi," *Palazzo Ducale storia e restauri*, ed. Giandomenico Romanelli (Verona: Arsenale Editrice, 2004), 83; Howard, "Civic and Religious Architecture in Gothic Venice," 122; Manfred Schuller, "Il Palazzo Ducale di Venezia. Le Facciate Medievali," *L'architettura Gotica Veneziana*, eds. Francesco Valcanover and Wolfgang Wolters (Venezia: Istituto Veneto di Scienze, Lettere ed Arti, 2000), 353.

10. Norwich, *A History of Venice*, 183–84; Lane, 111–14, 208; Crouzet-Pavan, 213; Franzoi, 83; Howard, "Civic and Religious Architecture in Gothic Venice," 122; Schuller, "Il Palazzo Ducale di Venezia," 353.

11. Lane, 100, 114; J. R. Hale, *Florence and the Medici* (London: Phoenix Press, 1977), 18; Lewis, 33, 92; Goldthwaite, *The Building of Renaissance Florence*, 1; Larner, 238.

12. Lane, 109–11.

13. Ibid., 110–11; Norwich, *A History of Venice*, 166.

14. Lane, 129–31, 145, 163–64; Norwich, *A History of Venice*, 240, 272; McAndrew, 88; Benjamin Z. Kedar, *Merchants in Crisis, Genoese and Venetian Men of Affairs and the Fourteenth Century Depression* (New Haven and London: Yale University Press, 1976), 47–49.

15. Norwich, *A History of Venice*, 155; Lane, 147, 150–51.

16. Lane, 151; Norwich, *A History of Venice*, 184; Rosch, 80; James Cushman Davis, *The Decline of the Venetian Nobility as a Ruling Class* (Baltimore: The Johns Hopkins University Press, 1962), 36–37; Howard, *The Architectural History of Venice*, 74.

    Norwich estimates that there were 1,212 members of the Great Council in 1340 (*A History of Venice*, 184), and Rosch (80) states that this number was reduced to 897 by the great plague epidemic of 1348–1350. Given this twenty-five percent mortality rate among the patriciate at mid-century, it seems unlikely that the ranks of the governing nobility would have numbered much more than twelve hundred three decades later, in 1379. Thus, Davis' assumption (37) that there were two thousand patricians in 1379 seems excessive, particularly since the addition of thirty families for services rendered during the Fourth Genoese War did not happen until 1381. Even after this expansion, Norwich estimates that there were only fifteen hundred members of the Great Council in 1400 (*A History of Venice*, 282).

17. Norwich, *A History of Venice*, 186–95; Lane, 114–16.

18. Norwich, *A History of Venice*, 192–99, 282; Lane, 115–17.

19. Norwich, *A History of Venice*, 197, 282; Lane, 96, 185, 201; Crouzet-Pavan, 203–204; Giorgio Cracco, "Patriziato e oligarchia a Venezia nel tre-quattrocento," *Florence and Venice: Comparisons and Relations*, 1:83–84, 1:86; Robert Finlay, *Politics in Renaissance Venice* (New Brunswick, N. J.: Rutgers University Press, 1980), 39.

20. Franzoi, 95, 103; Ruskin, 2:1, 2:125.

21. Franzoi, 81–83; Norwich, *A History of Venice*, 184; Lane, 208; Howard, "Civic and Religious Architecture in Gothic Venice," 122; Crouzet-Pavan, 213; Schuller, "Il Palazzo Ducale di Venezia," 353.

22. Ruskin, 2:294–95; Norwich, *A History of Venice*, 211; Franzoi, 83–84; Schuller, "Il Palazzo Ducale di Venezia," 353.

23. While there continues to be intense scholarly debate about whether Calendario was, in fact, the architect appointed to design and oversee construction of the new Ducal Palace, the arguments presented by Wolfgang Wolters that he was and that he executed his commission brilliantly seem much more compelling than those of his opponents. At the heart of Wolters' case is the testimony of numerous early Venetian chroniclers who praise Calendario as the architect and chief sculptor of the project. Wolters argues that until someone presents a good reason for doubting these traditional sources (which has not happened), they should form the basis of modern opinion on the subject. *La sculptura veneziana gotica (1300–1460)* (Venezia: Alfieri Edizioni, 1976), 40–41. For relevant material from the chronicles to which Wolters refers, see Vittorio Lazzarini, "Filippo Calendario, l'architetto della Tradizione del Palazzo Ducale," *Nuovo Archivio Veneto*, Vol. 7 (1894), 429–46. Wolters also argues that a stylistic analysis of the building's sculptural figures strongly support the view that Calendario was the project's principal sculptor during the period 1340–1355. "Venetian Figurative Sculpture: 1300–1450," *Venice Art and Architecture*, 1:160–61. Moreover, as readers will learn in Chapter Nine, Calendario died in disgrace a half century before the Ducal Palace was completed. Why would the many early chroniclers on whom Wolter relies, whose testimony comes well after his ignominious death, unanimously refer to him

as the architect and chief sculptor of the project unless there were simply no way to deny this inconvenient truth?

Edoardo Arslan, who also relies on the same early chronicles, tends to arrive at the same conclusion as Wolters, i.e., that Calendario was the architect responsible for the Ducal Palace. *Gothic Architecture in Venice*, trans. Anne Engel (London: Phaidon Press, 1971), 152–53.

Others remain skeptical. For instance, Umberto Franzoi believes that too little is known to give Calendario the full credit that Wolters affords him, but he does agree that, at a minimum, Calendario had a high degree of responsibility for organizing the building site. "Per la storia del Palazzo: origini e sviluppi," 86. Deborah Howard is also unwilling to go as far as Wolters, but she does state that Calendario was at least the project building master. "Civic and Religious Architecture in Gothic Venice," 123.

Others take a much more negative view of the Wolters thesis. John Julius Norwich, following Ruskin's lead, specifically states that an entirely different figure, Pietro Baseggio, was the Ducal Palace architect (*A History of Venice*, 212; Ruskin, 3:199), although the oldest chronicles never mention him in that capacity. Arslan, 152–53. Lionello Puppi regards the Wolters thesis with extreme skepticism. "Geografia di un cinale. Filippo Calendario tra storia e leggenda," *L'architettura Gotica Veneziana*, 103.

Yet, in spite of this ongoing debate about Calendario's specific role, there is general agreement with Ruskin's celebrated statement (2:232) that the architectural design of the Ducal Palace was "the great and sudden invention of one man, instantly forming a national style, and becoming the model for the imitation of every architect in Venice for upwards of a century." For instance, Arslan (141, 143, 148–49) holds that the extraordinary architectural unity of the completed Ducal Palace can only be explained if it is seen as the brilliant creation of a single artistic genius whose original conception was faithfully followed over an unusually long, frequently disrupted construction period.

24. In all succeeding references, the Republic's post-1340 governing complex will be called the Ducal Palace or Doge's Palace or just Palace (employing an intentionally upper-case D and P) to distinguish it from the Ziani ducal palace and its predecessor, the ducal fortress.

25. Franzoi, 83–84; Schuller, "Il Palazzo Ducale di Venezia," 353, 415, 420; Arslan, 141, 152–53; Wolfgang Wolters, S*toria e politica nei dipinti di palazzo ducale* (Venezia: Arsenale Editrice, 1987), 16–18; Lane, 182, 208; Lauritzen, *Venice: A Thousand Years*, 67–68; Howard, "Civic and Religious Architecture in Gothic Venice," 123; Schulz, "Urbanism in Medieval Venice," 429–30, 432 (fns. 32, 40, and 52).

26. Ruskin, 1:17, 2:232.

27. Franzoi, 86, 91, 103; Goy, *The House of Gold*, 61, 77–81, 90; Wolters, *La sculptura veneziana gotica*, 45; Manfred Schuller, "Le facciate medievali: storia, costruzione, effeti cromatici," *Palazzo Ducale storia e restuari*, 234, 236; Schuller, "Il Palazzo Ducale di Venezia," 417–18; Francois Icher, *Building the Great Cathedrals* (New York: Harry N. Abrams, Inc., 1998), 86–89, 96–111.

28. Franzoi, 86, 103; Franca Marina Fresa, "Monumenti di carta, monumenti di pietra," *Palazzo Ducale storia e restuari*, 207–10, 213 (figs. 2, 3, 4, and 9); Goy, *The House of Gold*, 61, 63–64, 82, 84–86.

29. Lauritzen, *Venice: A Thousand Years*, 66; Lane, 185, 201.

30. Larner, 97–98, 103, 105, 138.

31. Franzoi, 84, 86, 95–97, 101, 103, 105, 114; Manfred Schuller, "Le facciate medievali: storia, costruzione, effeti cromatici," 234, 236; Schuller, "Il Palazzo Ducale di Venezia," 416–18; Lorenzetti, 238; Samona et al., illustration 18.

32. Schuller, "Il Palazzo Ducale di Venezia," 353; Wolters, *La sculptura veneziana gotica*, 40; Franzoi, 83, 101, 103, 105; Arslan, 142–43, 146, 148–49; Pincus, *The Arco Foscari*, 35 (fn.1); Tuchman, *A Distant Mirror*, xiii, 95; Norman Cantor, *In the Wake of the Plague: The Black Death and the World It Made* (New York: Perennial, 2001), 6, 25; Laurentis de Monacis, *Chronicon de Rebus Venetis*, trans. John Aberth (unpublished, 2006), 315; Norwich, *A History of Venice*, 184, 215–16; Larner, 124; Howard, "Civic and Religious Architecture in Gothic Venice," 122; Rosch, 80; Lauritzen, *Venice: A Thousand Years*, 70; Mario Brunetti, "Venezia durante la peste del 1348," *Ateneo Veneto 32* (May–June, 1909), No. 1:289.

Notes to Chapter Nine

1. Tuchman, *A Distant Mirror*, 24–25; Cantor, 198–99; Joan Acocella, Review of *The Great Mortality: An Intimate History of the Black Death, the Most Devastating Plague of All Time* by John Kelly, *The New Yorker*, March 21, 2005: 82–83; John Aberth, "Chapter Five: Welcome to the Apocalypse," *A Knight at the Movies, Medieval History on Film* (New York: Rutledge, 2003), 202.

2. Norwich, *A History of Venice*, 217; Lane, 128, 174–75; Tuchman, *A Distant Mirror*, xiii, 93–95, 98; Norwich, *The Middle Sea*, 208–10; Aberth, *A Knight at the Movies*, 197–98; Acocella, 82; Goy, *The House of Gold*, 5–6, 14; *Chronicon Estense cum additamentis usque ad annum 1478*, eds. Giulio Bretoni and Emilio Paolo *Vicini, Rerum Italicarum Scriptores*, XV/3 (Castello and Bologna, 1908–1937), 162; Franzoi, 106; Reinhold C. Mueller, "Peste e demografia. Mediœvo e Rinascimento," *Venezia e la peste 1348–1797*, ed. Orazio Pugliese (Venezia: Marsilio Editori, 1979), 94; Reinhold C. Mueller, "Aspetti sociali ed economici della peste a Venezia nel Medioevo," *Venezia e la peste 1348–1797*, 71–72; Acocella, 82.

3. All quoted material is from de Monacis, *Chronicon de Rebus Venetis*, trans. John Aberth, 313–14. Non-quoted information is drawn from Tuchman, *A Distant Mirror*, 92-93, Acocella, 82, and Aberth, *A Knight at the Movies*, 200–201.

4. de Monacis, 314.

5. Mueller, "Aspetti sociali ed economici della peste a Venezia nel Medioevo," 71; Lauritzen, *Venice: A Thousand Years*, 70; Giovanni Boccaccio, *The Decameron*, trans. Frances Winwar (New York; Modern Library, 1955), xxiv; Tuchman, *A Distant Mirror*, 92–93, 101; Aberth, *A Knight at the Movies*, 203; Cantor, 23; Brunetti, 1:291, 1:294.

6. This classic tale by Boccaccio (1313–1375) recounts how ten young Florentines spent their voluntary exile to a countryside retreat in the plague year of 1348. The book's preface contains a justifiably famous description of the course of the pestilence in Florence, an

account that no doubt influenced chronicles written about the epidemic in other locations, including Venice.

7. de Monacis, 314–15.

8. Tuchman, *A Distant Mirror*, xiii, 95; Cantor, 6, 25; Norwich, *A History of Venice*, 184, 215–16; Franzoi, 83; Howard, "Civic and Religious Architecture in Gothic Venice," 122; Rosch, 80; Lauritzen, *Venice: A Thousand Years*, 70; Brunetti, 1:289; Mueller, "Aspetti sociali ed economici della peste a Venezia nel Mediœvo," 72–73; Mueller, "Peste e demografia. Mediœvo e Rinascimento," 93.

9. Brunetti, 1:290, 1:301–308, 2:10, 2:14–18, 2:21, 2:24; Cracco, 1:83–86; Lane, 185; Mueller, "Peste e demografia. Medioevo e Rinascimento," 93; Arslan, 208; Wolters, *La sculptura veneziana gotica*, 40; Franzoi, 111–12; Norwich, *A History of Venice*, 184; Franzoi, 83; Howard, "Civic and Religious Architecture in Gothic Venice," 122; Rosch, 80; Mueller, "Aspetti sociali ed economici della peste a Venezia nel Medioevo," 74–75.

10. Goy, *The House of Gold*, 5–6; Mueller, "Peste e demografia. Mediœvo e Rinascimento," 93; Lane, 170, 174–79; Norwich, *A History of Venice*, 216–23, 230–31; Kedar, 15.

11. Arslan, 141, 143, 148–49; Franzoi, 111–12; Arslan, 149; Ruskin, 2: 305–307; Wolters, *La sculptura veneziana gotica*, 41–43; Wolfgang Wolters, "Venetian Figurative Sculpture: 1300–1450," *Venice Art and Architecture*, 1: 160–62, 1:173; Janson, 325.

12. Lane, 181–83, 185; Norwich, *A History of Venice*, 223–29.

13. Wolters, *La sculptura veneziana gotica*, 48; Lazzarini, 436, 438, 441; Lane, 182; Lionello Puppi, "Vischiosita della leggenda e levita della storia," *Palazzo Ducale storia e restuari*, 147.

14. Franzoi, 111–12; Ruskin, 2:296; Schuller, "Il Palazzo Ducale di Venezia," 353; Schuller, "Le facciate medievali: storia, costruzione, effeti cromatici," 237; Norwich, *A History of Venice*, 228–29, 231–33, 239; Arslan, 142; Lane, 208; Pincus, *The Arco Foscari*, 34 (fn. 1).

15. Norwich, *A History of Venice*, 243–47; Lane, 184, 186, 189–91.

16. Lane, 186, 189–91.

17. Ibid., 191–92; Norwich, *A History of Venice*, 248–49.

18. Lane, 191–92; Norwich, *A History of Venice*, 249–50.

19. Lane, 192; Norwich, *A History of Venice*, 243, 250–52; Schuller, "Il Palazzo Ducale di Venezia," 354.

20. Lane, 192–95; Norwich, *A History of Venice*, 252–54.

21. Lane, 194–95; Norwich, *A History of Venice*, 254–55.

There is a memorial to Vettor Pisani in the church of Santi Giovanni e Paolo in the district of Castello; it can be found on the right-hand wall of the first apse to the right of the central apse. However, when one compares this modest testimonial with the much larger, more artistically appealing memorials that surround it, one thought becomes inescapable: there must be an almost perfect inverse relation between the historic indispensability of the men remembered in this huge memorial church and the artistic care and expense devoted to their shrines.

22. Lane, 195–97; Norwich, *A History of Venice*, 256, 259; Mueller, "Peste e demografia. Mediœvo e Rinascimento," 93; Larner, 237–40.

23. Lane, 196–201, 252; Norwich, *A History of Venice*, 256, 259–60, 282; Rosch, 80; Diehl, *La République de Venise*, 78–79; Larner, 237–40; Mueller, "Aspetti sociali ed economici della peste a Venezia nel Mediœvo," 74–75; Kedar, 7.

24. Lane, 198, 200–201, 229; Norwich, *A History of Venice*, 260–61, 267–69, 294; Larner, 237–40; Goy, *The House of Gold*, 8.

25. Arslan, 149; Howard, "Civic and Religious Architecture in Gothic Venice," 126; Ruskin, 2:296; Samona, et al., illustration 18.

26. Howard, "Civic and Religious Architecture in Gothic Venice," 122; Concina, *A History of Venetian Architecture*, 89; Arslan, 147; Lane, 208; Hills, 60; Schuller, "Le facciate medievali: storia, costruzione, effeti cromatici," 236–37; Lorenzetti, 238; Hills, 65–68; Gattinoni, 13.

27. Honour, 45, 47; Mitchell, 13; Howard, "Civic and Religious Architecture in Gothic Venice," 127–28; Howard, *The Architectural History of Venice*, 94; Hills, 67; Geoffrey Scott, *The Architecture of Humanism: A Study in the History of Taste* (London: Constable, 1914), 81, 83; Arslan, 152; Hills, 67–68; John Pemble, *Venice Rediscovered* (Oxford and New York: Oxford University Press, 1966), 121–22.

28. Ruskin, 2:297, 2:301; Norwich, *A History of Venice*, 212, 282; Arslan, 208; Howard, "Civic and Religious Architecture in Gothic Venice," 122, 126; Janson, 307; Norwich, *A History of Venice*, 212; Rubenstein, *The Palazzo Vecchio*, 1, 5–6, 8–17; Diehl, *La République de Venise*, 128; Lane, 197; Mueller, "Peste e demografia. Mediœvo e Rinascimento," 94; Goy, *The House of Gold*, 5–6; Mueller, "Aspetti sociali ed economici della peste a Venezia nel Mediœvo," 74–75; Mueller, "Peste e demografia. Mediœvo e Rinascimento," 93–94; Norwich, *The Middle Sea*, 209; Larner, 67–70, 124–26, 128–29, 133–35, 237–40; Tuchman, *A Distant Mirror*, 96; King, *Brunelleschi's Dome*, 5–6.

29. Ruskin, 2:232.

30. Lane, 208; Goy, *Venice: the City and Its Architecture*, 63; Honour, 47; Howard, *The Architectural History of Venice*, 90, 93; *Knopf Guide to Venice*, 224; Atta Macadam, ed., *Blue Guide Venice* (London and Tonbridge: Ernest Benn, 1980), 84; Ruskin, 2:232, 2:280–81.

31. Janson, 282–97; Nikolaus Pevsner, John Fleming and Hugh Honour, *A Dictionary of Architecture* (Woodstock, N.Y.: Overlook Press, 1976), 212; Alec Clifton-Taylor, "Gothic," *Great Architecture of the World*, John Julius Norwich, ed. (New York: Random House, 1975), 115; Marilyn Stokstad, *Art History* (Upper Saddle River, N.J.: Pearson, 2005), 515; Paul Frankl, *Gothic Architecture* (New Haven and London: Yale University Press, 1962), 86, 105; Otto von Simson, *The Gothic Cathedral, Origins of Gothic Architecture and the Medieval Concept of Order* (New York: Pantheon, 1956), 3–4.

32. Ruskin, 2:239, 2:285–86; Howard, "Civic and Religious Architecture in Gothic Venice," 126; Janson, 284, 287; Howard, *The Architectural History of Venice*, 208.

33. Ruskin, 2:153–54, 2:158–62, 2:166, 2:172, 2:175–76; 2:178; Schuller, "Il Palazzo Ducale di Venezia," 416–18; Schuller, "Le facciate medievali: storia, costruzione, effeti cromatici," 234, 236.

If one wishes to see a Venetian secular building that is basically consistent with what Ruskin describes as the external forms and internal elements of Gothic architecture, one needs to turn to an opulent private residence built some years after the Ducal Palace.

Although much of the decorative vocabulary used on the Ca d'Oro palace, erected between 1421 and 1440 along the northern bank of the Grand Canal, was appropriated directly from the Ducal Palace, the result is a much more convincingly Gothic edifice. To begin with, since Marin Contarini, the patrician merchant who commissioned the project, had no need or desire to furnish his house with an extraordinarily huge upper-story room, the result is a building that follows the typical Gothic pattern of ever lighter, thinner walls as the eye moves from lower to higher levels. Also, in contrast to the state's careful oversight of the Ducal Palace project throughout a prolonged construction period, Contarini never felt it necessary to create a controlling master plan for his new residence. This meant that the teams of independent contractors hired to complete different parts of the edifice were much freer to exhibit the playful novelty and irregularity that Ruskin identified as critical Gothic characteristics. For instance, the handsome ground-floor portico and the arresting .....Gothic tracery of the two upper-story loggia screens are entirely confined to the left half of the palace front, with no attempt to impose visual symmetry across the entire facade. In addition, a close examination reveals that the Ca d'Oro displays a great deal more of the perpetual variety of ornament that Ruskin says we should expect to find in a genuinely Gothic building. Goy, *The House of Gold*, 49–57, 139–45, 148, 164–67, 174, 209–12, 261; Hills, 68–74.

34. Ruskin, 2:125, 2:285; Howard, "Civic and Religious Architecture in Gothic Venice," 123, 126; Johnson, 94; Pemble, 121–23.

35. Ruskin, 1:17.

36. Ruskin, 1:36, 1:40.

Notes to Chapter Ten

1. Ruskin, 2:297, 2:301; *Goy, The House of Gold*, 7–8; Diehl, *La République de Venise*, 85–86; Norwich, *A History of Venice*, 26, 296, 298–301; Lane, 248; Thubron, 82; Schuller, "Il Palazzo Ducale di Venezia," 354.

2. Goy, *The House of Gold*, 8; Lane, 228–29; Norwich, *A History of Venice*, 298–99, 301.

3. Norwich, *A History of Venice*, 300; Finlay, 118, 130, 133. For a description of the intricate complexity of the ducal electoral system, see the material preceding note 13 of Chapter Eight.

4. Lane, 225–26, 228–29; Norwich, *A History of Venice*, 301; Goy, *The House of Gold*, 8–10.

5. Lane, 226, 228–29; Goy, *The House of Gold*, 8–9; Martines, 164, 170–71; Norwich, *A History of Venice*, 302–303, 306, 308, 321.

6. Schuller, "Il Palazzo Ducale di Venezia," 354, 404; Samona, et al., illustration 18; Ruskin, 2:297–99; Pincus, *The Arco Foscari*, 34–36.

7. Ruskin, 2:298–300; Schuller, "Il Palazzo Ducale di Venezia," 354; Arslan, 6–7; Wolters, *Storia e politica nei dipinti di palazzo ducale*, 18–19; Pincus, *The Arco Foscari*, 34–36; Concina, *A History of Venetian Architecture*, 91–92; Demus, *The Church of San Marco in Venice*, 207.

   Those wishing to gain further insight into the character of Tommaso Mocenigo would do well to visit the Gothic tomb monument erected in his honor on the northern wall of the magnificent Dominican church of Santi Giovanni e Paolo located in the northern precincts of the Castello district *(Fig. 60)*. Carved in the 1420s by two Tuscan sculptors, Niccolò di Pietro Lamberti of Florence and Giovanni di Martino of Fiesole, this small, simple memorial sheds light not only on Mocenigo personally but on an entire generation of Venetian leaders, the men who guided the late medieval Republic back to economic and political health after the devastating blows of the fourteenth century. Looking up, we see curtains pulled apart to reveal the doge laid out in the absolute finality of death; our attention is immediately drawn to his lifeless, sunken cheeks, his fallen nose and chin. No attempt is made to disguise the fact that Mocenigo as he was in life is cold and still and gone. But however stark the image before us may be, we are moved by the knowledge that as one of his final acts, the doge had the courage to commission an effigy of himself in the very grip of death. We sense the dignity and earnestness of his life; we feel very strongly that his religious faith and deep commitment to his country made him ready for the end and left him unafraid to die.

Tommaso Mocenigo's tomb makes a vivid contrast with a wall monument designed for another member of the Mocenigo family and installed in the same church a half century later. On the wall to the right of the main entrance, there is a large marble shrine raised to the memory of Pietro Mocenigo, a Venetian general in the Turkish wars who was doge for fourteen months, before dying in 1476. Carved by Pietro Lombardo (one of the most prolific sculptors of the early Venetian Renaissance) and finished in the 1480s, the goal of this later work is to glorify the earthly accomplishments of a single vainglorious individual. Accordingly, every effort is made to avoid the physical facts of death. At the center of the composition, Pietro Mocenigo, dressed for warfare under his ducal robes, stands proudly upright as in life. Consistent with this stance of unaltered martial vigor, he is surrounded by anonymous images of youth and middle age. The work is a virtuoso demonstration of Lombardo's great gifts as a sculptor and composer of small-scale architectural ensembles, but its prevailing attitude of cold, unvarnished egotism fails to stir our emotions.

8. Demus, *The Church of San Marco in Venice*, 207; Freeman, 101; Guido Tigler, "The Gothic Decoration of the Copings," *The Basilica of St. Mark in Venice*, 66–67; Wolters, "Venetian Figurative Sculpture: 1300–1450," *Venice Art and Architecture*, 1:166–68; Hills, 63–64.

9. Ruskin, 2:68.

10. King, *Brunelleschi's Dome*, 1, 12, 19, 32–33, 41, 93, 129; Ludwig H. Heydenreich and Wolfgang Lotz, *Architecture in Italy 1400–1600* (Harmondsworth, England: Penguin Books Ltd, 1974), 5; Janson, 388; Lewis, 142–43.

11. *Henry James on Italy*, 16.

12. Ruskin, 2:71.

13. Janson, 388–89; Heydenreich and Lotz, 6-8; King, *Brunelleschi's Dome*, 33–34; Giovanni Fanelli, *Brunelleschi*, trans. Helen Cassin (Florence: Scala Instituto Fotografico Editoriale, 1980), 64; Erwin Panofsky, *Renaissance and Renascences in Western Art* (New York: Harper & Row, 1972), 123.

14. King, *Brunelleschi's Dome*, 21–25; Janson, 388–91; Howard Burns, "Quattrocento Architecture and the Antique: Some Problems," *Classical Influences on European Culture A.D. 500–1500*, ed. R. R. Bolgar (Cambridge: Cambridge University Press, 1971), 277, 283–84; Johnson, 92; Giorgio Vasari, *Lives of the Artists*, ed. Betty Burroughs (New York: Simon & Schuster, 1946), 72–73; Goldthwaite, *The Building of Renaissance Florence*, 355;

Goldthwaite, *Wealth and the Demand for Art in Italy*, 215; Hyman, "The Venice Connection: Questions about Brunelleschi and the East," 1:194–98, 1:202; Heydenreich and Lotz, 6–7, 11, 305; Paolo Fontana, *Brunelleschi and Classical Architecture*, reprinted in *Brunelleschi in Perspective*, ed. Isabelle Hyman (Englewood Cliffs, N. J.: Prentice-Hall, Inc., 1974), 1:101–104.

15. Hans Baron, *The Crisis of the Early Italian Renaissance* (Princeton, N. J.: Princeton University Press, 1966), 444–45; King, *Brunelleschi's Dome*, 23; Janson, 379; Goldthwaite, *The Building of Renaissance Florence*, 33; Lane, 305; Goy, *The House of Gold*, 8, 10; Martines, 168; Gene A. Brucker, *Renaissance Florence* (New York: John Wiley & Sons, 1969), 52, 238–39; Fanelli, 10–11; Heydenreich and Lotz, 11; Masson, 78.

16. Hyman, "The Venice Connection: Questions about Brunelleschi and the East," 1:194, 1:196–97; King, *Brunelleschi's Dome*, 10, 29–30, 52–53, 97–99.

17. Heydenreich and Lotz, 6–7, 10, 90–91; Hyman, "The Venice Connection: Questions about Brunelleschi and the East," 1:197–202.

18. Janson, 389–90; Hyman, "The Venice Connection: Questions about Brunelleschi and the East," 1:195, 1:201–202; Burns, 277; Ackerman, *The Architecture of Michelangelo*, 155; Johnson, 94; Borsook, 216–17; Goldthwaite, *The Building of Renaissance Florence*, 18–19; Fanelli, 4-5; Heydenreich and Lotz, 11; Lewis, 141–42.

19. Panofsky, 7, 10–11, 37; Roberto Weiss, *The Renaissance Discovery of Classical Antiquity* (Oxford: Basil Blackwell Ltd., 1988), 3, 31; Janson, 350–51; Johnson, 32–34.

20. Panofsky, 11–15, 18–19, 39; Janson, 350, 390; Wittkower, *Architectural Principles in the Age of Humanism*, 29, 68–69, 101–102, 104, 113, 123; Johnson, 94–97.

     However, it is important to note that as fresh and life changing as it must have seemed to fifteenth-century Italian humanists, this core Renaissance belief that true architectural beauty required man-made art objects to conform to the underlying mathematical order of the cosmos was a rediscovered, rather than a new, idea. The proper correspondence between divine macrocosm and human microcosm had been a central tenet of church design and construction throughout the preceding Gothic period; thus, a theory of strict mathematical harmony lay at the heart of Abbot Suger's plan for the abbey church of St.-Denis, widely regarded as the first Gothic building. Von Simson, xx–xxi (fn. 3); Janson, 285.

21. King, *Brunelleschi's Dome*, 156, 159.

22. Vasari, 219.

23. Janson, 380, 417–18; Hale, *Florence and the Medici*, 55; Scott, 26–27.

24. Panofsky, 10.

25. Wittkower, *Architectural Principles in the Age of Humanism*, 9.

26. Martines, 197, 206; Burckhardt, 71, 108, 114–15, 138–39, 149, 162; Goldthwaite, *Wealth and the Demand for Art in Italy*, 202; Goldthwaite, *The Building of Renaissance Florence*, 98; Lane, 218–19.

27. Hyman, "The Venice Connection: Questions about Brunelleschi and the East," 1:206; Panofsky, 41; Weiss, 20; Lane, 218–19, 311; Richard J. Goy, *Building Renaissance Venice*, 22; Felix Gilbert, "Humanism in Venice," *Florence and Venice: Comparisons and Relations*, 1: 14–21; Vittore Branca, "Ermolao Barbaro and Late Quattrocento Venetian Humanism," *Renaissance Venice*, ed. J. R. Hale (London: Faber & Faber, 1954), 220; Andrew Hopkins,

Italian Architecture from Michelangelo to Borromini (London: Thames & Hudson, 2002), 128; John Steele Gordon, A*n Empire of Wealth, the Epic History of American Economic Power* (New York: Harper Perennial, 2005), 7; Norwich, *A History of Venice*, 221, 236, 458; Lane, 180, 217; Patricia Fortini Brown, *Venice & Antiquity: The Venetian Sense of the Past* (New Haven: Yale University Press, 1997), 49, 65–66; Crouzet-Pavan, xix, 180–81; Myra Nan Rosenfeld, "Sebastiano Serlio's Contributions to the Creation of the Modern Illustrated Architectural Manual," *Sebastiano Serlio*, ed. *Christof Thoenes* (Milano: Electa, 1989), 102; Concina, *A History of Venetian Architecture*, 202; Kenneth Clark, *Civilization* (New York: Harper & Row, 1969), 145.

28. Johnson, 76–77; Janson, 387–88, 408–409; Frederick Hartt, *History of the Italian Renaissance*, 4th ed. (New York: Harry M. Abrams, 1994), 246–48, 326; Pincus, *The Arco Foscari*, 47; Lane, 233; Norwich, *A History of Venice*, 355.

29. Johnson, 120–28, 138–40; Janson, 353–57, 409–11, 411; Hartt, 395–406, 530; Panofsky, 114; William H. McNeill, *Venice: the Hinge of Europe* (Chicago: University of Chicago Press, 1974), 156; Patricia Fortini Brown, *The Renaissance in Venice, A World Apart* (London: Weidenfeld & Nicolson, 1997), 31, 48; Lane, 212; Hills, 133, 136–38; Peter Humfrey, *Painting in Renaissance Venice* (New Haven and London: Yale University Press, 1995), 4, 9, 37, 40, 64, 71–82, 108, 279.

30. Norwich, *A History of Venice*, 301, 335, 341, 352, 363, 388–89; Lane, 251–52, 268–70; Finlay, 27–29, 109, 111, 124, 196–205, 221, 226; Donald E. Queller, *The Venetian Patriciate, Reality Versus Myth* (Urbana and Chicago: University of Illinois Press, 1986), 50, 104, 168, 172–74, 179, 190, 195, 201, 250; Brown, *Venice & Antiquity*, 268.

31. Franzoi, 120; Goy, *Building Renaissance Venice*, 102, 105, 108-9; Pincus, *The Arco Foscari*, 39-45, 48-49; Concina, *A History of Venetian Architecture*, 93; Hills, 83-86; Howard, "Civic and Religious Architecture in Gothic Venice," 128-132.

32. Pincus, *The Arco Foscari*, 44, 51–53, 56, 58, 380–83, 387, 394–95; Concina, *A History of Venetian Architecture*, 93; Norwich, *A History of Venice*, 301, 334–35; McAndrew, 91; Goy, *Building Renaissance Venice*, 108, 113–14; Brown, *Venice & Antiquity*, 268.

33. Pincus, *The Arco Foscari*, 2, 8–15, 58–60, 63, 76–78, 91, 131, 141–45, 161, 186–88, 208–10, 297–98, 379, 512, 514–16, 526–27; Howard, *The Architectural History of Venice*, 123; Hills, 86–87; McAndrew, 5.

34. Pincus, *The Arco Foscari*, 12–15, 297–98, 379; Goy, *Building Renaissance Venice*, 217–22; McAndrew, 62–63, 72, 82–83, 86–87, 99; Norwich, *A History of Venice*, 362.

35. McAndrew, 83–86, 89, 232–35; Samona et al., 135; Ruskin, 3:16, 3:25; Norbert Huse and Wolfgang Wolters, *The Art of Renaissance Venice, Architecture, Sculpture and Painting* (Chicago and London: University of Chicago Press, 1990), 26–28; Goy, *Building Renaissance Venice*, 14, 151, 157; Pincus, *The Arco Foscari*, 16–17, 449, 451.

36. McAndrew, 87–89, 102.

37. McAndrew, 89–99; Goy, *Building Renaissance Venice*, 182–225; Brown, *Venice & Antiquity*, 164–66.

38. McAndrew, 87, 99–100, 105; Goy, *Building Renaissance Venice*, 223–25, 255; Pincus, *The Arco Foscari*, 380–82; Norwich, *A History of Venice*, 363, 388–89; Howard, *The Architectural History of Venice*, 124–26; Samona et al., 112; Finlay, 28–29, 111–12, 124; Brown,

Venice & Antiquity, 167–69, 268.

39. McAndrew, 99–100; Goy, *Building Renaissance Venice*, 221, 227–28; Howard, *The Architectural History of Venice*, 134; Norwich, *A History of Venice*, 388; Finlay, 25, 109, 112, 124, 220, 226; Queller, *The Venetian Patriciate*, 168, 172–74, 179, 190, 195, 201, 250.

40. McAndrew, 99–106, 112–17; Concina, *A History of Venetian Architecture*, 146.

41. McAndrew, 381–82, 384, 389, 391–92; Howard, *The Architectural History of Venice*, 146–49; Lane, 223; Goy, *Building Renaissance Venice*, 234–35, 238–39, 254; Concina, *A History of Venetian Architecture*, 148; Vittorio Polli, *Mauro Codussi, architetto bergamasco 1400–1504* (Bergamo: Edizioni Bolis, 1993), 35.

42. Goy, *Building Renaissance Venice*, 33, 233–34, 237, 240; Deborah Howard, *Jacopo Sansovino Architecture and Patronage in Renaissance Venice* (New Haven and London: Yale University Press, 1975), 8–9; Mueller, "The Procurators of San Marco in the Thirteenth and Fourteenth Centuries," 112–13; Brian Pullan, *Rich and Poor in Renaissance Venice* (Cambridge, Mass.: Harvard University Press, 1971), 210; McAndrew, 394–97, 415, 422, 510.

Notes to Chapter Eleven

1. Diehl, *La République de Venise*, 140; Lane, 241, 305; Goy, *The House of Gold*, 8–10; Norwich, *A History of Venice*, 269, 272, 280; Alberto Tenenti, "The Sense of Space and Time in the Venetian World of the Fifteenth and Sixteenth Centuries," *Renaissance Venice*, 20; Ackerman, *Distance Points*, 453–54.

2. *The Portable Machiavelli*, Peter Bondanella and Mark Musa, trans. and eds. (New York: Penguin Books, 1979), 277.

3. Kedar, 50, 58, 66; Norwich, *A History of Venice*, 269, 293–94; Thubron, 80–81.

4. Lane, 237, 306-7, 324; Finlay, 165–66; S. J. Woolf, "Venice and the Terraferma: Problems of the Change from Commercial to Landed Activities," *Crisis and Change in the Venetian Economy in the Sixteenth and Seventeenth Centuries*, Brian Pullan, ed. (London: Methuen, 1968), 181, 187; Martines, 172; Goldthwaite, *Wealth and the Demand for Art in Italy*, 22, 201, 217–18; William J. Bouwsma, *Venice and the Defense of Republican Liberty: Renaissance Values in the Age of the Counter Reformation* (Berkeley: University of California Press, 1968), 105–106; James S. Ackerman, *Palladio* (Baltimore: Penguin Books, 1966), 36, 39.

5. Hale, *Florence and the Medici*, 51, 55, 81, 155–57; Goldthwaite, *Wealth and the Demand for Art in Italy*, 164–66, 168, 192–94, 201; Ugo Tucci, "The Psychology of the Venetian Merchant in the Sixteenth Century," *Renaissance Venice*, 351–52; Burckhardt, 100–15.

6. Burckhardt, 149.

7. Demus, *The Church of San Marco in Venice*, 145; Ettore Vio, "The Porta da Mar," *The Basilica of St. Mark in Venice*, 90; Guido Tigler, "The Sculpture," *St. Mark's, the Art and Architecture of Church and State in Venice*, 184.

8. Tenenti, 25–26; Tucci, 356–57; Thubron, 101; Martines, 171–72; Bouwsma, 106; Stanley Chojnacki, "Identity and Ideology in Renaissance Venice, the Third Serrata," *Venice Reconsidered, the History and Civilization of an Italian State 1297–1797* (Baltimore and London: The Johns Hopkins University Press, 2000), 263–75; McNeill, 82; Davis, 37.

9. McNeill, 77, 80–81; Paul Kennedy, *The Rise and Fall of the Great Powers* (New York:

Random House, 1987), 9–11; Thubron, 83, 95; Norwich, *A History of Venice*, 348–52, 356–57; Lane, 236; Goy, *Venice: the City and Its Architecture*, 74–79.

10. Norwich, *A History of Venice*, 383–86; Lane, 242, 359–61; Diehl, *La République de Venise*, 176–76; Thubron, 101–13, 116.

11. Norwich, A History of Venice, 386–87; Lane, 285–94; Diehl, *La République de Venise*, 178–79; Pullan, *Rich and Poor in Renaissance Venice*, 15; McNeill, 127–29; Thubron, 165; Davis, 37.

12. McNeill, 77, 123, 125; Tenenti, 20–21, 29; Lane, 242–45, 324–25, 348–52; Tucci, 354; Norwich, *A History of Venice*, 390–402.

Amazingly, there is a large gilded monument erected to the memory of Niccolò Orsini, the count of Pitigliano, in the south transept of the church of Santi Giovanni e Paolo. This is in honor of a man whose desperation to avoid battle and obliviousness to the fate of his engaged army was responsible for the single greatest military disaster in Venetian history. It is staggering proof, if any were needed, that there is no dependable relationship between the material grandeur of a memorial shrine and the intrinsic worth of the man in whose honor it was erected.

13. Lane, 241, 245, 248, 293; Norwich, *A History of Venice*, 403–33, 438; Howard, *The Architectural History of Venice*, 149; Howard, *Jacopo Sansovino Architecture and Patronage in Renaissance Venice*, 8–9, 14; Norwich, *The Middle Sea*, 265; McNeill, 88–89, 125; Woolf, 190; Johnson, 44–46, 57, 174–75; Janson, 478–79; Pevsner, et al., *A Dictionary of Architecture*, 315; Goldthwaite, *Wealth and the Demand for Art in Italy*, 159; Kennedy, 31–36, 45–46; R. R. Palmer and Joel Colton, *A History of the Modern World* (New York: Alfred A. Knopf, 1965), 65–68; Leon Satkowski, Giorgio Vasari, *Architect and Courtier* (Princeton, N. J.: Princeton University Press, 1992), 45.

14. Norwich, *A History of Venice*, 400–402; Tenenti, 22, 25–26, 29, 31, 36; Finlay, 35; Tucci, 356.

15. Woolf, 193, 195, 198; Davis, 42; Manfredo Tafuri, *Venice and the Renaissance*, trans. Jessica Levine (Cambridge, Mass.: MIT Press, 1989), 161; Diehl, *La République de Venise*, 169; Tucci, 352; Brian Pullan, "The Occupations and Investments of the Venetian Nobility in the Middle and Late Sixteenth Century," *Renaissance Venice*, 381.

16. Deborah Howard, "Jacopo Sansovino and the Romanization of Venetian Architecture," *Venice Art and Architecture*, 1:324.

17. Martines, 298.

18. Norwich, *A History of Venice*, 429, 434; Howard, *The Architectural History of Venice*, 149–50; McAndrew, 415, 510–19; Gattinoni, 13, 36.

The Campanile visitors see today is not the one Bon completed in 1514, although it is virtually identical in every detail to that ninth- to sixteenth-century structure. The victim of many centuries of lightning strikes, earthquakes, and ground subsidence, as well as a very poorly executed reinforcement project, the original tower crashed to the ground in a heap of rubble and dust on July 14, 1902, but was rebuilt with exacting fidelity *dov'era e com'era* (where it was and as it was) within ten years. Because Bon's tower virtually collapsed upon itself without toppling over, adjacent architectural monuments such as the Basilica, the

Marciana Library, and the Ducal Palace were not injured. As the Venetians say, it fell like a gentleman.

19. McAndrew, 404–23, 510–13; Howard, *The Architectural History of Venice*, 149–52; Howard, *Jacopo Sansovino Architecture and Patronage in Renaissance Venice*, 8–9, 14; Mueller, "The Procurators of San Marco in the Thirteenth and Fourteenth Centuries," 113, 122; Concina, *A History of Venetian Architecture*, 149–50; Lane, 223; Huse and Wolters, 40; Goy, *Building Renaissance Venice*, 254; Norwich, *A History of Venice*, 457.

20. Howard, *The Architectural History of Venice*, 149–52; McAndrew, 404–407, 411, 413–14, 513; Ackerman, *The Architecture of Michelangelo*, 155.

21. McAndrew, 411–14, 513.

Notes to Chapter Twelve

1. Giovanni Mariacher, ed., *Il Sansovino* (Arnoldo Mondatori Editore, 1962), 13–15, 20, 28, 30, 33, 42–43, 50, 178; Pevsner et al., *A Dictionary of Architecture*, 440; Howard, *Jacopo Sansovino Architecture and Patronage in Renaissance Venice*, 1–2; Howard, *The Architectural History of Venice*, 164–65; Freeman, 171; Ackerman, *Distance Points*, 364; John Pope-Hennessy, "The Relations between Florentine and Venetian Sculpture in the Sixteenth Century," *Florence and Venice: Comparisons and Relations*, 2: 327–28; Hopkins, 42–43.

2. Norwich, *A History of Venice*, 441; Barbara Tuchman, *The March of Folly from Troy to Vietnam* (New York: Alfred A. Knopf, 1984) 61, 68, 78, 82, 91–104, 113–14, 122–23, 125–26; Luigi Guicciardini, *The Sack of Rome*, trans. and ed., James H. McGregor (New York: Italica Press, 1993), xxxii, 123–25, 126; Ross King, *Michelangelo and the Pope's Ceiling* (New York: Walker & Co., 2003), 3–9; Ackerman, *The Architecture of Michelangelo*, 26–27; Hibbert, *Florence*, 171; R. A. Scotti, *Basilica, the Splendor and Scandal of Building St. Peter's* (London: Plume, 2006), xviii, 153, 155, 183.

3. Mariacher, 50, 178; Howard, *Jacopo Sansovino Architecture and Patronage in Renaissance Venice*, 1, 7–8, 36; Deborah Howard, "The Golden Age, Jacopo Sansovino and the Romanization of Venetian Architecture," *Venice Art and Architecture*, 316, 338–39; Hartt, 482; Janson, 422; James Lees-Milne, *Saint Peter's* (Boston: Little, Brown, 1967), 165–68.

4. Howard, *Jacopo Sansovino Architecture and Patronage in Renaissance Venice*, 9, 81–82; Heydenreich and Lotz, 235; McAndrew, 535, 538; Howard, *The Architectural History of Venice*, 151, 166; Howard, *Jacopo Sansovino Architecture and Patronage in Renaissance Venice*, 81–82; Howard, "The Golden Age, Jacopo Sansovino and the Romanization of Venetian Architecture," 316; Tafuri, *Venice and the Renaissance*, 108, 111; Concina, *A History of Venetian Architecture*, 175–77; Pullan, *Rich and Poor in Renaissance Venice*, 4–5.

5. Tafuri, *Venice and the Renaissance*, 8; Ackerman, *The Architecture of Michelangelo*, 137, 144, 308–309; Heydenreich and Lotz, 153–56, 235, 249–50; Hartt, 629.

6. Schulz, "La piazza medievale di San Marco," 140; Howard, "The Golden Age, Jacopo Sansovino and the Romanization of Venetian Architecture," 317; Howard, *Jacopo Sansovino Architecture and Patronage in Renaissance Venice*, 10–12.

7. Howard, "The Golden Age, Jacopo Sansovino and the Romanization of Venetian Architecture," 323–24; McAndrew, 381–82; Howard, *Jacopo Sansovino Architecture and Patronage in Renaissance Venice*, 11, 14–15; Howard, *The Architectural History of Venice*, 175; Concina, *A History of Venetian Architecture*, 187.

8. Howard, *Jacopo Sansovino Architecture and Patronage in Renaissance Venice*, 9, 14–15, 17–19; Howard, "The Golden Age, Jacopo Sansovino and the Romanization of Venetian Architecture," 322; Howard, *The Architectural History of Venice*, 175; Mueller, "The Procurators of San Marco in the Thirteenth and Fourteenth Centuries," 113, 122.

9. Brown, *Venice & Antiquity*, 145.

10. Lane, 219; Tafuri, *Venice and the Renaissance*, 16; Pincus, *The Arco Foscari*, 113; Howard, *Jacopo Sansovino Architecture and Patronage in Renaissance Venice*, 17–19, 22, 163 (fn. 44); Masson, 319–20.

11. Norwich, *A History of Venice*, 221, 236; Lane, 180, 217; Crouzet-Pavan, xix, 180; Brown, *Venice & Antiquity*, 9, 49, 65–66.

12. Norwich, *A History of Venice*, 330–33, 342–46; Brown, *Venice & Antiquity*, 145.

13. Norwich, *A History of Venice*, 333; Concina, *A History of Venetian Architecture*, 183; Norman O. Brown, *Life Against Death, the Psychoanalytical Meaning of History* (Middletown, Ct.: Wesleyan University Press, 1959), 266–83.

14. Heydenreich and Lotz, 237.

15. Howard, *Jacopo Sansovino Architecture and Patronage in Renaissance Venice*, 26–28.

16. Howard, *The Architectural History of Venice*, 176–78; Hartt, 481; Pevsner et al., *A Dictionary of Architecture*, 219, 342, 372–73, 511; *Knopf Guide to Rome* (New York: Alfred A. Knopf, 1994), 94; Howard, *Jacopo Sansovino Architecture and Patronage in Renaissance Venice*, 19–20 (illustrations 14 and 15); Howard, "The Golden Age, Jacopo Sansovino and the Romanization of Venetian Architecture," 322–23; Concina, *A History of Venetian Architecture*, 184; Heydenreich and Lotz, 236; Tafuri, *Venice and the Renaissance*, 64, 110.

17. *Knopf Guide to Rome*, 94; Howard, *Jacopo Sansovino Architecture and Patronage in Renaissance Venice*, 27–28; Huse and Wolters, 44; Concina, *A History of Venetian Architecture*, 184, 200–202, 205; Hartt, 625; Howard, "The Golden Age, Jacopo Sansovino and the Romanization of Venetian Architecture," 318–19, 322; Hopkins, 130, 132–33; Rosenfeld, 102–103; Sabine Frommel, *Sebastiano Serlio* (Milano: Electa, 1998), 15, 68, 71; Brown, *Venice & Antiquity*, 278–79.

18. Hartt, 625; Heydenreich and Lotz, 236; Concina, *A History of Venetian Architecture*, 184; Howard, *Jacopo Sansovino Architecture and Patronage in Renaissance Venice*, 27.

19. Hopkins, 111 (illustration 112), 130 (illustration 135), 132–33; Ackerman, *Distance Points*, 531; Rosenfeld, 102; Howard, *Jacopo Sansovino Architecture and Patronage in Renaissance Venice*, 19, 22–23, 36.

20. Howard, *Jacopo Sansovino Architecture and Patronage in Renaissance Venice*, 15–16, 19; Howard, "The Golden Age, Jacopo Sansovino and the Romanization of Venetian Architecture," 323; Ruskin, 2: 232; Wolters, "Venetian Figurative Sculpture: 1300–1450," 162; Lane, 441.

21. Howard, *Jacopo Sansovino Architecture and Patronage in Renaissance Venice*, 29, 31, 34; Howard, "The Golden Age, Jacopo Sansovino and the Romanization of Venetian Architecture," 323; Howard, *The Architectural History of Venice*, 178–80; Concina, *A History of Venetian Architecture*, 186–87.

22. Howard, *Jacopo Sansovino Architecture and Patronage in Renaissance Venice*, 31, 33–34; Howard, "The Golden Age, Jacopo Sansovino and the Romanization of Venetian Architecture," 366, 368, 371–72; McAndrews, 100; Concina, *A History of Venetian Architecture*, 187; Goy, *Building Renaissance Venice*, 255; Howard, *Venice & Antiquity*, 281; Pincus, *The Arco Foscari*, 382–83.

23. *Geschicte der Renaissance in Italien*, 1st ed. (Stuttgart, 1867), Section 53, quoted in Heydenreich and Lotz, 237.

24. Howard, *Jacopo Sansovino Architecture and Patronage in Renaissance Venice*, 19–26, 29; Howard, "The Golden Age, Jacopo Sansovino and the Romanization of Venetian Architecture," 322, 324; Heydenreich and Lotz, 236; Howard, *The Architectural History of Venice*, 173–75; Concina, *A History of Venetian Architecture*, 187.

25. Howard, *Jacopo Sansovino Architecture and Patronage in Renaissance Venice*, 1, 19, 25–26, 82–84; Morresi, 17, 19 (illustration 14), 20 (illustration 15), 24 (illustration 19), 40 (illustration 42), 74 (illustration 67); Mariacher, 181; Concina, *A History of Venetian Architecture*, 187; Howard, "The Golden Age, Jacopo Sansovino and the Romanization of Venetian Architecture," 324; Tafuri, *Venice and the Renaissance*, 167–68, 171, 173, 175; Gabriele Morolli, " Vincenzo Scamozzi e la fabbrica delle procuratie nuove," *Le Procuratie Nuove in Piazza San Marco* (Roma: Editalia, 1994), 19; Samona et al., 36, 57; Agazzi, 112, 115-19.
    San Geminiano, Sansovino's gleaming white Renaissance reincarnation of an original Byzantine church that reached back to the city's earliest beginnings (it was built in the sixth century by the Greek general Narses), was razed by Napoleon in the early nineteenth century. In 1797, when Bonaparte extinguished the Republic as part of his conquest of northern Italy, he vowed to be "an Attila to the State of Venice." Having succeeded in this destructive political goal, he then proceeded to act with equal barbarity toward the Piazza San Marco and the city's other historic art treasures. He began by stripping the Piazza of its Marcian icons, including the gilded four-horse chariot team which had stood guard over the Basilica San Marco for more than five centuries. He shipped the *quadriga* off to Paris along with thousands of paintings looted from Venetian churches, monasteries, convents, and guilds (these were deposited in Europe's first public art museum, the Musée Napoleon, later to become the Louvre). Then, to provide a royal ballroom for his son-in-law, Eugène de Beauharnais, whom Napoleon had named Italian Vice-Roi and Prince of Venice, he destroyed the entire western façade of the Piazza, including Sansovino's church. The replacement building that we see today is known as the Napoleonic Wing. To accommodate second-floor orchestra pits constructed out of sight above the ballroom floor, an extra half-story was added to the structure, and the large attic screen that was installed at the top of the exterior elevation to cover this added height was lined with statues of twelve Roman emperors. Originally, the center of the attic was to hold a life-size effigy of Napoleon, but this was never executed. Instead, the Italian sculptor Domenico Bandi produced an eight-foot-tall freestanding marble

statue of Bonaparte naked from the waist up and wearing a toga-like cloth draped over his lower torso. Although by 1811, when the commission was awarded, Napoleon was becoming quite portly, Bandi portrayed him as extremely muscular and fit. Installed on the Molo in front of the Ducal Palace in 1811, the statue remained there until 1814, when, after an attack by angry Venetians, it was removed from public view. Its whereabouts remained unknown for almost two centuries until it was rediscovered in 2002 by a group known as the French Committee to Safeguard Venice, which donated Bandi's statue to the city as a vital piece of missing Venetian history. The Venetian reaction was less than enthusiastic. One resident compared the Gallic gift to a committee of Germans asking the Israelis if they would like to have a statue of Hitler to help them recall the events of World War II. Bandi's Napoleon is currently housed in the Correr Museum where it may sometimes be seen in a glass case at the end of long, remote hallway.

26. Thubron, 121, 165–66; Norwich, *A History of Venice*, 466–67, 473–88, 490–91, 494; Lane, 245, 248, 324, 372–74, 377; Howard, *The Architectural History of Venice*, 203; Johnson, 162.

Following the fall of the last Cypriot citadel, Marcantonio Bragadin, the Venetian commander, was stripped and bound to a column, and the Ottoman executioner began to slowly carve his skin and flesh away from his body. After silently enduring this for thirty minutes, Bragadin expired, and his corpse was beheaded and quartered. The skin of the martyred Venetian general was deposited with the sultan in Istanbul, but was later stolen and returned to Bragadin's sons in Venice. There is a memorial to him in Santi Giovanni e Paolo, the Westminster Abbey of Venice; it is the first monument along the long south wall to the right of the main door. Although artistically undistinguished, it does contain a niche (behind an urn), which, when opened in 1961, was found to contain several remnants of tanned human skin.

27. Pullan, "The Occupations and Investments of the Venetian Nobility in the Middle and Late Sixteenth Century," 381, 385; Thubron, 165; Lane, 245–46, 248, 297, 306, 309, 331, 348, 377, 392, 400–401; Norwich, *A History of Venice*, 491, 508–509; Tafuri, *Venice and the Renaissance*, 161.

28. Lane, 256, 293, 391–96, 402–404; Tafuri, *Venice and the Renaissance*, 113, 126–29, 137, 161, 176–79; Pullan, *Rich and Poor in Renaissance Venice*, 6–7; Finlay, xv–xvii; Norwich, *A History of Venice*, 491, 498–501, 503–504, 507–509; Bouwsma, 65, 75–78.

29. Janson, 455; Heydenreich and Lotz, 303, 306, 310–11; Pevsner et al., *A Dictionary of Architecture*, 210, 378–80, 439; Ackerman, *Palladio*, 14–15, 27, 34, 78, 81, 87, 90–92, 118–20, 185; Guido Beltramini and Antonio Padoan, *Andrea Palladio: The Complete Illustrated Works* (New York: Universe Publishing, 2001), 9, 30–32, 37; Hartt, 625–26; Ackerman, *Distance Points*, 467, 469–472; Bruce Boucher, *Andrea Palladio: the Architect in His Time* (New York: Abbeville Press, 1994), 7, 11–12, 107, 112–15; Hopkins, 85; Lionello Puppi, "The Potential Venice of Palladio and Scamozzi," *Venice Art and Architecture*, 1:349; Wittkower, *Architectural Principles in the Age of Humanism*, 63, 86.

30. Janson, 455; Hartt, 627–28; Tafuri, *Venice and the Renaissance*, 10, 128–29; Wittkower, *Architectural Principles in the Age of Humanism*, 62, 68–69, 101–102, 113; Heydenreich and Lotz, 303; Ackerman, *Palladio*, 160, 162, 182; Puppi, "The Potential Venice of Palladio and Scamozzi," 345; Beltramini and Padoan, 77.

31. Tafuri, *Venice and the Renaissance*, 3, 10, 113, 122, 126–29, 137, 177–78; Puppi, "The Potential Venice of Palladio and Scamozzi," 341–45, 349; Huse and Wolters, 54; Howard, *The Architectural History of Venice*, 191; Morresi, 81 (illustrations 76–77); Boucher, 217–24; Loredana Olivato, "Architecture in Eighteenth-Century Venice," *Venice Art and Architecture*, 2: 712–13.

32. Ackerman, *Palladio*, 14–15, 130, 135, 138–46; Howard, *The Architectural History of Venice*, 190–204; Howard, *Jacopo Sansovino Architecture and Patronage in Renaissance Venice*, 64-74; Puppi, "The Potential Venice of Palladio and Scamozzi," 349, 352; Tafuri, *Venice and the Renaissance*, 10, 128, 137, 156, 175; Huse and Wolters, 95–96, 99; Beltramini and Padoan, 221–56; Ackerman, *Distance Points*, 479–85; Heydenreich and Lotz, 306–10; Wittkower, *Architectural Principles in the Age of Humanism*, 68–69, 72, 76, 89–97; Janson, 457; Hartt, 629; Norwich, *A History of Venice*, 494; James Ackerman, "Observations on Renaissance Church Planning in Venice and Florence, 1470–1570," *Florence and Venice: Comparisons and Relations*, 2: 303–304.

33. Goy, *Venice: the City and Its Architecture*, 127.

34. Howard, *The Architectural History of Venice*, 207–208; Puppi, "The Potential Venice of Palladio and Scamozzi," 354–56; Ackerman, *Palladio*, 160; Boucher, 284–86.

35. Tafuri, *Venice and the Renaissance*, 113, 126–29, 137, 161, 176–84, 272 (fn. 78), illustration 137; Concina, *A History of Venetian Architecture*, 225; Ackerman, *Palladio*, 182; Boucher, 286–88, 319 (fn. 51); Puppi, "The Potential Venice of Palladio and Scamozzi," 349, 355–56; Goy, *Venice: the City and its Architecture*, 127; Davis, 23, 34–35, 39–40, 54–58; Finlay, 21, 59–61, 281–83, 285–86, 288; Queller, *The Venetian Patriciate*, ix–x, xi, 30, 33, 113–14, 138, 152–53, 156, 158–60, 251.

36. Puppi, "The Potential Venice of Palladio and Scamozzi," 359–60; Tafuri, *Venice and the Renaissance*, 137, 166–68; Hopkins, 138–40.

37. Puppi, "The Potential Venice of Palladio and Scamozzi," 360.

38. Ackerman, *Palladio*, 94, 112, 118; Boucher, 50, 121; Tafuri, *Venice and the Renaissance*, 103, 122, 124–25, 137, 168; Wittkower, *Architectural Principles in the Age of Humanism*, 123; Hopkins, 137, 144.

39. Puppi, "The Potential Venice of Palladio and Scamozzi," 361; Concina, *A History of Venetian Architecture*, 220, 223, 225; Tafuri, *Venice and the Renaissance*, 167–71, 179–84; Morresi, 103; Boucher, 239–42; Hopkins, 136.

40. Puppi, "The Potential Venice of Palladio and Scamozzi," 361; Tafuri, *Venice and the Renaissance*, 169–79; Concina, *A History of Venetian Architecture*, 225; Hopkins, 143; Goy, *Venice: the City and its Architecture*, 142.

41. Goy, *Venice: the City and its Architecture*, 142; Tafuri, *Venice and the Renaissance*, illustration 128; Concina, *A History of Venetian Architecture*, 226; Hopkins, 143; Goy, *Venice: the City and its Architecture*, 142; Samona et al., 17; Morresi, 105 (illustration 109); Sarah Quill, Ruskin's *Venice: The Stones Revisited* (Aldershot, England: Lund Humphries, 2003), 166.

42. Lane, 378, 391, 393–94, 396–98, 400; Pullan, *Crisis and Change in the Venetian Economy in the Sixteenth and Seventeenth Centuries*, 8–9; Tafuri, *Venice and the Renaissance*, 130, 165, 170, 172, 177–79, 188; Norwich, *A History of Venice*, 508–17.

43. Tafuri, *Venice and the Renaissance*, 177; Claudio Rendina, *The Popes, Histories and Secrets* (Santa Ana, Cal.: Seven Locks Press, 2002), 483–91; Hartt, 482; Lees-Milne, 234–41; Masson, 445–46; Lanciani, 122, 253; Scotti, 231–37.

44. Norwich, *A History of Venice*, 397–98, 401, 510–13; Lane, 393, 396–98; McNeill, 192; Mary McCarthy, *Venice Observed* (New York: Harcourt, Brace, 1963), 70.

45. Norwich, *A History of Venice*, 509, 513–16; Lane, 397–98; McCarthy, *Venice Observed*, 64.

46. Norwich, *A History of Venice*, 516–17; Lane, 398; McCarthy, *Venice Observed*, 66–67, 69.

Notes to Chapter Thirteen

1. King, *Brunelleschi's Dome*, 156, 159.

2. Larner, 275.

3. Vasari, 219, 258.

4. Janson, 380, 417; Heydenreich and Lotz, 17; Edith Hamilton and Huntington Cairns, eds., *The Collected Dialogues of Plato* (Princeton, N. J.: Princeton University Press, 1987), 549; Hale, *Florence and the Medici*, 55; Jonathan Fineberg, *Art Since 1940, Strategies of Being*, 2nd ed. (Upper Saddle River, N. J.: Prentice Hall, 2000), 17; Clark, *Civilization*, 149-50.

5. Ackerman, *The Architecture of Michelangelo*, 271; Janson, 261–61, 298; Goldthwaite, *Wealth and the Demand for Art in Italy*, 179–80.

6. McCarthy, *The Stones of Florence*, 41.

7. Larner, 64; Hale, *Florence and the Medici*, 9, 16, 18, 115; McCarthy, *The Stones of Florence*, 40-41, 43-45; Goy, *Venice: the City and Its Architecture*, 111; Demus, *The Church of San Marco in Venice*, 45; Pincus, *The Arco Foscari*, 380–83; Brown, *The Renaissance in Venice, A World Apart*, 37, 51, 78; Borsook, 47.

8. Larner, 66, 113–15, 304–305, 353–54; Goldthwaite, *Wealth and the Demand for Art in Italy*, 180; Goldthwaite, *The Building of Renaissance Florence*, 90–93; Borsook, 34–35.

9. Lane, 90–91; Madden, *Enrico Dandolo*, 21, 94; Demus, *The Church of San Marco in Venice*, 50–56; Giuseppe Cappelletti, *Relazione storica sulle magistrature venete* (Venice: Filippi Editore, 1992), 15–21; Schulz, "Urbanism in Medieval Venice," 436.

10. Schulz, "Urbanism in Medieval Venice," 432–34; Schulz, "La piazza medievale di San Marco," 142–44; Demus, *The Church of San Marco in Venice*, 53; Goy, *Building Renaissance Venice*, 33; Mueller, "The Procurators of San Marco in the Thirteenth and Fourteenth Centuries," 108–12; Howard, *Jacopo Sansovino Architecture and Patronage in Renaissance Venice*, 8; Madden, *Enrico Dandolo*, 3, 5, 21, 94.

11. Goy, *Building Renaissance Venice*, 33; Mueller, "The Procurators of San Marco in the Thirteenth and Fourteenth Centuries," 108–109, 113, 120–21; Schulz, "Urbanism in Medieval Venice," 436; Schulz, "La piazza medievale di San Marco," 138, 140–41, 145; Goy, *The House of Gold*, 32; Howard, *Jacopo Sansovino Architecture and Patronage in Renaissance Venice*, 8–9, 30, 35; Goy, *The House of Gold*, 32.

12. Howard, *Jacopo Sansovino Architecture and Patronage in Renaissance Venice*, 8–9, 11–12; Demus, *The Church of San Marco in Venice*, 53; Schulz, "Urbanism in Medieval Venice," 436; Schulz, "La pizza medievale di San Marco," 138, 140–41, 145.

13. Howard, *Jacopo Sansovino Architecture and Patronage in Renaissance Venice*, 1, 9, 20–21; Goy, *Building Renaissance Venice*, 56.

14. Howard, *Jacopo Sansovino Architecture and Patronage in Renaissance Venice*, 14–15, 17–19; Mueller, "The Procurators of San Marco in the Thirteenth and Fourteenth Centuries," 219–20.

15. Pincus, *The Arco Foscari*, 42–43 (fn. 14); McAndrew, 88; Norwich, *A History of Venice*, 240; Goy, *Building Renaissance Venice*, 31, 34–36.

16. Pullan, *Rich and Poor in Renaissance Venice*, 7; Norwich, *A History of Venice*, 494; Lane, 252; Goy, *Building Renaissance Venice*, 31–32, 34–36; Finlay, 26, 51–53, 55, 57–58; Goy, *Venice: The City and Its Architecture*, 56; Pincus, *The Arco Foscari*, 42–43 (fn. 14).

17. Ruskin, 2:294–95; Lauritzen, *Venice: A Thousand Years*, 66; Arslan, 246; Lane, 185, 201; Finlay 42–43; Goy, *Building Renaissance Venice*, 31.

18. Goy, *Building Renaissance Venice*, 31–32, 35–36, 227–28; Pincus, *The Arco Foscari*, 34–36 (fn. 1), 113, 446–51, 453, 455–59; McAndrew, 83, 86–87, 89, 99–100.

19. Mueller, "The Procurators of San Marco in the Thirteenth and Fourteenth Centuries," 128; Schulz, "La pizza medievale di San Marco," 154 (fn. 70).

20. Ruskin, 2:294; Arslan, 246; Goy, *Building Renaissance Venice*, 35, 235, 239–40; McAndrew, 382, 391; Goy, *Venice: the City and Its Architecture*, 130; Howard, *Jacopo Sansovino Architecture and Patronage in Renaissance Venice*, 39, 41–43, 166 (fn. 89).

21. Howard, *Jacopo Sansovino Architecture and Patronage in Renaissance Venice*, 36, 161 (fn. 12); Pullen, *Rich and Poor in Renaissance Venice*, 351–54; Puppi, "The Potential Venice of Palladio and Scamozzi," 359–61; Tafuri, *Venice and the Renaissance*, 171–76.

22. Howard, *Jacopo Sansovino Architecture and Patronage in Renaissance Venice*, 36; Goy, *Building Renaissance Venice*, 33; Hartt, 482; Johnson, 102–106; Scotti, 271.

23. Finlay, 24, 28–29, 110, 139; Lane, 233; Norwich, *A History of Venice*, 355; Howard, *Jacopo Sansovino Architecture and Patronage in Renaissance Venice*, 81; Ackerman, *Distance Points*, 456.

24. Lane, 233–34; Norwich, *A History of Venice*, 354–55; Johnson, 76–78.

25. Lane, 233; Norwich, *A History of Venice*, 354–55.

26. Larner, 155, 263, 255; Martines, 18-29, 38–41, 47–51; Pullan, *Rich and Poor in Renaissance Venice*, 4–5; Ruskin, 3:60; Hartt, 465–66; Borsook, 43–44; Burckhardt, 8, 71; Goldthwaite, *Wealth and the Demand for Art in Italy*, 173.

27. Ackerman, " Observations on Renaissance Church Planning in Venice and Florence, 1470–1570," 303; Howard, *The Architectural History of Venice*, 203–204, 213–15; Ackerman, *Distance Points*, 482–84.

Notes to Chapter Fourteen

1. Queller and Madden, 108.

2. Schulz, "Urbanism in Medieval Venice," 441; Lewis, 85, 104–105; Borsook, 34–35; Hibbert, *Florence*, 49; Rubinstein, *The Palazzo Vecchio*, 9–10.

3. Ruskin, 2:17.

4.   Diehl, *Byzantium*, 256–57.

5.   Burke, 196, 198.

6.   Schulz, "Urbanism in Medieval Venice, " 432, 437–41; Ackerman, *The Architecture of Michelangelo*, 142, 144, 154, 308–309; Hyman, "The Venice Connection: Questions about Brunelleschi and the East," 1:194–95, 1:198–203; Burns, 272, 274, 277, 281–84; Schulz, "La piazza medievale di San Marco," 141–42; Johnson, 93–94.

7.   Hyman, "The Venice Connection: Questions about Brunelleschi and the East," 1:198, 1:200; Ackerman, *The Architecture of Michelangelo*, 197; Lees-Milne, 143; Heydenreich and Lotz, 90–91; Krautheimer, *Early Christian and Byzantine Architecture*, 12.

8.   Ackerman, *Distance Points*, 316.

9.   Vasari, 248, 253, 258, 274, 297.

10. Larner, 97; Rudolf Wittkower, *Gothic vs. Classic* (New York: George Braziller, 1974), 19; Hale, *Florence and the Medici*, 113, 132, 139–43; Brown, *Renaissance Venice, A World Apart*, 61; McCarthy, *The Stones of Florence*, 201–202, 217–19.

11. Burckhardt, viii, 51, 60–61.

12. Hartt, 152.

13. Ibid., 479.

14. Ibid., 419.

15. Ibid., 156–57.

16. Borsook, 215–17; Hyman, "The Venice Connection: Questions about Brunelleschi and the East," 1:203.

17. Hartt, 419, 624.

18. Ibid., 479.

19. Panofsky, 44; Ackerman, *The Architecture of Michelangelo*, 25; Vasari, 212.

20. All quoted material is from Vasari, 16, 219, 247. All non-quoted information is drawn from Johnson, 162, and Humfrey, 162, 164, 198–200, 203, 205.

21. Burke, 8.

22. Ibid., 196–97.

23. Ibid., 196–98.

24. Ruskin, 1:40.

25. Ackerman, *The Architecture of Michelangelo*, 69.

26. Manfredo Tafuri, *Interpreting the Renaissance, Princes, Cities, Architects*, trans. Daniel Sherer (New Haven and London: Yale University Press, 2006), 54–55.

27. Vasari, 72–73.

28. Panofsky, 108–109, 111–13.

29. Hartt, 152.

30. Goldthwaite, *Wealth and the Demand for Art in Italy*, 215, 225; McCarthy, *The Stones of Florence*, 47-48, 53; Heydenreich and Lotz, 305.

31. Vasari, 72.

32. Hyman, "The Venice Connection: Questions about Brunelleschi and the East," 1:194, 1:196–97; King, *Brunelleschi's Dome*, 10, 29–30, 52–53, 97–99; Cornel von Fabriczy, *Filippo Brunelleschi, His Life and Works*, reprinted in *Brunelleschi in Perspective*, 97; Mitchell, 141–43; Johnson, 92–93.

33. Panofsky, 10.
34. Ibid., 21, 37–38, 112–13; Janson, 351; Wittkower, *Gothic vs. Classic*, 85–86; Vasari, 185.
35. von Fabriczy, 98.

Notes to Chapter Fifteen

1. Burke, 198.
2. *The Republic of Plato*, trans. Francis MacDonald Cornford (New York and London: Oxford University Press, 1945), 22.
3. Hannah Arendt, "The Crisis in Culture" in *Between Past and Future, Eight Exercises in Political Thought* (New York: Viking Press, 1961), 215–16; Tafuri, *Interpreting the Renaissance*, 54–55; Scotti, 181.
4. Larner, 265; Goldthwaite, *Wealth and the Demand for Art in Italy*, 26.
5. Howard, *The Architectural History of Venice*, 208.
6. Eleanor Clark, *Rome and a Villa* (Pleasantville, N.Y.: Akadine Press, 1999), 265; Lees-Milne, 132, 135–36, 171–76; King, *Michelangelo and the Pope's Ceiling*, 3–6, 8–9, 310–11; J. R. Hale, *Machiavelli and Renaissance Italy* (London: English Universities Press Ltd, 1961), 97; Norwich, *A History of Venice*, 408–409, 414–15; Hartt, 487–88, 503–504, 545; Tuchman, *The March of Folly from Troy to Vietnam*, 96; Vasari, 264–65, 271–72, 275; Mariacher, 13.
7. Hartt, 480–85; Tuchman, *The March of Folly from Troy to Vietnam*, 96–97; Johnson, 103–106; Ackerman, *The Architecture of Michelangelo*, 30, 197–216; Lees-Milne, 137–39, 141–46; Vasari, 216; Goldthwaite, *Wealth and the Demand for Art in Italy*, 49; Scotti, 75, 97–98, 132–35, 140, 271.
8. Ackerman, *The Architecture of Michelangelo*, 34, 194, 197–203; Hartt, 636–37; Lees-Milne, 186–88, 235–41, 257–59; Hopkins, 94–97; Scotti, 234–37, 254–55.
9. Lees-Milne, 82–100, 200, 202, 233.
10. Ibid., 95.
11. Ruskin, 1:36.
12. Lees-Milne, 86, 95–96; Scotti, 38–39.
13. All quoted material is from Lanciani, 3. All non-quoted information is drawn from Lanciani, 3–4, 7–9.
14. Ibid., 33–34, 182, 190, 206; Goldthwaite, *The Building of Renaissance Florence*, 212–13, 216; Weiss, 57, 98–99, 104; Krautheimer, *Rome: Profile of a City*, 187.
15. Burckhardt, 134.
16. Lanciani, 182, 206.
17. Hale, *Florence and the Medici*, 104.
18. Lanciani, 182, 191–94, 205–208, 211, 234–35, 241, 245–46; Lees-Milne, 124; Burckhardt, 138; Scotti, 185.
19. Panofsky, 112–13.
20. Nicolai Rubinstein, "Oligarchy and Democracy in Fifteenth Century Florence," *Florence and Venice: Comparisons and Relations*, 1: 100–101, 103—104, 106–108; Hale, *Florence and the Medici*, 88–89; Brucker, 257.

21. King, *Brunelleschi's Dome*, 41–42, 46–48, 88–91, 141–45, 159.
22. Hale, *Florence and the Medici*, 93–113, 118–43; Brucker, 273–77; Hibbert, *Florence*, 176–85.
23. Pullan, *Rich and Poor in Renaissance Venice*, 4-5; Goldthwaite, *Wealth and the Demand for Art in Italy*, 245; Satkowski, 3–5, 8, 10–12, 45, 54–55, 59; Rubinstein, *The Palazzo Vecchio*, 40-41, 96; Borsook, 27-28; Hibbert, *Florence*, 174-175, 177-181; Hale, *Florence and the Medici*, 117–21, 123–25, 128–31, 133–43, 158; McCarthy, *The Stones of Florence*, 47, 217–19; Pope-Hennessy, 2: 333–35.
24. Hibbert, *Florence*, 175–76, 186, 194, 356–57, 360–61; Hale, *Florence and the Medici*, 123–24, 152; Lewis, 178–79; Goldthwaite, *The Building of Renaissance Florence*, 24; Borsook, 44–45, 47–47, 157–59, 208, 374; Satkowski, 28–30, 36–37, 41; Ackerman, *The Architecture of Michelangelo*, 300–301; Ugo Maccini, *Palazzo Vecchio* (Firenze: Scala, 1989), 9; Vasari, 253; Hale, *Florence and the Medici*, , 89, 128, 140–43, 149, 155; McCarthy, *The Stones of Florence*, 201–204, 206–209, 217–19; Brucker, 275; Lewis, 176, 179–80; Pope-Hennessy, 2:335.
25. Arendt, 218–25, 296–97 (fn. 14); Pope-Hennessy, 2:335; Clark, *Civilization*, 100–101.

INDEX